PAPERS ON THE 1962 ELECTION

Papers on the
1962 ELECTION

FIFTEEN PAPERS ON THE
CANADIAN GENERAL ELECTION OF 1962
EDITED BY

John Meisel

UNIVERSITY OF TORONTO PRESS

Reprinted in 2018

ISBN 978-1-4875-8146-6 (paper)

Printed in Canada

PREFACE

The origin of this book lies in one of the shortcomings of my study of the 1957 election. (1) In preparing that volume I was seriously handicapped by the almost total absence of primary works on the contests in any constituency, province, or region, of accounts of party organization and activity, and even of adequate analyses of the results. Except for the releases of the Canadian Institute of Public Opinion no acceptable survey data were available. I had to rely almost exclusively on newspaper and magazine reports and on such evidence as a single scholar could unearth while carrying a normal teaching load in an Ontario university. When planning a volume on the 1962 contest, the inauspicious circumstances in which my first full-scale election survey had to be written were still painfully in-scribed in my mind and I happily recalled the well-known adage about Mohammed and the Mountain. Why not prompt, encourage, and cajole some Canadian scholars into undertaking studies of those aspects of the election which interest them and so assure that a monograph on the 1962 contest would benefit from, and be supple-mented by, a series of local or otherwise specialized studies? In what seemed to be the reasonable expectation that financial support for such a project could be procured from a foundation, I approached about thirty individuals who had shown (or could be expected to show) some interest in Canadian electoral studies. The present volume attests to the generosity and enthusiasm of their response, particularly since, in the event, no financial assistance for the whole project was forthcoming and each contributor had to finance his or her own study.

This book does not follow the current North American fashion of writing with the aid of a pair of scissors and a glue-pot. It is not a set of "readings" in the sense that it makes available in a single volume numerous items published previously elsewhere: all of the contributions were originally written for inclusion in these Papers. This fact notwithstanding, the essays do not follow any one theme, nor are they given unity by a shared frame of reference. Each author dealt with some aspect of the 1962 election without any concern with what was being attempted by the others. As a result, the Papers do not pretend to give a complete and well-rounded account of the 1962 contest. A book attempting this task is under preparation and will, it is hoped, be completed late in 1964. The manner in which this collection has come into being is responsible for the occasional overlap in its content. This occurs exceedingly rarely, however, and then invariably brings somewhat divergent points of view or emphases on some important aspect of the election.

---

1. The Canadian General Election of 1957 (Toronto, 1962).

Obviously wasteful repetition was removed, whenever possible, by an editor fully aware of the magnanimous indulgence of his authors.

It was to be expected that the _Papers_ would add considerably to our knowledge of the 1962 election and to Canadian voting behaviour in general. Another notable contribution of this volume came as a surprise: it turned out to have become a veritable Mrs. Rombauer (2) of Canadian psephology. For while it does not prescribe every step necessary in a sound election study, it does illustrate an enormously wide range of approaches and techniques applicable in the study of elections. It is improbable that in the next decade anyone will seriously undertake to examine a Canadian election without first making a meticulous study of the techniques used by the various contributors to this book.

To find answers to the problems they have set for themselves, our authors have resorted to the use of such diverse expedients as surveys based on different kinds of samples, the application of electronic computers, analyses using election results ranging from national totals to minute variations by polling division; they have applied a variety of statistical tools to the analysis of official election returns, voters' lists, census data, and whatever else seemed relevant and accessible; they have interviewed candidates, party activists, and other, less immediately involved Canadians in every province, and they have made rewarding use of newspapers, party literature, and broadcasts. As a result they have documented convincingly a number of general impressions widely held about the 1962 election. Some of our previous knowledge of Canadian politics has been clarified and refined. In addition, they have produced completely new facts and insights and in some instances they have evaluated their findings in the light of some general concepts and propositions of sociology and political science, thus relating what has happened in Canada in 1962 to contemporary theories about human behaviour.

Before tackling the papers the reader will be well advised to fix firmly in his mind which election he is about to re-live. There has been such a plethora of national elections that it is easy to confuse the polling of June 18, 1962 with its twin of April 8, 1963. It will, therefore, be helpful to recall some highlights of each campaign, not because they were necessarily the most important but because they are particularly memorable features of the two elections. _Our_ contest is the one in which the dollar was devalued, which preceded the establishment of the Saskatchewan Medicare scheme, in which the Liberals held the Bomarc missiles to be useless, in which Premier Smallwood prevented Donald Fleming from addressing the St. J...n's Rotary Club, and which saw the rise of Réal Caouette in Quebec. It was in 1962 that Prime Minister Diefenbaker was prevented by rowdy demonstrators from being heard at his Vancouver rally and that, at Trail, BC, he was confronted by some

---

2. Irma S. Rombauer, _The Joy of Cooking: A Compilation of Reliable Recipes with an Occasional Culinary Chat_ (New York, numerous printings).

nude Doukhobor ladies.   In 1962 the party standings were Conservative 116, Liberal 100, Social Credit 30, and NDP 19.   We
are <u>not</u> concerned with the election in which the Liberals advocated
a nuclear role for Canada, nor with the one in which they launched
the Truth Squad.   The 1962 election antedates the appointment of
Senator McCutcheon to the cabinet and the later resignations of a
number of senior ministers from the government.   The number of
seats won by the parties in 1963 was: Conservative 95, Liberal
129, Social Credit 24 and NDP 17. (3)

When the careful and conscientious reader has put down the
<u>Papers</u> he will have within his grasp a sort of do-it-yourself kit
containing the materials out of which several election theories can
be constructed.   The authors hope that by unpacking and displaying
the kit, they will have tempted many readers into trying to put some
of the pieces together with the help of such additional equipment as
they have acquired in their own observations of Canadian elections.
To encourage an extensive use of this election kit, a special effort
was made to publish the <u>Papers</u> in a format and at a cost which
will make this volume accessible not only to a wide public but particularly to students -- both of the fee-paying and the armchair
variety.

                                                        J.M.

Kingston, January 1964

3. The reader who still finds it difficult to place the election in
its proper historical context is advised to consult John Saywell's
succint account, "Parliament and Politics" in J.T. Saywell, ed.,
<u>The Canadian Annual Review for 1962</u> (Toronto, 1963), particularly
pp. 3-39.

CONTENTS

x CONTENTS

CONTRIBUTORS

Robert R. Alford is Associate Professor of Sociology at the University of Wisconsin. He is the author of Party and Society, a comparative study of voting behaviour in the Anglo-American Countries.

Ivan Avakumovic is Associate Professor Political Science at the University of British Columbia.

Morris Davis teaches Political Science at Tulane University. He is the author of Iceland Extends Its Fisheries Limits: A Political Analysis (1963) and of several articles on interest groups and on public opinion.

Léon Dion is the head of the Department of Political Science at Laval University and is the author of numerous works on public opinion and contemporary politics.

William P. Irvine is a doctoral student in Political Science at Queen's University.

Vincent Lemieux is in the Department of Political Science at Laval University. He is a frequent contributor to Recherches Sociographiques.

K.A. MacKirdy is in the Department of History at the University of Waterloo. He is the author of a number of articles on political manifestations of regional sentiment in Canada and Australia, and is associated with T.H. Qualter in the analysis of the press coverage of the 1963 election.

John Meisel is in the Department of Political Studies at Queen's University.

George Perlin is a doctoral student in Political Science at Queen's University.

Tom Peterson is in the Department of Political Science and International Relations, University of Manitoba.

T.H. Qualter is in the Department of Political Science at the University of Waterloo. He is the author of Propaganda and Psychological Warfare (New York, 1962) and is doing an analysis of press treatment of the 1963 election.

Peter Regenstreif is Assistant Professor of Political Science and Canadian Studies at the University of Rochester.

Howard Scarrow is Associate Professor in the Department of Political Science at the State University of New York, Stony Brook, New York.

Mildred A. Schwartz is an Assistant Professor in the Department of Sociology and Anthropology at the University of Alberta, Calgary. She has written on ethnic groups and political behaviour and is currently studying the state of Canadian national identity.

Denis Smith is Assistant Professor of Politics at Trent University, Peterborough and managing Editor of the Canadian Forum.

CONTRIBUTORS

<u>Norman Ward</u> is Professor of Political Science at the University of Saskatchewan. He has written prolifically on Canadian politics, and humorously on Canadian society.

<u>Walter Young</u> lectures in political science at the University of British Columbia.

PART ONE:

CONSTITUENCY STUDIES

ST. JOHN'S WEST

George Perlin

I

Underlying the present two-party system in Newfoundland are the cleavages created by the constitutional referendum which led to union with Canada in 1949: the Liberal party was organized in Newfoundland by J.R. Smallwood, the successful leader of the confederation movement, while the Progressive Conservative party was established by former members of the two groups which had opposed union.

Although the new party system seemed to reify the conflict of the referendum campaign, the real focus of the differences between the parties in 1949 was not confederation; it was Mr. Smallwood. A skilful politician with wide popular support, the Liberal leader shaped and ruled his party with unquestioned personal authority. There was no broad set of principles to which the party was pledged; its members were united almost solely by their faith in Mr. Smallwood's leadership. In contrast, Conservative unity rested on a shared antipathy to the Liberal leader. To some Conservatives he was the personification of the union which they had bitterly fought against and still rejected; to others, who accepted confederation, he was a man of unproven administrative ability who displayed many of the characteristics of a demagogue.

The origins of the two parties still tend to blur whatever distinctions exist between them on matters of broad policy, but there has been some change since 1949, particularly in the attitude of Conservatives. While the Liberals experienced little difficulty in adapting themselves to the pattern of national politics, the Conservatives, for the first eight years of confederation, established no real identification with events outside Newfoundland. Mr. Diefenbaker's victory in 1957 gave them for the first time an opportunity to share in the prerogatives of power and a concomitant sense of participation in a larger political realm.

This broadening of the Conservative horizon has extended the range of discussion for both parties, but their dialogue reveals a lingering preoccupation with old feuds. Political debate in Newfoundland invariably seems to revolve around the figure of Mr. Smallwood. This is as true of federal election campaigns as it is of provincial campaigns. In attempting to understand the 1962 election in St. John's West, therefore, care must be taken to recognize the significance, at least for the competing parties, of

Premier Smallwood's dominant role in Newfoundland politics.

II

St. John's West extends over a fairly large geographical area
including about half of Newfoundland's capital city, St. John's, all
of the city's northern, southern, and western suburbs, and all of
the southern half of the Avalon Peninsula at the eastern tip of the
Island of Newfoundland.

Two-thirds of the riding's 32,000 voters live in St. John's or
the suburbs. Most of them derive their income from employment in
a variety of service industries, the federal and provincial civil
service, the transportation industry, or the distribution trade. Less
important sources of employment are the fishery and a few small
manufacturing and processing plants. (1)

The religious distribution of the population in the urban and
suburban sections of the riding is about equally divided between
Roman Catholics and Protestants with a slight Protestant majority.
Most of the Protestants belong to the Anglican Church or the
United Church, although the Salvation Army has a large number of
adherents and there are some smaller denominations.

The remaining third of the voting population of the riding live
in the three rural and semi-rural districts of Ferryland, St.
Mary's, and Placentia East. A majority of the people in these
districts are dependent on the fishery for their livelihood. Other
major sources of income are the United States Naval base and the
Canadian National Railways terminal at Argentia, in Placentia Bay,
and service industries in the nearby towns of Placentia, Fresh-
water, and Dunville. Some root-crop, dairy, and poultry farming
is also done on a very small scale near St. John's, and in the
Placentia area.

There is such a preponderance of Roman Catholics – an estimated ninety per cent of the population – in these three rural districts that the riding as a whole has a substantial Roman Catholic
majority. It has been customary, therefore, for candidates in the
riding to be Roman Catholics.

Other demographic and geographic factors influence the nature
of campaigning and, to a certain extent, the kinds of appeals which
the parties make. While there is a concentration of population in
St. John's and its environs, voters in the rural areas live in small

_____

1. The Dominion Bureau of Statistics has not at the time of
writing made available the data it collected in the 1961 census on the
occupational distribution of the riding's population. As a result this
part of the description of the demography of the riding has had to be
based on figures from the Newfoundland government census of 1945
and some speculative interpretation of later DBS figures. The
description of the religious distribution of the population has been derived from the 1961 census, although it, too, has had to be interpreted rather speculatively since there were no figures available for
the individual provincial districts within the riding.

settlements scattered along the coastline and can be reached only by driving over rather rough gravel roads. Not all settlements have electricity and where this utility does exist many homes are without television receivers. Thus the principal means of communication between the parties and the electorate are radio and public meetings in the villages. Door-to-door campaigning is difficult because houses in the smaller communities are often widely dispersed along fairly long stretches of coast. The small size of settlements also militates against the establishment of elaborate local organization, the cost being impracticably disproportionate to the number of voters in each community.

The absence of local government and a sparsity of public services, largely a result of the peripheral distribution of the population, reduce campaigning in the rural areas to parish-pump politics at its most elemental level. Each community has specific needs in the form of marine public works, the extension of rural electrification, or special aid in times of a poor fishery. There are constant demands for new roads or for improvements to existing roads and most communities still lack many of the basic amenities of modern living such as water and sewage systems. Candidates in both federal and provincial elections are expected to pay at least lip service to promises to remedy these conditions.

III

In the first federal election to be held in Newfoundland, in June 1949, the Progressive Conservative candidate in St. John's West was W. J. Browne, a district court judge who had been a minister in the last administration before the suspension of responsible government in 1933. Mr. Browne had been forced to resign his judicial position just after confederation when, apparently on the initiative of Premier Smallwood, the appropriation for his salary was not renewed. (2) The circumstances of his return to politics dictated the course of the campaign. It became a personal struggle between the Conservative candidate and the Liberal Premier, dramatically climaxed by Mr. Browne's attempt to have Mr. Smallwood arrested on charges of voter intimidation. Mr. Browne won the election, but it was a victory only in the first skirmish of a long battle. In the next encounter, the general election of 1953, he was defeated.

Within a few months of his defeat in 1953 Mr. Browne had found a by-election seat in the provincial legislature. However, he was anxious to return to federal politics and the Premier seems to

---

2. The St. John's _Daily News_ quoted the Premier on June 9, 1949, as saying: "Had (Mr. Browne) not resigned he would have been removed on the grounds that he has shown by his conduct during the past 12 months that he was unfit to exercise his (judicial) functions ...." The conduct to which the Premier referred apparently was Mr. Browne's participation in a petition to the Supreme Court to have the 1948 referendum declared unconstitutional.

have been equally anxious to remove from the provincial assembly
a man who had proved to be the Liberal administration's most
forceful and exacerbating critic. As a result, with the approach of
the federal election of 1957, Mr. Smallwood advised his adversary
that if he chose to return to St. John's West the Liberals would
offer him only token resistance. (3)

    Mr. Browne regained his seat in 1957 and was appointed a
minister without portfolio in the new Conservative government. He
was re-elected with a substantial majority in 1958 and subsequently
was appointed Solicitor General.

    In the elections of 1957 and 1958 the personal quarrel between
Mr. Browne and Premier Smallwood appeared to have mellowed, but
it was renewed with greater animosity than ever in 1958 when two
serious disagreements developed between the federal and provincial
governments. The first arose from a strike of loggers represented
by the International Woodworkers of America against the Anglo Newfoundland Development Company, one of the province's two big
newsprint producers. The strike was marked by several violent
physical exchanges between IWA members and non-union loggers
and, when over a period of several weeks the situation continued
to deteriorate, Premier Smallwood intervened to propose to the
loggers that he assist them in the formation of a new union. Un-
rest among the loggers continued and the Royal Canadian Mounted
Police, under contract to the Newfoundland government to police
the rural areas of the province, informed Ottawa that they needed
additional men to maintain order. The Mounted Police request was
refused by the federal Department of Justice and, as a consequence,
the province sued the federal government for breach of contract.

    Relations between the two governments were further strained
by the second disagreement which developed over the interpretation
of Term 29 of the amendment to the British North America Act by
which Newfoundland had entered Confederation. This term provided for the appointment of a royal commission within eight weeks
of union to review Newfoundland's financial position and to recom-
mend what additional financial assistance the province might require
to continue its public services at the levels and standards reached
at the time of the commission's hearings. The commission was
appointed in 1957 and recommended in 1958 that special federal
grants of eight million dollars a year be paid in perpetuity to the
Newfoundland government. In March 1959, Prime Minister Diefenbaker announced that the payments would be made only until 1962
when Newfoundland's position would be considered along with that
of all of the other provinces in a new review of Dominion-Provincial
fiscal relations. Mr. Smallwood denounced the decision as a vio-
lation of the Terms of Union and in July convened a special session
of the provincial legislature to debate it. The Premier made Mr.
Browne the focus of his attack, accusing the Solicitor General of
failing to fulfil his responsibility to uphold the interests of the province

_____

3. Mr. Browne is the source for this information.

in the Dominion cabinet. Seeking popular support for his position, Mr. Smallwood dissolved the legislature and called an election in which the Liberals and dissident Conservatives who organized themselves under the name United Newfoundland party, won all seven of the provincial districts which lie within St. John's West. The Premier described the result as a repudiation of Mr. Browne and vowed to defeat him in the next federal election.

IV

Richard Cashin, a twenty-five-year-old St. John's lawyer, was chosen by Premier Smallwood to oppose Mr. Browne in the general election of 1962. (4) Despite his youth, Mr. Cashin's name was well known in Newfoundland politics. His grandfather had been a Conservative prime minister of Newfoundland in the days of responsible government and his uncle had been for a short time the leader of the Progressive Conservative party in the post-confederation period. Mr. Cashin's other assets were his personal charm and his natural skill as an orator.

The Liberal candidate's campaign was built around a theme of loyalty to Newfoundland. The Liberals sought to discredit Mr. Browne as a member of a federal administration which they claimed had flouted the province's rights in the IWA and Term 29 disputes, a claim symbolized by the appointment of a United Newfoundland party member of the legislature as Mr. Cashin's campaign manager. Mr. Cashin was presented to the electorate as a candidate who would put the interests of his province before all else.

Mr. Browne ignored the issue of loyalty, at least in the form in which it was presented by the Liberals. He based his campaign on the record of federal government payments to, and disbursements in, Newfoundland, stressing that they had been more than doubled under the Diefenbaker administration. Mr. Browne implied that the eight million dollars a year provided for Newfoundland in the recommendation of the royal commission on Term 29 was of relatively minor significance when compared to the gross increase in federal subsidies and other assistance. The Conservative candidate also pointed to his success in securing federal financing for the extension of rural electrification, for the initiation of a harbour development project in St. John's, and for public works projects in rural sections of the riding.

A third candidate, Stanley Ross, running on behalf of the New Democratic party, took no part in this debate of primarily local

---

4. The method of selecting Liberal candidates for both federal and provincial elections is revealing of the nature of the Newfoundland Liberal party. Although a general nominating convention was held in 1949, candidates since then have been appointed by the party. In fact this has meant that the selection of candidates has been entirely the prerogative of Mr. Smallwood. There is nothing covert about the use of this process for the names of candidates always are announced either in personal statements by the Premier or in statements issued by his office.

issues devoting his limited campaign resources to an exposition of NDP national policies. (5)

Specifically national issues were given less emphasis by the Liberals and Conservatives although the electorate was exposed to campaign literature distributed by the old parties' national head-quarters and heard network broadcasts by Mr. Diefenbaker and Mr. Pearson.

The Conservatives found a new issue to exploit in the last two weeks of the campaign. On June 7, Finance Minister Donald Fleming, in St. John's to campaign on behalf of PC candidates, was invited by the local Rotary Club to be the guest speaker at its weekly dinner meeting. The Premier, learning of the invitation just before the meeting, sent a letter to the club's officers, while the meeting was in progress, advising them that if the Finance Minister were permitted to make his address the Newfoundland government would regard the club as a partisan organization and would be unable to sponsor a dinner and provide facilities for a district Rotary convention to be held later in the month. The club interpreted the Premier's letter as an ultimatum and informed Mr. Fleming that it had been forced to withdraw its invitation to him. Conservative leaders capitalized on the incident, declaring it to be unmistakable evidence of Mr. Smallwood's belief that he could act with impunity in any area he chose. To illustrate further their claim that the Premier was contemptuous of democratic processes they pointed to the apparently deliberate and methodical mutilation of campaign posters which they had erected throughout St. John's. (6)

In its closing days the campaign was marked by the exchange of increasingly intemperate attacks. A newspaper published by the Liberals, on the basis of the sale of Canadian wheat to China and the Canadian government's refusal to end trade relations with Cuba, described Mr. Browne as "the Communists' friend." (7) (This charge, in addition, to its obvious pejorative connotation, was calculated to undermine Mr. Browne's support among voters employed at the United States naval base at Argentia.) In turn, the Conservatives alluded to Mr. Smallwood as a new Hitler. (8)

It was with this cacophony of charges and counter-charges ringing in their ears that the voters of St. John's West went to the polls. Their decision reflected an obvious uncertainty. Mr. Cashin had 12,656 votes, Mr. Browne, 12,608, and the NDP candidate 280. Mr. Cashin's victory had been secured by the slimmest of

---

5. Mr. Ross was never regarded either by his own party or by his opponents as anything more than a token candidate.

6. Not to be outdone, the Liberals claimed that their campaign posters had also been destroyed which led to a ludicrous display of petty bickering over the question of which party had lost the larger number of posters.

7. The Liberal, published by the Liberal party of Newfoundland, June 1962, p. 4.

8. "The Truth Is," Evening Telegram, St. John's, June 6, 1962.

margins (9) but it was still a substantial accomplishment. Only four years before Mr. Browne had defeated another Liberal opponent by more than five thousand votes.

V

Analysis of the St. John's West election was based on data collected in a single-wave post-election sample survey. Returns were secured from 231 voters (a sample of 0.78 per cent) (10) and of this number 204 provided answers suitable for comprehensive study.

The accuracy of the demographic distribution of the sample, to the extent that it could be tested, was verified without significant error. There was a distinct bias, however, in the distribution of the voting choices of respondents. The Liberal vote was over-represented by 7.2 per cent and the Conservative vote was under-represented by 6.2 per cent. (11) Several factors contributed to this error, but the most significant appears to have been a post-election shift of support to the Liberal candidate. (12) The exaggeration that the error represents therefore is probably largely confined to respondents who indicated a preference for Mr. Cashin and if allowance is made for this exaggeration there seems to be no reason to suspect the results of the analysis.

The survey questionnaire was designed to gather information about the social characteristics of respondents, their interest in the election, their reaction to the issues, their views of the candidates, and the consistency of their voting habits. Very few of these

---

9. A recount in July reduced Mr. Cashin's majority to less than thirty votes. Later the Supreme Court of Newfoundland declared the election void on the ground that thirty-three servicemen had been improperly registered.

10. The original intention was to secure interviews with 320 people but this goal could not be realized. In the difference between the sample objective and actual returns refusals accounted for thirty-seven cases and the repeated absence of prospective respondents from their homes for twenty-five. Another ten people had moved and could not be traced. The breakdown of road communication to one section of the rural area of the riding and the inaccessibility of some smaller settlements accounted for the remainder of the difference. The percentage of complete returns is comparable to that in other studies. For example, see Bernard R. Berelson, Paul F. Lazarsfeld, and William N. McPhee, _Voting_ (Chicago, 1954), p.383.

11. In the election the Liberal candidate polled 49.5 per cent of the votes cast and the Conservative 49.3 per cent. Among the 204 respondents from whom a voting preference was secured 57 per cent favoured the Liberal candidate and 43 per cent favoured the Conservative.

12. The likelihood of the introduction of a systematic bias by the omission of a part of the rural area of the riding was found to be negligible.

Table 1
Associations between Voting Choices and Social Characteristics of
Respondents

	Number of cases	Percentage* Liberal	Association**
All respondents	204	57	
Age***			
21-33	32	72	+15
34-44	63	54	- 3
45-54	60	65	+ 8
55-64	34	41	-16
65 and over	14	36	-21
Unclassified	1		
Sex			
Male	114	53	- 4
Female	90	61	+ 4
Religion			
Roman Catholic	128	47	-10
Anglican	31	68	+11
United Church and other Protestant#	45	78	+21
Class##			
Upper and upper middle###	31	77	+20
Lower and middle white collar	34	59	+ 2
Skilled blue collar	58	64	+ 7
Fishermen and farm workers	21	48	- 9
Semi-skilled	20	35	-22
Unskilled	16	50	- 7
Pensioned or retired	17	53	- 4
Unclassified	7		

*For the sake of simplicity the percentage Conservative is not shown. It may be determined by subtracting the percentage Liberal from 100.

**The measure of association is explained in the text.

***The first division by age (21-33 years) is extended over a somewhat broader range (twelve years) than the other divisions because it was thought desirable to try to distinguish between respondents who had entered the electoral population before and after Confederation. Although a perfect distinction could not be made because respondents were not asked the exact date of their birth, it was assumed that persons of thirty-four had been of voting age before Newfoundland became a province.

#There were only five people in the "other Protestant" category. It was decided therefore to group them with members of the United Church. The "other Protestants" included two members of the Salvation Army, a Presbyterian, a member of the Pentecostal Assemblies, and one person who did not identify a specific denomination.

##The class scale was constructed on the basis of an occupational rather than a multi-factor status differentiation. Occupations were ranked as upper class, upper middle class, lower middle class white collar, skilled blue collar, fishermen and farm workers, semi-skilled and unskilled from a status scale adapted from the general ranking provided in Albert J. Reiss et al., Occupation And Social Class (New York, 1961). An eighth category not given a specific ranking was provided for persons who were pensioned or retired because there was evidence that their former occupations were not necessarily related to their current status. A separate category was provided for fishing and farm occupations because of the difficulty involved in trying to evaluate their status position in relation to urban occupations.

###Only four persons were ranked as upper class. Hence, it was decided to group upper and upper middle class people in a single division.

subjects could be treated satisfactorily within the limits of the space allotted to this paper. We shall therefore give a broad sketch of the findings with respect to two or three of the more interesting of them to illustrate some of the distinguishing features of voting behaviour in the riding. The discussion which follows will deal briefly with the relationship of some of the main social characteristics of respondents to their voting choices, the reaction of respondents to the issues raised in the campaign, and an attempt to explain the basis of the change in voting preferences which led to the Liberal victory in 1962. (13)

VI

Associations between the voting choices people made and their social characteristics have been found in all sociological studies of voting behaviour. The criterion for determining the strength of these associations in St. John's West was the extent to which the distribution of voting preferences of people with a particular characteristic deviated from that of the whole sample. In Table I, then, associations are measured by subtracting the percentage Liberal in each category from the percentage Liberal for the whole sample. A positive result indicates an association with a Liberal preference and a negative result an association with a Conservative preference. On this basis it can be seen that the association of sex with voting choice was rather weak, the tendency of men to vote Conservative and women to vote Liberal being measured as a deviation of only

13. A full report of the analysis of the survey data is contained in a master's thesis entitled "St. John's West, A Survey Study Of a Constituency in the Canadian General Election of 1962," submitted by the author of this paper to the University of Chicago.

4 per cent. On the other hand, with the exception of people of 34 to 44 years, age and voting choice were fairly strongly associated: young people and people from 45 to 54 tended to vote Liberal and people 55 and over tended to vote Conservative. The association for class was also fairly strong. Upper and upper-middle class people and higher-status blue-collar workers clearly favoured the Liberal candidate, while fishermen and farmers, the semi-skilled, the unskilled, and people pensioned or retired tended to vote Conservative. Only the Liberal preference of lower-middle-class white-collar workers was too weak to be considered very significant.

The one association which was free of ambiguity was that for religion. Being a Protestant was clearly associated with voting Liberal and being a Catholic was clearly associated with voting Conservative.

Tests for spuriousness, holding each characteristic and combination of characteristics constant in relation to each and combinations of the other characteristics, confirmed most of these findings but suggested that some sub-groups were under cross-pressures. Of particular interest was the fact that, when religion was controlled, lower-middle-class white-collar workers, the unskilled, and people who were pensioned or retired followed the preferences of their religious rather than their status-group memberships. Religion, therefore, appeared to have an association with voting choice which was quite independent of other variables.

If the relationships observed in Table I are more than coincidental a person whose social characteristics subject him to a preponderance of pressures weighted in favour of a particular preference should follow that preference when he votes. Table II shows that the chance that this would be so varied from better than average to good. Of the fifty-six respondents who possessed three or four of the characteristics associated with a Liberal preference 86 per cent actually voted Liberal, and of the sixty-six people who possessed three or four of the characteristics associated with a Conservative preference about six in ten actually voted Conservative. However, this criterion fails to distinguish the individuals most likely to vote Liberal or Conservative in the group of respondents whose social characteristics subject them to equally balanced countervailing pressures. Furthermore, as has been noted frequently, any attempt to understand electoral choice purely in terms of individual social characteristics will inevitably be frustrated by the fact that this highly static variable cannot explain the direction of change from one election to another. If social characteristics were the primary or only determinants of electoral choice, vote distributions would be expected to assume an almost inflexible pattern. The fact that they do not is evidence that other variables must be taken into account.

One factor which would have to be included in any enumeration of these additional variables is the impact on voters of the issues which constitute the substance of the party dialogue during the campaign. The precise relationship of voters' perceptions of the issues to their party preferences is by no means obvious. It may well be asked whether issues, in fact, influence vote decisions or whether

Table II

Percentages of Respondents Voting Liberal on a Scale of the
Social Characteristics Associated with a Liberal Preference*

| | Number of Characteristics Associated with a Liberal Preference** | | | | |
	4	3	2	1	0
Percentage voting Liberal	86	86	53	39	43
Number of cases***	14	42	68	43	23

*All associations - sex, age, religion, and class - observed
in Table 1, regardless of their strength, were used in con-
structing the scale.

**The scale, of course, also shows the extent of agreement
between the number of characteristics associated with a Conservative preference and a Conservative voting choice: to say
that a person has no characteristics associated with a Liberal
preference is the concomitant of saying that he has four
characteristics associated with a Conservative preference.

***Only those respondents who actually reported having voted are
included. Thus the total number of cases is 190 instead of
204.

they merely reinforce existing predispositions. Although the St.
John's West survey was not designed to seek an explicit answer to
this question, it did provide some more general information about
the importance which voters ascribed to the issues.

Respondents were asked to select from a list the three issues
which they thought had been most important in the election. (14)
On the basis of their replies each issue was ranked on a simple
percentage scale, the issue's score being determined by calculating
the number of times it was mentioned as a proportion of the number
of times it would have been mentioned if all respondents had thought
it important. The ordering of the issues on the scale, excluding
those which failed to achieve a minimum score of 10 per cent, is
shown by party preference in Table III.

Inspection of the Table reveals that there was general agreement between Liberals and Conservatives about which issues were

---

14. There were seventeen issues on the list. They were: the
St. John's harbour development, local roads, Mr. Browne's record,
the record of the Diefenbaker administration, Term 29, Canada's
trade with Communist China and Cuba, the IWA dispute, the extension of rural electrification, the Rotary incident, the destruction of
campaign posters, Mr. Cashin's age, nuclear weapons for Canada,
unemployment, the future of the United States bases in Newfoundland, public works, Mr. Smallwood's record, and the devaluation of
the dollar. The issues were chosen from the speeches of the principal participants in the campaign, literature distributed by the parties, and the materials used in newspaper, radio, and television advertisements. Both the Liberal and Conservative candidates in-
spected and approved the list before the final draft of the questionnaire was prepared.

Table III
Issues Mentioned Most Often as Important (by Voting Preference)

Liberal preference		Conservative preference	
Issue	Percentage*	Issue	Percentage*
Unemployment	54	Unemployment	53
Term 29	39	Diefenbaker record	32
Smallwood record	30	Browne record	24
Diefenbaker record	27	Term 29	23
Dollar devaluation	21	Harbour development	22
Browne record	21	Public works	21
Cashin's age	20	Dollar devaluation	16
Public works	17	Smallwood record	14
Local roads	12	Cashin's age	10
Harbour development	10	Local roads	(9)**

*The percentage is the number of times an issue was men-
tioned calculated as the number of times it would have been
mentioned if all respondents had thought it important.

** The percentage here is enclosed in brackets to indicate that
for Conservatives it did not achieve the minimum score, 10
per cent, established as the base for placing an issue on
the scale. It has been included because for the whole
sample it did achieve the minimum score.

most important in the campaign. However, the relative frequency
with which issues were mentioned varied considerably between
supporters of the two parties. Not surprisingly, issues which were
emphasized by the Liberal party during the campaign were mentioned
more often by Liberal voters than by Conservatives and those which
were emphasized by the Conservative party were mentioned more
often by Conservative voters. For example, Term 29 was described as an important issue by two of every five Liberal voters
as compared with only one in five Conservatives and, conversely,
the St. John's harbour development was mentioned by one in five
Conservatives as compared with only one in every ten Liberals.
There was only one issue, unemployment, for which there was no
significant inter-party difference and it was an issue about which
both parties had said a good deal during the campaign. However,
the fact that it scored at the top of the scale was inconsistent with
the ranking that it might have been expected to have, since the parties gave it far less attention in the campaign than, for example,
issues arising from the strained relations between the federal and
provincial governments. Possibly this was because Newfoundlanders,
living in a province with a backward and seasonal economy, are
constantly more conscious than current conditions may warrant of
the insecurity of their employment.

The kinds of issues which were mentioned suggest that people
in St. John's West do not make much distinction between federal
and provincial politics. Of the ten issues on the scale only three,
unemployment, the devaluation of the dollar, and the record of the
Diefenbaker administration, could be regarded as being of direct
importance to other Canadian voters and one of these, the record

of the Diefenbaker administration, had a peculiarly local connotation because of the emphasis in the campaign on Dominion-Provincial relations. The other issues, with the exception of the two (Mr. Cashin's age and Mr. Browne's record) which dealt with candidate qualifications and as such might be expected to concern voters in any constituency, were matters of primarily local interest. Indeed, two of them, Mr. Smallwood's record and local roads, had nothing to do with federal politics.

The explanation for the failure of respondents to make clear distinctions between federal and provincial issues remains uncertain. Are the voters' parochial views of the issues a reflection of their own biases or do they reflect attitudes acquired because of the parties' insistence on deliberately extending the provincial political struggle into the federal arena? It is likely that the relationship is one of interaction rather than of simple cause and effect (15), but the kind of data collected in the survey are too general to sub-stantiate this observation. An authoritative explanation will have to await further research.

VII

There are three factors which may produce electoral change: some members of the electorate may change their preferences; others who have voted in previous elections may decide not to vote; and others who have not had the opportunity to vote before or who have not used that opportunity may become voters. All of these factors contributed to the Conservative defeat in St. John's West in 1962, but the survey suggested that the most important of them was a shift in party preferences. Of the 190 respondents in the sample who reported voting, thirty-eight said that they had switched their preferences and of this number thirty-three voted Liberal.

Although, as it was observed earlier, knowledge of the asso-ciations between voting preferences and individual social character-istics cannot explain the direction of electoral change; it can be use-ful in identifying people with varying degrees of susceptibility to change. This was the case in St. John's West. As Table IV shows, 75 per cent of the thirty-three changers, as compared with only 48 per cent of other respondents who had voted Conservative in 1958 possessed two or more of the characteristics associated with a Liberal preference. Since social characteristics are pre-sumed to influence the individual's voting choice by exposing him to certain groups of people who express particular preferences, we infer that three-quarters of the people who changed were among the 1958 Conservatives most exposed by their social-group memberships to Liberal arguments.

---

15. One piece of evidence which suggests this interpretation is the fact that "the Rotary incident," to which the Conservative party devoted much of its publicity in the final two weeks of the campaign, was considered important by less than 3 per cent of the people who expressed a Conservative preference.

Table IV
Proportions of 1958 Conservatives Who Voted Liberal in 1962 and
of 1958 Conservatives Who Remained Loyal to the Conservative
Party in 1962 with Four, Three, Two, One, and No Social
Characteristics Associated with a Liberal Preference

	(N)*	Number of characteristics associated with a Liberal preference				
		4	3	2	1	0
1958 Conservatives who voted Liberal	(33)	3%	36%	36%	12%	12%
1958 Conservatives who remained loyal	(74)	2%	8%	38%	35%	16%

*The number of cases is somewhat smaller than in Table I
because non-voters in both 1958 and 1962 have been excluded.

A majority of the changers were also among the 1958 Conservatives most exposed to Liberal arguments from another source.
Sixty-one per cent of them, as compared with only 31 per cent of
the people who remained loyal to the Conservative party, actively
followed the election campaign by listening to radio and television,
reading newspaper stories and advertisements, and attending public
meetings. (16)
   On the basis of these two pieces of evidence it was hypothesized that in general the greater the exposure of a 1958 Conservative to Liberal arguments the greater was the chance that he
would vote Liberal in 1962. The hypothesis is substantiated by
Table V which shows the proportion of changers among 1958 Conservatives grouped by the extent to which they followed the campaign through the communications media used by the parties and by
the extent to which their social group memberships exposed them to
people with Liberal preferences. Changers comprised nearly eight
in ten of the group whose members possessed three or four of the
characteristics associated with a Liberal preference and who
actively followed the campaign and only one in twenty of the group
whose members had one or no characteristics associated with a
Liberal preference and who followed the campaign infrequently. (17)
   The fact of greater exposure is not in itself an inducement to
change. It merely ensures that when a party can present a convincing case it will be heard. The decision to change will depend
upon the success a party has in projecting a favourable image of itself while destroying those aspects of the image of its opponent
which have attracted the potential changers. Obviously there must

16. Data of this kind were used to measure interest in the
election. A full treatment is given in the thesis to which reference
was made in n. 13 supra.
   17. There was only one exception to the hypothesis. The percentage of changers among 1958 Conservatives possessing a majority
of the characteristics associated with a Liberal preference remained
constant as media used decreased from average to infrequent.

<u>Table V</u>

Percentages of Changers among 1958 Conservatives Grouped by the
Extent to Which They Used the Communications Media to Follow the
Campaign and the Extent to Which Their Social Characteristics Were
Associated with a Liberal Preference

Used media to follow the campaign	Number of characteristics associated with a Liberal preference		
	4 or 3	2	1 or 0
Actively	78% (N 9)*	44% (N 18)	33% (N 15)
With average frequency	50% (N 4)	25% (N 12)	18% (N 11)
Infrequently	50% (N 8)	10% (N 10)	5% (N 20)

*The number of cases in each grouping is the total number of 1958 Conservatives.

have been something in the Liberal campaign in 1962 which possessed sufficient cogency to achieve this end. Could it be iden- tified?

Fortunately, a large number of respondents (twenty of the thirty-three) who switched their preferences made explanatory com- ments about their decision. Sixty-five per cent of them gave reasons related to Mr. Browne's stand on the federal-provincial disagreements of 1959. These thirteen respondents made statements such as "Browne didn't do right for Newfoundland" or "Browne and Diefenbaker let Newfoundland down." (18) Assuming these respondents to be representative of all turnover voters it appears that in a large majority of cases it was the Liberal success in branding Mr. Browne as a disloyal Newfoundlander and in pre- senting Mr. Cashin as "a man who will fight for Newfoundland" that decided the 1962 election.

To understand the significance of this issue it is only necessary to recall that the post-confederation party system in Newfoundland

---

18. Of the other seven turnover voters who gave explanations for their decisions, two said that they felt that "a younger man should be given a chance," one said he had been influenced by the Diefenbaker administration's national policies, one mentioned unem- ployment, another, a civil servant, felt the Conservatives should have increased civil service salaries, one said that he "just felt the Liberals would do a better job of running the country," and one said he had been impressed by Mr. Cashin's television appearance. Turnover voters' perception of the importance of the issues had no necessary association with their reasons for changing. Unemploy- ment, for example, was described as important by seventeen of the nineteen respondents who gave other reasons for their decisions to change.

emerged from the cleavages produced by the constitutional referendum campaign of 1948.   The Conservative party was founded by
leaders of the movements which had opposed confederation and in
succeeding elections has relied largely for its support on areas
which voted against confederation.   While it is difficult to determine
precisely what motivated anti-confederation sentiment there is fairly
substantial evidence that it drew its impetus largely from local
patriotism. (19)   The Liberal choice of loyalty to Newfoundland as
the principal issue of the 1962 campaign, therefore, attacked the
very roots of Conservative support.

VIII

This paper has extended over a fairly wide range of topics
without thoroughly exploring or explaining any one of them.   While
this is not very satisfying, it is a necessity dictated first by the
use of rather crude tools of analysis and second by a desire to
provide a general background both for further studies of voting behaviour in Newfoundland and for comparative studies with voting
behaviour in other Canadian provinces.

Some of the specific findings of this research must be treated
with caution.   For example, the analysis of associations between
the social characteristics and voting choices of respondents did not
include an assessment of the influence of such important variables
as levels of educational attainment and primary group memberships.
There is clearly a need for additional research including these
variables.   Additional research should also make use of the more
psychologically oriented techniques developed in the studies identified
with the Survey Research Center of the University of Michigan. (20)

Despite the limited value of some of the data, the survey did
suggest one general conclusion: to a significant extent voting choices
in St. John's West are the function of local rather than national
stimuli.   This is not really very surprising.   Newfoundland, after
all, has been a province of Canada for little more than a decade
and the traditions of its people are traditions with deep historical
roots.   A constitutional act does not transform a society, particularly
one which has existed on an island largely cut off from other parts
of the world.   Assimilation of the Newfoundland culture within a
wider Canadian culture may never be fully realized, but as Newfoundland attains maturity as a province it may be expected to adapt
itself slowly to its new political status.

---

19. This was the view expressed by several persons prominent
in the referendum campaign during interviews conducted for a BA
thesis (now on deposit with the Department of Political Science,
Queen's University) by the author of this paper.

20. See, for example, Angus Campbell et al., The American
Voter (New York, 1960).

DID THEY VOTE FOR PARTY OR CANDIDATE IN HALIFAX?

Morris Davis

This article describes the distribution of ballots in the dual constituency of Halifax in the parliamentary election of June 18, 1962,
and the clues this distribution reveals about the bases of the electors' vote decisions. (1) A dual constituency is admittedly an oddity
in Canadian federal politics (2); but the complex decision with
which it confronts the elector yields the political analyst statistical
data far richer than that for any more usual single-member district.
For example, in 1962 the Halifax voter faced not twice as many
choices as a voter in a normal constituency but almost six times as
many. In most of the country a voter had at most five options:
he could mark his cross for the candidate of one of the four
political parties or he could so cast his ballot that it would be
counted for no candidate. In Halifax he had twenty-nine options; in
twenty-one ways he could pair any of the seven candidates with any
of the remaining six; or in seven ways he could vote for a single
candidate; or he could cast a null ballot. Indeed, had there been
the full roster of eight candidates (3) the Halifax voter would have
had some thirty-seven alternatives among which to choose.

Practising politicians in the Halifax area classify ballots under
three major headings: straights, splits, and plumpers. (4) These
categories are also useful to the academic student of politics.
Straight ballots (i.e., those on which the voter chose both

---

1. I am grateful to Professors John Graham, Alasdair
Sinclair, and James Aitchison, all of Dalhousie University, and to
Professor William Dalton of St. Mary's University, for their aid
and advice; and to the Atlantic Provinces Studies of the Social
Science Research Courcil of Canada, for a grant, which, though
primarily for another project, allowed me the time to gather the
data used here. Responsibility for the views expressed in this
article is, of course, solely mine.
2. Halifax in Nova Scotia and Queens in Prince Edward
Island are presently the only such federal constituencies. On the
subject of dual constituencies see Norman Ward, "Voting in Two-
Member Constituencies," Public Affairs, IX, Sept., 1946,
pp. 220-3.
3. The Social Credit party nominated only one candidate.
4. Rejected ballots and spoiled ballots are both null. Only
the former are tallied, however, since valid ballots have presumably
been cast in place of the latter.

candidates of a single party) he can assign primarily to the appeal of the party. (5)   Split ballots (i.e., those on which the voter selected candidates from two different parties) he can interpret as deriving primarily from the appeal of the candidates. (6)   Plumper ballots (i.e., those cast for only one candidate), though more difficult to interpret, at the least indicate weaker party loyalty than do straight ballots. (7)   By comparing the ballot profile of each nominee the political analyst can consequently develop certain indices of the comparative influence of party and candidate (8) on the vote decision.

Unfortunately, neither the number of straight, split, and plumper ballots, nor the configuration of candidates on them, can be deducted confidently from gross election statistics. (9)   Conventionally, the number of apparently split ballots for a party has been estimated as equal to the difference in votes between its higher and lower candidates. (10)   The lower candidate, in other words, supposedly receives all his votes on straight ballots, while the higher candidate alone appears on split ballots.   This assumption, of course, is systematically conservative; by precluding compensating splits and plumpers it necessarily overestimates the extent of straight party voting.

A comparison of Table I and II spotlights the inadequacy in such a method of computation.   Table I presents the number of apparently straight and split ballots computed according to this

---

5. The other possibility, that the voter favours both candidates of the same party because of their personal characteristics rather than their party label, is remote and (as our discussion of ticket balancing will later indicate) extremely unlikely.

6. Admittedly, the voter casting a split ballot might favour one nominee for reasons specific to the candidate while favouring the other for party reasons; such a voter, however, would certainly not be considered a loyal party supporter.   Furthermore, the explanation for his supporting one nominee for party reasons and not supporting the other candidate of the same party, likely also lies in the personal characteristics of the candidates.

7. Plumper ballots are difficult to interpret because they may primarily reflect ignorance (e.g., not knowing that there are two votes) or antipathy to the running mate not voted for.   They seem intermediary to straight and split ballots because, while not fully supporting the ticket of any one party, they do not at all support that of any other.

8. Other factors, such as ideological preferences, cannot be identified by the methods employed here.

9. Let whoever doubts this imagine a dual constituency with only four electors and two parties in which the vote is 2 and 1 for each pair of candidates.   Then let him calculate how many patterns of straight, split, and plumper ballots are consonant with these results.   The problem, of course, is vastly more complex when there are ninety thousand voters.

10. This estimation procedure is employed by Ward, "Voting in Two-Member Constituencies."

Table I

Distribution of Apparently Straight and Split Ballots as Computed from the Total Returns for the Halifax Constituency

Party	Apprently straight ballots (1)	Apparently split ballots (2)	(2)/(1)
PC	41,804	1,160	.028
Lib.	40,635	837	.021
NDP	5,653	811	.143
Total	88,092	2,808	.032

rationale from the total returns for the Halifax constituency, and also the ratio between these two kinds of ballots. For the Progressive Conservative party the ratio is 2.8 per cent; for the Liberal party, 2.1 per cent; for the New Democratic party, 14.3 per cent; and for all three parties combined, 3.2 per cent. (11) As Table II shows, each of these ratios, even that for the NDP, seriously underestimates the amount of ticket splitting in the election. Table II contains data analogous to that in Table I, but this time computed for each of a sample (12) of polling places in the Halifax constituency. Examination of such small units allows us to isolate many split ballots that would average out in the gross results for the entire electoral district. According to this analysis the Progressive Conservatives have a ratio of apparently split to apparently straight ballots of 5.0 per cent; the Liberals, 3.6 per cent; the New Democratic party, 35.5 per cent; and the three parties, 6.1 per cent. Using poll-by-poll figures in effect doubles the estimated ratio of split to straight ballots.

Table II

Distribution of Apparently Straight and Split Ballots as Computed from a Sample of Polling Stations in the Halifax Constituency

Party	Apparently straight ballots (1)	Apparently split ballots (2)	(2)/(1)
PC	3,482	174	.050
Lib.	3,244	118	.036
NDP	394	140	.355
Total	7,120	432	.061

Even poll returns, of course, average out many split ballots. In addition, they do not facilitate the separation of split from plumper ballots or the specification of pairings that occur on split ballots. Any deeper analysis of the vote distribution requires access not to

---

11. Since the Social Credit party ran only one candidate, it is omitted from consideration here.

12. This sample is identical with the "combined sample" discussed below.

grouped electoral statistics but to individual ballots.   Only then can one determine the proportion of straight, split, and plumper ballots, and the pattern of candidate votes among them.

The balance of this paper is based on a ballot-by-ballot count of a sample of polls in the Halifax federal constituency.   Since the sample we used is not mathematically random, an account of its selection might be in order.   The sample falls under two headings: systematic and preliminary. (13)   The systematic part was collected during my attendance, as agent for one of the candidates, at the recount held in Halifax during July 1962.   Press of other business and lack of assistants (14) permitted my attending the recount only every second morning.   All ballots on all polls examined during those mornings together comprise the systematic portion of the sample.   Though the selection procedure was admittedly not random, it was practicable and indeed analogous to choosing clusters of names at every n-th interval on a list.   In addition, even fully re-cording all the polls recounted would have provided inadequate in-formation about the whole Halifax constituency, the recount having been discontinued before any polling places outside the city of Halifax were examined. (15)

The preliminary part of the sample stems from the deputy returning officers of various polling stations having incorrectly com-pleted the "Statement of the Poll" (Form 53) which is delivered to the candidates or their agents.   The DRO's can hardly be blamed for their error, since these forms, like most of the machinery and

---

13. I use the term "preliminary" because I collected this sub-sample first and developed many of my procedures during its analysis. As we shall see, the purist might prefer the designation "haphazard."

14. No funds were budgeted for, or expended on, the re-search reported here.   Lack of money precluded interviewing.

15. The recount was held before Justice V.J. Pottier of the Halifax County Court.   In his concluding remarks at the recount Justice Pottier noted that examination was made "of the votes cast in 184 polling divisions, out of a total of what one might say com-prised 560 polling dividions.   I am including in this number the so-called service vote and the provision for advanced polls.   The re-count started on July 3rd and continued until July 17th, 1962. If a complete recount had been carried out I estimate it would have taken six weeks more." (Statement dated July 20, 1962).   The recount began on the initiative of the agent for the Liberal candidate, John E. Lloyd, and was discontinued after application to this effect on his behalf.   Cause of the application for discontinuance can probably be located in Liberal fears about the mounting costs they would face, given the unlikelihood, made evident as the recount proceeded, of snatching victory from the jaws of defeat.   (The question of costs is treated in an interesting statement of Justice Pottier dated July 16).

I should like to record here my gratitude to Justice Pottier and to the candidates' agents present at the recount for their cour-tesy and help.

regulations of federal elections, are constructed with single-member (rather than dual) constituencies in mind. The mistake consisted in the DRO's specifying, on the lines headed "Number of ballot papers cast for," not the seven candidates but rather the various ballot combinations they found when counting the poll: i.e., instead of stating that so many ballots were cast for candidate A, they reported so many for A and B, for A and C, for A and D, for A alone, and so on. (16) These incorrect completions of the "Statement of the Poll" furnished data similar to what we obtained for other polls at the recount. The preliminary sample also helped redress our geographical balance since it contained eight polls from the city of Dartmouth, one from the urban part of Halifax County, four from the rural part of the County, and only two (17) from the city of Halifax.

The systematic subsample includes the following thirty polling stations (all from the city of Halifax): 9 to 14, 46 to 54, 98 to 107, and 168 to 172. The preliminary subsample includes the following fifteen stations: 42 and 208 (city of Halifax); 220A, 220B, 239, 262, 286, 287, 292A, and 304 (city of Dartmouth); 333A (urban part of Halifax County) and 380, 403M-Z, 408, and 435H-Z (rural part of Halifax County). Taken together these forty-five polling stations comprise the <u>combined sample</u> hereinafter analysed.

As Table III indicates, this combined sample departs markedly from the geographical distribution of votes in the constituency as a whole. (18) With hindsight one can, of course, design far more elegant samples of polling stations. (19) But the gods of chance

---

16. Since the forms provided only seven lines for cast ballot papers and there were some twenty-eight possible combinations of candidates, DRO's often resorted to considerable writing between lines. One deputy returning officer managed to cram information on seventeen kinds of ballots within this restricted space.

17. A third polling station, already in the systematic subsample, was eliminated. Otherwise the preliminary subsample comprises all polls in which the DRO's mistakenly recorded all ballot combinations found. It does not, however, include polls where the DRO unhelpfully (for both me and the Returning Officer) grouped split ballots together under an omnibus category like "miscellaneous splits" or "miscellaneous ballots."

18. A word of caution on the figures for the combined sample. As specified earlier, these data come from two sources: from the recount and from Forms 53 completed by DRO's. Both these sources give figures slightly different from those certified by the Returning Officer. (Because the recount was discontinued, no corrections it would have made in any polls are official. Errors it uncovered were, however, slight: with 61,882 votes counted, the total net change for all seven candidates amounted to only 191 votes, or about 0.3 per cent. Gross changes, of course, were somewhat higher.)

19. With the co-operation of one or more of the parties, agents at a randomly selected set of polling places could record ballot-by-ballot voting on election night. This would be the best method to use

Table III
Geographical Distribution of Votes by Halifax Constituency
and by Combined Sample

Place	Constituency		Sample	
	Number	Percentage	Number	Percentage
City of Halifax	74,061	40.8	11,024	73.7
City of Dartmouth*	33,408	18.4	2,459	16.5
County of Halifax (Urban)	24,124	13.3	323	2.2
County of Halifax (Rural)**	41,560	22.9	1,126	7.6
Service Vote	8,304	4.6	0	0.0
Total	181,457	100.0	14,932	100.0

*Urban polling stations only.
**Includes 17 polling stations in rural Dartmouth, and one polling station on Sable Island.

sometimes smile on unworthy mortals; and, as Table IV indicates, there is an astoundingly close correspondence between the percentage of the vote obtained by candidates in the combined sample and the actual vote distribution in the total constituency. Instead of subjecting the sample to tests of significance, which might be hard to justify anyway given the non-random characteristics of the sample, let us simply note that in no case does the difference between a candidate's sample and constituency percentages differ by more than 0.8 per cent; and that this, or even the candidates appearing in the same rank order for both the sample and the constituency, is more than we had a right reasonably to expect. Henceforth we shall assume that the combined sample presents a profile of voting decisions similar to that for the entire electoral district.

It is appropriate here to introduce the nominees before we inquire about the extent to which electors voted for candidate or for party. Except for Social Credit the parties chose two nominees apiece. (20) In selecting its "team," each party obviously tried to balance certain religious, geographical, and perhaps ideological factors. The Progressive Conservatives renominated the two incumbent members of Parliament for Halifax, Robert McCleave and Edmund Morris. McCleave, a Protestant from the city of Halifax, was generally rated a moderate in politics; Morris, a Catholic whose home is in the urban part of Halifax County, was more openly and caustically controversial. Of the Liberal candidates, John E. Lloyd, a Protestant residing in, and at this time mayor of, the city Halifax, had long been an active politician; while Gerald A. Regan,

---

in any future replication of this report. A recount happened to provide the occasion for collecting data, but it is not at all essential for future studies.

20. The Social Credit party nominated Robert J. Kuglin, a Protestant clergyman from Truro, Nova Scotia (i.e., from outside the Halifax district). He conducted a rather perfunctory campaign.

Table IV

Distribution of Votes among Candidates by Halifax Constituency
and by Combined Sample

Candidate (Party)	Constituency		Sample	
	Number	Percentage	Number	Percentage
Aitchison (NDP)	6,464	3.6	524	3.5
Kuglin (Socred)	1,784	1.0	117	.8
Lloyd (Lib.)	41,472	22.9	3,328	22.3
McCleave (PC)	42,964	23.7	3,656	24.5
Morris (PC)	41,804	23.0	3,519	23.6
Regan (Lib.)	40,635	22.4	3,305	22.1
Ronayne (NDP)	5,653	3.1	428	2.9
(Rejected ballots)	681	.4	55	.4
Total	181,457	100.1*	14,932	100.1*

*Difference from 100.0% due to rounding.

a Catholic nominally from Halifax City (in fact from outside the geographic bounds of the constituency) and a young lawyer who often
represented labour unions, was still seeking his first victory in a
political campaign.   Finally, the New Democratic party nominated
James H. Aitchison, a Protestant from Halifax City and a professor
of political science at Dalhousie University, who was much concerned with defence policy and with United States-Canadian relations;
and Perry Ronayne, a Catholic labour union official from the city of
Dartmouth, who emphasized bread-and-butter issues.

With only two candidates to choose there were severe limits on
the extent of ticket balancing attainable, but the parties can hardly be
accused of not making an effort.   Each party (21) nominated one
Catholic and one Protestant.   Each party (with the nominal exception of the Liberals) chose one candidate from the city of Halifax
and one from some other part of the electoral district.   Each party
presented nominees who could reasonably be said to represent
different major components of that party.

How important factors like religion and geography (22) were
to the vote decision is difficult to assess.   Religion as we shall point
out shortly, seems to have been a prime motivating factor for about
2 per cent of the Halifax electors.   Geography evidently mattered
even less.   McCleave, for example, ran better than Morris in the
urban part of Halifax County (and in the rural part as well) (23);
Aitchison did his best in the city of Dartmouth, and indeed did
better there than Ronayne (24); and Lloyd received a higher percentage of the vote in the rural areas of Halifax County than he did

21. The Social Credit party is omitted from consideration here.
22. On ideology see note 8.
23. McCleave obtained 25.2 per cent of the vote in the urban
County areas, and Morris 24.4 per cent.   For the rural County
the figures were 23.0 and 22.5 per cent.
24. Aitchison received 3.6 per cent of the vote in Halifax City
and 4.2 per cent in Dartmouth; Ronayne had 4.0 per cent in Dartmouth.

in the city of Halifax. (25)

Further analysis of the motives behind the voting decision depends on an exact reckoning of voter behaviour. Table V lists the twenty-nine kinds of ballot decisions possible in the Halifax constituency and the number and percentage of each kind in the combined sample. Grouping these figures shows that 87.70 per cent of the electors cast straight ballots and 5.11 per cent cast plumper ballots. (26) The 6.11 per cent who split their votes between candidates of two different parties included 3.06 per cent who voted for two Protestants, 1.10 per cent for two Catholics, and 1.95 per cent for both a Catholic and a Protestant. (27)

One could say either that seven out of eight voters cast straight party ballots or that more than 11 out of 100 voters were not faithful party supporters. In either case, the ratio of non-straight to straight ballots is not 3.2 per cent, as customary analysis would have suggested (28), but 12.8 per cent. An examination of actual ballots, in short, shows between three and four times as much ticket splitting and plumper voting as would be predicted from the gross election returns. Some, but by no means most, of this ticket splitting is traceable to the religious background of the candidates, and presumably of the voters. The electorate included 4.16 per cent split voters who selected candidates of the same religion and 1.95 per cent those of different religions. Split ballots, in other words, exhibited more than twice as much religious homogeneity as heterogeneity. (29) Caution must be exercised in interpreting these figures, of course: the difference is small (2.21 per cent) and other factors may be responsible for the results. For example, each of the Protestant candidates may have been better known or more capable than his running mate. On the whole, however, it does not seem rash to suggest that religion did have a small but systematic effect on the election results. (30)

In gauging the appeal which each candidate exerted on voters apart from that of his party, it may seem reasonable to emphasize the number of plumper ballots he received. After all, these represent voters he attracted and his running mate did not: that is the

---

25. The figures are 23.7 per cent in the rural County and 21.7 per cent in Halifax City.

26. Since the Social Credit party had only one candidate, there is some difficulty in classifying ballots marked for Kuglin alone. If we consider them straight ballots, the total of such ballots would be 88.09 per cent; if we consider them plumpers, the total of plumper ballots would be 5.50 per cent.

27. If we omit Kuglin, the figures would be 2.13, 1.10 and 1.74 per cent respectively.

28. See note 2.

29. The exact ratio is 2.08. With Kuglin omitted it is 1.85. Protestantism, like Catholicism, is here considered as a single religious category.

30. The over-all election returns also reflect this fact. Each Protestant candidate did better than his running mate.

Table V
Behaviour in Combined Sample

Ballots marked for:	Number	Percentage
Aitchison (NDP) and Kuglin (Socred)	42	0.55
Aitchison (NDP) and Lloyd (Lib.)	22	.29
Aitchison (NDP) and McCleave (PC)	34	.44
Aitchison (NDP) and Morris (PC)	13	.17
Aitchison (NDP) and Regan (Lib.)	16	.21
Aitchison (NDP) and Ronayne (NDP)	368	4.78
Aitchison (NDP) alone	29	.38
Kuglin (Socred) and Lloyd (Lib.)	20	.26
Kuglin (Socred) and McCleave (PC)	9	.12
Kuglin (Socred) and Morris (PC)	3	.04
Kuglin (Socred) and Regan (Lib.)	10	.13
Kuglin (Socred) and Ronayne (NDP)	3	.04
Kuglin (Socred) alone	30	.39
Lloyd (Lib.) and McCleave (PC)	108	1.40
Lloyd (Lib.) and Morris (PC)	27	.35
Lloyd (Lib.) and Regan (Lib.)	3,053	39.62
Lloyd (Lib.) and Ronayne (NDP)	5	.06
Lloyd (Lib.) alone	93	1.21
McCleave (PC) and Morris (PC)	3,336	43.30
McCleave (PC) and Regan (Lib.)	64	.83
McCleave (PC) and Ronayne (NDP)	9	.12
McCleave (PC) alone	96	1.25
Morris (PC) and Regan (Lib.)	50	.65
Morris (PC) and Ronayne (NDP)	1	.01
Morris (PC) alone	89	1.16
Regan (Lib.) and Ronayne (NDP)	34	.44
Regan (Lib.) alone	78	1.01
Ronayne (NDP) alone	8	.10
Rejected	55	.71
Total	7,705	100.02*

*Difference from 100.00% due to rounding.

connotation of the term "plumper." And in fact the higher of the two candidates in each party did receive the higher number of plumper votes. The ratio of plumper to straight ballots for each candidate, as printed in the first column of Table VI, might then provide an index of a candidate's pulling power relative to that of his party. All candidates except Aitchison, it can be seen, obtained between two and three plumper votes for every hundred straight party votes; Aitchison obtained nearly eight per hundred. From this one might conclude that all nominees, except Aitchison, exuded personal appeal to relatively the same extent.

Unfortunately, as noted earlier (31), plumper votes are not unambiguous. A person may cast only one vote because he does

31. Ward is not unaware of the shortcomings in his method. See article cited in note 2, especially 223.

Table VI
Ratios by Candidate of all Plumper to Straight, and
Split to Straight, Ballots in Combined Sample

Candidate (Party)	Plumper/Straight	Split/Straight
Aitchison (NDP)	.079	.345
Lloyd (Lib.)	.030	.060
McCleave (PC)	.029	.067
Morris (PC)	.027	.028
Regan (Lib.)	.026	.057
Ronayne (NDP)	.022	.141

not know he has two votes. (The ballot itself contains no directions.) He may want to cast two votes for his party but not know
both candidates' names. He may vote for one candidate because of
his party and not vote for the other candidate for personal reasons:
in so acting he may not be a very loyal party supporter, but at
least he is not directly disloyal. In this sense plumper ballots may
reasonably be interpreted as party-instigated as well as candidate-
impelled.

The ratio of split to straight ballots is a much less ambiguous
measure of a candidate's pulling power. The elector who casts a
split ballot is being overtly disloyal to all parties: not only to the
parties he neglects but to the two parties for whose nominees he
does vote, because of having also voted for one of their opponents.
Candidate rather than party factors can thus be said to lie behind
the vote decision of the ballot splitter. The second column of
Table VI, which reproduces this preferable ratio, shows not merely that the more popular candidate in each party has the higher
score but also that there is a clear difference between the NDP and
the two larger parties. Both Ronayne and Aitchison, the latter especially, exhibit marked drawing power relative to their party. For
every 100 votes he received that are traceable to party affiliation,
Aitchison received 34 votes for personal reasons and Ronayne 14.
Other candidates amassed less than seven split votes for every
hundred straight, with Morris obtaining less than three per hundred.

Once again, the figures in Table VI are based on fairly small
numbers of split and plumper ballots and must be interpreted with
some caution. Position on the ballot, for example, seems to have
influenced the behaviour of certain voters. More than half of 1 per
cent of the voters marked their crosses for Aitchison and Kuglin,
the first two names on the ballot. Indeed, as Table V shows,
Aitchison was paired with Kuglin more than with any other candidate
except his running mate Ronayne. Conversely, Kuglin was paired
with Aitchison almost as frequently as with all other candidates combined - despite the openly critical attitude of Professor Aitchison to
the Social Credit party and the principles for which it reputedly ·
stands. Some politicians have suggested to me that Aitchison-Kuglin
ballots represent protest votes against the "establishment" or the
dominant socio-political forces in the Halifax region. Kuglin-Ronayne
ballots, however, would equally well express such protest, and only

Table VII

Ratios by Candidate of Plumper to Straight, and Split to Straight,
Ballots in. Combined Sample, All Pairings with Kuglin (Socred)
Having Been Eliminated

Candidate (Party)	Plumper/Straight	Split/Straight
Aitchison (NDP)	.079	.231
Lloyd (Lib.)	.030	.053
McCleave (PC)	.029	.064
Morris (PC)	.027	.027
Regan (Lib.)	.026	.054
Ronayne (NDP)	.022	.133

.04 per cent as against .55 per cent, of the ballots were in this form. Religion may account for some of this discrepancy – Aitchison and Kuglin are Protestants and Ronayne is Catholic – but the main factor in the Aitchison-Kuglin pairings seems to have been their occupying the first two places on the ballot. (32)

If we omit from our computations split votes in which Kuglin figures, an omission that can also be justified on classificatory grounds (33), the ratios in Table VI become those in Table VII. Column 1, of course, is the same but in column 2 Aitchison's ratio is reduced by about a third. Ratios for the other candidates remain virtually constant. None the less, though the range is considerably narrower, there is still a clear difference between the two NDP candidates, particularly Aitchison, and those of the other parties. Both the New Democratic party's nominees were less dependent on their party for their share of the vote than were the nominees of either the Liberal or Progressive Conservative parties.

An interesting insight into the voters' perception of a candidate can be gleaned from his ratio of plumper to split ballots. Table VIII provides these data with and without the Social Credit candidate Kuglin. The figures in the two columns vary considerably, but the rank order is identical. Ronayne and Aitchison received a rather large number of split votes in comparison to plumper votes. Morris, on the other hand, had by far the fewest number of split votes relative to plumper votes. A plausible interpretation of these figures is that Aitchison and Ronayne, while saddled with the least attractive party image in Halifax, were viewed by many electors as personable candidates, support for whom was not incompatible with support of

---

32. In his split ballots Ronayne was paired most with Regan. Although these are the last two names on the ballot, it would be difficult, because of both men being Catholics and identified with labour unions, to establish that ballot position was a major factor in this pairing.

33. Because the Socred party had only one nominee, any elector favouring that party and also wishing to utilize both votes to which he was entitled, would have to cast a split ballot. Those who favoured other candidates or parties were under no such compulsion. As a result, split ballots involving Kuglin may well have been qualitatively different in origin from other split ballots.

Table VIII

Ratios in Combined Sample of Plumper to Split Votes
by Candidates, Pairings with Kuglin (Socred)
Being Included or Eliminated

Candidate (Party)	Pairings with Kuglin included	Pairings with Kuglin eliminated
Aitchison (NDP)	.228	.341
Lloyd (Lib.)	.511	.574
McCleave (PC)	.428	.447
Morris (PC)	.947	.978
Regan (Lib.)	.448	.476
Ronayne (NDP)	.154	.163

some other candidate. Because their personal attractiveness was
not exclusive or controversial, there was little psychological strain
in voting for Aitchison, or to a lesser extent for Ronayne, and also
for someone not in the NDP. Towards Morris, however, most
voters seemed to have either a deep and exclusive commitment or
none at all. They voted for him and McCleave for party reasons
or they voted for him alone (34); but relatively few electors could
see their way clear to combining a vote for Morris with one for a
candidate from any other party. Aitchison's and Ronayne's com-
patibility with candidates of other parties had its mirror twin in
Morris's incompatibility. (35)

Finally, Table IX records the number of split ballots and the
ratio of split to straight ballots obtained by each party. In this
Table "NDP-Lib." should be read in column 2 as "the number of
ballots for either candidate of the NDP along with either Liberal
candidate divided by the number of straight NDP ballots"; "Lib.-NDP"
should be read as "the number of ballots for either candidate of the
NDP along with either Liberal candidate divided by the number of
straight Liberal ballots"; and so on. According to Table IX, the
NDP figured on almost half as many split as straight ballots; indeed,
almost a fifth of its votes (36) came from persons who were not
consistent supporters of that party. The NDP was associated in
split ballots more often with the Liberal party than with the Progressive Conservative party. In this sense the NDP may perhaps
be said to have hurt the Liberal party. It would be more accurate,
however, to say that the Liberals and PC's hurt each other; for
the Lib.-PC ratio of .081 and PC-Lib. ratio of .075 are based on
249 ballots in the combined sample, whereas the NDP-Lib. ratio of
.209 derives from 77 ballots and the NDP-PC ratio of .155 from

---

34. 1.16 per cent of the electors cast plumper ballots for
Morris in comparison to 1.21 per cent for Lloyd, 1.25 per cent
for McCleave, and 1.01 per cent for Regan.

35. This conclusion is consonant with political scuttlebutt around
Halifax concerning Morris's appeal among the electorate.

36. Each split vote is here computed to be worth half a straight
vote to a party.

Table IX
Number of Split Ballots and Ratio of Split to Straight Ballots in Combined Sample by Party Pairings

Pairings	Number of split ballots	Ratio of split to straight ballots
NDP-Lib.	77	.209
NDP-PC	57	.155
NDP-Socred	45	.122
Total NDP-All	179	.486
Lib.-NDP	77	.025
Lib.-PC	249	.081
Lib.-Socred	30	.010
Total Lib.-All	356	.116
PC-NDP	57	.017
PC-Lib.	249	.075
PC-Socred	12	.004
Total PC-All	318	.096
Socred-NDP	45	1.500
Socred-Lib.	30	1.000
Socred-PC	12	.400
Total Socred-All	87	2.900

57. The Liberals and Conservatives, in other words, split more than twelve times as many ballots as the net difference between NDP-Lib. and NDP-PC ballots. (37)

To the question posed at the beginning of this article the answer is now clear. (38) In the election of June 18, about 88 per cent of the voters in the constituency of Halifax chose both standard bearers of the same party. Another 5 per cent voted for a single candidate; and 6 per cent split their vote among candidates of two parties. The decision of perhaps a third of the ticket splitters can be traced to the religious affiliation of the candidates; and of another twelfth to the ease and simplicity of marking crosses for the first two names on the ballot. Some candidates seem to have exerted considerable drawing power apart from that wielded by their party. All nominees demonstrated this capacity to some extent, but those of the NDP stood out in this respect. James Aitchison, in particular, received a third as many votes for personal reasons as for party reasons. A candidate like Morris was more controversial in character; and while he drew considerable support from those who especially favoured him, he tended rarely to be paired with a candidate from another party. Loyal party support fails to explain the decision of one Halifax voter in eight, not just one in twenty-five or

---

37. In contrast to the NDP, both larger parties received almost all their support for party reasons, only a twentieth of their votes coming on split ballots. The Social Credit party's figures differ widely from those of the other parties because it ran only one candidate.

38. At least if our methods are assented to.

thirty as earlier methods of investigation would have indicated. In so close an election as this constituency experienced in 1962, factors other than party loyalty easily spelled the difference between defeat and victory for two, and perhaps even all four, of the top runners in the race.

Microscopic analysis of a case study is merely of curiosity value if it does not illuminate phenomena greater than itself in time or space. At the risk of appearing rash, I should like, therefore, to conclude what I hope has been a cautious presentation with some incautious generalizations from our findings. First, Canadians do not split their votes as often as electors in the United States reputedly do only because they do not have the opportunity. In a federal election most Canadians have only one vote and you cannot split one vote. Instead, many of them do the next best thing, voting one way at the national level and another way at the provincial. Second, the number of persons who vote for a new party for party reasons has probably been consistently overestimated. A party that is just beginning or that has recently been revived often nominates fresh and vibrant candidates; and much of the vote that the party supposedly attracts is actually due to the magnetism of these candidates. Third, the overlap of the Liberal and Progressive Conservative parties on the political scale, and the psychological ease with which many persons could switch from one party to the other, likely contributed much more to the final election results throughout Canada than did any systematic encroachment of the New Democratic party on the Liberals. Finally, it almost goes without saying that the election in Halifax, like politics in English Canada generally, yields virtually no clues at all about what goes on in the political world of Quebec.

ELECTION IN THE CONSTITUENCY OF LEVIS

Vincent Lemieux[*]

This paper attempts to explain the success of Social Credit in one of the Quebec constituencies where it was victorious. Lévis - the constituency chosen - is on the boundary of a block of twenty-six carried by Social Credit: the neighbouring constituency to the west, Lotbinière, elected a Conservative. As will be shown below, Lévis is predominantly urban, but there are areas in the back county where agriculture still predominates. In such a mixed constituency, we could study rural and urban "créditisme" at the same time. Lévis was also interesting because here Social Credit was confronted by an opponent of some stature, Maurice Bourget, who had been the member of Parliament since 1940. Finally, Lévis offered a particularly useful field for our research because we have already studied provincial elections in the constituency from 1912 to 1960.[1]

Since the federal election of 1949, the constituency of Lévis has been approximately the same at both the federal and provincial levels. The only difference is that the Saint-Henri area, including the municipalities of Saint-Henri, Saint-Henri-de-Lauzon, and Rivière-Boyer, is included in the federal constituency of Belle-chasse, whereas provincially it is part of Lévis.

In the federal riding, three ecological zones can be distinguished. The first lies along the river across from Quebec City and includes the constituency's two most populous urban areas - Lévis and Lauzon. A second zone, also urban, goes from Saint-David to Saint-Rédempteur, passing through Saint-Télesphore, Saint-Romuald, and Charny. Breakeyville would also have to be included, since very few farmers now remain here. The third zone, which, roughly speaking, forms a semi-circle around the two preceding ones, comprises areas which remained rural despite the increasing penetration of urban ways of life (Saint-Joseph, Pintendre, Saint-Jean-Chrysostome, Saint-Lambert, Saint-Etienne, and Saint-Nicolas). The population is more scattered in this third zone than in the other two. Also, these are the only settlements, with Saint-Télesphore, where masculine sex ratios are greater than 100. This is a good enough index of their rural character.

[*]In collaboration with Michel Chaloult and André Ouellet.
Translation by W.P. Irvine and John Meisel.
1. "Les Elections provinciales dans le comté de Lévis, de 1912 à 1960", Recherches sociographiques, II, no. 3-4 (July-Dec., 1961), pp. 367-399.

Table I
Population of Localities in the Constituency of Lévis
from 1948 to 1961, and Masculine Sex Ratios in 1961

	1941	1951	1961	Index of pop.growth 1961/1941	Masculine sex ratios (1961)
Lévis	11,991	13,162	15,112	126	94
Lauzon	7,877	9,643	11,533	146	96
Total, Zone 1	19,868	22,805	26,645	(134)	95
Saint-Romuald	4,027	4,797	5,681	(141)	94
Charny	2,831	3,300	4,189	(148)	98
Saint-David	875	1,147	1,968	(225)	96
Breakeyville	1,194	1,155	1,213	(102)	96
Saint-Rédempteur	680	757	1,035	(152)	97
Saint-Télesphore	254	232	385	(152)	116
Total, Zone 2	9,861	11,388	14,471	(147)	96
Saint-Nicolas	1,738	2,036	2,384	(137)	107
Pintendre	1,063	1,267	1,465	(138)	106
Saint-Jean C.	1,238	1,469	1,471	(119)	106
Saint-Lambert	1,202	1,233	1,444	(120)	107
Saint-Etienne	682	788	868	(127)	104
Saint-Joseph	299	293	299	(100)	123
Total, Zone 3	6,222	7,086	7,931	(127)	107
Grand total, Lévis	35,951	41,279	49,047	(136)	97

Source: Censuses of Canada.

Since 1940, Maurice Bourget has always been re-elected easily in Lévis. Even in 1958, admittedly while running against a fairly weak opponent, he received 58 per cent of the vote – the highest percentage obtained by a Liberal candidate in Quebec. If we compare it to the province as a whole, and to the two regions which immediately surround it on one side and the St. Lawrence River (2), Lévis constituency has recently been very "Liberal." Table II shows this well.

Never the less, on June 18, 1962, Lévis was won by the Social Credit candidate, J.A. Roy. The final count gave him 11,504 votes. Maurice Bourget received 8,826 votes, and the Conservative candidate, Jean-Marie Morin, 3,575.

Our task is to examine this Social Credit sweep in Lévis. Because we decided to do this study only after the June election, the campaign was not followed particularly closely and it will not be

2. We have included in the first region the constituencies of Quebec and its outskirts, i.e., Quebec-East, Quebec-West, Quebec South, and Quebec Montmorency; and in the second region, the constituencies adjacent to Lévis on the south shore of the Saint Lawrence, i.e., Bellechasse, Dorchester, and Lotbinière.

Table II

Percentage of Votes Cast for Liberals in the Province of Quebec,
in Lévis, and in the Two Regions round Lévis from 1940 to 1962

	1940	1945	1949	1953	1957	1958	1962
Province of Quebec	63	51	60	61	58	46	39
Lévis	68	71	61	72	72	58	37
Region to the north of Lévis (Q-East, Q-Montmorency, Q-West, and Q-South)	66	59	68	61	63	46	31
Region to the south of Lévis (Bellechasse, Dorchester, and Lotbinière	64	59	54	55	56	44	33

Source: Reports of the Chief Electoral Officer.

described here. We will, rather, relate the election results to a
number of political and other factors. (3)

The study will be divided into four sections. First we shall
give a provisional explanation of the Social Credit sweep in the constituency. Then we shall look for more particular factors to explain
the vote in certain milieux and geographic areas: the analysis of
these factors will occupy the second and third parties. In the fourth
section we will move from analysis to synthesis and attempt a general explanation of the Social Credit success in Lévis.

I. PROVINCIAL EXPLANATION OF SOCIAL CREDIT SUCCESS IN LEVIS

The Social Credit sweep in Lévis and in the part of Quebec
comprising the twenty-six constituencies won by it, can be related
to three series of occurrences, each of a different order. A
sweep of such magnitude would not have been possible without 1)
an economic climate which had been deteriorating for a number of

---

3. Our sources are public documents (the Census of Canada,
Reports of the Chief Electoral Officer, newspapers, etc.), over
eighty interviews done in Lévis during the summer, and our own
personal observations. We interviewed the three candidates and the
Returning Officer for Lévis, eleven Liberal organizers, eight Conservative organizers, and thirteen Social Credit organizers. We
also spoke with twenty voters in Zone 1 (Lévis and Lauzon), thirteen voters in Zone 2, (Saint-Romuald, etc.) and eleven voters in
Zone 3 (Saint-Nicolas, etc.). The voters were chosen at random
from the Voters' Lists. The author took part in some interviews,
but most were conducted by André Ouellet and Michel Chaloult.

years, a situation which was related to a set of political circumstances hardly favourable to the "old-line parties"; 2) the effective
exploitation of this situation and these circumstances by Réal
Caouette and some of his lieutenants, particularly on television; and
3) the diffusion of Social Credit by the large number of militants
and by an organization whose vigour contrasted with that of the
"old-line parties." Let us examine each of these occurrences.

In Lévis, as in the whole of the province, the number of unemployed had been increasing for four or five years. In both
urban and rural areas, but particularly in the latter, the prosperity
of the forties and early fifties gave way to a more trying economic
situation. The most tangible effect of this was the shortage of money
necessary to buy the ever more varied range of consumer goods
made increasingly attractive by advertising. Instalment buying was
an artificial solution to this shortage, a solution fostered by this same
commercial advertising.

During the war and in the immediate post-war years farmers,
encouraged by the then current prosperity, bought much costly agricultural machinery. For some years their profits decreased steadily, as agricultural prices remained stable, and prices of fertilizers,
feeds etc., increased constantly. The development of the "Chantiers
Maritimes" of Lauzon had also attracted rural dwellers to urban
settlements and to build houses there. Ever since, their debts and
their needs increased faster than their incomes.

At the political level, circumstances were hardly favourable to
the traditional parties. The Conservative party had disappointed its
followers after its stunning victory of 1958, and no longer had the
strong Union Nationale organization behind it. As far as the Liberals are concerned, the fact that their local organization was the
same federally and provincially meant that they were closely identified, in the popular mind, with the Lesage government, especially
since no federal leader held their interest. In many areas of the
constituency there was considerable dissatisfaction with the provincial government whose decision not to engage in patronage was
interpreted either as a sign of not understanding local problems or
as a disguised move to favour a few friends even more. (4)

These, then, were in rough outline the socio-economic situation and political conditions existing in Lévis well before the electoral

---

4. In the constituency, this disapproval was mainly directed
against the provincial Liberal member - Roger Roy - who was
accused of being unskilful and unco-operative in his relations with
organizers, associations, and individuals in various localities. For
Roger Roy to campaign alongside Maurice Bourget, as he felt he had
to, was to fan this resentment. Organizers for all three parties
stressed that this was one of the main reasons for the defeat of
Maurice Bourget. No one had much to criticize him for, except for
having supported Roger Roy's campaign in 1960 and for associating
himself with him again in this campaign.

campaign began. Réal Caouette's skill consisted of being able to exploit them on behalf of the Social Credit party. Many organizers are convinced that the weekly television talks of the Social Credit leader were an indispensable condition of the success of his party. They took place on Sunday night at supper time when families were all together. A very popular broadcast (l'Heure des Quilles) preceded Caouette. And, as a Liberal organizer remarked, people could not change stations: Caouette spoke on the only French-language channel in the area. The Social Credit quarter-hour was also followed by a very popular program (Robin des Bois): there was, therefore, a strong tendency to leave the set turned on during the Social Credit program regardless of one's attitude towards Caouette.

It seems that many people who were very hostile at first and who regarded Caouette as some sort of a deranged person, came in this way to agree with one or two of his ideas. During the week they would have the chance to discuss them with friends, neighbours, or fellow workers. It was in these primary groups that opinion leaders, who had previously been converted to Social Credit, built on a few appealing and retained ideas and convinced the others to pay closer attention to Caouette in the future. Many would do this the following Sunday, thus making themselves even more receptive to the Social Credit opinion leaders.

In a more general sense, the propagation of Social Credit seemed to have occurred in places where men meet and are united by social ties. A garage operator in Saint-Jean-Chrysostome did not like to admit that people stopping at his garage influenced his vote, which was cast for Social Credit. He did admit, however, that almost all of these people were Social Crediters. A truck driver from Lévis said that most of the other truck drivers he met during the campaign, and most of the people he met in restaurants, were Social Crediters and that it was through speaking with them that he became interested. A twenty-nine-year-old butcher from Saint-David discussed politics with his seven brothers and his father, a life-long Conservative. The seven brothers voted Social Credit but were not able to convince their father, who remained a Conservative.

Our interviews suggest that this diffusion through primary groups met with astounding success among workers at the "Chantiers Maritimes" of Lauzon, among the employees of the CNR, and Anglo Pulp (at Quebec), etc. The following are a few significant examples. A forty-five-year-old worker at the "Chantiers Maritimes" of Lauzon, who lived in Lévis, said that Social Credit was much discussed in the yards. He himself has never taken part in political discussions for he says he has a hard time expressing himself, but "after listening to them talking, and after watching television, I became convinced that Social Credit was the party of the future." A day labourer from Saint-Rédempteur, who was about fifty and who had always voted Liberal, did not take part in discussions with his fellow workers either, but admitted that they had an influence on him. Like them, he voted Social Credit. The

Liberal organizer at Saint -Rédempteur was of the opinion that very
few of the workers at the "Chantiers," the CNR, or Anglo Pulp
remained faithful to the old parties.   He cited the case of the local
mayor, who works in the CNR yards at Charny, and who, very
early in the campaign, gained the impression from his fellow workers that the Liberal party would be beaten in the constituency.   It is
also interesting to note that a large number of Social Credit organizers were employed in establishments where many workers
came together daily.   Of the thirteen Social Credit organizers we
met, no less than eight came from such an environment: three from
the "Chantiers" of Lauzon, three from the CNR, one from Anglo
Pulp, and one from a big dairy.   One can be sure that among these
people, the claims of Social Credit were reinforced by a class consciousness opposed to the management, to those who order them
about without explanation, and who, in many cases, are Anglo-
Canadians at the same time.   Among CNR employees, Donald
Gordon's $75,000 salary "for bringing about deficits" was a useful
symbol.

   Another important aspect of the propagation of the Social Credit message was that, in a good many cases, it was carried by the
young people.   One of the best election workers whom we were
fortunate enough to meet even told us that he always made a point,
when visiting a family to try and convert the younger members to
Social Credit, leaving it to them, after he left, to convert their
parents.   More sensitive than their elders to the needs raised by
commercial advertising, young people were also more aware than
they of the shortage of money, and were receptive to the solutions
put forward by Social Credit.   Nowadays they are also better informed than their elders, and because of their knowledge can influence their vote; in the past, it was the father who decided how
his sons and daughters would vote.

   A Liberal organizer also suggested to us that Maurice Bourget,
a former baseball player with a famous Lévis club, and a skilled
orator, did not mean as much to the young as to people over forty.
Younger people do not go to political meetings any more, and for
many of them, Maurice Bourget was no more than an "old man
from the past," in office too long.

   In certain places, several voters who favoured Social Credit
did not dare to declare their support openly.   This accounted for
some Social Credit organizers being among the most surprised at
the success of their party (this was the case at Saint-Rédempteur).
On this point, the MP, J.A. Roy, told us of having received
numerous telephone calls from unknowns, pledging him their vote
and apologizing for not being able to say it in public because of
pressures on them from the "old-line" parties.   The Liberals even
paid, for working on election day, several people who voted Social
Credit.   This "hidden créditisme" confirms our hypothesis that
Social Credit doctrines were disseminated mainly by primary groups,
whose silent action may well be hidden from partisan organizations.

   But this does not mean that the Social Credit organization was
useless.   Started one night in a basement with the advice of an

organizer from Quebec City, it was completely established for a
year before the election.   The candidate was chosen in September
1961 and could count on an organization of 400 members.

To ensure easier and more effective communication, the constituency was first divided into four territories: Lévis, Lauzon,
Saint-Romuald, and Charny.   Each of these territories included, in
addition to the place that gave it its name, several smaller localities.
Thus, Saint-Rédempteur, Saint-Etienne, Breakeyville, and Saint-
Lambert were part of the territory of Charny.   Each territory was
itself divided into ten or so sectors which did not necessarily correspond to villages or parishes.   Finally, each sector was made up
of from one to five or six polls.   Two people were responsible for
each poll, and there was a leader for each sector and each territory.   Thus the central organization only had to communicate with
four territory leaders instead of fifteen or twenty local or parish
organizers.   As to the territory and sector leaders, they only had
to communicate with ten or twelve subordinates at most.

The Liberal organization was not in as good a state.   From
the 1,200 members which it had at the time of Lesage's victory in
1960, no more than 200 were left by the time the campaign began.
In some places, they could count on only three or four workers
where they would have liked to have had ten.   The Liberals conducted an active but hardly enthusiastic campaign.   Several re-
proached the Montreal provincial leadership for having advised them,
as late as May 5, not to speak about Social Credit so as not to
seem to attach great importance to it.   Liberal strategists thought
that, in this way Social Credit would not be able to attract enough
Conservative votes to beat the Liberals.   This plan, formulated in
Montreal, may have had some merit for the province as a whole,
but in twenty-six constituencies it clearly proved mistaken.

The Conservative organization was in a state of even greater
disrepair.   Several organizers had left the Conservative for the
Social Credit party before the campaign began.   One of them, from
Saint-Etienne, told us how, when people saw him coming into a
house, they would say, believing that he was still a Conservative,
"This year, we are not voting for you, we are voting for Social
Credit."   He would reply that he, too, was voting Social Credit!
The Conservative candidate, Jean-Marie Morin, was one of the
last ones chosen in the province, and, from this late beginning,
never had a chance in the two-man battle between the Liberals and
Social Credit.

II. NON-POLITICAL FACTORS CONTRIBUTING TO
THE DIFFERENT LOCAL RESULTS

The three components of the Social Credit wave which we
have just examined had the same general impact on all the areas of
the constituency.   Everywhere the voters were conscious of an
economic situation and political conditions unfavourable to the "old-
line parties."   Caouette was heard and his message transmitted by
a number of workers whose ardour contrasted with the weariness

Table III
Results of the Federal Elections of 1957, 1958, and 1962 in the
Localities of the Constituency of Lévis (in percentages)*

		1957	1958	1962 Actual results	1962 Expected results
Lévis:	Participation:	81.4	83.7	87.7	87.7
	Lib.	59.7	50.2	34.4	33.5
	PC	21.7	33.5	14.8	12.2
	Socred			38.5	42.0
Lauzon:	Participation	85.4	87.5	90.7	90.7
	Lib.	65.5	55.0	39.5	36.7
	PC	19.9	32.5	10.9	11.9
	Socred			40.3	42.1
Saint-Romuald:	Participation	78.9	84.1	88.9	88.9
	Lib.	55.0	48.4	32.9	32.3
	PC	23.9	35.7	12.6	13.0
	Socred			43.4	43.6
Charny:	Participation	79.3	85.5	86.9	86.9
	Lib.	58.6	50.7	24.9	33.9
	PC	20.7	34.8	15.0	12.7
	Socred			47.0	40.3
Saint-David:	Participation	84.5	89.5	90.8	90.8
	Lib.	57.2	42.6	26.2	28.5
	PC	27.3	46.9	15.3	17.1
	Socred			49.3	45.2
Breakeyville:	Participation	82.6	86.0	89.2	89.2
	Lib.	50.7	40.2	24.3	26.9
	PC	31.9	45.8	11.2	16.7
	Socred			53.7	45.6
Saint-Rédempteur:	Participation	80.2	84.9	89.2	89.2
	Lib.	54.6	47.8	20.2	31.9
	PC	25.6	37.1	15.5	13.5
	Socred			53.5	43.8
Saint-Télesphore:	Participation	83.9	87.2	88.0	88.0
	Lib.	58.1	55.8	35.1	37.3
	PC	25.8	31.4	6.3	11.5
	Socred			46.6	39.2
Saint-Nicolas:	Participation	71.6	80.2	82.9	82.9
	Lib.	46.5	36.9	23.1	24.6
	PC	25.1	43.3	13.8	15.8
	Socred			46.0	42.5

Table III (Continued)

Pintendre:	Participation	84.4	83.7	92.6	92.6
	Lib.	51.6	35.5	23.2	23.7
	PC	32.8	48.2	13.7	17.6
	Socred			55.7	51.3
Saint-Jean	Participation	80.2	84.5	86.6	86.6
Chrysostome:	Lib.	47.1	39.0	28.7	26.1
	PC	33.1	45.5	10.1	16.6
	Socred			47.8	43.9
Saint-	Participation	82.7	87.6	91.0	91.0
Lambert:	Lib.	47.6	40.1	31.3	26.8
	PC	35.1	47.5	16.6	17.3
	Socred			43.1	46.9
Saint-	Participation	83.9	83.9	88.6	88.6
Etienne:	Lib.	62.4	30.5	23.5	20.4
	PC	21.5	53.4	12.1	19.5
	Socred			53.0	48.7
Saint-	Participation	87.4	87.9	94.8	94.8
Joseph:	Lib.	52.0	39.8	33.3	26.6
	PC	35.4	48.1	16.0	17.6
	Socred			45.5	50.6
Total	Participation	81.7	85.2	88.7	88.7
	Lib.	58.5	48.8	32.6	32.6
	PC	23.2	36.4	13.3	13.3
	Socred			42.8	42.8

Source: Reports of the Chief Electoral Officer
*The armed forces vote and rejected ballots are excluded.
Percentages are calculated from the total number of those
eligible to vote, in each election, not from those actually
voting.

and disaffection afflicting the Liberal and Conservative organizations.
Of the three factors, it was the second (Caouette's speeches) whose
impact was the most uniform. In connection with the other two,
small but significant differences occurred from locality to locality, as
will be indicated below.

But these small differences do not alone explain the much
larger differences in the election results in various parts of the
constituency. If we examine the list of areas in Table III we see
that the Liberal results (expressed as a percentage of the electorate) ranged from 20.2 to 39.5 per cent; the Conservative results,
from 6.3 to 16.6 per cent; and the Social Credit results, from
38.5 to 55.7 per cent. This table also gives the total Lévis vote
for the federal elections of 1957 and 1958, as well as what we are
calling the expected 1962 results. These will be referred to in observations to be made later.

To explain the voting differences among the various localities, we wish to examine some differentiating factors, whether or not they were considered by observers of the election, and see if they can be related to the local results.

A rapid increase in population is often a sign of a progressive area, and it has been argued that Social Credit strength was in non-progressive areas. However, no meaningful correlation arises from a comparison of the 1941-61 rate of increase in the various localities (Table I) with the voting results. Saint-David is the area with the greatest population increase by far (with an index of 225 compared to 1941, but it is one where Social Credit met with great success (49.3 per cent). The party is also very strong in Breakeyville, an area where the population has not increased since 1941), but not as strong as at Pintendre where the population increase was greater than that for the constituency as a whole.

Were men more responsive than women to the Social Credit appeal? If we compare the voting results and the masculine sex ratio (Table I) for each area, we do find a certain positive correspondence. Lévis, Lauzon, and Saint-Romuald are the three areas where the "old-line parties" most successfully resisted the Social Credit tide. They are also the areas having the largest proportions of women. On the other hand, Breakeyville and Saint-Rédempteur, which have approximately the same masculine ratio as Lauzon, are among the strongest Social Credit areas of the constituency. Never the less, the relationship is significant, particularly if the comparison is made by zones instead of localities. Table IV illustrates this well.

Table IV

Comparison of Social Credit Support with Masculine Sex Ratios by Zone

	Socred Support (1962)	Masculine sex ratio (1961)
Zone 1 - (Lévis, Lauzon)	39	95
Zone 2 - (Saint-Romuald, etc.)	47	96
Zone 3 - (Saint-Nicolas, etc.)	48	107

Source: Census of Canada (1961) and Report of the Chief Electoral Officer (1962).

But is this really a question simply of the relative proportion of men and women or rather, is it one of the ecological character of which this proportion is an index? It is here that we must present a simple proposition: the relationship seems to be between Social Credit support and the size of the locality rather than with just the masculine ratio. In the five largest centres of the constituency, i.e., (from largest to smallest) Lévis, Lauzon, Saint-Romuald, Charny and Saint-Nicolas, Social Credit obtained less than half of the votes east. On the other hand, the party polled more than half the votes in three of the five smallest villages: Saint-Etienne, Saint-Rédempteur, and Breakeyville, and in the other two, Saint-Télesphore and

Saint-Joseph, it received 46.6 and 45.5 per cent of the votes respectively. In the five most populous centres the Social Credit average was 41.1 per cent, in the five smallest localities it was 52.2 per cent.

Among the socio-economic factors we will examine only occupations. We have assumed from the outset that this was one of the principal factors influencing electoral behaviour, at least in the urban areas of zones 1 and 2. Therefore, we embarked on a fairly lengthy project to confirm or refute this hypothesis. All of the voters registered on the Voters' Lists for the eight urban areas were divided into two categories according to their occupation: the "higher" and the "lower" occupations. (5) They were also divided according to their electoral behaviour into two categories: those who supported the old parties, and those who supported Social Credit.

Table V
"Lower" Occupations and Social Credit Support, by Urban Locality

Localities	Percentage of electors with "lower" occupations	Actual percentage of Social Credit votes	Expected percentage of Social Credit votes
Lévis	50.6	38.5	37.8
Lauzon	67.6	40.3	45.5
Saint-Romuald	58.8	43.4	41.5
Charny	64.3	47.0	44.0
Saint-David	61.2	49.3	42.5
Breakeyville	73.9	53.7	48.2
Saint-Rédempteur	72.6	53.5	47.7
Saint-Télesphore	73.1	46.6	47.9
Total	59.7	41.8	41.8

Sources: Voters' Lists and Report of the Chief Electoral Officer (1962).

In the first two columns of Table V are placed the comparative percentages of "lower" occupations and of Social Credit voters. In all the eight areas taken together, the percentages of "lower" occupations is 59.7 per cent and the percentage Social Credit is 41.8.

_____

5. The "higher occupations" category included: professionals, members of religious orders, civil servants, office workers, secretaries, stenographers, merchants and tradesmen, manufacturers and entrepreneurs, as well as all people living on their income, and all widows. The "lower occupations" category included: all labourers, day-workers, clerks and craftsmen (grocers, butchers, restaurant workers, barbers, hairdressers who considered themselves as such and not as merchants or tradesmen) as well, naturally, as the unemployed. Wives and children whose occupations were not specified (housewives, oldest daughter) or whose occupation was not stated were classified with the father. Generally, we have felt that a "lower" occupation should be specifically identified in order to be counted. That is to say, in practice, that residual or doubtful cases

On the basis of these figures, we can suggest the following hypothesis (6): 60 per cent of "lower occupations voted Social Credit, but only 15 per cent of the "higher" occupations. If we add 60 per cent of 59.7 per cent (the percentage of "lower" occupations) and 15 per cent of 40.3 per cent (the percentage of "higher" occupations) we obtain 41.8 per cent which was the actual percentage Social Credit vote.

The percentages in the third column were thus obtained on the supposition that 60 per cent of the "lower" occupations and 15 per cent of the "higher" occupations voted Social Credit. This gives us the "expected" Social Credit vote as opposed to what the party actually received. We note that in Lévis, Saint-Romuald, and Saint-Télesphore the actual percentage and the expected percentages are very close. In Lauzon, on the other hand, there are appreciably fewer Social Crediters than we might have expected; while in Charny, Saint-David, Breakeyville, and Saint-Rédempteur, the opposite is true: Social Credit support is greater than our hypothesis would suggest. It is worthy of note that these four areas each include a high proportion of the "lower" occupations. According to the law of "social gravitation" originally formulated by Tingsten, we can expect that the percentage support from any social group for a party which represents the interests of that group will increase as the proportion of people from that group in the whole community increases. There is a strong possibility, given the nature of the diffusion of Social Credit propaganda described in the first part of this study, that this law operated in the four areas in question.

But why did it not apply in Lauzon, where there is a greater proportion of "lower" occupations than in Saint-David? To answer this question, we thought it advisable to extend the analysis, which was made possible by our data. Lévis and Lauzon are in fact huge settlements, having little in common with others in the constituency. Whereas each of the others corresponds to a single parish, Lévis and Lauzon include six parishes, Notre-Dame, Christ-Roi, and Sainte-Jeanne d'Arc in Lévis; Saint-Joseph (7) and Sainte-Bernadette in Lauzon, and Bienville which is three-quarters in Lauzon and one-quarter in Lévis. If we divide Lévis and Lauzon, following the parish boundaries as closely as possible, we see in Table VI that our six areas differ significantly with regard to both occupations and voting.

For the six parishes as a whole, we find that 59.7 per cent of the voters classified into "lower" occupations; 39.3 per cent voted Social Credit. Both these percentages are lower than for the whole of the eight urban localities in the constituency. We thus have to suggest a new hypothesis concerning the percentages of people with "lower" and "higher" occupations who supported Social Credit in our six parishes. I would suggest the following: 58 per cent of the

---

were classified more among the "higher" occupations than among the "lower" ones. Thus it would be more appropriate to say "others" rather than "higher" occupations.

6. This hypothesis seems the most plausible we could formulate on the basis of our interviews and of our personal observations.

7. Not to be confused with the locality of Saint-Joseph.

Table VI

"Lower" Occupations and Social Credit Support in the Six Parishes
within Lévis and Lauzon

Parishes	Percentage of electors with "lower" occupations	Actual percentage of Social Credit votes	Expected percentage of Social Credit votes
Bienville (Lévis and Lauzon)	55.8	34.1	38.4
Notre-Dame (Lévis)	41.9	29.1	32.1
Christ-Roi (Lévis)	56.9	46.5	38.8
Sainte-Jeanne d'Arc (Lévis)	66.7	51.4	43.2
Saint-Joseph (Lauzon)	65.8	35.3	42.8
Sainte-Bernadette (Lauzon)	77.4	49.3	48.0
Total	57.9	39.3	39.3

Source: Voters' Lists and the Report of the Chief Electoral
Officer.

"lower" occupation group and 13.5 per cent of the "higher" voted
Social Credit, accounting for that party's 39.3 per cent. The
"expected" percentages of Social Credit voters in the third column
of Table VI were calculated on the basis of this hypothesis.

In a general way, the figures in this table confirm the effects
of social gravitation suggested by the preceding table. In parishes
such as Sainte-Jeanne d'Arc and Sainte-Bernadette where the proportion of the "lower" occupations is high, the actual Social Credit
vote was higher than might have been expected. Note, however,
that Saint-Joseph was a deviant case: we shall discuss it later.
Conversely, in the two parishes where the number in "lower"
occupations was relatively small (Bienville and Notre-Dame) the
actual Social Credit vote is significantly lower than might have been
expected. This phenomenon illustrates the counterpart to the law of
gravitation cited above: the number of voters in a social category
who support a party acting for that category's interests decreases
as the percentage of people from that group in the whole community
decreases.

In order not to complicate unnecessarily this rather summary
explanation, we can dispose of this matter of amplification and atten-
uation due to social gravitation by suggesting the following. If, on
the average, 60 per cent of "lower" occupations and 15 per cent of
"higher" occupations supported Social Credit in the urban areas of
the constituency, these percentages may have risen to as high as
66 per cent and 18 per cent in places like Saint-Rédempteur,
Breakeyville and Sainte-Jeanne d'Arc, as they may have fallen to
55 per cent and 10 per cent in places like Bienville and Notre-Dame.

But the whole explanation cannot be based on the effects of social gravitation. There are almost as many in the "lower" occupations category in Saint-Joseph as in Sainte-Jeanne d'Arc, yet far fewer Social Credit voters (only 35.3 as opposed to 51.4 per cent in Sainte-Jeanne d'Arc). There are a few more in the "lower" occupations in Christ-Roi than in Bienville (56.9 to 55.8 per cent) but far greater Social Credit support in the first parish than in the second (46.5 as against 34.1 per cent).

These deviations are highly suggestive. Saint-Joseph, Bienville, and Notre-Dame are old parishes, most of whose families have lived there for a long time. These three occupy the centre of the area contained within Lévis and Lauzon. Christ-Roi and Sainte-Bernadette, on the other hand, and Saint-Jeanne d'Arc to a lesser degree, are peripheral and newer parishes, populated since 1940 by numerous young people who were attracted by the war-time development of the "Chantiers Maritimes" of Lauzon. In many cases, these newly-arrived people are now mortgagees making monthly payments on their houses, and on many things inside them! It is obvious from our interviews and personal observations that, where occupation is held constant, the new residents in the outlying districts of Christ-Roi, Saint-Bernadette, and even Sainte-Jeanne d'Arc were more sensitive to the Social Credit appeal than the older residents of Notre-Dame, Bienville, and Saint-Joseph.

The same phenomenon can be observed also at the poll level Thus, the poll containing the greatest proportion of "lower" occupations in Notre-Dame (59.6 per cent) is also one of the ones where Social Credit was least successful (only 30 per cent of those voting supported Social Credit). Voters in this poll live in the commercial district of Lévis in one of the oldest parts of the city and are members of some of the oldest local families. Not very far from them, in the parish of Christ-Roi, approximately the same proportion of "low" occupations is found in polls containing people who have settled there much more recently, but here 50, 60, or even 70 per cent of those voting did so in favour of Social Credit. The same phenomenon can be seen in Saint-Romuald. Of two polls, one in the old section, one in a new part, where there are 58.3 per cent and 56.3 per cent in the "lower" category respectively, fewer than 40 per cent of the voters in the first voted Social Credit, but 54 per cent did in the second.

To all of these non-political factors, we must now add the political ones if we are to give an adequate sociological analysis of the voting results.

III. POLITICAL FACTORS INFLUENCING THE LOCAL RESULTS

If we retain for a moment the somewhat restricted scope of our six parishes, we note a fairly close connection between the Social Credit vote of 1962 and the Conservative vote of 1958.

Concomitant with this positive relationship is a negative inverse relationship between the Liberal vote in 1958 and the Social Credit

Table VII

Comparison of the Results Obtained by the Liberals and
Conservatives in 1958 and by the Social Crediters in 1962,
in the Six Parishes within Levis and Lauzon (in percentages)

Parishes	Liberals 1958	Conservatives 1958	Social Credit 1962
Bienville (Lévis and Lauzon)	56.0	31.2	34.1
Notre-Dame (Lévis)	52.2	30.0	29.1
Christ-Roi (Lévis)	48.8	36.4	46.5
Sainte-Jeanne d'Arc (Lévis)	44.7	39.8	51.4
Saint-Joseph (Lauzon)	57.6	29.3	35.3
Sainte-Bernadette (Lauzon)	48.7	36.8	49.3

Source: Reports of the Chief Electoral Officer.

results of 1962. This suggests the fact, evident to any observer of the election in Lévis, that the Social Credit party recruited its support more from the Conservatives than from the Liberals.

The data in Table III will enable us to amplify this proposition. Here again, we will make a hypothesis which, although perhaps altogether too simple, will, by revealing some significant deviations, put us on the track of new explanations. Let us hold the electorate constant and suppose that only three types of switches took place from 1958 to 1962: (1) from Conservative to Social Credit, (2) from Liberal to Social Credit, and (3) from non-voter to Social Credit. This ignores six other possible types of switches (Conservative to Liberal, Liberal to Conservative, non-voter to Conservative, non-voter to Liberal, Conservative to non-voter, and Liberal to non-voter) but these seem to be unimportant, except perhaps for Conservative to Liberal. (8)

If, then, we consider only the three types of switching listed above, the following would have taken place in the constituency between 1958 and 1962: 63.5 per cent of the Conservatives switched to Social Credit, leaving the Conservatives with their 1962 percentage of 13.3 per cent, 33.2 per cent of the Liberals would have switched to Social Credit, leaving the Liberal party with its

_____

8. At least, this is the impression we received from interviews with thirty-six voters in the constituency. Of those who gave answers which were precise enough to be useful, none switched in any of the ways which we consider unimportant. Of those who switched from "old-line" parties to Social Credit, two out of three had voted Conservative 1958, and one out of three for the Liberals, which corresponds approximately to the hypothesis we are making below.

percentage of 32.6 in 1962; and, finally, 3.5 per cent of non-voters in 1958 would have voted Social Credit in 1962. These three categories of switchers add up to Social Credit's actual percentage in 1962 - 42.8 per cent.

By doing the same sort of calculation as before we can see what would have happened in each area if, in fact, Social Credit had received the support of all the non-voters of 1958 who voted in 1962, of 63.5 per cent of the Conservatives, and of 33.2 per cent of the Liberals. The results of these calculations appear in Table III.

We note first that in Lévis and Lauzon Social Credit did not obtain quite the percentage expected. This is due to the fact that the central parishes of Notre-Dame, Bienville, and Saint-Joseph outweigh the peripheral and, on the whole, less populous parishes of Christ-Roi, Sainte-Jeanne d'Arc, and Sainte-Bernadette. If we were to calculate the expected percentages for the six parishes as we did for the other areas of the constituency, we would find that Social Credit obtained quite a bit less than would have been expected in the first three parishes, and that in the other three, the opposite was the case.

Since Lévis and Lauzon between them account for more than half the population of the constituency, their vote has great weight in the riding as a whole. For Social Credit to have obtained less support than might have been expected, according to our hypothesis, means that in the other areas, their actual percentages will, for the most part, exceed the expected proportion. The reverse will be true of Liberal and Conservative fortunes.

With this precaution in mind, we can now turn to a review of the actual and expected voting percentages for each of the three parties for each area outside Lévis and Lauzon.

One salient fact emerges about the Conservatives. Their actual percentages fall considerably short of what we would have expected in areas where they were very strong in 1958. This is most obvious in Breakeyville, Pintendre, Saint-Jean Chrysostome, and Saint-Etienne, but can also be observed elsewhere. The small village of Saint-Télesphore is the only deviant case. Except for Lévis, the actual Conservative vote exceeds the expected vote only in Charny and Saint-Rédempteur.

The Liberals' behaviour was quite different from one ecological zone to another. In 1958, they withstood the Conservative threat better in Zone 2 (Saint-Romuald, etc.) than in Zone 3 (Saint Nicolas, etc.). In 1962, their actual results in the latter zone, were almost everywhere higher than expected, while the reverse was true in Zone 2.

This again suggests that a sort of law of gravitation was in operation. That is, the hypothetical Conservative losses were greater than 63.5 per cent in areas where they were most successful in 1958, and less than 63.5 per cent where they were proportionally weaker. In the same way, the Liberals lost more than 33.2 per cent of their support in Zone 2 where they had remained strong in 1958, and less than 33.2 per cent in Zone 3 where they every-

where came second to the Conservatives in 1958.   This proves
again that election phenomenon, like social phenomena generally,
are not distributed normally like physical phenomena.   They operate
according to their own laws, including this law of social gravitation
enunciated by Tingsten.

As for the Social Credit results, outside Lévis and Lauzon
they are almost universally better than might have been expected.
In the last analysis, the Social Credit vote only fell short of what
our hypothesis suggested in Saint-Romuald, Saint-Lambert, and
Saint-Joseph.   It should be said that they fell considerably short in
the last two areas.

We can discard here an explanation which does not hold for
Lévis, despite the fact that it seemed important to us in a setting
such as that of the Island of Orleans. (9)   We refer to the explanation of the Social Credit vote of 1962 by that obtained in Lévis
during the forties.   If we examine that vote we see that the increase in the size of the 1940's Social Credit pockets as revealed
by the 1962 election was not proportionate to their original strength
This is confirmed by the fact that the organizers for Social Credit
in Lévis include almost no partisans from the forties.

To explain the few deviant cases which still remain, we have
to look rather at the more purely local political factors which were
pointed out to us in our interviews.

The relative weakness of Social Credit in Saint-Joseph can
be explained by the fact that the party organizers, confident of
victory as were most people, campaigned less vigorously and
effectively than was the practice in other areas.   In Saint-Lambert,
the entrenched position of the chief Liberal organizer no doubt
partly explains why his party was more successful here than elsewhere in stemming the Social Credit tide.   Local political influences
also help to explain, along with the reasons already discussed, the
results of the election in the three largest areas: Lévis, Lauzon,
and Saint-Romuald, which are also the three which remained most
faithful to the Liberals.   It seems that the party is better thought of
and better organized there than elsewhere.   There is also the fact
that Maurice Bourget has always found his strongest support in
Lauzon where he was born and in Lévis where he has lived for
several years.   Similarly, the Conservative candidate, Jean-Marie
Morin was hardly known, except in Lévis where he taught.   It is
not surprising then that the Conservatives retained their support
more successfully there than we would have expected by our hypothesis on the voting shifts.   As for J.A. Roy, the Social Credit
candidate, he himself told us that the fact that he was well known
as a general merchant in the parish of Sainte-Bernadette (included
in Lauzon) explained the fine results he obtained there (49.3 per
cent of eligible voters, as shown in Table VII.

---

9.   "L'élection fédérale du 18 juin 1962 à l'Ile d'Orleans,"
unpublished paper read to the ACFAS Convention (1962) by Michel
Chaloult and Vincent Lemieux.

We should note finally that although as we suggested in the first section, the discontent with the policy of the provincial Liberal government and with the attitude of the Liberal member, Roger Roy, was very strong in several places, it seems to have hurt the Liberals most in Breakeyville, Saint-Rédempteur, and Saint-Etienne, either by offsetting the work of the local organizations or by discouraging them from acting. Also, these three areas, as well as Saint-Lambert, Pintendre, and Saint-Joseph gave majorities to the Union Nationale over the Liberals, who carried the constituency as a whole, in the provincial elections of November 14, 1962.

IV. CONCLUSION

In addition to the general factors contributing to the Social Credit tide, described in the first section of this study, two additional circumstances seem to bear a relationship to most of the local results in Lévis. The first is related to the size of the localities: the Social Credit vote was in inverse relationship to the size of the population. On examination, it seems that a large or small population implies two factors which relate to the Social Credit results. In the first place, the largest centres are also generally the most prosperous, and therefore find it easier to resist the Social Credit propaganda. In the second place, their very size means that these places cannot be uniformly covered by the spread of Social Credit. Primary group ties are weaker than in the smaller centres. So, Social Credit which, as we have seen, spread through these primary group linkages was not diffused as effectively as elsewhere. Another factor which seems to have a direct bearing on the Social Credit vote is the support received by the Conservatives in 1958. We have even seen that the larger the Conservative vote in 1958, the larger the proportion of Conservatives who swung to Social Credit in 1958. For, as with the Social Credit tide in 1962, the Conservative swing in 1958 had been strongest in the smaller centres. This leads to the presumption that even though the two movements of opinion had, at bottom, been quite different, they were, none the less, both strengthened by the same factors: a somewhat depressed economic climate, and the effects of primary group linkages.

In the urban areas of the constituency, a division of the registered voters into two broad occupational groups: the "lower" occupations, and the others, or "higher" occupations (in our terminology) seems to be directly related to a political division of the voters into supporters of Social Credit and supporters of the "old-line" parties. There again we find the law of gravitation in operation: there is a greater chance that a member of a "lower" occupation will vote Social Credit if 70 per cent of the voters are of "lower" occupation than if only 40 per cent are. We might add here that some subcategories of the "low" occupations were probably stronger supporters of Social Credit than others. For example, there were the blue-collar CNR employees who played a large and unexpected role in the Social Credit success in Charny and Saint-Rédempteur. Subdividing Lévis and Lauzon into six parishes also enabled us to see that where the percentage of "low" occupation was held constant, newly settled areas were more favourable to Social Credit than older ones. Finally, we note in the results the play of local political factors: traditional voting, the state of the organizations, the personality of the candidates and their organizers, etc. This was particularly apparent in Lauzon, a traditional Liberal stronghold where Maurice Bourget had strong roots.

But these local political influences are best seen in the smaller rural localities of the constituency, as also in the smaller urban areas like Breakeyville and Saint-Rédempteur. Because they are less prosperous and less well organized, these smaller districts are specially dependent on government patronage. This means that parties are judged not so much on what they promise or do not promise, but on what the local political organizer obtained or did not obtain. With the Liberal organizers being the same federally or provincially, and the provincial Liberal member out campaigning, we can understand that the Liberal candidate in 1962 was judged on the well-perceived and carefully weighed record of the provincial administration rather than on an abstract and poorly known program at the federal level, where the Liberals were in opposition. So in most of these smaller localities, the local organizers were blamed either for having obtained almost nothing or for looking too well after themselves personally after sixteen years of privation.

In this context it is interesting to note that in the November 1962 provincial election, the Union Nationale was to obtain more votes than the Liberals in almost all of these small rural and urban centres. In the five largest centres, on the other hand, the Liberals were everywhere stronger than the Union Nationale, and in the sixth, Saint-David, a traditionally "blue" area, the Liberal upsurge was very impressive. This leads us to ascribe a dual nature to Social Credit: alongside an urban "créditisme" (or, to speak more generally, a créditisme of large centres) there seems also to be a rural "créditisme" (or, again, one of the small centres). Both these "créditismes" entail disaffection in the political sphere, against the "old-line" parties. They also involve discontent with the economic order. This is stronger in the smaller centres and in those lacking in prosperity than in the cities where the "créditisme" on the other hand, implies a third element almost non-existent in rural "creditisme": disaffection with the social order. A "low" occupation is not defined so much by the level of salary as by the status of being dominated, implied by it. In other words, it is a social phenomenon even more than an economic one.

This discontent with the social order, more or less paralleled by nationalistic discontent, was manifested among the workers at the "Chantiers Maritimes" of Lauzon and among the employees of the CNR who were the backbone of the Social Credit organization in the urban centres of the constituency. From this point of view, the federal election of 1962 and the provincial election of November 14, 1962 threw light on each other. For the Union Nationale was strengthened by the economic discontent and so won the small rural and urban centres of the constituency. But its past and its position as an opposition party made it difficult for it to utilize the social and national discontent at the expense of the Liberals. The Social Credit voters from the smaller centres thus tended towards the Union Nationale, whereas those of the larger areas were disposed to support the Liberal party.

The hypothesis which we have formulated about the double nature of Social Credit, as revealed in the provincial election of November, is based on a study of only one constituency. It seems to us, however, that it could fruitfully be applied to other constituencies in the whole region swept by Social Credit in June 1962. Simplified and provisional though it is, it seems useful in shedding light on the election, and to be suggestive with regard to the probable evolution of Social Credit in Quebec.

THREE DIMENSIONS OF A LOCAL POLITICAL PARTY

Howard A. Scarrow *

A local political party may be seen as embracing three dimensions:
the association, in whose name the nomination is bestowed; the organization, which stages the election campaign; and the supporters,
who cast votes for the party candidate on election day. The study
of a single riding in the period surrounding a general election provides an opportunity to examine these dimensions in some detail.
The riding chosen for the present study is "Urban" riding, located
in the Province of Ontario.

I. THE LIBERAL NOMINATION

The nomination of parliamentary candidates is undoubtedly the
most important single function entrusted to the local party association.
This is true from the standpoint of democratic society, which is in
need of some agency to narrow down election day choice; from the
standpoint of the national party, which is only as strong as the candidates who are nominated and elected; and from the standpoint of
the individual candidate, who at one swift stroke becomes the personal embodiment of all the symbolism conveyed by the party label.
If little is known about the workings of the nomination process
in Canada, or if many local associations appear to pay little attention to the procedures which are followed, it is not because of the
lack of importance of this stage of the political recruitment process.
Rather, it is because the "natural" selectors have proved so severe
that the problem for the party leadership has more often been that of
finding persons willing to accept the nomination than it has been that
of establishing procedures for regulating competition for it. These
selectors include societal values and prejudices, as well as the eco-
nomical realities associated with running for, and accepting a seat in
Parliament. Long periods of party tenure, combined with the practice of rather automatic renomination of incumbent MP's, have also
served to reduce the importance of the formal nomination procedures.
Not infrequently, however, events conspire to produce keen
competition for a party nomination, and to focus attention upon the

* The author wishes to express his appreciation to the candidates of all parties whose co-operation made this study possible. Because, in order to encourage frank discussion, the author promised
anonymity to these and other sources, it has been necessary to with-
hold the name of the constituency. Hence the fictitious name "Urban"
riding.

mechanics of candidate selection. Such was the case for the 1962 Liberal nomination in Urban riding. The Liberals had held the seat from 1935 until 1958, and not since 1945 had it been necessary for the association to find a new standard bearer. By 1962, however, not only was there no Liberal incumbent, but death had removed from possible contention the Liberal member who had met defeat in 1958. The significance of the vacuum was made all the more apparent by the fact that this traditional Liberal stronghold was an area of high unemployment, and thus of political discontent. It is hardly surprising that under these circumstances a record number of aspirants dropped hints of their availability. Four months before the nomination meeting the local newspaper counted seven possible contenders. Even so, the "natural" selectors were conspicuously at work. A month prior to the meeting one of the leading contenders dropped out of the race because of the pressures within his own business; and each of the four aspirants whose name was finally placed before the convention either came from a wealthy family or commanded an income which would place him well within the top 5 or 10 per cent of the community. (The same could be said of the candidates finally adopted by all three parties).

The role of the Liberal association was to select a candidate from the remaining eligibles. The method which was prescribed by the constitution, and which as long as anyone could recall had always been followed in both the federal and the comparable provincial riding, was the open convention. Under this procedure, anyone who lives in the riding and who is a "Liberal supporter" can attend the convention and cast a ballot. Proof of the former can be found in the city directory; proof of the latter is possible only in the negative sense that scrutineers placed by the competing candidates can spot persons who have been conspicuously identified with another party. With this important qualification, there is a resemblance to the "open primary" as used in some states in the United States; and to judge by the number of persons who attended the Liberal convention in 1935 – an estimated 4,000 compared with 11,000 Liberal votes cast in the subsequent general election – it is possible for turnout under the two types of procedures to be about the same.

The open convention is not the procedure one might have expected to find used, particularly by a party which had controlled a seat for a long period of time. At least one reason for the retention of the system, however, is that any change in favour of a more structured procedure is likely to be regarded with suspicion. This became apparent in the spring of 1961 when, it being evident that there was going to be strenuous competition for the nomination, the president of the association suggested an amendment to the constitution whereby the executive could use its own discretion in determining the method of nomination. However, the proposal was defeated at a spring meeting of the association which had been called mainly to consider the question and which was attended by about 100 persons. The proposal was favoured by one of the aspirants, whose announced campaign manager sat on the executive, but was opposed by other aspirants, including the ultimately successful candidate and elected member.

The open convention system had the effect of placing a premium upon the initiative and energy of the competing aspirants. In some respects their campaigns resembled those of a general election, beginning as much as six or eight months in advance and reaching a peak on the eve of the nomination meeting, and featuring campaign managers and phalanxes of workers. In other respects, however, the campaigns differed sharply from those associated with general elections. They received no coverage in the press (although editorials and "political columns" speculated on who the front-runners might be), and since the goal was only 500 or 600 votes the candidates themselves made little use of the mass media. Instead, they directed their appeals to audiences provided by established civic, ethnic, and social groups in the community. Since the enemy was not a rival party, and since there was nothing in the way of ideological differences to separate the candidates, most appeals had to be focused upon individual traits. Finally, and most important, appeals had to be directed to those persons who could be made sufficiently interested in the outcome of the contest to brave a cold winter night and, as it turned out, to arrive at the rented theatre early enough to get in the door.

Because of the campaign strategy which the situation required, the new Canadian voters (1) were seen by the contenders as being especially crucial. Here were persons who could be reached through their social clubs; who were likely to take cues from their leaders, if only the leaders could be identified and won over; and to whom, observers feel, it is a matter of particularly great importance to have a member of Parliament, regardless of party, who can be liked and trusted. It is hardly surprising, therefore, that an estimated 70 to 75 per cent of the 1,200 persons who crowded into the nomination meeting were from the new Canadian side of the community, even though they constitute only 35 per cent (2) of the total population of the metropolitan area. (The major non-British and non-French ethnic groups are: Italian, 8 per cent; German, 5 per cent; Polish, 3 per cent; Ukranian, 3 per cent.)

Another explanation for the disproportionate number of new Canadians at the meeting was the fact that two of the four candidates who survived as serious contenders had roots in the Ukrainian community, one being a well-known doctor and the other being a woman renowned for her social work activities. The declaration of availability by the doctor, four weeks prior to the nomination meeting, illustrated that while an open convention might minimize the influence exerted upon candidate selection by persons recognized as party leaders, it does not eliminate it. At least so it was believed by informed observers, who interpreted the doctor's entry into the race

---

1. In this paper the term "new Canadian" is used to refer to those persons listed by the census as being of neither British nor French origin. Although the term is not completely satisfactory - many of these persons are no longer "new" in Canada - it seems preferable to the more commonly employed "ethnic groups."

2. Figures are from the 1961 census. British-origin population totals 47 per cent; French-origin, 18 per cent.

as reflecting the urging not only of some local Liberal leaders, but of Ottawa Liberals as well. The favourable comments on his behalf which appeared in the local press were similarly interpreted. On the other hand, the entry of the social worker illustrated how unimportant months of hard campaigning could become. Declaring herself in the running three weeks before the scheduled meeting, and confining her campaign to about ten days, she was dismissed by the press as hardly a serious candidate and accused in some quarters of simply trying to split the "ethnic vote" – some even said at the instigation of the other candidates. Never the less, partly because she delivered what was unanimously regarded as the best speech given at the convention meeting, and partly because she received the support of the candidate whose name was dropped after the first ballot but who was still able to control his followers, she went on to the third and final ballot where she lost out by a handful of votes. Her failure to win support from the Ukranian doctor after he himself had been eliminated on the second ballot, was but one illustration of the subsystem of personal rivalries and local politics, the roots of which extended far back into the past, which was operating just below the surface of the convention.

The outcome of the nomination contest points to what is perhaps the strongest argument which can be advanced in favour of the open convention system, viz., the likelihood that the winner will be someone skilled in organizing a campaign. There is no question that the Liberal nominee was the aspirant who had worked hardest and longest, and that he had entered the nomination meeting with twice as many pledged delegates as the closest rival; or that in the subsequent election contest he waged one of the best organized campaigns ever seen in the riding. On the other hand, objection to the system might be raised on these very grounds; that if there are few people who have the time and resources to stand for Parliament, there are still fewer who can in addition see their way clear to contest an open nomination.

However, any complete evaluation of the open convention system can be made only in relation to alternative methods, ones which rest upon stricter definitions of party membership. Candidate selection by dues-paying party members is one possibility. The difficulty, of course, is that given the limited between-election activity by most associations, the idea of dues-paying membership is rather artificial; and it is hardly surprising that few party associations can boast of more than a handful of members in this sense.

Another possible alternative is to entrust selection of candidates to those who have acquired the reputation of "key" party spokesmen in the area. These are persons who have held or are holding office in the association, or who have been candidates for office, or who in some less conspicuous way have taken an active interest in association affairs. They are usually lawyers, businessmen, or other persons high on the socio-economic scale, and frequently occupy other positions of community leadership. Regardless of the formal nomination procedure adopted, leaders such as these usually huddle together to decide on who would make a good candidate, and follow through with persuasive efforts. Even ruling out the possibility of deliberate "in-group" selection, the objection which can be made against this method of nomination - from the standpoint of the aspirant, the party, and democratic society - is that the attributes of the "good candidate" are liable to turn out to be the very attributes which are dominant in the selection clique. Thus the Liberal candidate who emerged victorious from the open convention described above was distinguished by the two traits which were not shared by most of the key Liberals in the area, viz., his age (he was only thirty), and his religion (a minority religion).

II. THE PARTY ELECTORAL ORGANIZATION

A final and frequently used nomination alternative is the delegate convention, whereby voting is restricted to accredited delegates chosen (in an urban riding) from the various polling divisions or groups of polling divisions. Ideally this procedure assumes that there exists a rather permanent network of poll captains and area chairmen (3) spatially distributed across the riding, who can legitimately be said to constitute the party organization, and who stand ready at election time to respond to the directions given by the candidate and his manager. As with the precinct captains in the United States, they are persons who might be pictured as providing the real connective link between a vast and impersonalized party and state apparatus, on the one hand, and the individual citizen, on the other.

A comparison of the United States and Canada suggests that the development of such a network of workers depends in part upon certain institutional factors. In the United States, particularly in the older eastern sections, the extension of partisan politics into county and municipal affairs, together with complicated registration and voting procedures, encouraged the emergence of a permanent, multi-purpose network of precinct, ward, and county party workers, long nourished by the awards of spoils, and in most states now selected through the state-run election machinery. In Canada, aside from the necessity of making nominations, there has been (1) the legal requirement that each urban polling division be enumerated by a pair of canvassers selected by the two parties which polled the first and second highest vote at the last election; (2) the practice of placing the actual election day machinery in the hands of incumbent party supporters, with the consequent patronage opportunities; (3) the resulting necessity for opposition parties to post scrutineers; and (4) the practice, vigorously advocated by all parties, of door-to-door canvassing during the election campaign. (4)

---

3. In addition to a captain for each polling division, it is usual for the parties to divide the riding into a number of areas (15 to 30) and to appoint supervisory chairmen for each.

4. Because of the smaller population, and because of this emphasis upon the door-to-door canvass, it seems likely that citizen contact with party organization is much more common in Canada than in the United States. In 1949, for example, the Canadian

It is obvious that constituency organizations in Canada vary widely, and that they usually fall far short of conforming to the idealized party structure sketched above. None the less, some of the features of this aspect of a local political party may be suggested by an examination of certain traits of the Liberal and Conservative poll captains who participated in the 1962 contest in Urban riding. An examination of these traits is justified not only because these workers constitute a possible alternative nominating body, but also because they constitute the largest single group of party actives.

General Characteristics of Liberal and Conservative Poll Captains

Seen from the viewpoint of poll captains as participants in the nominating process, there are three characteristics which need to be stressed. First, this network of party workers lacks the high degree of permanency and stability from one election to the next which the ideal model would suggest. This is due in part to the fact that for each party there are areas of obvious weakness where the party has never been able to build up a following of workers, and in part to normal population shifts, or to dissatisfaction with past worker performance. Perhaps more important, however, is the fact that election campaigns tend to be highly personalized operations, being run by the candidate and his own appointed campaign manager; a new candidate is likely to introduce major alterations in the ranks of the workers. Thus it was estimated that about half of the Urban riding Liberal poll captains were new appointees for the 1962 campaign.

A second characteristic of the phalanx of poll captains is that, to varying degrees and differing by party and circumstance, they tend to be regarded as paid canvassers, under a contractual relationship to the manager, rather than as voluntary members of a party organization. Although the most extreme manifestation of this tendency, i.e., working for one party and voting for another, is no doubt limited to a relatively few persons on either side, the financial rewards associated with the job definitely influence the way poll captains are perceived by other persons associated with the party. The honorarium for canvassing and election day activity may be modest, but the $50-$75 payment by the government for being the party nominee for the voters list enumeration makes the job financially attractive. In nearly every polling division the Liberal and Conservative poll captains served in this capacity. If your party happens to be victorious. moreover, other opportunities may be available, such as census-taker or, at the next election, having your house used as a polling station.

A third characteristic of the poll workers is that they are nearly all women, usually married or widowed. In the 1962 campaign neither the Liberal nor Conservative organization could boast of more

---

Institute of Public Opinion reported that 22 per cent of those who voted in the 1949 election had been driven to the polls in a car provided by a political party (CIPO release of Aug. 6, 1949).

than about half a dozen male poll captains out of a total of over 230 for each party. (5) The predominance of women is explained by the fact that the parties see as the main task of each poll captain the canvassing of the neighbourhood at least once, and sometimes twice or three times, as well as being on the job throughout election day to get out the vote. Such work presumably cannot be done by a male holding a full-time job. Of all the traits of the poll captains, the sex imbalance is the one most stressed by those who would argue against entrusting candidate selection to this group. Not only does it make the workers unrepresentative of the total community of party adherents, but also, observers believe, women themselves are the ones most likely to stand in the way of a women ever winning the nomination.

Characteristics of NDP Poll Captains

At this point it should be observed that the workers for the New Democratic party differed from those of the two major parties in three respects. A partial list of the party's poll captains and area chairmen reveals that practically 100 per cent were males, and that six of the nine executive officers of the party association were active in this capacity (a seventh was the candidate himself). Furthermore, the patronage opportunities associated with the enumeration were not available to this third-ranking party.

In the latter connection, Liberals and Conservatives discount the poverty plea of the NDP by pointing out that some salaried personnel from the union headquarters served as full-time organizers for the NDP during the election campaign, and that the NDP candidate had the use of the union's regular radio and television program - in terms of both personal appearances and "free plugs." None the less, the failure of the NDP to have available for its use the normal patronage opportunities, and (it seems fairly certain) its failure to pay its poll workers, must have significantly affected the type of poll organization which it was able to field, and the style of campaign it was able to wage. Indeed, it is difficult to account for the virtual absence of women from the NDP organization if the remuneration variable is ignored.

Occupational Status

A significant characteristic of the poll captains of all parties, and one which especially distinguishes them from those who are leaders in the affairs of the respective associations, is that a high percentage of them are from manual labour households. On the basis of information provided by the city directory and the voters list, the occupation of the households, where this could be determined,

---

5. Among the area chairmen there was only one male. There were, of course, a large number of male workers who participated in other phases of the campaign, e.g., drivers on election day, clerical work, advisory committees.

Table I

| | Poll captains | | | Nine key leaders | | |
	PC	Lib.	NDP	PC	Lib.	NDP
Labour:						
Skilled or supervisory	61	60	61	1		1
Unskilled or doubtful*	57	49	46			
White-collar, sales, managerial	49	50	12	2	2	1
Independent business	5	2	1	1	2	1
Professional	1	1	7	5	4	6
Fire, police	6	9				
Retired, widow	29	39	7		1	
Unemployed	7	2	3		1	
	215	212	137	9	9	9

*Includes imprecise job descriptions, e.g., "works at plant X."

was as shown in Table I. (6)   The preponderance of manual workers can be explained by the highly industrialized nature of the community, the conscious attempt by parties to have workers "fit" the
neighbourhood, and, probably also, by the remuneration associated
with the job.   Whatever the explanation, however, the consequence
is that election campaigns serve to inject a high degree of personal
involvement into a stratum of the community which otherwise has
been shown to be low on the scale of political participation.

Other Traits

In order to discover certain other traits, questionnaires were
sent to the poll workers (captains and area chairmen) for both the
Conservative and Liberal parties.   Although the number of usable
returns - thirty-nine Conservative and thirty-one Liberal - was too
small to allow confident generalizations concerning the total population
of party "actives" at this level, the fact that sixty of the seventy respondents had participated in campaign activity for their party at least
once before, and the fact that the responses came from thoroughly
scattered polling divisions, justifies mention of the major findings. (7)

---

6. The actual names of the poll captains were taken from lists
supplied by the party headquarters or from lists of enumerators submitted by the parties to the local returning officer (both types of lists
were substantially the same).   The nine key Conservatives and nine
key Liberals are persons who, in the opinion of an informed local
observer, came closest to meeting this description.   The nine NDP
leaders are the major office holders in the local association.   Incidentally, five of the seven professional occupations shown for the
NDP represent teachers.
     7. Strictly on the ratio of the number of usable questionnaires
returned to the number delivered (498), the return was very small -
just over 14 per cent.   However, as already suggested, poll captains vary widely in their motivation, experience, and loyalty to the

(a) Only sixteen of the respondents affirmed that they had attended a meeting or activity sponsored by the party during the calendar year 1961. This finding underscores the relative autonomy of the electoral organization as opposed to the local association. (8)

(b) Eighteen respondents were able to give an example of personal contact with voters during the year 1961 which, in their opinion, might have helped to influence votes in the 1962 election (e.g., talking with newly enfranchised neighbours). When asked to estimate the number of persons in their polling division who could call them by name, twenty-nine respondents estimated fifty or more persons. If the latter figure may be taken as a rough index of thorough integration into the neighbourhood, then these respondents may be viewed as performing well the function of personal link between citizen and state. (9)

(c) Over one-third of the respondents indicated that at least one parent had been active in partisan activity, a finding which tends to confirm the proposition that the family serves to transmit not only partisan preferences, but active interest in partisan activity as well. (10)

Policy Attitudes

A major purpose of the questionnaire was to learn whether or not persons actively identified with the major parties could be distinguished by any differences in attitudes towards public policy questions. Possible differences in attitudes are important both in

---

party, some being little more than hired canvassers for the particular election. Thus the responses which were received undoubtedly represent a much higher percentage of those who realistically can be regarded as part of the party electoral organization.

8. Two possible activities would have been attendance at business meetings of the associations, or activities sponsored by the women's groups. It should be noted that the extent of autonomy of the electoral organization depends much upon circumstances. If a party loses an election, or if the elected MP takes little interest in the affairs of the party, the extent of autonomy is likely to be maximized. On the other hand, an energetic MP will become the main directive force in the affairs of the local association, and the workers which he has gathered around him are likely to attend functions sponsored by him in the name of the association.

9. For comparison with the United States for this and other traits of poll captains, see Phillips Cutright and Peter R. Rossi, "Grass Roots Politicians and the Vote," American Sociological Review, XXIII, 1958, pp.171-9; Daniel Katz and Samuel J. Eldersveld, "The Impact of Local Party Activity upon the Electorate," Public Opinion Quarterly, XXV, 1961, pp. 1-24; and Robert S. Hirschfield et al., "A Profile of Political Activists in Manhattan," Western Political Quarterly, XV, 1962, pp. 489-506.

10. See Dwaine Marvick and Charles Nixon, "Recruitment Contrasts in Rival Campaign Groups," in Marvick, ed., Decision-Makers (Glencoe, 1961), pp. 208-10.

Table II
Policy Attitudes of Conservative and Liberal Poll Workers

Topic	PC			Liberal		
	Favour	No opinion	Oppose	Favour	No opinion	Oppose
Old age pensions	71.8	10.3	17.9	93.5	–	6.5
Public works	53.8	25.7	20.5	56.4	40.4	3.2
Medical care	33.3	28.2	38.5	45.2	29.0	25.8
Govt. & unions	61.5	30.8	7.7	45.2	29.0	25.8
Govt. & business	51.3	30.8	17.9	41.9	35.5	22.6
Tariff increase	74.4	15.3	10.3	71.0	9.6	19.4
Conscription	82.1	10.1	7.7	61.3	22.6	16.1
Provincial rights	46.2	30.7	23.1	51.6	38.7	9.7
French langugage	25.6	30.8	43.6	45.2	22.5	32.3
Red China trade	33.3	35.9	30.8	19.4	25.8	54.8
Nuclear weapons	20.5	43.6	35.9	29.0	42.0	29.0

explaining support for one party rather than another, and in indicating possible differences in types of pressures which might be exerted on a Liberal as opposed to a Conservative MP. Thus the respondents were asked to indicate whether they generally tended to agree, to disagree, or had no opinion on a number of policy items. (11) The results (see Table II), though subject to varying interpretation, suggest the following conclusions:

(a) On questions related to increases in government services and expenditures, a liberal-conservative pattern emerges, as these terms are popularly understood. More Liberals favoured, and more Conservatives opposed, increases in old age pensions, increases in government financed public works, and a plan for government sub-sidized medical care. Yet there was no conflict of opinion on these questions, since majorities on both sides favoured pensions and public works, while on the question of medical care there was no majority sentiment in either party.

(b) On two questions relating to government intervention in the economy, the results are not consistent with the liberal-conservative stereotype. Conservatives were more in favour of increased government control over trade union activity, as well as more in favour of increased government control over business practices.

(c) On four questions designed to probe into the historic differences between the two parties, the results conformed with the traditional policy positions. More Conservatives favoured, and more Liberals opposed, "tightening up the tariff to protect Canadian manu-facturers," and "compulsory military conscription in times of national emergency;" while more Liberals favoured "more rights for the the provinces; less power concentrated in Ottawa," and making the French language and culture a more conspicuous part of

---

11. Ten respondents failed to express an opinion on one or more questions. These were coded "no opinion."

Canadian life." Again, however, agreement was more evident than conflict in that healthy majorities of both parties favoured tariff increases and military conscription. The more conspicuous difference revealed on the question of the French language and culture undoubtedly reflects the much higher proportion of French Canadians within the Liberal organization (see below).

(d) Just as the somewhat greater Liberal fear of centralized power at Ottawa is consistent only with a position once strongly identified with the Liberal party (and perhaps also with local French-Canadian opinion), and not consistent with contemporary small "l" liberalism, so too the great Conservative approval of increased trade with Red China is consistent not with the ideological stereotype, but rather with the lead given on this question by the national Conservative government. Perhaps it is significant too that the question on which there was the highest percentage of "no opinion," i.e., nuclear arms for Canada, was the question on which both major parties have taken highly ambiguous positions. However, here too the greater Conservative disapproval might be interpreted as being consistent with the strong stand on disarmament taken by External Affairs Minister Howard Green. On the other hand, the more militant attitude by Liberals on the question of trade with Red China and on nuclear arms might be interpreted as reflecting the greater Liberal support among Catholics and new Canadians (see below).

In summary, the policy attitudes of the party actives reveal patterns rather similar to those obtained in national opinion surveys: consensus is more evident than conflict, and the popular liberal-conservative stereotype often does not fit the respective party labels. The rather large percentage of "no opinion," moreover, would suggest that policy preference is not a very strong determinant of partisan adherence and activity, at least at this level of participation.

III. PARTY SUPPORTERS

The final dimension of the local political party to be examined is the core of electoral support. That each does lay claim to a rather permanent core of supporters is confirmed by analysis of the 1957, 1958, and 1962 election results. These results show that regardless of how well or how poorly a party performs at a given election, the geographic areas (and by implication the sociological groups) showing greatest support, average support, and lowest support, remain virtually the same. (12)

Nature of Core Strength

An approximate picture of the core strength of the respective

------

12. Comparison of the ranking of the nineteen census tracts (see below) by percentage of vote polled in 1958 compared to 1957, and 1962 compared to 1958, yields rank order correlations of +.96 and +.96 for Conservative; +.91 and +.91 for Liberal; and +.94 and +.88 for the CCF-NDP.

parties may be seen by examining the vote in terms of the census
tracts into which the metropolitan area has been divided by the Dominion Bureau of Statistics. The picture can, of course, only be
approximate since the census tracts, although designed to be "fairly
homogeneous with respect to economic status and living conditions,"
are invariably too heterogeneous to permit a neat isolation of each
demographic dimension. What can be discerned, however, is the
relative strength of the parties among certain groups.

Altogether the riding contained nineteen census tracts which
could be utilized. (13) These were ranked according to three demographic characteristics: (1) percentage of population of British origin; (2) percentage of population of neither British nor French origin (i.e., new Canadians); and (3) the median earnings of head of
the family. Because the census tracts varied widely in population,
it was not practical to analyse the vote in terms of each of the nineteen ranked tracts. Instead, for each of the three demographic variables the vote was computed for four tract groupings: a first quartile grouping containing the several top-ranked tracts, a second quartile grouping containing the next several ranked tracts and so forth.
The number of tracts included in each quartile grouping was such as
to yield groupings which were as nearly as possible representative of
of equal numbers of voters, although the groupings were held constant for all three elections analysed. (14) The results are shown
in Table III and may be summarized as follows:

(a) <u>Conservative</u> The table confirms that Conservative
strength is correlated most closely with the portion of population of
British origin. In all three elections there was a progressive relationship from the first to the fourth quartile, and a 15 to 20 percentage point differential between them. Clearly, then, Conservatism depends heavily upon the British-origin element within the population: even in the 1958 victory the Conservative candidate was not
able to win over his Liberal rival in those polling divisions having
the lowest portion of British-origin voters with them.

To some extent the figures relating to the new Canadian electorate are reciprocal to those relating to the British-origin (i.e.,
non-new Canadian and non-French) electorate, and thus predictably
they show the Conservatives having far less support in areas most
densely populated by new Canadians than in areas least populated by
them. However, the relationship is not so pronounced as with the
British-origin variable, suggesting that anti-Conservatism is somewhat more intense among the French than among the new Canadian
electorate.

---

13.   The metropolitan area is divided into forty-five census
tracts. Twenty-one of these are wholly or partly outside Urban
riding and have thus been omitted. Five others, on the fringe
areas have been omitted because of their having only one or two
polling divisions within them and because the polling division
boundaries cut across the census tracts. In the more populous
areas, polling division boundaries cut by census tract boundaries
are counted in the census tract in which the majority of voters reside.

14.   Each quartile contains from three to six census tracts.

Table III
Percentage of Party Vote by Census Tracts Grouped into Quartiles,
Elections of 1957, 1958, and 1962

Percentage of British origin	Conservative			Liberal			CCF-NDP		
	1957	1958	1962	1957	1958	1962	1957	1958	1962
1st (highest)	43.4	55.9	35.4	41.1	30.3	44.5	15.3	13.6	20.0
2nd	37.6	51.2	31.5	40.6	30.4	44.4	21.7	18.3	24.1
3rd	28.8	45.9	24.7	44.0	31.1	44.8	27.1	22.8	30.5
4th (lowest)	22.2	35.1	19.1	51.2	41.3	52.5	26.4	23.5	28.4
Percentage of neither British nor French origin									
1st (highest)	23.8	37.1	20.6	48.6	38.3	50.6	27.6	24.6	28.8
2nd	40.4	52.6	32.3	39.1	29.8	42.1	20.6	17.6	25.6
3rd	33.3	48.0	28.8	45.7	34.5	46.4	21.0	17.5	24.8
4th (lowest)	38.3	50.6	31.6	41.7	31.6	45.6	20.0	17.8	22.7
Median income									
1st (highest)	45.4	56.5	35.7	42.1	32.5	47.2	12.5	11.0	17.1
2nd	34.3	47.2	29.5	43.2	33.7	45.0	22.4	19.1	25.5
3rd	25.3	40.2	21.5	48.1	37.1	48.3	26.6	22.8	30.2
4th (lowest)	30.8	43.9	26.1	42.5	31.6	44.8	26.7	24.4	29.1

Urban Riding Results

	1957	1958	1962
Liberal	43.4	34.3	45.6
Conservative	32.2	45.8	27.7
CCF-NDP	22.1	19.1	24.5
Other	2.4	0.9	2.2

The table confirms that Conservatism is positively correlated with income. In each election the Conservative candidate was considerably stronger in the highest income areas than in the lowest income areas. However, it will be noted that the correlation is not so high as in the case of the British-origin variable: in each election the Conservative candidate polled stronger in the fourth income quartile than in the third. The reason apparently is that there is a higher proportion of British-origin population in the lowest income quartile than in the third (54 per cent as opposed to 43 per cent).

(b) Liberal The most impressive aspect of Liberal support is its relative undifferentiated appeal to all elements of the electorate. Usually less than 10 percentage points separate the top and bottom Liberal quartiles, either in victory or in defeat. Particularly noticeable is the undifferentiated support in all income groups. The most obvious points of Liberal strength are among the population of non-British origin. The advantage is somewhat less among new Canadians alone. The magnitude of the 1962 Liberal victory is underscored by the fact that, unlike 1957, the Liberal candidate carried every quartile for each of the three demographic variables studied.

(c) <u>CCF-NDP.</u> Electoral support for the CCF-NDP is the most closely correlated with income. The largest differential occurs between the first and the second quartile; thereafter the influence of income is less marked. In 1962 the NDP strength in the two lowest income quartiles surpassed that of the Conservatives. On the two ethnic scales, the table shows the CCF-NDP picking up support as the areas become less heavily concentrated with British-origin voters.

Table IV

	Conservative	Liberal
Non-Catholic	166	100
Catholic	35	95
	201	195

<u>Inter-relationship of Supporters and Actives</u> The difference in ethnic origin of Liberal and Conservative party supporters has been extended into the ranks of the party actives. An examination of the names of the Liberal poll captains reveals at least fifty-two obviously French surnames, while only fifteen French surnames dot the Conservative list. The Liberal group also may have contained a higher number of other non-Anglo-Saxons; however, on the basis of the names alone this fact cannot be established.

The religious affiliation of the party actives was determined by consulting the municipal voters list for separate school supporters. Where religious affiliations could be thus determined, the results were those in Table IV. It should be noted that the greater concentration of Catholics among the Liberals was more than a reflection of ethnic origin. Forty-two of the ninety-five Catholics in the Liberal column had names which were neither obviously French nor obviously new Canadian. This is an aspect of core party strength which census tracts cannot reveal. (15)

Among the key party leaders in the respective associations, the ethnic and religious differential is again apparent. A list of nine key Liberals reveals seven non-Anglo-Saxons and five Catholics; while the comparable group of Conservative leaders contains only two non-Anglo-Saxons and one Catholic.

<u>Voting Swing</u> The final aspect of voting behaviour in the 1957, 1958, and 1962 federal elections which merits attention is voting swing. The most impressive feature of the swing between 1957 and 1958, and between 1958 and 1962, was its uniformity across

---

15. The complete breakdown, based on probable surname origin, is as follows: Conservative Catholic - 13 French, 8 new Canadian, 14 English Canadian; Liberal Catholic - 46 French, 7 new Canadian, 42 English Canadian.

16. Thus in 1958 the standard deviation from the mean percentage point gain for the Conservatives in the nineteen census tracts was 2.5; while in 1962 the standard deviation from the mean percentage point loss for the Conservatives was 2.1.

the riding. In 1958 each census tract in the riding recorded a swing towards Conservatism, while in 1962 each tract swung in the opposite direction. In both instances, moreover, there was little variation among the census tracts in the degree of swing. (16) Thus whatever it was that motivated change in partisan choice, it knew no geographical-sociological boundaries. The uniformity is particularly impressive in view of the fact that each candidate devotes consider-able energy at aiming specialized appeals to particular groups, and often through specialized media designed to reach a particular group. This is especially true of the new Canadian groups, who have their own language media as well as their own networks of cultural re-lationships.

A final question to be posed, therefore, is the one often put by political correspondents: "Is there an ethnic (i.e., new Canadian) vote?" The ambiguity of the question is such that there are several possible answers. In one sense the answer is in the affirmative. As has been shown, the new Canadians do not distribute their voting preferences in random fashion. Rather, they have inclined towards the non-Conservative parties more than have voters who are not new Canadians, just as voters of British origin and of the highest income levels have inclined towards Conservatism more so than have voters not so characterized.

The question "Is there an ethnic vote?" may also be interpreted as asking whether, to the extent that new Canadians do reveal a distinctive voting preference, they do so because of their being new Canadian (e.g., particularly with such questions as immigration policy and anti-Communism), or rather because of some other trait which might characterize them. It should be stressed, therefore, that finding a positive relationship between Liberalism and new Canadianism, as between Conservatism and British origin, does not necessarily establish that the operative variable is the ethnic one.

The evidence would deny the existence of an "ethnic vote" if by that is meant that new Canadians (a) persistently stick to one partisan preference; or that they (b) distinctively shift partisan pre-ferences; or that they (c) vote in a massive bloc. As already pointed out, the census tracts with the highest concentration of new Canadians (a) swung back and forth between contending parties and (b) did so in the identical direction and in no greater or lesser de-gree than the census tracts of lowest new Canadian concentration. Also, it may now be added, (c) these areas recorded a greater CCF-NDP support.

One last qualification must be inserted. If the question "Is there an ethnic vote?" is meant to ask "Is there an Italian vote, as distinguished from a German vote, as distinguished from a Ukrainian vote, and so forth?" then there is little in this paper which bears upon the answer; much more refined data is required.

THE CAMPAIGN IN EGLINTON*

Denis Smith

I. PRELIMINARIES

The campaign in Toronto Eglinton attracted as much national interest as any constituency campaign in the country. This was so partly because of the intrinsic interest of the local campaign, and partly because of Eglinton's location in Metropolitan Toronto. (1) The Liberal party saw Toronto as a prime target because of the number of urban ridings it contained (many of them Liberal from 1949 to 1957), and because of the city's concentration of ministers. If the Government were to be threatened, it could best be done in those urban ridings where the Prime Minister's stock had plummeted most since 1958. The Liberal intention to stake leading candidates in crucial urban seats had become clear by the end of 1961.

The New Democratic party, too, was ready to give unusual attention to city and suburban constituencies, in its effort to establish a new foundation of working-class and middle-class support. The public and the press, sensing a close national campaign and the importance of the city vote, turned their focus more directly than usual upon strategic Toronto. (2) The glow of national interest upon Toronto penetrated Eglinton riding, illuminated the campaigns of two candidates who were substantial figures of interest in their own right, and gave to the battle there the intensity and fascination of a ritual duel.

Donald M. Fleming, Minister of Finance in the Diefenbaker ministry from its formation in June, 1957, was by 1962 the most controversial member of the cabinet (apart from the Prime Minister himself). His peppery and self-righteous manner on the front bench made him a favourite target of the Liberal opposition; his early

---

*In addition to the sources acknowledged in the footnotes, I am grateful for opportunities to discuss the Eglinton campaign in interviews and letters with numerous persons involved in the campaign, including Warren Armstrong, Basil Duggan, Dr. David Gauthier, Eamonn Martin, Mitchell W. Sharp, and Robert Wright.

1. In 1958, the Progressive Conservative party captured every seat in Metropolitan Toronto, and at dissolution it still possessed seventeen of eighteen seats, including those of three cabinet ministers and the Speaker of the House of Commons.

2. See, for instance, Douglas Fisher, MP, "Watch Toronto For Fireworks," Toronto Telegram, Jan. 1, 1962.

statements on economic policy stimulated critics to question his grasp of contemporary economic theory; his denial of responsibility for the policy of the Bank of Canada and the views of its Governor for more than two years, followed by his sudden reversal and demand for Mr. Coyne's resignation in 1961, appeared enigmatic or worse to the opposition; his promise of 1957 to balance the budget had been belied by five substantial deficits; and his relations with the Prime Minister were widely believed to be cool. (3) Mr. Fleming, whose temperament invited parliamentary storms, had not had an easy time in office. Since the Coyne affair, he had been the object of fervent antagonism among Liberals. As the election approached, many Liberals and independents expressed the vehement desire to "get Fleming out." Antagonism was frequently accompanied by curiosity. How could Mr. Fleming defend his public record on the hustings? How could he support the Prime Minister after facing apparent humiliation at his hands in the Coyne controversy and the December cabinet affair in Quebec City? Few observers expected a dull campaign in Toronto Eglinton.

Mr. Fleming had held the constituency, with little difficulty, since 1945, and his strong local organization expected no serious challenge in the general election of 1962. (4) But the Liberal party was not discouraged by Conservative complacency. The riding had become noticeably more commercial since the 1958 general election and the number of apartment dwellers had increased substantially. The constituency was less settled and less solidly middle class than it had been. Liberals wondered whether recent changes in the riding's character had caused any weakening of traditional support for the sitting Conservative member. (5) Could the widespread dissatisfaction with Mr. Fleming's tenure of the Ministry of Finance be focused in the constituency? With a strong candidate in opposition, perhaps. In December, 1961, strongly supported by both the national Liberal leader and the local Constituency Association Executive, Mitchell W. Sharp announced that he would contest the Liberal nomination in Eglinton. Mr. Sharp, an experienced economist and former senior civil servant, had been touted by the press for

---

3. See, inter alia, H.S. Gordon, "The Bank of Canada in a System of Responsible Government," Canadian Journal of Economics and Political Science, XXVII, no. 1, Feb., 1961, pp. 1-22; J. Duncan Edmonds, "The Coyne Affair: Principles and Implications," Canadian Forum, Sept., 1961, pp. 121-2; Toronto Star, Dec. 27, and 28, 1961.

4. Mr. Fleming had been a political representative of Eglinton riding since his election as a Toronto school trustee for Ward 9 in 1938. (The boundaries of Ward 9 were the same as those of Eglinton.) From 1939 to 1944 he was an alderman for Ward 9, and in the federal general election of 1945 he was elected to the House of Commons with a majority of 7,890. This majority increased at each subsequent election to its peak of 19,097 in 1958.

5. Ralph Hyman, "Liberal Thrust into PC Stronghold," Toronto Globe and Mail, June 14, 1962.

several months as one of the new Liberal "brains trust" and as likely candidate for Minister of Trade and Commerce in a Liberal government. (6)

A provincial by-election in Eglinton constituency was fortuitously called for January 18, 1961, and for it the Liberal party nominated a popular municipal politician, Mrs. Jean Newman. (7) The party conducted a vigorous campaign, and members of the federal riding association watched with concern for clues to political feeling in the constituency. Mr. Sharp took a discreet part in the campaign for Mrs. Newman, in an attempt to assess for himself his chances of success against Mr. Fleming. The result of the by-election was encouraging for the federal Liberals. The Conservative candidate, Mr. Leonard Reilly, defeated Mrs. Newman by only thirty-eight votes. (8) The Liberal party tasted blood, and Mr. Sharp was

---

6. Mr. Sharp had been a member of the federal Department of Finance for nine years, and was Director of its Economic Policy Division from 1947 to 1951. In 1951 he became Associate Deputy Minister of Trade and Commerce, and in 1957 Deputy Minister of Trade and Commerce. In 1958, he resigned to become Vice-President of Brazilian Traction, Light and Power Company in Toronto. At the time of his resignation from the civil service, he was approached to accept a position in the Liberal party, but declined. In 1960, Lester B. Pearson invited Mr. Sharp, as a liberally-minded independent, to organize the Kingston Conference, a Liberal-sponsored but independent meeting on Canadian problems, to be held in September, 1960; and Mr. Sharp accepted the invitation. By the summer of 1961 Mr. Pearson was urging Mr. Sharp to become a federal candidate for the Liberal party in the forthcoming campaign. Several Liberal constituency associations in Toronto and area approached Mr. Sharp with offers of nomination when it became known in the party that Mr. Pearson favoured him; but Mr. Sharp declined these invitations because he had not yet decided to seek a nomination. He lived just south of Eglinton riding, and by October had determined to contest the Liberal nomination there. National and local party support followed quickly upon this decision.

7. Mrs. Newman had been, since 1951, successively a trustee for Ward 9 on the Toronto Board of Education, an alderman for Ward 9, and a member of the Toronto Board of Control for two terms, from 1956 to 1960. In 1960 she was defeated in the election for the mayoralty by the incumbent Nathan Phillips.

8. The result was: Leonard Reilly (PC) - 11,366; Mrs. Jean Newman (L) - 11,328; Eamonn Martin (NDP) - 2,695 (Globe and Mail. Jan. 20, 1962). Mr. Martin had the Irish romantic in him. He had come to Canada in 1953 from Ireland after a full young career as law student, actor, member of the Irish Republican Army, and politician, and was at the time of the election an inspector with the Toronto Transit Commission. He commented after the by-election: "I fought for the poor, the weak and the oppressed, but since there were none of those in Eglinton, I lost. None the less, we shall rise again."

encouraged that victory was possible. But Liberal optimism was still restrained. Mrs. Newman had a personal following in the riding that Mr. Sharp did not yet have; and Mr. Fleming, too, had a strong local following that might sustain him in spite of the bitterness of Liberal feelings. By February, however, the lines were being drawn for a mighty battle.

The Executive of the Eglinton Liberal Association prepared for an early nomination meeting on Feb. 12, 1962. (9) In the background there were awkward noises. A thirty-year-old pharmacologist and medical doctor, Dr. Russell Taylor, was determined to contest the nomination against Mr. Sharp, rejecting any suggestion that the convention would automatically choose Mr. Sharp. To counter the official endorsement of Mr. Sharp by the Executive, Dr. Taylor had conducted a door-to-door drive for new memberships in the constituency association, in the hope of carrying the nomination convention with his own recruits. Mr. Sharp was inclined to think Dr. Taylor a nuisance; privately he applied even less complimentary epithets to his challenger. Dr. Taylor said that he was drawn to Eglinton by the desire to defeat Mr. Fleming for "letting his principles get" bent in the Coyne case. (10) His activity, and the public's lively interest in Mr. Sharp's challenge to the Minister of Finance, drew an overflow audience of about nine hundred persons to the nomination meeting at North Toronto Collegiate on February 12. Mr. Sharp was nominated by Mrs. Newman, and won the nomination against Dr. Taylor by 343 to 111 votes. The significance of Mr. Sharp's nomination for the Liberal party was made clear by the presence of the party leader Lester B. Pearson, who delivered the main address after the nomination. (11)

9. The Riding Association Executive was in an anomalous position of its own making, which may reflect the casual nature of party organization in Canada. The constitution of the Association required that a new Executive be elected by the Association by November 30, 1961; but the old Executive had remained in office beyond the end of its constitutional term. "Some dissension" was reported in the Association over this nice point. (Toronto Star, January 31, 1962).

10. But Dr. Taylor had more general political ambitions. He had been president of the Spadina Riding Liberal Association, had considered contesting the Spadina nomination, but had decided against doing so because he "couldn't get mad at Rea" (the sitting Conservative member). "I'm the kind of politician who wants to get identified with the man I run against," he told a reporter. He was able to get mad at Fleming. Dr. Taylor was devoted to his methodical campaigning techniques, and explained that he had learned them from his uncle, Frank Trafford Taylor, once Liberal organizer in Manitoba, whose creed was to take political issues to the doorsteps. Dr. Taylor accepted his uncle's political golden rule: "The only way you can win in politics is by good organization and hard work. Always suspect a candidate that isn't willing to knock on doors. (Ibid., Jan. 31, 1962).

11. Ibid., Feb. 13, 1962.

Soon after his nomination, Mr. Sharp announced that he had
resigned from his position with Brazilian Traction, Light and Power
Company to devote himself fully to his campaign. (12)   By the end
of March, the Liberal organization was optimistic that it would make
a strong campaign, based on the work of many volunteers, most of
them young, who had already offered their services to Mr. Sharp.
They were drawn predominantly from business, the professions, and
the university community, and a substantial number confessed to
having voted Conservative in 1958. After the dissolution of Parliament on April 19, the Liberal campaign crystallized. Mr. Sharp
gained as his campaign manager a young lawyer and recent graduate
of Osgoode Hall, Robert Wright, and Mr. Wright began working on
salary for the Liberal party early in May.

Mr. Fleming's organization possessed more seasoned leadership and less amateur enthusiasm. Before the dissolution of Parliament, its preparatory activities were conducted under the direction
of Warren Armstrong and William Allan, two Conservatives familiar
with the constituency. Mr. Armstrong had acted as the Progressive
Conservative campaign manager in Eglinton in three previous campaigns: the federal campaigns of 1957 and 1958, and the provincial
campaign of 1959. Mr. Allan, who had served as Mr. Fleming's
executive assistant after his appointment to the Ministry of Finance
in 1957, had been Mr. Fleming's official agent in the 1957 federal
election, and previously had been the organizing chairman of the
Eglinton Young Conservatives. (13)   The Fleming committee rooms
opened on North Yonge Street in May, staffed with a growing number of workers. Almost all were long-time residents of the riding
who had worked before for Mr. Fleming.

Mr. Fleming's nomination, unanimous and uncontested, was
made at a meeting of the Progressive Conservative riding association on May 2, 1962, in Lawrence Park Collegiate Institute. The
meeting was attended by about three hundred persons. (14)   Mr.
Fleming, in his acceptance address, emphasized his long, close,
and devoted attachment to the Eglinton community: residence since
1933, public service either at the municipal or the federal level since
1957, association with the founding of the North Toronto Branch of
the YMCA and with numerous local community and athletic clubs.
He accused Mr. Sharp of scurrilous attacks on the Prime Minister,
and of contesting the seat to seek revenge, but the burden of his
speech concerned his own local service. "If anything has been
lacking in my public service," he concluded, "it has not been for
lack of knowing this Riding and its people, or want of devotion to
them and their interests." (15) This theme of Mr. Fleming's local
service became familiar as the campaign advanced.

----
12. Ibid., Feb. 15, 1962.
13. Ibid., July 22, 1957.
14. Ibid., May 3, 1962.
15. Federal Election Issues - A Report to the People of Eglinton by the Hon. Donald M. Fleming, Eglinton Riding Progressive
Conservative Association (June, 1962), pp. 24-6.

By the time of the Parliamentary dissolution, the Eglinton New Democratic Party Association had not yet decided whether to contest the seat. Eamonn Martin, the provincial candidate in January, urged the Association not to nominate. He and others in the organization preferred Mr. Sharp to Mr. Fleming, and did not wish to split the anti-Fleming vote. Some members of the executive considered that the effort and money of the Eglinton organization would be better used in York South and York Centre, where the party expected to make serious challenges. A small NDP group approached Mr. Sharp in April to seek some public commitments of policy from him in return for a decision not to nominate against him. Mr. Sharp insisted that the NDP would have to make its decision on its own, without any specific commitments from him. The national and provincial offices of the NDP felt that the party should nominate in as many constituencies as possible, even hopeless ones, since the NDP was especially concerned to produce a significant national total of voters. This was the first general election since the founding of the party in 1960; the party wished to justify its existence by producing a substantial increase over the previous national vote for the CCF, and for this purpose, every NDP vote was important. Against the advice of Mr. Martin, and in deference to the national party, the Eglinton association decided to nominate. On May 18, at a small meeting, by previous arrangement, Dr. David Gauthier, a thirty-year-old lecturer in philosophy at the University of Toronto, was nominated for the party. (16) Like the Progressive Conservative and Liberal parties, the NDP established its committee rooms a few days later on the Yonge Street commercial strip, in quarters less spacious and affluent than those of its rivals. (17)

The Social Credit party produced a candidate for Eglinton by more mysterious means than the other parties. The central Toronto

16. Dr. Gauthier was invited to contest the seat by David Lewis at the beginning of May. Although he had doubts about both the electoral prospects and the programme of the NDP, he agreed to run "to do what little I could to falsify my doubts, and to help the NDP to succeed." Dr. Gauthier had been an active participant in the nuclear disarmament campaign, and naturally saw the election as an opportunity to express his views on this subject. He also saw, through rose-coloured glasses, the prospect that the NDP might pick up the social ideas of the New Left movement in English politics (which he favoured) and concern itself not only with the economic environment, but with the total cultural and social quality of life. And he was attracted by a general curiosity to taste political life.

17. The NDP headquarters, crowded with four battered desks, was the only committee room to decorate its walls with original paintings. The party acquired, on loan, three large abstracts which gave the otherwise drab room a droll vitality. The influence of the paintings on the NDP campaign was uncertain. Mr. Martin reported that "not all our workers approve. Some of our ladies think we should take them down."

office of the party announced in May that Mr. Basil Duggan, the
comptroller of a plumbing firm, would contest the seat for the party.
Mr. Duggan's campaign had an elusive charm. Mr. Duggan made
no public speeches in the constituency, no committee rooms for the
party were opened, and no pamphlets were printed by the candidate.
The only evidences of Social Credit in Eglinton were a few
scattered window stickers in Yonge Street stores in the last days
of the campaign.

II. THE CAMPAIGN

Mr. Sharp gave notice from his nomination day forward that
he criticized the government and Mr. Fleming on both general and
specific grounds. In Ottawa, on March 19, at a Liberal nomination
meeting, Mr. Sharp accused the Conservative government of using
a confidential civil service report, the famous "hidden report" on
economic prospects, as a stepping stone to power in the 1958 general election campaign. The use of the report, he said, "had destroyed the confidential relationship between civil servants and the
ministry." The Coyne affair, too, had revealed the government's
lack of principle, "... its willingness to do anything - however
sordid - to attain its political ends." In his first campaign pamphlet,
Mr. Sharp wrote: "Like many others, over the past few years I
have felt a growing concern with the Diefenbaker Government - concern with its indecision and lack of leadership, and its mismanagement of our country's economy ... The present Minister of Finance
must assume a large share of the responsibility and blame for (this)
mismanagement ...: of our trade relations with Britain and the
Common Market; and for the Coyne affair." The emphasis of Mr.
Sharp's remarks throughout the campaign remained within fields of
his own competence, economic affairs and public administration: but
always with an undertone of more sweeping criticism. Canada was
drifting, and had lost both self-confidence and international
prestige. (18)
On the evening of Mr. Fleming's nomination, the government,
in circumstances of crisis in Canada's exchange reserve fund,
announced a decision which offered Mr. Sharp an unexpected chance
to illustrate his claims of economic mismanagement. The Department
of Finance issued a statement, in Mr. Fleming's name, announcing
the devaluation of the Canadian dollar to nine-two and a half cents in
American currency. (19)
Whatever the economic merits of devaluation, the crisis in which
it occurred, and its coincidence with the general election campaign,
made it a decision embarrassing to justify. The benefits would not
be revealed for weeks or months, and then not without ambiguity;

18. Toronto Star, March 20 and 23, 1962; Mitchell Sharp-
Liberal-Eglinton, Eglinton Liberal Association (May, 1962).

19. Mr. Fleming's nomination meeting did not hear the news of
the dollar devaluation; the Department did not issue the Minister of
Finance's statement until late that evening. (Toronto Star, May 3,
1962.)

the surprise and apparent insult to Canadian pride were immediate.
Mr. Sharp quickly added a new arrow to his quiver. In his
second campaign pamphlet, distributed after May 10, he concluded
that the dollar had lost value because of "loss of confidence in the
Diefenbaker government's economic and financial policies. In an
effort to hold the Canadian dollar at 95¢ ... the government used
up $400 to $500 millions of our federal reserves of U.S. dollars.
The attempt was unsuccessful. The government devalued again,
not by plan but by panic. Any government acting in this way is
obviously in trouble." (20) Mr. Sharp saw the government
stumbling blindly from crisis to crisis.

Mr. Fleming made his first public defence in the constituency
at a reception on May 15. While primly rejecting an offer of 8¢
from an NDP heckler ("Here's what's missing out of a Diefen-
buck!"), he defended devaluation on the grounds that it would result
in increased exports and domestic sales, higher returns for wheat
producers, increased employment, and a boom in the tourist trade.
The previous Liberal government, he told his audience, had not delivered such benefits to the country. On the contrary, it had im-
posed a "wretched tight-money policy"; it had created uncontrolled
inflation and thirteen budget deficits in twenty-two years; it had
played off one part of the country against another. There was not
much wrong with the Conservative administration, and there was
not much right with its Liberal predecessor. Recently the Liberal
party had plunged further into error, by allowing "an extreme
ranting and roaring Socialist" into its midst. (21)

On the same day Mr. Fleming published his reply to a request
made by Mr. Sharp on April 30 for a public debate between the two
candidates. Mr. Fleming's reply was testy: Mr. Sharp had issued
the challenge as a publicity stunt, and had exploited its news value
before Mr. Fleming was officially nominated and in a position to
reply. The challenge was rejected. (22)

While party solicitation picked up pace, the clash of candidates
in Eglinton subsided during the next two weeks, while both leading
candidates made campaign visits to other parts of the country. From
May 28, the Eglinton campaign moved excitedly, and in the end
frantically, to its climax.

Mr. Fleming appeared on a fifteen-minute political broadcast on
the CTV network (in Toronto on CFTO) on May 28, and the same
evening addressed more than five hundred persons in the North Toronto Memorial Arena. In both the television interview and the public address, he emphasized the beneficial effects of devaluation and
the pegging of the dollar, argued that "we have a good, solid, one
hundred cent dollar," and accused the Liberal party of "a mon-
strous hoax - a hoax the Liberals are attempting to perpetrate upon

20. Eglinton Voters Are Asking These Questions: Here Are
My Answers, Eglinton Liberal Association (May, 1962).

21. Globe and Mail, May 16, 1962. (The socialist was Hazen
Argue.)

22. Ibid.

the Canadian people and the Canadian housewife" - the hoax that
devaluation would increase the cost of living. Mr. Fleming turned
devaluation further to his party's credit with the argument that, since
1946, the Canadian government had defaulted on its agreement with
the International Monetary Fund to stabilize the dollar; only now was
Canada at last in good standing with the Fund. The dollar was
stable and its value would be maintained. (23)

Mr. Fleming was now on the warpath against his opponent.
Mr. Sharp's second campaign pamphlet, containing the answers to
six questions about the economy, the dollar, budget deficits, the
Coyne affair, and Mr. Pearson, was, said Mr. Fleming, "full of
false and base assertions that besmirch Canada." He doubted that
Mr. Sharp could have seen or approved it. (24)

The Toronto Globe and Mail, which had not yet made a clear
commitment for or against the government of Mr. Diefenbaker, devoted its leading editorial on June 1 to Mr. Sharp. The Globe
accused Mr. Sharp of using the methods of the Grand Old Duke of
York. "He marches the Liberal Party, with cliches flying, right
up to the major problems facing Canada and marches right back
down again." Mr. Sharp, said the Globe, speaks of "the solution
of our budgetary problems," "a better life for Canadians," "strong,
responsible government that will pull the country together and get it
moving forward again," but never explains the meaning of these
phrases. "Does he mean that we shall have to tighten our belts,
work harder and longer, postpone welfare plans until we can afford
them? If these are the thoughts behind the phrases, let Mr. Sharp
tell the voters so, boldly and courageously." Whether this was a
challenge for clarification or a disdainful rejection of Mr. Sharp was
not quite clear; but the tone was less than sympathetic. (25)

Mr. Sharp, meeting with about one hundred campaign workers
in his committee rooms a few days later, made his reply to the
Globe and Mail and to Mr. Fleming. "I was feeling a little low
after I saw the editorial on Friday; perhaps it was right, and I
hadn't explained our policies clearly enough. But then when I saw the

---

23. Toronto Star, May 29, 1962: television broadcast on
CFTO, May 28, 1962.

24. Globe and Mail, June 1, 1962. The phrases in the pamphlet most likely to arouse the Finance Minister's anger were these:
"Under the Diefenbaker Government, Canada has been drifting, our
national finances are in disorder, our economy sluggish, and our
trade policies negative and sterile ... Around the world, people
are asking when will the Diefenbaker government stop going into
debt? When, if ever, will it balance the budget? No other important world government is being so reckless, irresponsible and
shortsighted ... Our unemployment problem is about the worst in the
world ... It could get even worse ..." (Eglinton voters are asking
these questions ...)

25. "The Duke of Eglinton," Globe and Mail, June 1, 1962. A
cartoon on the editorial page the next day confirmed the Globe's
anti-Liberal inclinations.

cartoon on Saturday - with the so-called "Brains Trust" sitting behind Pearson, and me with a crown and shield saying "Duke of Eglinton," I knew it was all right: everyone will remember the cartoon and forget the editorial." (26) Besides, he said, one of his assistants had done some homework for him, and reported that after the march up the hill, the Grand Old Duke of York had become Commander-in-Chief of the British Army, and in that position, according to Sir Arthur Bryant, "he wasted no time. The first need was to restore the vanished prestige by ending the scandal of juvenile command." (27) Touché.

The campaign pamphlet to which Mr. Fleming had referred, said Mr. Sharp, was his own. He had prepared it and he took full responsibility for its contents. "If Mr. Fleming is so certain these are blatant lies, I challenge him again to meet me publicly to debate these matters. (28) Mr. Sharp, though calm, confident and unpompous, nevertheless did not elaborate his party's specific economic policies, as the Globe and Mail had demanded he should.

Prime Minister Diefenbaker had previously classed Mr. Sharp among the "bright bureaucratic boys" surrounding Mr. Pearson. As the campaign advanced, the Prime Minister used more picturesque language to describe the group of advisers to Mr. Pearson. At Cobourg, on June 4, Mr. Diefenbaker named Mitchell Sharp as one of "Pearson's menagerie." "... Mr. Pearson held a meeting in January 1960 (sic). It was just a conference, he said, not a political meeting. And the chairman of that conference was Mitchell Sharp, the man who is now the candidate in Toronto ... The man who sat in the gallery of the House of Commons during the pipeline debate in 1956 ... The man who was the right-hand man of C. D. Howe, who pushed Canadians around ..."(29) The theme was repeated with variations throughout the country. Mr. Pearson had behind him "these powers behind the throne - pushers-about-of-people, controllers, authoritarians, dreamers, your masters," (30) the persons the public should fear in a Liberal administration, the source of the Liberal party's corruption. The Liberal party, in Mr. Diefenbaker's eyes, had a basic flaw of pride which made it unsuitable for office in the Canadian parliamentary system; Mr. Sharp, among others, personified this flaw.

Mr. Fleming, after his hurried appearances in the constituency at the end of May, departed again to fight the national party's wars for eight days in Quebec and the Maritime provinces. He kept himself at the centre of controversy, with the assistance of Premier Smallwood of Newfoundland. On June 7, Mr. Fleming appeared at a meeting of the St. John's, Newfoundland, Rotary Club to speak on

---

26. The Conservative campaign committee did what it could to keep both editorial and cartoon before the voters of Eglinton by reprinting both for wide distribution.

27. Globe and Mail, June 5, 1962.

28. Ibid.

29. CBC-TV News, National edition, June 5, 1962.

30. Toronto Star, June 7, 1962.

the subject of devaluation.   During the meal preceding his address,
Premier Smallwood informed the executive of the Club that his
government's financial support for a forthcoming Rotary meeting
would be withdrawn unless the Club prevented the Finance Minister
from delivering his address.   Under this threat, the Club persuaded
Mr. Fleming not to speak. (31)   Mr. Fleming made appropriate
use of the incident as an example of Liberal arrogance and autocracy
in the remaining ten days of the campaign. (32)

    Mr. Fleming's repeated assurances that the ninety-two-and-one-
half cent dollar would be maintained were unexpectedly put in doubt
on June 8 when the Minister of Agriculture, Mr. Alvin Hamilton,
said in Vancouver that he favoured further devaluation to ninety
cents, "a natural peg which is defensible with our negative trade
balance."   The government could hardly avoid an explanation or a
denial.   On June 10 Mr. Fleming issued a press release from
Ottawa designed to squelch the awkward suggestion of his own col-
league: "After consultation with the Prime Minister, I wish to make
it clear beyond question that the rate of 92 1/2¢ in U.S. funds is
definite and final ... We are determined to maintain the 92 1/2¢
rate against pressure of any sort ... The government's policies
will be of a character which involves no further reduction in the
exchange value of the Canadian currency." (33)

    Mr. Hamilton's blunder gave Mitchell Sharp yet another ex-
ample of the confusion of the Conservative administration and in a
crowded public meeting on June 11 he accused the cabinet of "inept
amateurish bungling."   The government obviously did not know
where it was going; it had no policy for defence, no policy for the
dollar, no policy for trade.   Mr. Sharp made a careful and restrained appeal for support to his attentive, though profusely per-
spiring audience.   He denied that he was violently partisan, or that
Liberal times would always be good times (as Robert Winters had
claimed in introducing him).   He hoped that Liberal economic
measures (an Economic Advisory Council, improved tax incentives,
a municipal loan fund, and extended jurisdiction for the Industrial
Development Bank) would be effective.   But they might not overcome
the imbalance of Canada's foreign payments, and they might not cure
domestic unemployment; if they did not do so a Liberal government
would be ready to take "other steps."   This veiled allusion was the
closest that any Eglinton candidate came to advocating emergency
economic measures; Mr. Sharp made no clearer definition of his
meaning.   But the tone of his address was restrained, for a speech
on the hustings.   Mr. Sharp was confident. (34)

---

31. Toronto <u>Telegram</u>, June 7, 1962; <u>Toronto Star</u>, June 8, 1962.
    32. Not only the fact of Premier Smallwood's threat, but the
origin of the topic for Mr. Fleming's undelivered address, was controversial.   Premier Smallwood and the St. John's Rotary Club insisted that Mr. Fleming had suggested his own topic; Mr. Fleming
called this a "vicious lie"; he said he had been invited by the Club
to discuss devaluation. (<u>Toronto Star</u>, June 11, 1962.)
    33. <u>Globe and Mail</u>, June 11, 1962.
    34. Speech of Mr. Sharp at Blythwood School, June 11, 1962.

The final printed statements for both Mr. Sharp and Mr.
Fleming had now appeared.   Mr. Sharp's sought to capitalize on
the enthusiasm and optimism his campaign had generated in the
riding.   It was titled Report on Eglinton - The Riding That Is
Making Election History, and it praised Mitchell Sharp as a man
who "inspires confidence."   Testimonials from Grant Dexter of the
Winnipeg Free Press, Professor W.L. Morton of the University of
Manitoba, and John Bird of the Toronto Star lauded his ability,
courage and public service.   The statement by John Bird concluded:
"In 1958, Mitchell Sharp went into business.   Brazilian Traction in
Toronto, headed by Conservative Henry Borden, thought sufficiently
high (sic) of this "bureaucrat" to promptly offer him a job as vice-
president."   While Mr. Sharp's previous two pamphlets had contained Mr. Sharp's own statements, this one contained only comments of praise about him.

Mr. Fleming published one major campaign document, a more
conventional election manifesto of thirty-five closely printed pages. (35)
It was divided into three sections, "Donald Fleming Discusses: The
Issues"; "Donald Fleming Discusses: Personal Service in Eglinton";
and "Donald Fleming Discusses: The Opposition Campaign in Eglinton."   The document set down unmistakably Mr. Fleming's attitude to Mr. Sharp and the Liberal party.

Under "The Issues," Mr. Fleming justified devaluation, his
government's expansionist economic and fiscal policies, development of
resources policy, foreign policy, trade and employment policies, increased aid to the provinces, social insurance, and the government's
attitude to Parliament.   The Board of the International Monetary
Fund, he wrote, had "not only approved ... but expressed itself as
heartily welcoming" the Canadian decision to peg the dollar on May 2.
The decline in the exchange value of the dollar would have no more
than "a very slight fractional effect" on Canadian prices. (36)

The second section of the manifesto repeated Mr. Fleming's
address in accepting the nomination for the riding; the third section,
of eight pages, contained the sting.   Without once mentioning Mr.
Sharp's name, Mr. Fleming attempted to demolish his opponent with
a variety of accusations.   "This gentleman," "a member of the

---

35. Federal Election Issues - A Report to the People of Eglinton by the Hon. Donald M. Fleming, Eglinton Riding Progressive
Conservative Association (June, 1962).

36. In a direct reference to Mr. Sharp, the manifesto accused
him of speaking of "a loss of $400 million in our exchange reserves.
The Liberal candidate in my riding ... spoke of our spending between $400 million and $500 million.   The truth is that in these
transactions we have simply converted U.S. dollars to Canadian
dollars.   For every U.S. dollar sold we have received in exchange
more than a dollar in Canadian funds.   It is entirely misleading to
talk about these transactions as losses or spending."   Mr. Sharp's
statement had been that "the government used up $400 to $500
millions of our limited reserves of U.S. dollars."   (Eglinton voters
are asking these questions ...)

Party's bureaucratic brain trust," had been imported into the riding by the Liberal high command. "The Liberals have passed over the local people to accept an outsider." The Liberal candidate had entered Eglinton "with a personal axe to grind ... seeking to make himself an issue ... seeking personal revenge." The Liberal candidate had spoken in Ottawa on March 19, 1962, of his shock that the Prime Minister had disclosed the "Hidden Report" to Parliament in 1958. Mr. Fleming was not surprised that Mr. Sharp was shocked: "... I am sure that he was. So were all the other bureaucrats, the coterie of the late Mr. C. D. Howe, and those of like mind with the Liberal Government who had come to treat Parliament with undisguised contempt ... The Report was the property of the Canadian Government. The Canadian taxpayers paid for it. The use made of it was the responsibility of the Government, and a matter for its decision. The Liberal candidate appears to think that as a civil servant he had the right to veto the use of that Report by a new Government. This is a new theory of copyright. The present Government is quite prepared to defend its course of action ... notwithstanding the disapproval of a civil servant who set himself up as master and judge of the government he was employed to serve. The whole episode illustrates some of the burdens we inherited from our Liberal predecessors." (37) Mr. Sharp, the manifesto continued, suggests that the civil service needs to be protected against the Government. On the contrary, "the Civil Service is doing very well, thank you. It is just as good a Civil Service as it was when the Liberal candidate was a member of it; indeed many people think it is better."

Finally, Mr. Fleming criticized Mr. Sharp for his defence of James Coyne: "... This country is deriving great advantage today from the change brought about by the Government last year. We now have effective co-operation between the Bank of Canada and the Department of Finance ... The course which the Government took in this case was a duty it owed to the Canadian people, regardless of the full torrent of abuse, lies, and vituperation heaped upon the Government, and myself in particular, by the Liberals. My only regret in the light of hindsight is that we did not take this course four years sooner."

"With the departure of the former Governor has gone the tight money policy which was applied in the days of the Liberal Govern-

_____

37. An observer might be excused for concluding that in the heat of battle Mr. Fleming had missed the point of Mr. Sharp's criticisms. Mr. Sharp had objected to the publication of a confidential civil service document as material for partisan criticism of the previous government, protesting that the possibility of publication might inhibit government economists in future from making honest appraisals of the economic outlook. Mr. Fleming had detected political bias in, or read it into the civil servant's legitimate protest. It was true that Mr. Sharp, no longer a civil servant, but now a party candidate, had introduced the issue into the campaign. Mr. Fleming, in retrospect, may understandably have doubted the civil servant's impartiality.

ment and which did so much to stifle enterprise and restrict employment. We want neither of them back." The Liberal party was no
longer representative of the Canadian people; it had "developed an
attitude and a philosophy foreign to the spirit and the outlook of the
Canadian people"; it was the "prophet of gloom and doom." The
Diefenbaker government, in refreshing contrast, had "an unshake-
able confidence in Canada's destiny." Mr. Fleming repudiated what
he considered to be the Liberal party's national pessimism and its
special relationship with the federal civil service. His pungent views
reflected those of the Prime Minister, and of many Conservative
enemies of William Lyon Mackenzie King.

In the last week of the campaign, Mr. Fleming appeared more
and more strained. Both candidates held their final rallies on
Friday, June 15: Mr. Sharp, an outdoor picnic in a high school
sports field, and Mr. Fleming, a formal meeting in the Capitol
Theatre on North Yonge Street. Both meetings were failures, for
different reasons. At Mr. Sharp's rally, there were too many outdoor distractions on a summer evening to keep the interest of a
casual and good-humoured audience; and several hundred children
succeeded in drowning the speeches in their roars for Coca Cola
and balloons. As the evening grew dark many curious visitors dispersed up Yonge Street to the Capitol Theatre.

Mr. Fleming's meeting was a misfortune. The theatre, dimly
lit, recollected a fading vaudeville theatre in an early Fellini movie:
the stage, cramped with straight-backed chairs, two wicker flower
baskets, and a lectern decorated with flags, and backed by a worn
grey curtain; the loudspeakers, muffling out "Love Is a Many Splen-
doured Thing" and "Exodus," as the audience rambled into the
gloom. Mr. Fleming entered late with his party, to an ambiguous
standing ovation, and was accompanied to the platform by eight
prominent supporters, including Henry Borden, the President of
Brazilian Traction. (38) Intermittent heckling began with the first
speech of endorsation by Senator Joseph Sullivan, and mounted in
intensity as five of the guests praised Mr. Fleming, and painfully
noticed signs of unfaithfulness in the constituency. The audience was
sceptical. (Cries of "Let him speak.")

At last Mr. Fleming was introduced, already tense from the
heckling. He was honoured, he said, to have with him his old
friend Henry Borden, whose father, Sir Robert, had done so much
at the Versailles Peace Conference in 1919. "As he signed the
Treaty in the Hall of Mirrors at Versailles," recalled Mr. Fleming,
"he had tears in his eyes." Mr. Fleming had no chance to continue before the cries from the audience began once more. ("What
are you doing?" "You don't look too happy, Don." "What about
Mr. Coyne?")

"There are some animals who make noises like cows down
there," responded the Minister of Finance. He began a disquisition
on free speech and Mr. Smallwood. There were groans, cries of
"Tell us something new, Donald," and mocking cheers for Mr.
Smallwood.

---

38. "When he speaks, he speaks for Brazilian Traction," explained one of the platform guests, enigmatically.

"You are not going to take free speech from me," said Mr. Fleming, his voice high-pitched; his followers applauded. One of them, brandishing a stave that once held a Fleming poster, walked menacingly toward a persistent heckler until warned off by friends. Mr. Fleming's narrative was broken by shouts, and his remarks skittered from subject to subject in response to provocative questions from the audience. "... Mr. Coyne subsidized an attack on the government while holding public office ..." "Mr. Diefenbaker is the fearless challenger of the power of Soviet Communism. They (the Russians) prefer Mr. Pearson, the man who - much as he may regret it - once said "better red than dead ...""

In response to groans at his mention of the latest report on reduced unemployment, Mr. Fleming pounced with delight: "There. This is a dead giveaway. They are the howlers!" When unemployment was reduced, he claimed that Liberals groaned. This caught the hecklers off guard, and Mr. Fleming regained tenuous control over the meeting.

Mr. Sharp, continued Mr. Fleming, had written the famous economic report, and then "hidden it under the rug until we found it." The men around Mr. Pearson, who go about the world running down Canada, "don't deserve to be called Canadians." The Liberal party was harming Canadian credit at home and abroad. Recently Robert Winters had intervened in the campaign in the Maritimes to say that Canada was nearly bankrupt. Now he was here in the riding introducing the Liberal candidate. "Robert Winters ... ought to be ashamed of himself ... He should not come into a decent riding like this."

More angry references to the hecklers; to Hazen Argue; to Liberal inflationism; and a peroration on the Conservative challenge to self-reliance and toughness, and Mr. Fleming retired, in a stale-mate with his hecklers. The campaign had worn his expossd nerves, and his countenance was sad. (39)

The points at issue between the two leading candidates had been repeatedly aired and embellished; the public would never be in a better position to judge between them than it was on June 15. Mr. Fleming had scored the last and certainly the most unrestrained blows. Now, on the weekend, the candidates could finally lower their guards and relax, while their campaign organizers made their last efforts to influence the decision on polling day.

For the previous month, the NDP candidate had conducted a quiet, relatively unobtrusive campaign. Dr. Gauthier had addressed one club meeting with Conservative and Liberal spokesmen, but had

---

39. A number of Toronto investment firms sent representatives to the meeting to hear the Minister's remarks on the exchange crisis. (The outflow of dollars had continued after devaluation, and had reached its peak on the previous day. Globe and Mail, June 15, 1962.) When Mr. Fleming said nothing about the crisis, some of the investment men, without premeditation, joined in heckling Mr. Fleming. One of them, challenged by Mr. Fleming to identify himself, refused to do so for fear of embarrassing the government.

limited his other addresses to weekly talks to small groups in his committee rooms on Thursday evenings.   Eamonn Martin, his mentor, was his constant spur, and together they canvassed at bus stops for eight days from June 8, meeting (they estimated) from 250 to 400 persons daily.   A haphazard canvass was carried out, mostly by the candidate and Mr. Martin, of stores on Eglinton Avenue and Yonge Street, of Merton, Balliol, and Davisville Streets in the southern part of the riding, and of Alexandra and Lytton Boulevards in the more prosperous north, where, according to Mr. Martin, "a university candidate might appeal."   Gauthier pamphlets were distributed more widely, along with one thousand window signs and twenty large lawn photographs of the candidate. A few small coffee parties were held for Dr. Gauthier, and an auto cavalcade of about two dozen cars was organized to take supporters to the T.C. Douglas rally at the O'Keefe Centre on June 12.

Dr. Gauthier did not expect to win.   His organization was equipped neither with the volunteers nor the finances to make a showing.   The campaign was virtually conducted by David Gauthier, Eamonn Martin, and two volunteers in the committee room.   The candidate's $200 deposit was paid by the provincial NDP office; the committee budgeted for expenditures of about $1,500.   There are no local unions in the constituency to support the party, and the Eglinton committee received only a small sum from the Metropolitan Toronto union campaign fund.

While the NDP candidate gave some attention in his remarks to an expanded economy, the Common Market, and health insurance, he considered the main issue to be "a sane nuclear policy."   He concentrated in his few speeches on the issue of nuclear weapons for Canada and related problems of the Western alliance: "... We ought to work for goals which will not increase tension.   Our best hope is to work for strong conventional forces: this would assure that German forces would remain conventional, not nuclear ... Once I thought Canada could do better outside NATO, but I no longer do.   Now I think there are trends of non-nuclear thought in NATO which Canada should be encouraging ... One plan I have is for Canada and the United States to set up a joint arms-control research organization.   It would embarrass the United States to refuse.   A well-financed group in the United States with a vested interest in arms control would be more influential than Canadian complaints.   I'm a supporter of Alcock (of the Canadian Peace Research Institute), but I believe governments will be more influential ... This idea is just mine ... "   These thoughts of Dr. Gauthier were ignored in a campaign which centred on economic policy and the record of Mr. Fleming.

Mr. Sharp's organization, almost entirely voluntary, consisted of several hundred canvassers (the organization itself estimated "over 1,500" workers).   The majority of these were under forty, and many did not live in the constituency.   The organization was able to make a complete canvass of the riding, and to cover most polls with more than a single canvass.   The instructions to workers noted that "this is an exciting development considering that there has been nothing like it in the past twenty years." (40)

The Liberal campaign was notable not only because the Sharp volunteers were young and numerous, but because they were high-spirited and well-briefed.   The local organization depended largely for its advice to canvassers on American examples, particularly materials used by the Kennedy organization in the 1960 presidential campaign.   To produce its advertising pamphlets and posters, the party engaged an advertising agency employee, Mr. Paul Break, and the results were rakishly attractive.   The entire Liberal effort was a mixture of amateur enthusiasm and advertising professional-ism.   Mr. Sharp's meetings, for instance, were smoother produc-tions than Mr. Fleming's.   They were opened with facetious crayon sketches by George Feyer, described glibly by Mr. Break: pro-fessional entertainments, designed to set the audience at ease.   Mr. Fleming's meetings were more stodgy, and his campaign pamphlets were not designed for aesthetic appeal.

A member of the Eglinton Liberal party's fund-raising commit-tee estimated that $26,500 was raised for Mr. Sharp.   What was spent was probably considerably greater.   No comparative figure was available from the Conservative organization.   The Sharp or-ganization considered its main task to be to make Mr. Sharp's name and face familiar in the riding.   For this purpose, from the time of his nomination, Mr. Sharp attended frequent coffee parties in the constituency, where he both addressed and chatted informally with hundreds of persons.

In the opinion of the campaign committee, the youth of the Sharp volunteers reflected the support for Mr. Sharp.   Robert Wright, Mr. Sharp's campaign manager, said a few days before

---

40. The workers' instructions contained "a few rules to be kept in mind when the canvass is being done": "1. Be courteous.   Never argue with the voter.   That may lose more votes than it will gain. 2. Simply say 'I am calling on behalf of Mitchell Sharp, your Lib-eral Candidate in Eglinton in the June 18th Federal Election, and I am wondering if we can count on your support at the polls.' 3. Having said that, watch the response and reaction very closely. Most people will simply say 'Thank you' or 'Oh yes' but will not tell you how they intend to vote.   Some will say 'No' or 'I'm Conser-vative' or some such expression which indicates that they do not in-tend to vote Liberal.   Opposite their names on the Voters List mark 'PC' or 'NDP' as their definite preference so that you will not have to waste time going after them again.   Some will say that they have not made up their minds – mark them 'D' for doubtful.   However, some people will say 'We're Liberal' or 'He's my man' or 'I'm for Sharp' or 'I hope he wins.'   Mark him 'L' on your list.   4. You must never mark the Voters List in the presence of the voter – wait until you have left the door and before you get to the next door. 5. Leave a pamphlet with each voter.   6. Ask if they know how others in the house are going to vote.   7. If any of the Liberal voters have a special request such as for transportation on Election Day, make a note and pass it along to Campaign Headquarters." (Poll Organization, mimeographed, May 9, 1962.)

the campaign ended: "We have the young, under forty; Fleming has the over-55 vote. In between, we have the businessmen and professionals in the 50-group. Fleming has those in this group who are clerical and semiskilled: that's a paradox. Those who should be voting Liberal in this age group are not - perhaps because voting Conservative is a status symbol, a means of lifting themselves up ... The Conservatives have the area south of Eglinton and east of Yonge that we should have."

Five days before the poll, Mr. Wright was cautiously optimistic. "Our canvass, as of last week, shows we are in the lead ... But the Conservatives say their canvass gives them the same result. Monday will show whether someone is talking hot air." There was doubt about the reliability of the canvass, since about one-third of the voters were marked "doubtful." The doubtfuls, apparently, would decide the outcome.

The Conservative organization, protected from self-doubt like any political organization by its egocentricity and its hopes, shielded itself from the trends of Liberal campaigning until the last ten days. "We're doing all right in this constituency. I'm not sure about the rest of the country, but here we're O.K.," said Warren Armstrong, Mr. Fleming's campaign manager, on June 6. The party had an efficient door-to-door and telephone canvass in operation. But suddenly, by June 13, Progressive Conservative optimism disappeared. Canvassers from all parts of the constituency reported the break-up of traditional Conservative support. The old were solid for Fleming, but the Sharp organization had captured the young. Those who remembered what Mr. Fleming had done for the riding, it was said, would vote Conservative, others might not. Because the distinction between parties was one of age rather than income or profession, it was not possible to speak of strong Conservative areas: there seemed to be none. Would a low poll hurt Mr. Fleming? No, thought Mr. Armstrong. "If the doubtfuls stay home, we have it. There are more declared Conservatives than Liberals in the riding. The doubtfuls will decide."

Conservative workers, in their extremity, saw two things that weakened the Fleming campaign: Mr. Fleming's association with Prime Minister Diefenbaker, and Mr. Fleming's absence for much of the campaign while fulfilling national commitments. But he had returned for the last week, and was running hard, attending coffee klatches almost continuously. Conservative canvassers distributed large numbers of party pamphlets in the last week. Even this final effort might not be enough. A senior campaign official remarked in the last days, in sudden exasperation: "This is going to be a bitch of a fight."

III. THE RESULT

1958			1962		
Fleming	(PC)	28,565	Fleming	(PC)	18,648
Wilson	(Lib.)	9,468	Sharp	(Lib.)	17,888
Grube	(CCF)	2,646	Gauthier	(NDP)	4,113
			Duggan	(Socred)	341

Mr. Fleming's personal activity and the barrage of Conservative pamphlets distributed in the last week of the campaign, along with an efficient Conservative operation to get out the vote on June 18, apparently saved the constituency for the Minister of Finance. Mr. Fleming squeaked back into the House of Commons with 760 votes more than Mr. Sharp. It is impossible to say how many individuals decided to vote for Mr. Fleming in the last week of the campaign, but the external evidence – of the last-minute Conservative blitz, of the number of doubtfuls encountered by each major party in its canvass, of the apparent easing of the Liberal campaign in the last days – suggests that Mr. Fleming retrieved victory at the last possible moment.   Campaign timing was one significant factor in the outcome.   Partly, the timing of each party's greatest effort was unplanned.   The buoyancy of Liberal organizers after June 11 could not have been predicted; neither could the desperation of the Conservatives.   And these contrasting moods were above all what determined the intensity of the campaign in the last week.   But partly, the different peaks in the two campaigns may also have reflected the different natures of the two organizations. The Sharp organization was predominantly young, amateur, and inexperienced: it may have misjudged the importance of intense effort at the last moment.   The Fleming organization was experienced: its final panic may merely have reinforced its professional sense of timing.

The NDP candidate also influenced the result.   About 2,500 votes in the constituency were regarded as reliable NDP votes. But Dr. Gauthier gained 4,113 votes, considerably more than either Mrs. Grube in 1958 or Mr. Martin in January, 1962.   Dr. Gauthier, like Mr. Sharp, sought to capitalize on the unpopularity of Mr. Fleming.   It is likely that a substantial majority of his votes were, in one sense, votes against Mr. Fleming.   The potential alternative for NDP voters who opposed Mr. Fleming was to vote Liberal.   If the NDP had not contested the riding, it is conceivable that the Liberal party might have gained enough of Dr. Gauthier's votes to upset Mr. Fleming.   The NDP committee itself thought that it received an infusion of strength in the riding on Friday, June 15, when the Toronto Star's popular independent columnist, Pierre Berton, declared himself for the New Democratic party. (41)   This declaration, in a Liberal newspaper, could not have helped Mr. Sharp.

Mr. Fleming received 45 per cent of the popular vote in the riding, Mr. Sharp 44 per cent, and Dr. Gauthier 10 per cent. (This represents a "swing" of 23 per cent of the 1958 popular vote to the Liberal candidate.)   Mr. Fleming's stronghold was his own neighbourhood: in other parts of the riding, as both the Liberals and the Conservatives expected, the outcome was close.   Mr. Sharp had no unusually strong areas and no unusually weak areas.   In the less prosperous district south of Eglinton Avenue and east of

---

41. Pierre Berton, "Why I Intend to Vote for the NDP," Toronto Star, June 15, 1962.

Yonge Street, Mr. Fleming did slightly better against Mr. Sharp than in the whole riding, but still only two percentage points separated the leading candidates (Mr. Fleming gained 43 per cent of the vote here, and Mr. Sharp 41 per cent). This was Dr. Gauthier's area of relative strength, but his position even here was weak (he gained 14 per cent of the vote in the area). In thirty-three polls where more than half the voters were apartment or duplex dwellers, Mr. Fleming received 46 per cent of the vote, Mr. Sharp 44 per cent and Dr. Gauthier 10 per cent. There was no special advantage for Mr. Sharp in the apartment vote, as some Liberals vaguely expected.

IV. REFLECTIONS

The dialogue between Mr. Fleming and Mr. Sharp in the 1962 Eglinton campaign offers some signs of how the two main parties see themselves, each other, and their respective places in national history.

Mr. Fleming's essential case in 1962 was that the Liberal party was in some sense disloyal to the country, arrogant towards the opponents and the public, ignorant of the proper role of politicians and Parliament, and inclined to blur the lines between administration and politics, and to turn the country into a non-political state managed by administrators or "bureaucrats." This image of the Liberal party was intertwined with criticisms of Liberal policies. Mr. Coyne, the civil servant, had been the advocate of tight money; Mr. Sharp, the civil servant turned politician, had objected to the publication of a civil service document on the economy for partisan reasons. Mr. Fleming tended to turn the discussion of economic policy and the Bank of Canada into discussion of the subordinate role of civil servants, and of the impropriety of the Liberal party's friendly ties with the senior civil service. The passion with which Mr. Fleming expressed his views on this subject indicates its importance to him. Mr. Fleming on the platform was the parliamentary constitutionalist with a sharp tongue, believing in the profession of politics, the competence of politicians to govern, and the non-partisan position of their civil service advisers.

Mr. Sharp, by implication, seemed to offer another interpretation of the constitution, and he was accused of doing so by Mr. Fleming. For Mr. Sharp, the Conservative government was not only "inept" and "bungling," it was "amateurish," not administratively neat and professional. It did not do the sensible things which Mr. Sharp (and others) thought it should do, and it did not maintain good relations with the civil servants who could advise it what to do. (42)

_____
42. Mr. Sharp had discussed his experience in the civil service, and his conception of the proper relationship between politicians and civil servants, in an article in the Toronto Star, July 27, 1961. He thought that civil servants should not concern themselves with party politics ("Indeed, with one or two exceptions I hadn't the slightest idea of my colleagues' political persuasions, if they had any."), but emphatically that they should be consulted and should

But what appeared to Mr. Sharp to be weakness appeared to Mr. Fleming to be strength. To say that a government was "amateurish" meant to say that it was under the control of House of Commons men. Mr. Sharp's view was that of a thoughtful administrator, who considered the messiness and hypocrisy of politics to be something tiresome, and perhaps something inappropriate for governing a nation in the mid-twentieth century. From early in the campaign, when he showed his impatience with his legitimate opponent for the Liberal nomination, to his careful and calculatedly undemagogic remarks about the economic situation on June 11, Mr. Sharp appeared to be the administrator and reluctant politician. He gave the clear impression that he was running, not for a seat in the House of Commons, but for a seat in the cabinet, the body that would make decisions and govern the country. A seat in the House of Commons was incidental. Not so for Mr. Fleming, who had plunged into the turbulent life of the House of Commons from the moment he entered it in 1945, and was shaped by it.

In Mr. Fleming's eyes, Mr. Sharp's personal history stamped him as a "bureaucrat," one of C.D. Howe's boys, a man who would not treat the House of Commons with the deference it deserved if he came to power. This, of course, was an easy charge to make because no evidence could be presented to refute it. Mr. Sharp had never sat in the House of Commons and shown how he would treat it. But Mr. Fleming, still strongly affected by the contempt for the House displayed by C.D. Howe, was ready to suspect any of Mr. Howe's associates of the same attitude.

Was there any constitutional validity to Mr. Fleming's accusations against Mr. Sharp? It cannot be improper for the senior civil service to be on terms of mutual respect with the ministry. It seems essential, if a government is to produce workable and appropriate legislation, that it should rely on its civil servants for advice and even initiatives. Mr. Fleming was inclined to disregard this necessity, in his public statements if not in practice, because he suspected some civil servants of Liberal bias. The fact that Mr. Sharp had been a civil servant, and had now entered politics as a Liberal, seemed to confirm Mr. Fleming's image of the Liberal party and its civil service. The party, in Mr. Sharp's case as in others, had violated the traditional Parliamentary practice of

---

play a major role in the initiation and formation of policy. A good public servant would loyally support his minister, and try "to keep his minister out of trouble," and this would involve offering advice about the political implications of policies; so a senior civil servant, though formally non-partisan, must be interested in "politics," in that sense. If the civil servant is encouraged to offer advice, a close relationship of mutual respect and friendship is bound to arise between him and his minister, but this will have "nothing to do with party politics." Mr. Sharp believed that this non-political friendship was demonstrated in 1957. "... The present permanent heads of Departments in Ottawa ..., from my observation, behaved in a most exemplary manner when the change of government occurred."

non-partisanship in the public service. If Mr. Sharp had protested against an act of the Conservative government while he was a deputy minister, and had subsequently left the civil service and become a politician, perhaps he <u>had</u> all the time been a Liberal in disguise; perhaps his attitude in the case of the "hidden report" <u>had</u> been politically motivated. Or perhaps Mr. Sharp did not consider that he had become a partisan by becoming a Liberal party candidate. It would have been difficult for Mr. Sharp to clear himself of the suspicion of partisanship, except by remaining permanently neutral in politics. He had not done so. (43)

Mr. Fleming's statements in the Eglinton campaign, taken with those of Mr. Diefenbaker and with the evidence of other events, suggest that Conservative suspicion of the civil service made cooperation between the civil service and a Conservative government difficult. To the extent that this suspicion arises from the entry of former senior civil servants into the senior and active ranks of the Liberal party, the party's inclination to blur the line between politics and administration has been unwise. The civil service, to be non-partisan, must be non-partisan to both sides. The Liberal party has not faced squarely the political implications of drawing civil servants into the party leadership, and certainly did not do so in the 1962 Eglinton campaign. Mr. Sharp did not appear publicly to comprehend the nature of the problem. Mr. Diefenbaker's and Mr. Fleming's criticisms of the practice, though phrased in rhetorical language for the political platform, deserve to be treated seriously.(44)

---

43. Mr. Sharp's timing in resigning from the civil service offered further reason for Conservative suspicion of his neutrality. He submitted his resignation on the evening of March 31,1958, election night, after it appeared certain that the Diefenbaker government had been returned to office. (Ibid., April 7, 1958.)

44. Mr. Sharp has since commented upon the practice. While he does not believe that it is good constitutional practice for a government to appoint senior civil servants directly to the Cabinet ("... notwithstanding the Pearson and Pickersgill appointments which turned out so well ..."), he sees positive merit in the fact that some senior civil servants have resigned from the public service and entered politics. In a political system which does not efficiently train House of Commons men to take public office in their maturity, Mr. Sharp believes that sometime civil servants provide an experience of government which all cabinets need. For the Liberal party, this approach seems to offer an efficient compensation for the failure of the Canadian House of Commons to bring forward capable political cadres; but it may also help to explain why little has been done by the Liberal party to make the House a vigorous political training ground. The assumption of such a view is that administration, not parliamentary politics, takes precedence. In a parliamentary system this attitude is not altogether orthodox, to say the least. The Liberal party's attitude does nothing, of course, to explain the Conservative party's indifference to the weakness of Parliament; and the Conservative party lacks even the excuse that

On the other hand, the Conservative party too must reconsider its public attitude to the professional civil service.   The Minister of Finance must have expert advice, and to gain it he must treat his civil servants with respect.   This involves a degree of restraint on the hustings that Mr. Fleming frequently lacked in 1962.   If a minister refers scathingly in public to "bureaucrats," some normally loyal civil servants are likely to be offended.   Conservative politicians could avoid creating opposition gratuitously in the civil service by avoiding careless and sweeping public statements of this kind. Just as the civil service has a duty of loyalty to the government, whatever its politics, the government has a duty of respect and trust to the civil service; neither side can break the bargain.   If the civil service is to be non-partisan, as parliamentary tradition demands and as Mr. Fleming wished it to be, it must be immune from attack by politicians.

These, at least, are two of the constitutional lessons to be drawn from the Fleming-Sharp battle.   Eglinton in 1962 thus offered its citizens a basic Canadian political conflict in microcosm: a conflict which is sometimes ignored in the suggestion that there are no significant differences between the two major parties. (45)

---

it finds capable leaders in the civil service as substitutes for those unavailable in the House of Commons.   Each party, in its own way, has failed to perceive clearly what has happened to Parliament in this century.

45. The last flutter of the campaign occurred late in 1962, when Dr. Gauthier, now convinced that his earlier doubts about the policy and prospects of the New Democratic party were justified, offered his resignation from the party.   Mr. Martin followed him out the door.

A RETURN TO THE STATUS QUO: THE ELECTION IN WINNIPEG NORTH CENTRE*

T. Peterson and I. Avakumovic

Stretching like an irregular wedge from historic Point Douglas on the Red River westward out to the city's ragged edge on the prairie, Winnipeg North Centre is one of Canada's most cosmopolitan ridings. From the last decades of the nineteenth century, immigrant Ukrainians, Chinese, Jews, Russians, Poles, Germans, and countless others streamed into it through the old CPR station and mingled together in an ethnic kaleidoscope. Many settled there, getting jobs in the nearby stock and rail yards. Some of their descendants still remain, amid the remnants of the older Anglo-Saxon community. In time, those who could moved south to Winnipeg's better neighbourhoods. Their places were taken by newer immigrants and by the quiet trickle of Indians from northern reserves.

The riding gradually divided into four distinct parts. In its centre close to the CPR tracks, houses have steadily decayed and the sooty tenements have become dismal slums. A second region, some twelve blocks to the south, is markedly different. Here, neat rows of middle-class homes face quiet elm-lined streets. On the western periphery, a third district is characterized by occasional fields, heavy industry, and the box-like housing of railway and factory workers. Last, at the opposite narrower end to the east, is downtown Main Street, flanked by old hotels, pawnshops, and remodelled diners. These in turn serve as a facade for the garment and wholesale district, the city's Chinatown, and congested rooming houses. Beside the Red River, near the former site of Lord Selkirk's Fort Douglas, are more factories and the gas works. These four parts together comprise a constituency generally poor in appearance but rich in history and diversity.

Over the years, it won a reputation as a socialist stronghold. In 1900, it helped elect one of Canada's first Labour members to the House of Commons. As part of Winnipeg Centre in 1921, it first

_____

*This study was made possible by a grant from the University of Manitoba's President's Research Fund and by the considerable assistance of the following graduate students: M. Glassman, G. Knysh, W. Neville, D. Stephens, and J. Woods.

The authors are grateful to Professor W.H.N. Hull for his many helpful suggestions. He will be preparing a subsequent study when further material becomes available from the Dominion Bureau of Statistics.

sent James S. Woodsworth to Ottawa. It became a separate constituency following the Redistribution Act of 1924, and thenceforth for
seventeen years remained Woodsworth's faithful seat. His proportions of the popular vote varied from three-quarters in 1930 to less
than half in 1940, when even his unpopular pacifism could not defeat
him. After Woodsworth died, Stanley Knowles inherited this traditional strength.

The depression had led Knowles, like many others, from the
pulpit to the platform. A contemporary of T.C. Douglas he studied
theology at United College and worked for a time at one of the
poorer missions in North Centre. By 1934, he was active in the
newly-formed CCF. Rising rapidly, within five years he reached
the National Council. In the 1942 by-election following Woodsworth's
death, he won 70 per cent of the vote cast and began the persistent
work that was to establish his parliamentary career.

Succeeding elections built a legend of Knowles' invincibility in
North Centre. His opponents were weak: of the total vote, Liberals usually got less than a third, and the Conservatives trailed
with less than a fifth. What strength they mustered was limited
mainly to the southern middle-class part of the constituency. In
1945 and in 1953, Communists also ran, but each received under
two thousand votes. Against this feeble and fragmented opposition,
there was a united socialist block numbering over ten thousand
voters. Its strength was concentrated in the western working-class
district and the poorer areas in the riding's centre. Showing remarkable fidelity, this block returned Knowles with substantial majorities in the three elections of the post-war decade. As he established his parliamentary reputation in Ottawa, it was understandable
that the security of his seat was increasingly taken for granted.

But his faithful party organizers aged, and prosperous workers
moved to better homes outside the old riding. Following the Redistribution Act of 1952, a fifth part north of the tracks was added to
the original four. Almost wholly East European in origin and character, it brought with it an element of political extremism compounded
from the majority's bitter anti-Bolshevik memories and the tough
faith of a Communist minority. Meanwhile, the central blight spread
and worsened. The ignorance or apathy of slum dwellers was reflected in declining turnouts, markedly below the provincial average.
After 1953, as well, the over-all population slowly began to fall.
All these factors combined almost imperceptibly to change North
Centre from what it had been in Woodsworth's time.

To contest the Knowles legend in 1957, the local Conservative
association, then numbering less than fifty, nominated John MacLean.
A month out of the Law School and twenty years younger than
Knowles, MacLean was practically unknown in politics. His chief
asset was the hopeful energy of youth. The election predictably saw
Knowles again exceed his opponents' combined total. A departure
from the traditional pattern, however, was the tripling of the Conservative vote, placing MacLean ahead of the Liberal candidate.
But the socialist block of ten thousand still kept him from victory.

Yet ten months later in March 1958, North Centre voted Con-

servative for the first time in its history. Running hard a second
time, John MacLean had done the seemingly impossible. Shock and
disbelief reverberated beyond Winnipeg across Canada. A legend
had died, and "post mortems" were myriad. One enigmatic aspect
of the upset was the spectacular turnout of four thousand new voters,
even though the electoral roll was substantially unchanged from 1957.
This curious phenomenon, combined with relatively slight CCF and
Liberal losses, gave MacLean a narrow majority of fewer than
fourteen hundred votes. Knowles' loyal block remained essentially
intact; a hitherto unknown group had defeated him. Although fairly
evenly distributed, most of the new Conservative voters came from
the riding's southern district. Their past fatalism or inertia had
evidently been overcome by Prime Minister Diefenbaker's evangeli-
cal fervour. Also partly responsible was the invigorated Conservative organization. Managing MacLean's campaign, Barry Gibbons,
a local sales executive, built a machine that was to serve as a
model for Conservatives throughout the province. With decisive
central direction, unprecedented advertising expenditure, massive
telephone and postcard recruitment of over five hundred new association members, and extensive canvassing for the first time, this
new organization made an impact on the old socialist riding for which
it was wholly unprepared. Returning belatedly from the national
campaign circuit, Knowles on election night was stunned by the un-
foreseen result.

To some it appeared that his parliamentary career was finished.
But some weeks after his defeat, Knowles became Executive Vice-
President of the Canadian Labour Congress, and while in that capacity he worked over the next three years to broaden the foundation
of the CCF. His efforts were rewarded in the summer of 1961 by
the formation of the New Democratic party, based on a closer
association of many CLC unions with the old socialist movement.

The following March, a month before Prime Minister Diefenbaker dissolved the twenty-fourth Parliament, Knowles had already
been nominated to contest North Centre. At a downtown theatre
rally attended by almost six hundred persons, T.C. Douglas, the
New Democratic leader, indicted the old parties and argued vigorously for more comprehensive economic planning. The response of
the audience was optimistic. Reflecting it, Knowles subsequently expressed the hope that the New Democrats would gain as many as
six or eight Manitoba seats in the forthcoming election.

The party's determination to regain North Centre was demonstrated by the appointment of a special full-time campaign manager on
April 18, the day before the dissolution of Parliament. He was
Frank Chafe, thirty-nine year old CLC Regional Director of Education for the prairies, transferred from Regina on two months'
leave of absence. Unfamiliar with the constituency and its old CCF
personnel, he began slowly rebuilding an organization based on the
provincial riding associations.

There were seven provincial ridings wholly or partly within
Winnipeg North Centre. Four of these, flanking the CPR yards,
were held by the CCF. Two of the others, located further south

and in the downtown area were Conservative, as was the seventh which attached the western working-class district to a large rural riding. Chafe's strategy was to increase Knowles' vote in the western and central CCF areas sufficiently to offset the Conservative strength in the south-east, and at the same time at least break even in the predominantly Ukrainian district north of the tracks.

Accordingly, he scheduled meetings of the provincial constituency associations in late April and early May. These meetings were attended by about two dozen persons each. They were held in Knowles' campaign headquarters, a modest frame house owned by the party in the western part of the riding. Filled with the memory of past triumphs and disappointments, it symbolized the strength of tradition and the weakness of age affecting Chafe's efforts and Knowles' fortunes.

A week after the appointment of the NDP organizer, the Conservative nominating convention was held. Well publicized by store-window placards, it attracted over three hundred persons. They crowded into a hot and smoky club hall in the southern part of the riding. On the platform, backed by Veterans Affairs Minister Gordon Churchill, Postmaster General William Hamilton joked at length, defended the government and advised Knowles to go back east to the CLC. MacLean was nominated without opposition, and joined the battle by declaring: "Knowles may be a fighter, but this year he's going to get the fight of his life." (1)

Indeed, from virtual anonymity in 1957, MacLean had become a substantial party figure, solicitous of his constituents, skilled in organization and notably active in Parliament. In recognition of his ability, he had been elected National President of the Young Progressive Conservatives and had already been given a major role in co-ordinating the Conservative campaign in Manitoba. Noisy enthusiasm acclaimed his renomination. After the formal meeting, refreshments, music, and colourful Serbian dancing accompanied the quiet taking of names for volunteer canvassing. Barry Gibbons, the dynamic 1958 manager, was back and confident of victory.

Under his direction, two separate committee rooms had already been rented: a spacious former restaurant in the riding's centre, and a former store in the district north of the tracks, designed to attract the local Slavic vote. On May 4, at a reception in a downtown department store, some seventy members of the local women's association pledged their support and began to work. The next day, about fifty Young Conservatives attended a day-long campaign school and were assigned part of North Centre as a special project. Gibbons' organization within two weeks had caught up and passed the NDP. Money did not appear a major problem.

Other nominations followed. The Communist party in late April nominated Don Currie, a professional party organizer. Twenty-seven years old, Currie was a well-trained speaker and had won some notice as an opponent of higher municipal taxation. With the party candidate in Winnipeg North, he shared a cramped committee

_____
1. Quoted in the Winnipeg _Tribune_, April 26, 1962.

room in the northern district, across the street from the Conservative auxiliary office. Currie's chief aim was publicity, which he
pursued with anti-American sallies, appeals to pacifism, and accusations that the NDP had betrayed the working class.

On May 10, about three hundred Liberals met in a school
auditorium and formally nominated Barry Krawchuk, an aggressive
twenty-nine-year-old lawyer of Ukrainian origin. Many of those
present came to hear the guest speaker, Paul Martin, excoriate
the Conservatives, and the nomination was little more than a by-
product. Martin's mission was, partly to conciliate the candidate,
who threatened to withdraw after the Free Press printed rumours
that top Liberals had "written off" the constituency. After the nomination, the campaign lapsed not so much for lack of funds as for
lack of help. The local constituency association was moribund, the
provincial party was weak in the area, and Krawchuk accordingly
had mainly to fight his own battle. He was unable to recruit more
than a dozen reliable workers, most of whom were university students; and he afterwards expressed the belief that his chief asset
had been his name.

A Social Credit candidate was nominated last. At a meeting
arranged by the Manitoba Social Credit League, forty-five persons
chose all four candidates for the Winnipeg ridings, including David
Webster for North Centre. A draughtsman and bank clerk, originally from Alberta, Webster was young and completely inexperienced
in politics. His party's weakness in the riding had been demonstrated in 1957, when its candidate obtained fewer than nineteen
hundred votes; and this time, Webster's diffidence further frustrated
any serious hopes he might have had. His campaign was at best
limited and hesitant.

All of the nominations were virtually foregone conclusions. Decisions were prearranged by small groups at the provincial or
national level, with the formal votes being little more than ritual con-
cessions to grass-roots democracy. The local meetings' real purposes were to raise morale, recruit workers, get publicity, and
launch the campaign as vigorously as possible. In achieving these,
the Conservative convention was the most successful.

Once launched, the campaign inevitably focused on the struggle
between Knowles and MacLean. The old challenger and the young
incumbent were a study in contrast. A big, shrewd, three-hundred
pounder, MacLean mingled freely with his constituents, shaking hands,
joking and asking their personal support. His speeches emphasized
that the contest was between free enterprise and socialism: "Too
often in the past, a free enterprise candidate has been defeated by a
minority of socialists ... We cannot let this happen on June 18.
People all over the constituency who believe in freedom of initiative,
enterprise and thought are crossing party lines and joining our
cause." (2)

Beside MacLean, Knowles was a thin, almost ascetic figure,
earnest but aloof. He made a point of never mentioning MacLean by

_____
2. Quoted in the Winnipeg Free Press, June 11, 1962.

name, and his campaign literature, omitting direct references to socialism, stressed the Woodsworth tradition and his personal record. His pledge to the voters ended simply: "I will continue to serve you, and all the working people of Canada, with everything that I have." (3)   To some of Knowles' supporters, this approach lacked fire and failed to attack with sufficient force. Many voters might well have thought him the incumbent rather than the challenger; and indeed canvasses indicated that some even thought him a Liberal or a Conservative.

The campaign was fought on many fronts. By mid-May, the major parties were advertising heavily in all available media. Billboards appeared suddenly: six for the NDP, twelve for the Conservatives, and three for the Liberals. Several in the latter two groups prominently displayed the national leaders; those of the NDP, in keeping with Knowles' general strategy, concentrated on publicizing the candidate himself. In Catholic and ethnic weeklies, Conservative advertisements appeared first, and were quickly followed by the NDP. (4)   Both also sent out special Ukrainian pamphlets to attract the vote in the northern district or at least to prevent its monopoly by Krawchuk, the Liberal candidate. Conservative advertising in the daily press, largely sponsored by the national headquarters, exceeded that of all other parties, with the Liberals running second.

Pouring from each committee room, there was another continuous flow of propaganda. On a prearranged timetable, the Conservatives mailed to every household in the riding five major releases; a recruiting postcard in late April, a printed letter from MacLean in May; and in the final two weeks, a Diefenbaker-MacLean card, a letter that skilfully appeared to be handwritten, and a where-to-vote card. Similarly, but not on as consistent a schedule, the NDP issued four releases: a Douglas pamphlet, a Knowles pamphlet, a typed letter, and also a final where-to-vote card. Unlike the Conservatives, the NDP relied mainly on voluntary delivery, mailing only in the areas missed. In addition, there were countless other pamphlets given less general distribution, plus calendar cards, bumper stickers, window placards, matches, buttons (sold by the NDP to raise almost $500), combs (Liberals: "Comb Dief out of your hair"), a fortune in Diefendollars, and even Conservative darning kits. Much of this propaganda probably had little effect on the ad-weary public, and many pamphlets were undoubtedly discarded unread.

One that did deserve attention was an offensive Canadian Intelligence Service smear-sheet identifying prominent New Democrats as Communists. Rashly distributed in several areas of North Centre

---

3. Campaign pamphlet.
4. E.G. MacLean: "Heartiest Anniversary Greetings! May the State of Israel continue to flourish in an atmosphere of peace and security." (<u>Western Jewish News</u>, May 10, 1962). Knowles: a "relentless fighter for freedom and social justice and a foe of Communism." (<u>Sunday Herald</u>, June 10, 1962).

by Richard Seaborn, a right-wing Conservative MLA, its anti-Semitic overtones aroused a storm of protest. Damage was undeniably done to both sides before Premier Roblin publicly forced Seaborn to apologize.

While propagandist advertising became, by past electoral standards, more frenetic and profuse, public meetings continued their relative decline. Open assemblies formally addressed by the candidate were rare: Knowles held three, attended by audiences of between fifty and a hundred and twenty persons each; and the Communist, claiming to be the only candidate who dared to face the public, harangued at length a dozen persons in a school room one sultry June evening. The others evidently felt that such poorly attended local meetings were a waste of effort.

Semi-private social gatherings were more common. Including informal teas, receptions and dances, these were inclined to be repetitive and saccharine, although exceptions proved revealing. At a dance in Point Douglas, a group including ethnic and veterans' representatives presented MacLean with an inscribed scroll commending his efforts. Curiously, the scroll's cost was later included among his campaign expenses. At a packinghouse union meeting on Main Street, after Chafe and Knowles pointedly noted the NDP's need for greater financial support, violent argument erupted between those in favour and others wanting to preserve the meagre union fund for a scholarship and study program. At length, after being reminded of heavy business contributions to the old parties, the union delegates voted fourteen hundred dollars, to be divided evenly among the seven metropolitan Winnipeg constituencies. The lesson was clear that union contributions were often neither easy to obtain nor very substantial once obtained. Less stormy were the frequent teas: Knowles attended over thirty, and MacLean incredibly over sixty. But whether these actually won any votes, or simply involved affirming the faithful, remains conjectural.

A third type of meeting was the mass rally, with nationally prominent speakers. All the parties staged these with varying success. Tim Buck and Leslie Morris each spoke at Communist gatherings of about two hundred supporters; Premier W.A.C. Bennett spoke for Social Credit to a somewhat larger audience, including many who were obviously merely curious. The biggest rallies, all held in Winnipeg Auditorium, came near the climactic close of the campaign. On May 23, Prime Minister Diefenbaker spoke to a disappointing four thousand, promising among other things a second Trans-Canada highway. Five days later, Liberal leader L.B. Pearson addressed about five thousand, concentrating his attack on unemployment. Finally, four days before the election, New Democrat leader T.C. Douglas spoke mainly on the same issue to slightly less than four thousand. All three rallies had motorcades, banners, and other fanfare to stimulate a last desperate effort by flagging party workers. It is again doubtful whether many voters were influenced by the respective shows of strength. The party with the biggest rally won only one seat in the province.

Debates among the candidates were generally shunned. This

was, of course, partly because of their dangerous unpredictability
and partly because of the low attendance at all local public meetings.
At a union-sponsored multilateral debate, for example, there were
ten Liberal and New Democrat speakers, but only sixty in the audience. A greater but still limited success was a debate arranged
by a welfare committee in North Centre. Four of the candidates
attended, and Chafe spoke for Knowles, who was detained and
arrived late. But little effective debates occurred. Instead, unfortunately for the meeting's purpose, the Communist was roundly
abused by the other four, with each seeking to surpass his rivals
in patriotic fervour. The poll where the meeting was held ultimately voted Conservative.

Unobtrusive door-to-door canvassing was meanwhile proceeding spasmodically. Every campaign handbook insisted that it was
the key to victory, with the purpose being mainly to identify party
supporters and make sure they voted. To this end, managers
chose district leaders who in turn appointed poll captains. The
latter were then periodically checked and encouraged. But the
task was wearisome, and no party realized the ideal of complete
coverage. Gibbons claimed that his association had almost a thousand members, of whom about two hundred canvassed at one time
or another; while the NDP claimed about half of the association
membership but an equal number of canvassers. It seems likely,
however, that neither had many more than fifty reliable workers.
Poll captains for MacLean included businessmen, lawyers, housewives, and members of the provincial legislature, and for Knowles
included railway workers, teachers, and union agents. Both sides
recruited help from outside the riding. For additional canvassing in
the southern section, the NDP also had a full-time assistant from
the Steelworkers, partly paid by the party. When regular methods
failed, both parties organized special "blitzes," or in default, sent
out extra mail.

Supplementing these collective efforts, Knowles and MacLean
did some personal canvassing. The latter's original intention to
visit every fourth household proved impossible, but he claimed at the
end to have contacted every business firm in the constituency. For
his part, Knowles maintained an old Woodsworth tradition by making
about twenty-five early morning appearances at factory and railway
shop gates. In the cold Winnipeg dawns, he distributed pamphlets
among the hurrying workers, some of whom paused to shake hands
and wish him well. To an observer, it is a stirring ceremony,
but with the drastic reduction of modern work forces by mechani-
zation and the arrival by car of many employees from outlying suburbs, it seems now to have more symbolic than practical value.

Greater use of radio and television to a degree compensated for
the decline of personal contact. Generally, radio was used in the
mornings and television in the afternoons and evenings. Regrettably,
there were no true debates or independent interviews; instead the
voters were treated to talks of varying length, fulsomely staged
interviews, or artificial panel discussions, and to a spate of noisily
urgent spot announcements. Within the context of these techniques,

both major candidates appeared to advantage and what Knowles gained in his brief, clear, and moderate talks, MacLean balanced with the vigour and frequency of his appearances. As in press advertising, the Conservatives, possibly sensing defeat, launched a last desperate drive on television which at times approached saturation. It would seem that such campaigning must surely reach a point of diminishing or even negative effects on a public already inured to commercials. Yet both candidates indicated after the election that in any future campaigning they would make even greater use of television. Their intention appeared part of the general trend towards massive impersonal communication which would inevitably inflate further the already swollen campaign budgets, and aggravate the problem of fund-raising.

Regarding these budgets, each candidate is required by the Canada Elections Act to appoint an official agent in charge of campaign finances. Within two months after the election, the latter is required to submit to the returning officer a sworn statement of contributions and expenses. The returning officer must then publish a summary of the statement in a local newspaper. The intent of this procedure is apparently to deter irresponsible or corrupt practices. Unfortunately, the law is not fully enforced and the submitted statements virtually defy verification by an outsider.

In North Centre, only two statements were deposited on time, two were late, and the Liberal agent neither presented any statement nor was he penalized. According to them, the Communist spent over nine hundred dollars, all contributed by the party; the Social Crediter spent slightly less, apparently largely out of his own pocket; Knowles spent almost five thousand, partly borrowed and partly raised from about twenty-five individuals and unions; and MacLean spent over nine thousand, two-thirds of which was evidently contributed by a Conservative Senator who headed the law firm in which MacLean practised. The NDP statement appeared the most thorough, while those of the Conservative and Communist agents had appreciable omissions either by intent or oversight. All statements, of course, excluded national party expenditure and were therefore inherently incomplete.

In terms of the amount spent per vote obtained, the Communist led with a dollar and forty cents. MacLean equalled Social Credit at slightly less than a dollar, while Knowles secured the greatest number of votes at thirty-seven cents each. Distribution of expenses was roughly as given in Table I. The Communist statement was misleading because Currie apparently pooled expenses with the candidate in Winnipeg North; hence he reported no figure for the committee room rental nor any for radio and television, while the figures for press expenses covered some joint advertising. The Social Credit gap in press, radio and television was filled by national expenditure, as were discrepancies in the statements of the other parties. For example, the third Conservative item excluded the twelve billboards rented by the provincial party, and the staff costs for the NDP did not cover the salaries of Chafe and his Steelworkers assistant, presumably paid partly by the CLC and the provincial party.

Table I

Item	NDP	PC	Socred	Comm.
Staff & premises	907.57	2217.82	–	10.00
Literature	2252.78	4103.87	765.64	372.78
Billboards & posters	645.70	642.33	98.89	150.96
Press	370.64	725.98	–	378.58
Radio & TV	575.00	1410.00	–	–
Total	4571.69	9100.00	864.53	912.32

By June 18, campaign funds and workers alike were exhausted. The day dawned in Winnipeg warm and sunny, speciously auguring a heavy turnout. The two main rival party organizations feverishly sought to provide poll scrutineers, cars for transporting supporters, and tried to check frantic calls regarding doubtful practices or belated complaints from citizens who discovered themselves omitted from the voters' lists. Each headquarters was a-quiver with nervous anxiety, while undistributed pamphlets lay reproachfully on the littered tables.

By twilight, both the Conservative and the New Democratic committee rooms were thronged with well-wishers, many of whom had appeared seldom if at all during the campaign. The chief contestants were clearly tired, and MacLean appeared exhausted. Certainly he could have done no more. After initially uncertain returns, Knowles' victory was clear and by eleven had been conceded. He won with three and a half thousand votes more than MacLean, but less than an absolute majority. The other candidates all lost their deposits.

Table II shows the percentage of the vote won by each party in 1958 and in 1962 in the five main parts of North Centre. It is clear that Knowles' strength was still greatest in the western working class district, and elsewhere lower but consistent. The Communist candidate apparently hurt the NDP in the northern part, and was correspondingly weaker in the western sector. Both Krawchuk and Webster evidently took some of MacLean's 1958 votes, the former notably in the north and the downtown area.

Paradoxically, with all the New Democratic effort, its total was 672 votes lower than what the CCF had received in its previous defeat. Similarly, despite the strenuous exertion of the Conservative machine, MacLean's total dropped by 5,603 votes. These anomalous results hinted that the local campaign was largely futile sound and fury. One obvious reason for MacLean's loss was the Liberal recovery of over 2,000 votes, but an even deeper factor was the generally reduced turnout. Somehow, it was clear, Prime Minister Diefenbaker in 1958 had aroused and won a normally apathetic section of the electorate. This time, his magic simply had not worked. With the lower turnout and the more even split in his opposition, Knowles' victory was assured by the law of socialist solidarity.

Table II
Percentage of Vote

		CCF NDP	PC	Lib.	Socred	Comm.
South	- 1958	39	49	12	-	-
	1962	40	36	19	4	1
Downtown	- 1958	42	50	8	-	-
	1962	39	39	18	2	2
Centre	- 1958	39	49	12	-	-
	1962	41	36	18	2	3
West	- 1958	54	38	8	-	-
	1962	59	24	13	3	1
North	- 1958	43	47	10	-	-
	1962	41	30	22	2	5

The day after the election, over three thousand questionnaires were mailed to North Centre voters, one to every fourteenth name on the electoral roll. (5) With each went an explanatory signed letter and to allay resistance further, the questionaire's purpose was publicized on radio and television. A stamped self-addressed envelope was enclosed as well to encourage replies: but no follow-up by telephone or mail was used. By the deadline, July 7, 567 or almost 19 per cent usable completed questionnaires had been returned. The resulting sample was 1.34 per cent of the total electorate (42,328), and the 535 who indicated their actual votes comprised 1.82 per cent of the actual turnout (29,368). That it was not completely representative, however, is shown by the disparity in voting proportions (see Table III). None the less, the questionnaire results afforded some tentative clues to the nature of the major parties' support and to the campaign itself.

Table III

	NDP	PC	Lib.	Socred	Comm.
Actual:	43.8	31.7	19.3	3.0	2.2
Sample:	47.1	33.3	16.0	3.4	0.2

The NDP appeared to attract more men than women (52:48), and was relatively stronger among those claiming (a) to have had some secondary education, (b) to be from 35 to 55 years old, (c) to be members of the Anglican, United, or Lutheran churches, (d) to be of Anglo-Saxon or Scandinavian origin, and (e) to be

5. For the questionnaire used, see Appendix A.

employed as skilled or unskilled labour.   Of those claiming union membership, almost 70 per cent voted for Knowles.

In contrast, the Conservative party apparently attracted fewer men than women (44:56) and was relatively stronger among those claiming (a) to have had only elementary education (possibly these respondents were more candid), (b) to be 55 or older, (c) to be members of the Greek Orthodox, Ukrainian Catholic, or Mennonite churches, (d) to be of Ukrainian or German origin, and (e) to be employed in clerical work, as housewives or currently unemployed.

While those respondents voting Liberal were fewer (86 replies), the group indicated that the party did relatively well among the age group under 35, among university graduates, among Roman Catholics, and, to a lesser extent, in the professional class. (6)   Other samples were not large enough to justify generalizations, and even those tentatively made here regarding relative party strength may well be modified in the light of further studies.   A point deserving emphasis in this respect is that block voting by ethnic or other groups, at least as indicated by the questionnaire, was much less solid than is commonly believed to be the case.   The NDP, for example, received significant support from Catholics and Ukrainians, as did the Conservative party from those earning less than four thousand dollars a year.   There is undeniable ethnic and class consciousness in North Centre, but it does not appear to be reflected in exclusive political alignments.

Regarding the campaign, many of the respondents appeared to have been influenced by it only slightly.   About 6 per cent claimed membership in a party, but some probably confused this with voting support; party membership figures approximated 5 per cent of the turnout in 1962.   Almost three-quarters said that they had not been contacted by any party, and almost nine-tenths believably admitted that they attended no meetings.   Over 80 per cent said they had decided to vote before May 15, while of the remainder, half apparently decided in the last week.   In judging the relative influence of the various campaign techniques, half felt that the most effective was television.   The proportion reading newspaper articles was somewhat higher than that watching television, however, but this was qualified by the vehement expression by several of their hearty dislike for an alleged Liberal bias in the Free Press.

The reasons given for voting were at once the least classifiable and most lively.   Some proudly proclaimed that they voted as their grandfathers had; while some wives humbly confessed that they followed their husbands' advice for the sake of conjugal harmony.   To Currie's credit, the single Communist respondent voted for him in the conviction that only his party could always be relied upon to tell the truth.   For sheer irrelevance, one unforgiving crediter voted NDP because his Liberal brother-in-law had never repaid a loan of four thousand dollars.   Lacking space to illustrate further the infinite variety of human nature, we must be content

---

6. As is customary across Canada, the service vote had favoured the Liberals by a substantial majority.

with noting some general indications: candidate personality, current
domestic issues, and national leadership ranked in that order of
importance. This may well not be applicable to many constituencies
other than Winnipeg North Centre. Among the NDP supporters
there, the most common reasons were Knowles' qualities (59 per
cent), the belief that the party served the workingman (34 per cent),
while the national leader, T.C. Douglas, was referred to in only
2 per cent of the replies. Despite the Diefendollars, devaluation
was seldom mentioned; and less than 1 per cent considered nuclear
weapons an issue. For Conservative voters, the main reasons
given were Prime Minister Diefenbaker's leadership (21 per cent),
the increase in pensions (13 per cent), MacLean's work for the
riding (11 per cent), and general anti-Liberalism (45 per cent).
The latter frequently focused on the notorious twenty-two years
and, surprisingly often, on the leader's television appearances.

Of all the replies, those of the Liberal voters most consistently echoed the standard campaign slogans about devaluation, unemployment, cabinet indecisiveness, and Canada's international prestige.
Since the Liberal voters also most frequently claimed secondary
education or better, a cynical correlation suggested itself. It was
that education increased voter susceptibility to sophisticated propaganda, while those with narrower awareness necessarily voted on
the simpler bases of emotional allegiance to a man or straightforward
mercenary hopes. If there is any validity to this, the schools bear
looking into. They may be habituating students to indoctrination, not
preparing them for citizenship.

Any assessment of the voting reasons must, of course, be
tempered by the realization that many were simply rationalizations of
long-standing allegiance. Party consistency since 1953 was understandably strongest in the CCF-NDP, and weakest in the Liberal
party. Although the relevant sample was small, there was an indication that workers in the clerical class swung most decisively from
the Liberals to the Conservatives.

In view of the limitations of the type of mail-questionnaire survey conducted in Winnipeg North Centre, however, the above findings
can only be accepted with considerable caution.

APPENDIX A*

Election Questionnaire
Winnipeg North Centre, June 1962

Please check (✓) the appropriate space for each question. We would appreciate answers to all questions, if possible. Please do NOT sign your name. Thank you very much.

1. Sex: Male_____
                                               Female _____

2. Marital status: Single_____
                                              Married_____
                                              Widowed_____

3. Education completed: Elementary_____
                                              High School___
                                              University_____

4. Age: 21=24____   35-44____   55-64_____
          25-34____   45-54____   65-69_____
                                            70 and
                                            over___

5. Religious preference: if any, please name_____

6. Racial or ethnic origin: if possible, please name_____

7. a) Occupation or type of work in 1962:_____
    b) Are you a member of a labour union?   Yes_____
                                                No _____

8. Annual income in 1951: under $1,000_____ $5,000-5,999_____
                          $1,000-1,999_____   6,000-6,999_____
                          $2,000-2,999_____   7,000-7,999_____
                          $3,000-3,999_____   8,000 and
                          $4,000-4,999_____   over_____

9. Length of residence in Winnipeg North Centre: under 2 years___
                                                    2-5 years_____
                                                    over 5 years___

10. Do you read political articles in the press: Yes_____
                                                  No _____

---

*The following was based partly on that used by Professor P. Jewett in her valuable electoral study of the by-elections in Peterborough and Niagara Falls, <u>Canadian Journal of Economics and Political Science</u>, XXVIII, Feb., 1962. Our indebtedness to her efforts is hereby acknowledged.

If yes, please state which newspaper(s)_____

11. Do you watch political programmes on TV Yes_____
                                           No _____

12. Did you attend any political meetings in the past year?
                                         Yes_____
                                         No _____
    If yes, please state meetings of which party or parties
                                         _____

13. Were you personally contacted by any candidate or party
    worker? If "yes", please state which party (parties)
                                         _____

14. Are you a member of any political party? Yes_____
                                             No _____
    If "yes", please state which party: _____

15. How did you vote in the federal general election in Winnipeg
    North Centre on June 18, 1962?

    Don Currie (Communist)_____
    Stanley Knowles (NDP) _____
    Barry Krawchuk (Liberal)_____
    John MacLean (Progressive Conservative)_____
    David Webster (Social Credit)_____

16. What were the main reasons why you voted the way you did on
    June 18, 1962? (If you did not vote, please indicate why not).
    _____
    _____
    _____
    _____
    _____
    _____
    _____
    _____

17. If possible, please indicate when you decided to vote as you
    did._____
    What do you feel persuaded you?_____
    _____
    _____
    _____

18. Please check (✓) how you voted in these federal general
    elections.
                      1953   1957   1958
    Conservative   ____   ____   ____

    Liberal   ____   ____   ____

	1953	1957	1958
CCF	____	____	____
Social Credit	____	____	____
LPP/Communist	____	____	____
Did not vote	____	____	____
Do not remember	____	____	____

When you have completed the questionnaire would you return it to the sender; Professor Ivan Avakumovic, Department of Political Science and International Relations, University of Manitoba, Winnipeg 19.

PART TWO:

REGIONAL STUDIES

THE ELECTION IN THE PROVINCE OF QUEBEC

Léon Dion

Preamble

During the first semester of the academic year 1962-1963, Profess-
or Vincent Lemieux and I conducted a weekly seminar on the subject of the 1962 federal election in Quebec. (1)   All the basic material used in the seminar was taken from the newspapers, which,
due to the conditions of the study, were the only sources available. (2)   The speeches of the four party leaders during the campaign, party advertising in the newspapers, pre-election polls, the
"Chronique d'une campagne" by André Laurendeau, the interventions of MM. René Lévesque, Jean Marchand, and André Laurendeau, as well as the general attitudes towards the Social Credit party during the last days of the campaign, the interpretations of the
election returns given by the candidates and by the party organizations, and the letters to the newspapers concerning the election
outcome: such were the main topics which were extensively covered during the seminar.   Unfortunately, it is impossible, in the short
space at our disposal here, to present and to comment upon the
many tables and graphs which accompanied the presentation of each
topic.   However, each time quantitative data are mentioned in the
course of the present study the implicit reference will be to one or

---

1. The following students, all of them in their third year leading to the MA in political science, took an active part in the seminar and were responsible for specific research work: MM. Denis
Belleville, André Busque, J.-Y. Chenel, Louis Chouinard, Denis
de Belleval, Jean Deschenes, Louis Duclos, Marcel Gilbert, Ger-
main Julien, Michel Juneau, Pierre Lemire, André Ouellet.   M.
Michel Chaloult, research assistant in political behaviour and M.
Paul Cliche, MA in political science, a journalist with La Presse
also helped in this seminar.   To all these people, as well as to
Professor Lemieux, I wish here to convey my thanks for the work
they have done.

2. La Presse, the Montreal Star and Le Soleil (Quebec City)
were the newspapers chosen for most topics.   However, in some
cases, for example for the study of the post-electoral interpretations
by the candidates, other newspapers, including regional newspapers,
were also used.   Le Devoir was used for the study of the post-
electoral letters to the newspapers, for the study of the attitudes
towards the Social Credit party at the end of the campaign and for
the study of the "Chronique d'une campagne," by André Laurendeau.

another of these tables.   The three tables presented here have been drawn from some of the original tables in the relevant papers.

Although some of the research techniques applied in the course of the seminar have very seldom if ever been used in electoral studies, it is impossible to explain here how we used them.   Because one of our primary objectives was the training of students, it is certain that errors and mistakes were made in the treatment of several topics.   We are confident, however, that they do not impair the validity of the general comments which are here presented. We also beg the reader to excuse the very skimpy way in which each topic will be touched upon in the following pages.

I. THE PARTY LEADERS' SPEECHES

Since our purpose was the study of the campaign speeches delivered in the Province of Quebec as reported in the three newspapers chosen we did not check the accuracy of the reports against the speeches as they were actually delivered or against one another: in general, there were no substantial divergences between the three newspapers.   For all four parties, the Star tended to be more factual and to give more details on the external aspects of the meetings; Le Soleil generally provided better coverage for speeches delivered in the Quebec district, and in areas such as Beauce, Lac Saint-Jean, and the Lower St. Lawrence where it enjoys a large circulation.   It generally paid less attention to speeches made in the other regions of the province.   All in all, La Presse devoted the largest space to campaign speeches. (3)

Since it would have been cumbersome and fruitless to consider the speeches of all candidates which the newspapers had reported, we restricted the study to addresses made in Quebec by the four party leaders, i.e., Messrs. Diefenbaker, Pearson, Thompson, and Douglas.   To these four, our plan was to add two main candidates for each party.   Since some of our first choices of party lieutenants proved not to have been given a single column in any of the newspapers, we had in some cases to shift to other names.   Even then it was found that for three of the parties no candidate had been given substantial consideration in the newspapers.

On the Conservative side, we finally picked M. Balcer and M. Flynn, both ministers in the Diefenbaker cabinet.   However, even they were almost completely ignored by the Star throughout the campaign.   M. Balcer was given only a few marginal comments on one occasion in La Presse and Le Soleil; M. Flynn received more attention, although even he received no more than 15

3. It is often asserted that the party leaders speak a different language in the Province of Quebec and in the other provinces. Originally, we aimed at assessing this view by comparing the themes touched upon in Ontario and Quebec by the different speakers as reported in the three Quebec papers.   Although the data for the study of this question are available the work of correlation has not been completed and this subject will not be discussed in the present study.

per cent of the total space devoted to the campaign speeches made in Quebec by Mr. Diefenbaker.

For the Liberals, M. Lionel Chevrier and M. Maurice Lamontagne were selected as the only two men who could possibly have received more than local treatment in the press. The _Star_ reported, in a more concise manner, as many speeches of these two candidates as did _La Presse_ and _Le Soleil_, while M. Chevrier was given more columns in _La Presse_ and M. Lamontagne in _Le Soleil_. However, both men together were allowed only a small percentage of the total space in the three newspapers given to Mr. Pearson's campaign speeches in Quebec.

As for the NDP, it was found impossible to discover any candidate who had aroused the attention of the newspapers. At the end we chose M. Fernand Daoust who was given four short columns in _La Presse_ and one in _Le Soleil_ and Mme. Thérèse Casgrain who received three short columns in _La Presse_ and none in _Le Soleil_. Both were ignored by the _Star_. Although Mr. Douglas, being the leader of a party whose influence and dynamism were very low in Quebec, was given only about 20 per cent of the space attributed in our newspapers to both Mr. Diefenbaker and Mr. Pearson, he received about 80 per cent of the total space allocated to the three NDP candidates.

The Social Credit party presents a striking contrast to the three others in that one Quebec candidate, M. Caouette, was given more total space than the national leader, Mr. Thompson, although one daily, _Le Soleil_, allocated a little more space to Mr. Thompson. M. Caouette was, admittedly, the deputy leader. However, our two possible second choices, M. Gregoire and Dr. Marcoux, were ignored by the press. Dr. Marcoux received only a single column in _Le Soleil_ and M. Gregoire none in all three dailies. In general terms, the two Social Credit candidates were given about three times as much space in the news columns of the newspapers as the three NDP candidates and about 65 per cent of the space attributed to the two other parties' main candidates.

One conclusion to be drawn from the preceding analysis is that, except for M. Caouette who succeeded in retaining the attention of the campaign reporters and who on occasion even stole the show from Mr. Thompson, no Quebec candidate aroused more than local interest and none was able to find his way into the metropolitan press unless he accompanied his leader at a party meeting. The impact of this fact is momentous since, in a federal election, the national party leaders can afford to devote only a few days of the campaign to Quebec (in the June election it was from five to nine days, depending on the various party leaders, out of a total of about forty days). During the few days when the national party leaders were campaigning in Quebec a flood of information poured from the metropolitan press. However, during the rest of the campaign the news columns of the metropolitan press were almost silent on the struggle waged by three parties out of four within the Province of Quebec. (4)

_____

4. During the campaign, the Social Credit candidates com-

In his "Chronique d'une campagne" (5) M. Laurendeau appears to have been even more parsimonious in his mention of the candidates we selected than were the newspapers themselves in their routine campaign reports. Four of those we have chosen, MM. Flynn, Balcer, Marcoux, and Daoust are ignored in the Chronicle. M. Lamontagne is mentioned three times, M. Chevrier twice, and Mme. Casgrain once. The "Chronique d'une campagne" is atypical, however, in that M. Caouette's name appears only four times which is probably explained by the fact that, as in the case of so many other people, M. Laurendeau became conscious of the significance of the Social Credit party very late in the campaign. (6)

In one of his articles, M. Laurendeau expressed the view that no one central theme emerged during the election. Our study of the campaign speeches as reported by our three newspapers confirms this comment. (7) As is shown in Tables I-III, of all the main themes discussed in the campaign, economic policy received the largest percentage for all parties. However, it was not mentioned so much more often than the other themes to permit the conclusion that questions of economic policy were central in the campaign speeches. Furthermore, the theme is in first place only because it constitutes 35 per cent of the total of topics mentioned by the Social Credit party. This high percentage itself is a faithful reflection of the ideology of this party which attributes so much importance to questions of finance and banking. By contrast, economic policy ranks second for the Conservatives, third for the Liberals ("ex aequo" with Anglo-French relations), and only sixth for for the NDP. (8) In so far as the Conservatives expressed a preference

---

plained that the press did not give them fair treatment and even ignored them. On analysis, however, this charge proves to have been without foundation. Considering the fact that the Social Credit party was expected to be only a small third force one must conclude that it was given at least its fair share in the news columns of the metropolitan press. The probable reason for this was the newsworthiness, in the eyes of the press, of M. Caouette.

5. The "Chronicle of a Campaign" appeared 32 times on a total of 34 issues of Le Devoir between May 13 and June 18. A very extensive content analysis has been made of the 29 articles which were written by M. André Laurendeau.

6. In the "Chronique d'une campagne," Mr. Diefenbaker is mentioned by name seventeen times, Mr. Pearson twelve times, and Mr. Douglas and Mr. Thompson four times each.

7. After many efforts at a general classification, we arranged the themes discussed in the campaign speeches, the publicity and the "Chronique d'une campagne" into the following categories: (1) social measures; (2) unemployment; (3) economic policy; (4) capacity for governing; (5) Anglo-French relations; (6) problems of Confederation; (7) nuclear armaments; (8) external policy. The percentages are presented in Tables I-III.

8. This fact may look strange in view of the NDP program. However, the data in our possession permit us to furnish the following information: Mr. Douglas concentrated more on economic policy

at all they gave it to themes related to Confederation, followed by economic policy. The Liberals stressed questions concerning aptness for government and then unemployment; as to the NDP, its main interest was in the direction of social measures, closely followed by Anglo-French relations. Nuclear armament and foreign policy were given little consideration by all four parties.

The Conservatives waged an essentially negative campaign. While they scarcely mentioned themes pertaining to aptness for government, they defended their policies on unemployment, Anglo-French relations, and social security. A closer study of the campaign themes showed that they were unwilling to make positive commitments in these fields. Their campaign technique was as follows: first they clarified and justified the Conservative attitudes and policy of the last four years and then they pledged themselves to their continuation if re-elected.

The Liberals also took a negative stand in that they were mostly satisfied with opposing the Conservatives on the various themes without presenting an alternative practical program of their own. They scarcely mentioned social policy. However, they showed great enthusiasm in expressing their capacity for governing the country (32 per cent of all themes).

By contrast, the "Créditistes" conducted an essentially positive campaign. They felt confident they could govern the country. While they violently attacked both "old parties" in matters of economic and social policy, they time and again explained their own formula for permitting "liberty and security through money." They scarcely mentioned unemployment as such and were little concerned with problems related to Confederation.

That the NDP did not conduct a dynamic campaign and felt beaten from the start is indicated by the fact that it was almost silent on its capacity for government (3 per cent). One must recall that the percentage distribution of the themes was almost entirely drawn from Mr. Douglas' speeches in Quebec, since our three newspapers scarcely mentioned any of Quebec's NDP candidates. This fact probably reflects Mr. Douglas' conviction that the NDP had no chance in the province. It may also express a kind of inferiority complex which seemed to have been characteristic of this party. In other respects, the NDP manifested a willingness for positive commitment, insisting on matters of social policy and Anglo-French relations; it also made much of unemployment.

In general terms, three considerations arrest our attention. First, if we couple our eight themes according to general areas of interest, we are struck by the fact that the themes which were particularly highly charged with emotion (no. 5 and no. 6) were given as much or almost as much importance by the Liberal and the Conservative parties as themes related to questions of national policy (themes no. 1, 2, and 3). By contrast, the NDP and the Social

---

in Ontario (4 times more) and more on unemployment in Quebec (1 1/2 times more).

Table I
Campaign Themes, as Revealed by Reported Speeches*

	PC no.	%	Lib. no.	%	Socred no.	%	NDP no.	%	Total no.	%
1. Social measures	13	12	2	2	13	14	9	28	37	10
2. Unemployment	13	12	21	16	4	4	5	16	43	13
3. Economic policy	21	20	20	15	33	35	2	6	76	20
4. Capacity to assume government	6	6	42	32	21	22	1	3	70	19
5. Anglo-French relations	18	17	20	15	12	13	8	25	58	16
6. Questions pertaining to Confederation	25	24	15	11	3	3	3	9	46	13
7. Nuclear armaments	4	4	8	6	2	2	3	9	17	5
8. Foreign policy	5	5	4	3	7	7	1	3	17	5
Total	105	100	132	100	95	100	32	99	364	101

Table II
Campaign Themes, as Treated in "Chronicle of a Campaign"*

	PC no.	%	Lib. no.	%	Socred no.	%	NDP no.	%	Total no.	%
1. Social measures	2	8	2	9	1	12	2	13	7	10
2. Unemployment	2	8	1	5	1	12	2	13	6	9
3. Economic policy	7	29	3	14	2	25	3	20	15	22
4. Capacity to assume government	2	8	4	18	0	0	0	0	6	9
5. Anglo-French relations	5	21	4	18	1	12	2	13	12	17
6. Questions pertaining to Confederation	1	4	3	14	0	0	1	7	5	7
7. Nuclear armaments	4	17	4	18	2	25	4	27	14	20
8. Foreign policy	1	4	1	5	1	12	1	7	4	6
Total	24	99	22	101	8	98	15	100	69	100

Table III
Campaign Themes, as Used in Party Advertising*

	PC no.	%	Lib. no.	%	Socred no.	%	NDP no.	%	Total no.	%
1. Social measures	2	5	1	2	0	0	4	18	7	6
2. Unemployment	2	5	3	5	0	0	1	5	6	5
3. Economic policy	14	37	11	20	1	9	1	5	27	21
4. Capacity to assume government	19	50	32	57	10	91	13	59	74	58
5. Anglo-French relations	1	3	5	9	0	0	1	5	7	6
6. Questions pertaining to Confederation	0	0	1	2	0	0	0	0	1	1
7. Nuclear armaments	0	0	0	0	0	0	2	9	2	2
8. Foreign policy	0	0	3	5	0	0	0	0	3	2
Total	38	100	56	100	11	100	22	101	127	101

*We give the absolute numbers as well as the percentages because these are central to our analysis. We are well aware of the possible danger of gross errors that may enter in our comments on account of the simple fact that we sometimes deal here with extremely small numbers. The percentages have been rounded up for reasons of convenience.

Credit parties (9) dealt far more often with the latter problems than with those of the first category. This confirms the remark often made by the third party's spokesmen to the effect that the representatives of the two older parties tend to delude the citizens of Quebec by emotional appeals rather than presenting practical programs. Second, the fact that a bare 10 per cent of the themes dealt with matters related to foreign affairs (themes 7 and 8), the highest percentage being only 12 per cent for both the Liberal party and the NDP, indicates that all four parties were agreed that these would not weigh very much in the orientation of the popular vote. Third, the Conservatives had the greatest influence in the total distribution of the eight themes, followed by the Liberals and the Social Credit, the NDP sorely trailing behind. (10)

During and chiefly after the campaign many expressed the view that journalists and other commentators did not reflect the main themes set forth by the political parties. Although this comment was prompted by the seemingly low awareness of the Social Credit upsurge - a subject which will be discussed in a subsequent section - it is interesting to assess the validity of the more general accusation. Since M. André Laurendeau, whom I consider to be the most outstanding French-Canadian journalist, made day-to-day campaign comments in his "Chronique" it is worth presenting here a brief analysis of his performance. Before discussing this point, however, one must recall that since no single theme emerged as central during the campaign and since there was a great discrepancy between the parties themselves in the importance given to each theme, the problem of reflecting faithfully the campaign themes was insuperable. However, if one compares the percentages attributed to all parties

---

9. The performance of the Social Credit party is particularly striking, the percentages for both categories of themes being 53 per cent for questions of national policy and only 16 per cent for those related to nationalist attitudes.

10. In so far as one can venture any hypothesis here it could be suggested that the relative degree of influence exerted by one party in the total distribution of themes establishes its share in giving the tone to the campaign (as reflected in the newspapers). The calculus is made by establishing the deviation in percentage points between the percentage of each theme for each party with the total percentages for the four parties without taking account of the plus and minus signs and dividing the totals by two. We thus get the following percentage figures: Conservatives, 14.5; Liberals, 18.5; Social Credit, 23.5; NDP, 36.0. The same calculus for the "Chronique" also indicates that the total distribution of themes is closer to that for the Conservative party which could be taken as an indication that M. Laurendeau reflected rather faithfully the general physiognomy of the campaign. However, here the NDP ranks second, which may be taken as a tendency on M. Laurendeau's part to see the campaign through his avowed NDP sympathies, followed by the Liberals and the "Créditistes." The deviations in percentage points are as follows: Conservatives, 11.5; Liberals 18; NDP, 15; and Social Credit, 20.

for each of the eight themes with the same percentages for all four
parties in the "Chronique" one must conclude that M. Laurendeau
was rather close to the mark, the total deviation (plus or minus)
being 18.5 percentage points.   He overstressed the issue of nuclear
armaments by the wide margin of 7.5 percentage points and under-
valued aptness for government by 5 points. (11)   On the other hand,
he won a perfect or almost perfect score in the treatment of themes
no. 1 (social measures), no. 3 (economic policy), no. 5 (Anglo-
French relations), and no. 8 (foreign policy).   He underestimated
by a small margin the importance of unemployment and the questions
concerning Confederation.

By contrast, if we take his own frequency of themes in percentages and compare it with our distribution of themes for each
party, we get a completely different picture.   M. Laurendeau was
widest of the mark in his dealing with the Social Credit (plus or
minus 37 percentage points), with a deviation of minus 11 points for
theme no. 4 (aptness for government) and of plus 11.5 points for
theme no. 7 (nuclear armaments).   Then he also was off minus or
plus 35.5 percentage points in his treatment of the NDP, misjudging
the theme of social measures by minus 7.5 points and that of nuclear
armaments by plus 9 points. (12)   He misrepresented the Conservative party by plus or minus 28.5 percentage points, and was most
wrong on the theme of nuclear armaments (plus 6.5 points) and
that of questions pertaining to Confederation (minus 10).   His best
party performance was towards the Liberals (plus or minus 26.5
percentage points), the largest deviation being minus 7 points for the
theme of aptness in assuming government and plus 6 points for that
of nuclear armaments.   For all parties the "Chronique" shows the
largest deviation for nuclear armamements (for all four parties), aptness for assuming government (for two parties), and questions pertaining to Confederation and social measures (for one party each).
The questions he reflected more faithfully were foreign policy and
Anglo-French relations.

---

11. M. Laurendeau mentioned this last theme only in connection
with the two main parties, the Conservatives and the Liberals, a
fact which may be taken as an indication of political realism.

12. Given the importance of the theme of nuclear armaments in
the NDP platform the low percentage   which is attributed to it in our
table is striking.   This may be due to the fact that Mr. Douglas overlooked the question in his Quebec campaign speeches while those
candidates, such as Mme. Casgrain, the "Peace candidate" who may
have treated this theme, were not quoted in the metropolitan press.
However, even in general terms, M. Laurendeau correlates only to
an extremely low degree with the NDP campaign speeches.   This fact
is the more striking since M. Laurendeau avowed his own sympathy
for the NDP.   The distribution of the themes for that party in the
"Chronicle" might be considered as expressing the author's views
concerning the relative importance a NDP campaign speech should
attach to the various themes.   However, between the ideal picture in
M. Laurendeau's mind and the actual behaviour of the NDP speakers
there appears to have existed an enormous difference.

II. PARTY ADVERTISING

The study of party advertising in our three newspapers proved highly suggestive. (13)   The first advertisements began to appear on May 12.   However, the period extending from that date to May 31 accounts for only 22 per cent of total advertising, leaving 78 per cent for the last 16 days.   Seventeen per cent of all advertising appeared on June 16, the last day on which space could be bought in the newspapers.   The Conservative party had only four different large advertising pages while the Liberal party had seven.   Le Soleil was given by far the largest amount of advertising (240 advertisements), followed by the Star (67) and La Presse (45). This distribution appears to be inversely proportional to the circulation of the various newspapers.   Le Soleil carried a greater amount of regional and constituency advertising than the other two. In terms of total space covered, however, Le Soleil still ranks first (55 per cent), followed by La Presse (33 per cent) and the Star which gets a bare 12 per cent of the total space.   The Liberals bought by far the largest advertising space (66 per cent), the Conservatives only 27 per cent while the NDP and Social Credit secured a bare 3 and 2 per cent respectively.   One may note, however, that while the NDP spread its advertising in about the same proportion in all three newspapers, Social Credit concentrated on Le Soleil with all advertisements but two appearing on June 16.

Another noteworthy characteristic of party advertising is the fact that the picture of Mr. Pearson never appeared while that of the Conservative leader was almost always present.   The typical Liberal advertising gave preference to the "team of the 75 candidates" and contained a scene from daily life and an extract from the party platform.   The Liberals were the only party to present a coloured advertisement in a daily newspaper.   It appeared once in La Presse and in Le Soleil.   The Star usually offered more text than the two French-language dailies.   Conservative advertising gave pre-eminence to Mr. Diefenbaker's picture, contained little text and illustrated the "great prosperity of the Canadian common man."   A large part of an issue of "Perspectives," which is distributed every Saturday by Le Soleil and many other French-language dailies, was bought by the Conservative party and contained magnificent coloured advertising pages.   Here again the advertising in the Star differed from that of the other two dailies.   It contained more text: occasionally the Parliament buildings stood in the background.   The other two parties did so little advertising that it is unnecessary to discuss it here.

On the whole advertising was used more by the parties for disseminating information than for mere propaganda.   About 40 per

---

13. For reasons of brevity we shall not consider here party advertising in regional newspapers, magazines, leaflets, and pamphlets.   The Social Credit party made extensive use of these last-named media.

cent of the total advertising was devoted to such items as the announcement of party conventions, the location of committee rooms,
and the place of meetings. In addition, more than 35 per cent announced a TV speech; this attests to the great importance attributed to that medium in the conduct of a campaign. A bare 25 per
cent of total newspaper advertising was thus left for mere propaganda, the Conservative party scoring below that percentage and
the Liberal party above.

That part of the advertising which was devoted to propaganda
(or persuasion) has been studied and its content classified according to our eight main themes (Table III). Since the NDP and
Social Credit bought very little newspaper space they may be ignored. Let us recall, however, that Social Credit did all its advertising in Le Soleil and most of it in the issue of June 16, while
the NDP spread its advertising throughout the campaign and in all
three newspapers. A similar remark applies to the distribution of
themes. While Social Credit concentrated on almost only one
theme, aptness to assume government, the NDP offered a distribution which is even more scattered than that of the Conservative
party. Thus 9 per cent of total NDP advertising was devoted to
nuclear armament, a theme completely absent in the other three
parties' advertising. Furthermore, 18 per cent of total NDP advertising dealt with social measures, which scarcely appeared in
the advertising of the other parties. As to the Conservative party,
the main insistence was on the capacity of the party to govern and
to a less marked degree on economic policy. The same remark
also applies to the Liberal party although here some mention was
made of foreign policy and of questions pertaining to Confederation
which were overlooked by the Conservative party.

No general correlation between the distribution of themes for
the party speeches and for advertising can be established, although
it is to be noted that the two themes which received the highest percentages for all parties (themes 3 and 4) also account for the higher
advertising percentage.

III. CONSCIOUSNESS OF THE SOCIAL CREDIT UPSURGE

A study of pre-election polls, as shown in Table IV, would be
most rewarding. However, the space allowed us here permits us
only to note that as from January 1961, the Gallup poll recorded an
increase in popular favour of the Social Credit party. However, a
Gallup poll taken as late as May 26, 1962, and published in the Star
and La Presse on June 9, underestimated the strength of the Social
Credit party by a margin of 6.5 percentage points, that of the Conservative party by 5 percentage points and overestimated the strength
of the Liberal party by a wide margin of 13 percentage points. The
forecast of Gruneau Ltd., published on June 16 in Le Soleil, was
even more off the mark: the election performance of Social Credit
was underestimated by 15.9 percentage points while that of the Liberals was overestimated by 14.9 percentage points and that of the
Conservatives by 3.8 percentage points. In spite of their wide

Table IV
Distribution of Popular Vote in Province of Quebec as Given by
Election Returns and Opinion Polls (Undecided Votes Excluded)
(in percentages)

General elections and opinion polls	PC	Lib.	Socred	NDP	Other
1953 election	29.5	64.5	0.0	2.5	3.5
1957 election	31.5	62.5	0.5	1.5	4.0
1958 election	49.5	46.0	0.5	2.0	-
Gallup poll: January 1961	25.0	65.0	8.0	2.0	-
Gallup poll: September 1961	32.0	47.0	16.0	5.0	-
Gallup poll: November 1961	33.0	50.0	13.0	4.0	-
Gallup poll: May 1962	32.0	53.0	12.0	3.0	-
Gallup poll: May 26 published June 9, 1962	25.0	52.0	19.0	4.0	-
Gruneau Ltd: June 16, 1962	33.8	53.9	9.6	27.0	-
1962 election	30.0	39.0	25.5	4.5	1.0

margins of error, the pre-election polls indicated a notable increase in the popularity of the Social Credit party one year and a half before election day, but they failed to record what may have been a last-minute change of party allegiance especially among those who on May 26 indicated their intention to vote Liberal.

Some newspapers carried their own polls, the Montreal Star being the first daily to note the Social Credit upsurge, closely followed by Le Nouveau Journal and La Presse; Le Soleil and L'Action, which stood at the centre of the storm, failed to notice it throughout the campaign.

Among the journalists themselves, Gérard Pelletier and Richard Daignault of La Presse (29 May), Amedée Gaudreault of Le Nouveau Journal (9 June), Fernand Bourret of Le Devoir (11 June) and Max McMahon and Peter Desbarats of the Star, showed awareness of the Social Credit wave. However, it was left to an American-based Canadian political scientist, S. Peter Regenstreif, to predict with incredible accuracy the outcome of the elections. On May 19 he published an article in the Star in which he said that, while the Social Credit party did not command more than 10 per cent of the Quebec electorate, in the twenty-eight constituencies east of Three-Rivers, they had "won" 15 per cent of urban and 30 per cent of rural "voters" in those constituencies. On June 16, in the same daily, he predicted that a minority government would be elected and for Quebec he gave 10 seats to the Conservatives, 35 to the Liberals, at least 20 to the Social Credit party; 10 seats were left as doubtful. (14)

---

14. The actual returns were 14 Conservatives, 35 Liberals and 26 Social Crediters.

In general, the _Star_, in its editorial and other sections, furnished the best information concerning the activities and the personalities of the Social Credit party: _La Presse_ wrote the largest
number of articles about the movement; and _Le Devoir_, which had
scarcely mentioned that party up to the last week of the campaign,
then showed that, of all newspapers, it sensed with the greatest
intensity what Social Credit was about to do.

We may conclude from this analysis that, with the exception
of a few isolated journalists, the newspapers were not aware of
the Social Credit upsurge until the very last week and that this
awareness was manifested only by the Montreal press.

It is well known that the Liberal and Conservative candidates
in the constituencies affected by the Social Credit wave were at an
early date aware of the seriousness of the threat it represented to
them. However, except for a few remarks by M. Maurice
Lamontagne, we find nothing in the press concerning this awareness on the part of the other seven candidates we have selected
for our study. We can, nevertheless, appreciate how acute had
become the fear of Social Credit during the last days of the campaign, by studying three last-minute denunciations of the party made
respectively by the Chairman of CSN (Confederation des Syndicats
Nationaux), M. Jean Marchand, in a declaration made on June 11,
by M. Laurendeau in an editorial of _Le Devoir_ on June 13, and
finally by the provincial Minister of Natural Resources M. René
Lévesque, in a French TV program from Quebec City, sponsored
by the federal Liberal party on June 14. However, it was too
late for these interventions to receive much press notice. Only
La Presse and _Le Devoir_ published entirely or in part the
Marchand declaration. Some comments on it were also published
in these newspapers, but it received no mention in the _Star_ and
Le Soleil. The editorial published by M. Laurendeau provoked
no comment on the part of any other newspaper. As to M.
Lévesque's TV appearance, _La Presse_ and _Le Devoir_ granted it
a big first-page headline, summarized the content of his declaration,
and commented favourably on it. On the other hand, the _Star_ and
Le Soleil were satisfied with a brief summary. In conclusion, it
might be suggested that it is a matter of conjecture whether the
three last-minute interventions affected the outcome of the elections
at all. (15)

---

15. A score of other influential people, notably M. Gérard
Picard, also denounced the Social Credit party during the last days
of the campaign. As late as June 16, the FTQ (Federation des
travailleurs du Quebec), issued a violent indictment of that party.
The Social Credit leaders had little time left to answer the accusations hurled at them. However, on June 14, _La Presse_ reported a comment by M. Caouette to the effect that "M. Laurendeau
and M. Marchand are two public liars."

IV. POST-ELECTORAL INTERPRETATIONS

That most people were astonished by the Social Credit performance is shown in the fact that all post-electoral comments dealt
in one way or another with that theme. With 25.5 per cent of the
popular vote it won twenty-six seats, taking seventeen seats from
the Conservatives and nine from the Liberals. All the seats taken
from the Conservatives had been Liberal in the elections of 1957
and 1953. (16) The Social Credit party owes its high number of
seats to the fact that its vote was well concentrated in five regions
where it obtained the highest proportion of the popular vote and won
twenty-two seats of a possible total of twenty-six; Quebec (48.3 per
cent), Lac St-Jean-Saguenay (53.2 per cent), Côte-Nord-Nou-
veau-Quebec (49.9 per cent), Abitibi-Témiscamingue (54.6 per
cent) and Cantons de l'Est (44 per cent). In all these regions the
Liberals came second. The Social Credit party also took three
seats out of a possible eight in Gaspésie-Rive-Sud, and one seat
out of a total of five in the region of Three Rivers. Social Credit
received a bare 6.2 per cent of the popular vote in the Montreal
metropolitan area, 14.4 per cent in the Montreal region, 29.8 per
cent in the region of Three Rivers, 26.9 per cent of the Ottawa
region, and 30.4 per cent in Gaspésie-Rive-Sud.

On the morrow of election day a flood of comments by candidates and party managers, journalists, and correspondents presented their interpretations of the event. We have made a study of these
comments as they appeared in the newspapers.(17)   All the
twenty-one elements of interpretation contained in Table V are ex-
pressions drawn from the various commentators themselves. Our
own classifications of the themes into three levels - ideological,
psychological, and technical - must be taken as representing some
effort at systematization on our part. However, we feel that they
correspond "grosso modo" to the nature of the themes classified

---

16. The Liberals obtained 39 per cent of the popular vote and
won 35 seats, the Conservatives 30.0 per cent of the popular vote
and 14 seats, and the NDP with 4.5 per cent of the popular vote
was unable to elect a single candidate.

17. For comments made by the candidates, party leaders and
managers, we perused Le Devoir, La Presse, the Montreal Star,
Le Soleil, L'Action, La Tribune (Sherbrooke), Le Nouvelliste
(Three Rivers), and Le Progrès du Saguenay (a bi-monthly).
For the first five newspapers we covered the period extending from
June 19 to July 31; for the other newspapers, from June 19 to
July 5. We also meant to study the four party caucuses, but press
releases were issued only in the case of the Social Credit party.
In all, 23 party comments appear to have been made in the fore-
mentioned newspapers, 12 by the Social Credit party, 6 by the
Conservatives, 3 by the Liberals, and only 2 by the NDP. The
comments by the journalists were taken from the editorials of

under each category. The general categories may be considered
as convenient and useful tools for comparative analysis. In our
discussion, the Liberal and NDP parties should normally be overlooked, all comments which could be made about them being probably without significance because of the scarcity of data concerning
them. The almost complete silence of the Liberals and the lack of
substance in the observations of the three spokesmen for the party
(one of them being an anonymous party manager) might be taken as
a reaction to the fact that they were the first and only real victims
of the Social Credit upsurge. It is interesting to note that from a
total of seven mentions attributed to that party, two (and these were
the only ones made) observations attributed the success of the
Social Credit to dissatisfaction among the population with the Liberal
provincial government. The absence of comment by the NDP (only
two statements found their way into the newspapers, one from a
defeated candidate and the other from the leaders of the party) is
hardly surprising; it waged a very weak campaign in Quebec. It
might be of interest to note, however, that of the four comments
attributed to the NDP, one is to the effect that Social Credit "offers
easy solutions" (read: "ours are very difficult"), and another
states that the Social Credit success was due to "many years of
propaganda" (read: "our program is not known").

　　In general, the interpretation found in the newspapers attributed less importance to questions pertaining to ideology (23 per cent)
than to psychology (44 per cent) and technique (34 per cent).

　　The Social Credit party was alone of all parties (except for
one mention each by the Conservatives and the NDP) to lay some
stress on questions of ideology. However, these were more often

---

Le Devoir, La Presse, the Montreal Star, the Gazette, Montreal
Matin, Le Soleil and L'Action. Since many of these comments
were not signed it is impossible to establish the number of people
who contributed them. For the letters to the newspapers, Le
Devoir, La Presse, Le Soleil and three bi-monthly papers, Le
Progrès du Saguenay, Le Progrès de Rouyn-Noranda and Le
Lac St-Jean were scrutinized during a period extending from
July 4, date of publication of the first letter, to July 25. Some
letters were duplicated in two or more newspapers and were
counted only once. In all, 27 letters were retained, a large proportion of them being drawn from Le Devoir, which, as always,
got more than its share of "correspondence." Originally, we
wished to retain the name of the region from where the letters came
and the occupations of the correspondents but, because of lack of information, this project was dropped. However, it seems that all
correspondents were males. Among the 27 correspondents, 7
avowed "Créditiste" allegiance, 5 expressed their satisfaction at the
turn of events while saying they were not "Creditistes," 6 affirmed
they had no party allegiance while 3 expressed their opposition to
the Social Credit party. It was impossible to get any clues about
the party allegiance of 6 correspondents. We regret that no letters
to the English-language newspapers were studied.

Table V

Interpretations of the Social Credit Upsurge

Elements of Interpretation	Candidates and other party commentators					Newspapers				Sign of motivation
	PC	Lib.	Socred	NDP	Total	Letters	Articles	Total	%	
I - Ideological Level										
1. Victory of the common man			4		4	7	3	14	8.0	+
2. Nationalism or separatism			2		2	2	1	3	2.0	+
3. Socialism rejected			2		2	1	1	3	2.0	−
4. Doctrine of Socred			1		1			1	1.0	+
5. Wish for socio-economic betterment and opposition to the trusts						7	3	10	6.0	−
6. Appeal of new ideas	1				1		2	3	2.0	+
7. Socred offers easy solutions				1	1	1	1	3	2.0	−
Total	1	0	7	1	9	17	11	37	23.0	4 (21) 3 (16)

Table V (Continued)
Interpretations of the Social Credit Upsurge

Elements of Interpretation	Candidates and other party commentators					Newspapers				Sign of motivation
	PC	Lib.	Socred	NDP	Total	Letters	Articles	Total	%	
II– Psychological Level										
1. Aversion toward old parties	5	3	5	2	15	21	12	48	28.0	–
2. Last hour upsurge	1				1			1	1.0	+
3. Dissatisfaction with the provincial govt.		2			2			2	1.0	–
4. Mistrust of newspapers			2		2			2	1.0	–
5. Leaders' estrangement from the people	1		1		2	1		3	2.0	–
6. Revolt against the established order and social (class) unrest	1				1	2	18	21	11.0	–
Total	8	5	8	2	23	24	30	77	44.0	1 5 (1) (76)

Table V (Continued)
Interpretations of the Social Credit Upsurge

Elements of Interpretation	Candidates and other party commentators					Newspapers		Total	%	Sign of motivation
	PC	Lib.	Socred	NDP	Total	Letters	Articles			
III-Technical level										
1. TV Influence	1	1	6		8		2	10	6.0	+
2. Result of many years of propaganda			4	1	5			5	3.0	+
3. Appeal of the leader: Caouette						2	8	10	6.0	+
4. Zeal of membership	2		4		6	4	3	13	8.0	+
5. Slogans and demagoguery	2				2	6		8	5.0	–
6. Lack of electoral machine, candidates close to the people and Socred organization	1		8		9			9	5.0	+
7. Ignored by old parties	1	1			2		1	3	2.0	–
8. Impact of Union Nationale			2		2			2	1.0	–
Total	7	2	24	1	34	12	14	60	34.0	5 3 (47)(13)
Grand Total	16	7	39	4	66	53	55	174	101.0	10 11 (69)(105)

mentioned, at least in absolute numbers, in letters to newspapers and by journalists. The comments regarding the state of mind of the electorate which has been more or less correctly labelled here as the psychological level have come in higher numbers from the journalists than from the correspondents to newspapers and in a lesser degree from the parties. However, one should note here that half the mentions originating with the Conservative party and with the NDP, as well as five out of seven mentions by the Liberals, were classified under this label. More than two-thirds of the mentions put under the technical category came from Social Credit spokesmen. Letter-writers and journalists generally have not stressed any of the themes under this label except the impact of "slogans and demagoguery" (correspondents) and of "the appeal of the leader" (journalists).

For the Conservatives, three interpretations account for a little more than half of the total comments (9/16) coming from that party. They are: "aversion toward old parties," "zeal of membership," and "slogans and demagoguery." For the Social Credit party, comments concerning the "party organization," "TV influence," and "aversion to old parties" coupled with either "victory of the common man" or "wish for socio-economic betterment" exceed half of the total mentions (28/53). With two interpretations, "revolt against the established order" and the "appeal of the leader" constitute more than half of the journalists' mentions (30/55). The only interpretation to emerge first more than once in the mentions of our four different informants is "aversion to old parties" (twice). This recurs more than once among the two or three which account for at least half of the total mentions of each of our four sources.

"Aversion to the old parties" was the most frequently mentioned interpretation (28 per cent) and was the only one cited by all categories of commentators. The second place was held by "revolt against the social order" (11 per cent) but only because it owed eighteen of its twenty-one mentions to journalists. Third came "victory of the common man" (8 per cent) mentioned seven out of fourteen times by the newspaper letter-writers; fourth was "zeal of the membership" (8 per cent cited four times by Social Credit spokesmen and newspaper correspondents; fifth, "TV influence" (6 per cent), mentioned six times out of ten by Social Credit spokesmen; sixth, the "wish for socio-economic betterment" (6 per cent) which received seven mentions out of the ten in the newspaper correspondence; and "ex aequo," the "appeal of the leader" (6 per cent), a theme which was not mentioned at all by the spokesmen of the four parties and which struck the imagination of the journalists who contributed eight of the ten mentions it won; seventh, "Social Credit organization" (5 per cent), the spokesmen of this party being responsible for eight out of nine mentions; and eighth, the impact of "slogans and demagoguery" (5 per cent), mentioned six times by the newspaper correspondents and twice by Conservative spokesmen. (It is interesting to note that the theme of

---

18. The fate of party campaign slogans in the June federal

"nationalism or separatism" was not mentioned once by any of the political parties. Thus it appears that only two important elements of interpretation are located on the ideological level, equally two on the psychological level, and as many as five on the technical level.

As reported in the newspapers, there seemed to have been very little evidence of an ideological positive commitment to the Social Credit doctrine. Only 5 per cent of total mentions could be considered as expressing the opinion of commentators that the Social Credit votes were given for doctrinal reasons. However, before concluding that the commentators in general held that the Social Credit votes were motivated in a negative rather than a positive way, one should make a closer study of the data in Table V. There, in the last two columns a positive or negative sign is attributed to each theme, according to our more or less subjective appreciation of the nature of the attitude to which it seemed to be related. We thus arrived at a total of ten positive and eleven negative themes, making a total of 69 (40 per cent) positive and 105 (60 per cent) negative mentions. However, the preponderance given to negative attitudes is due only to the fact that all themes on the psychological level except one ("last-hour upsurge," which received only one mention) were considered as referring to reasons for not voting for a party other than Social Credit. On the two other levels, the positive motives outweigh the negative ones. It is interesting to note that 19 per cent of all mentions made on the ideological level, which is predominantly positive, came from known Social Credit commentators; 40 per cent of all mentions on the technical level, which are predominantly positive, also came from Social Credit sources; while only 10 per cent of the mentions on the psychological level (predominantly negative) were due to known "Créditiste" sources. In conclusion, one may say that the general configuration of the themes does not show a pronounced negative character. The generally higher percentage given to negative motivations is only due to the fact that one single element of interpretation, i.e., "aversion toward old parties" received so many mentions (48 or 28 per cent of the total). However, the possible elements of discontent and even of rebellion against the political "status quo" on the part of those who voted Social Credit has struck many of our observers. Some of the interpretation to which we have given a positive motivation, such as "nationalism or separatism," "victory of the common man," and "appeal of the leader, Caouette" contain unmistakable signs of dissatisfaction. If we take this into account, we get the astonishing figure of 128 mentions or 74 per cent of the total which can be taken as indicative of dissatisfaction.

---

elections in Quebec would make an interesting study: the various slogans were: for the Conservatives: "There is no error with Diefenbaker"; for the Liberals: "The 75" (candidates); for the NDP: "It's time for new leadership with the New Democratic party"; and finally, the Social Credit party put forward its famous: "You have nothing to lose in voting Social Credit."

CONCLUSION

Our study is far from presenting a complete over-all view of the political behaviour manifested during the long May-June campaign. The conditions under which our survey was undertaken forced us to limit our attention to the content found in the newspapers. Our analysis should have been supplemented by interviews with the many people whose speeches and comments found their way into the news-papers. We should have endeavoured to lay hands upon the full speeches and comments as they were originally written. Party organizations, campaign strategies, the expectations of the candidates themselves concerning the outcome of the elections, and many other aspects should have been used if we had had in mind a complete campaign analysis. Furthermore, other media in addition to the newspapers should have been thoroughly scrutinized, notably the radio and television, which latter has come to be the most important means of campaigning in recent years. We should also have had a research team in the field during the campaign and on election day, covering the party meetings, visiting the committees and surveying the elections polls. Finally, we should have conducted permanent opinion polls and mass observation throughout the campaign in order to establish who intended to vote for which party and for what rea-sons. The post-electoral comments we found in the newspapers offered meagre information on that aspect of the election.

In general, one may state that most observers thought the Social Credit vote to have been given predominantly by farmers, blue- and white-collar workers, low-paid and poorly educated people. Some of the journalists who became conscious of the Social Credit upsurge in the later period of the campaign advanced interesting hypotheses in that respect. Thus, Richard Daignault, on May 29, stated in La Presse that the "Créditistes" came predom-inantly from the petty bourgeoisie, the village shopkeepers and tradesmen, the city white-collar people, the unskilled workers, the poorer farmers and "colons." He added that few professionals, in-tellectuals and people in the highest income brackets took Social Credit seriously. S. Peter Regenstreif, writing in the Star on June 16, said that partisans of Social Credit were living on an in-come below $3,000 a year, had an elementary (primary) school training, and were in possession of no specific professional skills. He added that the slogan "you have nothing to lose" reflected per-fectly the situation of those people. It is superfluous to object here that these remarks have no scientific value. However, since they were made by observers who bested the Gallup poll in their elec-toral forecasts and since we have nothing else to offer, one may be justified in giving them some consideration.

AN ANALYSIS OF VOTING SHIFTS IN QUEBEC

W.P. Irvine

I. THE SOCIAL CREDIT PARTY

The most spectacular result of the 1962 election in the province of
Quebec was, of course, the extraordinary and quite unheralded
rise of Social Credit. From having contested sixteen seats in
1958 as Social Credit or Union des Electeurs, the Social Credit
party was able to nominate a full slate of seventy-five candidates in
1962, increase its vote in all constituencies, and capture twenty-six
seats. The Liberals, with a keen sense of the past, were confident that they would again benefit from Quebec's disenchantment
with the Conservatives. To their dismay, they found that the Liberal vote increased in only five (of fifty-four) constituencies off
Montreal Island, and in eleven (of twenty-one) on it. In eight of
these sixteen seats, their increase was less than the combined increase of Social Credit and "others." (1) The Progressive Conservatives were unable to maintain their strength and lost support in
all seventy-five constituencies, but managed to retain fourteen of
them. "Other" candidates contested fifty-three seats, increasing
their support in thirty-seven, just over half (nineteen) being on
Montreal Island. In fifteen seats, their vote increased by more
than that of the Social Credit candidate. Fourteen of these were
on Montreal Island.

    Another essay in this collection (2) has distinguished two
sources of support for Social Credit - one based on economic protest, the other on nationalistic protest. The economic protest was
particularly important in rural areas too remote for market-garden-
ing near Montreal, and in areas dependent on a stagnant industry -
base metals, textiles, etc. The various elements of the nationalistic
protest are similar to the elements which have generally animated
movements of the "radical right": white-collar frustration at limited
opportunities for advancement in industries controlled by absentee
owners and managed by English-speaking managers, frustration

---

1. In this paper, the term "other" shall refer to NDP candidates, and to Independents of various leanings. There were forty
NDP candidates, and seventeen Independents, or minor party candidates. Of these, four were Independent Liberals, and four Independent Conservatives.
    2. Vincent Lemieux, pp. 33-52.

among intellectuals subject to similar lack of opportunities; resentment of fringe areas against the metropolis, or of small entrepreneurs against big business, and so on. (3) There may even have been a religious aspect to this movement of the right. Many of the areas showing greatest Social Credit strength are places where the Roman Catholic clergy and hierarchy have kept to their traditional ideas with growing uneasiness caused by the attitudes of Cardinal Léger and Pope John XXIII. To all of these frustrations, a political movement of the right provides an apparent solution, or means to a solution.

Social Credit probably had greater difficulty eliciting as positive a response in areas of mainly economic protest. Constituencies whose economies stagnated under both the Liberals and Conservatives might well have agreed with M. Caouette that they had nothing to lose by voting for him. With such negative motivation, abstention could have been as meaningful a form of protest as a vote for Social Credit. (4) Widespread failure to vote was not as likely in constituencies which saw Social Credit as a vehicle for social and nationalistic protest. Of the fifty-two constituencies where Social Credit gained by more than 20 percentage points, seventeen had a population growth of less than 5 per cent between 1956 and 1961 while ten grew by more than 10 per cent. In the more stagnant constituencies, there was a median turnout loss of 2.0 per cent, and a median Social Credit gain of 39.2 per cent. The corresponding figures for the ten more prosperous constituencies were -0.95 per cent and 48.75 per cent. This seems to support the hypothesis that Social Credit benefited more from nationalist than from economic discontent.

Table I shows the movement of a number of variables in relation to various ranges of shift to Social Credit. The lack of any stable relationship between turnout and Social Credit shift is understandable in view of the various motives for voting Social Credit discussed previously. That there is no apparent relationship in Table I between Social Credit voting and population growth may be attributed to the mixture of motives with respect to Social Credit voting. While stagnant economic conditions would certainly give rise to a protest, better economic conditions may simply make protest on other grounds more thinkable, especially if it is believed that

---

3. For a similar analysis of Social Credit movements in other parts of Canada see, D.V. Smiley, "Canada's Poujadists: A New Look at Social Credit," Canadian Forum, XLII, pp. 121-3.

4. Suitable economic statistics on a constituency basis are seriously lacking in Canada. In this paper, median earnings as reported in the 1961 Census will be used as indicators of economic status. Population growth will be taken as an index of economic prosperity or stagnation. This Malthusian approach has many weaknesses, especially when applied to essentially residential constituencies (e.g., because of a decline in population, St. Antoine-Westmount becomes classified as stagnant). On the whole, however, population growth nevertheless appears to be a useful index.

Table 1
Social Credit Gain and Population Characteristics
(in Median Values)

% Socred gain	0.0 to 4.9	5.0 to 9.9	10.0 to 19.9	20.0 to 34.9	35.0 to 49.9	Over 50.0%
Turnout (1962 cf. 1958)	-1.0	-3.6	-3.05	-3.15	-0.1	1.25
% Anglo-Saxon	24.6	4.65	12.05	5.0	2.2	2.65
% French	62.5	84.1	80.3	88.9	96.7	96.2
% Pop. growth	7.2	7.25	13.15	4.65	5.0	8.25
Median earnings ($)	3,656	3,456	3,038	2,716	2,826	3,134
% No schooling	4.0	4.5	6.85	7.1	7.4	8.55
% University	8.0	3.65	3.6	2.6	2.8	2.6
N low education (5) (N=21)	1	0	2	5	7	6
N medium education (N=32)	4	4	8	7	4	5
N high education (N=22)	8	6	4	0	3	1
Total no. of constituencies	13	10	14	12	14	12

Sources: Reports of the Chief Electoral Officer, 1958, 1962.
Census of Canada, 1961.

the benefits of prosperity are being shared unequally. Although there does seem to have been a vote of economic protest, it is blurred by the nationalist protest and possibly by the inefficiency of the economic indicator.

Fairly stable relationships emerge between ethnicity and Social Credit voting. The jog which appears in the 10.0 to 19.9 per cent range is really a regional effect. The two smallest ranges of Social Credit shift are dominated by Montreal constituencies. Eleven of the thirteen in the first group, and eight of the ten in the second are on Montreal Island. What these figures say, in effect, is that the more English Montreal constituencies shifted less to Social Credit than the less English Montreal constituencies. Starting with the 10.0 to 19.9 per cent range of Social Credit gain, there is, to all intents and purposes, a straight-line relationship between increasing Social Credit gain and decreasing percentage of Anglo-Saxon. The trend for median percentage of French-Canadians can be read in the same way. Adding these pairs of median percentages, we note a relationship between increasing gains for Social Credit and decreasing percentages of people who are neither Anglo-Saxon nor French. A large segment of this group is the Jewish community of Montreal, which might well be leery of the

5. An index was constructed by making three ranks: percentage no schooling, percentage with more than 12 years of school, and median years of schooling for the constituency population. Values ranging from 0 to 3 were assigned to constituencies according to the quartile in which they fell, in such a way that a high score indicates high education. The highest possible value for a constituency is 9. Scores of 0 to 2 are low education constituencies, 3 to 6, medium, and 7 to 9, high.

Social Credit movement. Anti-Jewish sentiment had been quite strong in its Quebec branch in the past. Thus, the ten most heavily "ethnic" constituencies on Montreal Island gave Social Credit a median gain of 3.0 per cent. The ten least "ethnic" saw a median increase of 6.55 per cent.

The relationship between median earnings and Social Credit gains shows that the shift to Social Credit was less pronounced in economically well-off constituencies. Median income increases in the highest range of Social Credit shift which includes a number of highly urbanized and industrialized constituencies: Chicoutimi, Lac St. Jean, and Lapointe, for example. The constituencies which shifted to Social Credit by less than 10 per cent are, again, predominantly those of Montreal Island, where incomes are appreciably higher than in other sections of the province. Voting in the twenty-one constituencies on the Island shows the same trend as the province as a whole. The ten constituencies with the lowest level of income had a median shift to Social Credit of 7.9 per cent, more than double the 3.45 per cent shift in the ten highest income constituencies. The rank correlation between increasing shift to Social Credit, and increasing economic standing is -.472, significant at the 5 per cent level.

The key to understanding protest voting lies in identifying the group with which the dissatisfied voter is comparing himself. Montreal constituencies may tend to use the Westmount or Notre-Dame-de-Grâce areas as points of reference, and the protest may thus vary in intensity according to the perceived discrepancy between the style of life in these areas as opposed to the voter's own. This, apparently, is what happened. Higher-status and better-educated constituencies outside Montreal, exposed to communication from the metropolis, may use these high-status Montreal areas as reference groups. They could still be dissatisfied then, despite their own high standing relative to their region, or relative to the province as a whole. On the other hand, low-status and remote areas such as the Gaspé may, by virtue of their lower level of education, have a more limited scope of reference. Not being exposed to communication from outside their region, people in these areas may have lower expectations, and thus be less dissatisfied than other more prosperous areas.

Table II
Median Social Credit Vote by Earnings and Ethnicity
(outside Montreal Island)

	Over 85% French	Under 85% French
Lowest status	29.2	18.25
	(N=10)	(N=6)
Highest status	47.1	13.05
	(N=10)	(N=6)

From Table II we see that, in the more French constituencies, it was the higher status areas which rejected the two-party system

most forcefully by switching to Social Credit. In less French constituencies, the reverse was true. (6) Where upper-status Anglo-
Saxons control an economy to the extent that they do in Quebec,
they obviously have the greatest stake in maintaining the existing institutions. The lower-status French, who probably have least to
lose from radical change, are less susceptible to the appeal of such
a movement because their lower status tends to blind them to the
possibilities of change.

When measured both in terms of percentages of the population
with no schooling, with more than twelve years of schooling, and
in terms of an education index, there appears to be a distinct relationship between lack of formal education and propensity to vote
Social Credit. Social Credit candidates gained less than 20 per
cent of the vote in only 3 of 21 "low education" constituencies, as
opposed to 16 of 32 "medium education" constituencies, and 18 of
22 "high education" constituencies. Eighteen of the 38 constituencies where Social Credit gained over 20 per cent were in the "low
education" group. Only four were "highly educated" in terms of
the general index, these deviant cases being Lévis, Sherbrooke,
Quebec East, and Quebec-Montmorency. Closer study of these
four would probably yield results similar to those found by Professor Lemieux in Lévis. In these areas, the highly educated
people tend to be strongly nationalistic, for a variety of reasons,
which generally arise from extreme sensitivity to the power of
Montreal business, or the power of the federal government.

The phenomenon of rural and urban voting is quite interesting
in connection with the degree of support for Social Credit in each
type of area. In 1962, the province of Quebec contained thirteen
completely rural and twenty-five completely urban constituencies. (7)
The median shift to Social Credit was 27.0 per cent in the former
and 5.7 per cent in the latter, which were dominated by the twenty-
one Montreal constituencies. In the ten most urban constituencies
outside Montreal, the median shift was 48.05 per cent. Except for
Montreal, then, the presence of an urban centre in the constituency
perhaps contributed to the spread of Social Credit into that constituency by serving to focus discontent. In the thirty-three mixed
constituencies, (8) the median gain in the urban parts was 32.7
per cent, and 32.8 per cent in the rural parts. If we eliminated
the constituencies over 15 per cent non-French, the median figures
become 43.3 per cent and 42.2 per cent respectively. In either
case, the difference is negligible compared to the difference between
completely urban and completely rural constituencies. The city is
needed as the hub for the communication of Social Credit propagan-
da(especially if that city had a television station) but, given the

---

6. As there are only twelve constituencies less than 85 per
cent French outside Montreal, these figures must be considered
with great caution.

7. As defined by the Chief Electoral Officer.

8. A "mixed" constituency is one between 10 and 90 per
cent urban.

presence of the hub, the communication could be equally successful in the rural as in the urban areas.

Twenty-seven Quebec constituencies outside the Montreal-Longueuil area contain more than one urban centre, with a total of fifty-five "satellite cities" tributary to the twenty-seven major ones. In thirty-one of the fifty-five cases, Social Credit gains were greater in the satellite city. At least fifteen of the exceptions can be accounted for by special local support for one candidate, or by the fact that the satellite city is a residential (upper class) suburb of the main city. The interpretation of the Social Credit movement as a revolt of the fringes against the centre thus gains additional support.

Shifting to Social Credit was a product of nationalist and economic frustrations, which were probably prompted less by objective conditions than by the individual's own subjective estimation of his status. Certainly economic deprivation contributed a good deal to the dissatisfaction, but economically stagnant areas whose reference groups were other economically stagnant areas did not respond to Social Credit to the same extent as more prosperous areas whose horizons included Montreal. The highest Social Credit gains came mainly in the remote northern constituencies, in the Quebec city region, and in the Eastern townships. All of these areas had sufficiently large centres, and were sufficiently diversified, to encompass both nationalistic and economic dissatisfaction. Furthermore, in a number of cases there was the absence of a strictly two-party tradition. Nine of the twenty-six areas shifting over 35 per cent to Social Credit, had voted 20 per cent or more for an "other" candidate at least once since 1953. These areas generally depended on one dominant industry, which was in turn dependent on world markets: pulp and paper, aluminum, textiles, etc. In varying degrees, these industries had to cut production in the face of declining world demand. In virtually all cases, the industries were dominated by large, foreign-owned, and English-managed enterprises. The nationalism of these centres could easily be communicated to the more rural constituencies surrounding them.

II. THE LIBERAL PARTY

As illustrated in Table III, the Liberal shift was essentially a mirror image of the Social Credit shift, somewhat distorted perhaps, but still recognizable. We can identify exactly the same trends, and deviations within trends, with respect to Liberal losses, as we could with respect to Social Credit gains. Liberal gains, or small losses, occurred in those upper-status, English, better-educated areas on Montreal Island, which showed only a passing interest in Social Credit. Heavy Liberal losses marked the middle-status, moderately educated, and highly French constituencies so susceptible to the "Creditiste" appeal. Turnout showed generally the same fluctuation as it had for Social Credit, while the degree of population growth remained fairly stable over the whole range of Liberal losses.

The most interesting result of the 1962 election with respect to

Table III
Liberal Shift and Population Characteristics
(in Median Values)

% Lib. shift	Gain	0.0 to -4.9	-5.0 to -9.0	-10.0 to -19.9	Over -20.0
Turnout (1962 cf. 1958)	-1.3	-2.8	-3.15	-0.35	1.55
% Anglo-Saxon	19.4	4.2	5.2	2.5	2.6
% French	65.0	88.9	92.05	96.2	96.65
% Pop. growth	7.6	6.5	7.6	7.4	6.15
Median earnings ($)	3,376	3,448	2,780	2,840	3,156
% No schooling	5.7	5.7	7.1	8.55	7.1
% University	3.9	3.6	3.05	2.7	2.75
N low education (N=21)	1	3	5	8	4
N medium education (N=32)	7	7	6	8	4
N high education (N=22)	8	7	3	2	2
Total no. of constituencies	16	17	14	18	10

the Liberals is the strong support they received from the people of Anglo-Saxon and other non-French origin. Fourteen of the sixteen constituencies where the Liberals gained had populations less than 80 per cent French. Nine of the sixteen were less than 70 per cent French. Only Pontiac-Témiscamingue and Stanstead of the important Anglo-Saxon constituencies seemed willing to consider Social Credit as a possible alternative. In Mount Royal and Notre-Dame-de-Grâce constituencies, the Liberals did better in 1962 than in 1953. The rank correlation between increasing Liberal losses on Montreal Island and increasing percentage of French Canadians in the constituency is 0.702, highly significant at the 1 per cent level.

Table IV
Median Liberal Shift by Ethnicity and Economic Status

| | Over 85% French | | Under 85% French | |
	All of Quebec	Ex. Montreal	All of Quebec	Ex. Montreal
Lowest status	-5.8 (N=10)	-5.8 (N=10)	0.0 (N=10)	-5.6 (N=6)
Highest status	-5.05 (N=10)	-10.1 (N=10)	+1.45 (N=10)	-3.2% (N=6)

Table IV shows, in fact, that it was the upper-status French constituencies outside Montreal that were quickest to abandon the Liberal party. This continues the movement of upper-status French out of the Liberal party which was becoming very evident by 1959.(9) The new nationalist elites of French Canada were not being brought

---

9. A parallel table for Liberal shift by ethnicity and educational status shows a similar pattern with an even stronger support for the

into the federal party as they were into the provincial party at about that time.

In twelve of the twenty-one Montreal constituencies, the "other" (mainly NDP) shift was higher than the Liberal shift. In ten of these cases, the Liberals and the Conservatives were both losing to Social Credit and "other" candidates. The median percentage of French in these constituencies was 80.55 per cent while in the other nine constituencies, it was 38.3 per cent.

The thirteen completely rural constituencies saw a shift from the Liberals of -6.3 per cent, significantly higher than the loss of 1.2 per cent in the twenty-five completely urban constituencies. Both of these figures were lower than those for the mixed constituencies, where the median Liberal loss in the urban sections was 12.5 per cent and in rural sections, 8.9 per cent (10). This rather startling discrepancy underlines the urban (and particularly, urban French) protest against the Liberal party. In twenty-three of the thirty-three mixed constituencies, the Liberals did better in the rural than urban parts, with six cases of rural gains and urban losses in the one constituency. Of the ten exceptions, three were constituencies with substantial English minorities, largely inhabiting the cities. In at least three others, the Liberal candidate had especially strong support in the main urban area (the mayor of Rivière-du-Loup, for example, gained in the city, but lost the country). In Quebec-Montmorency all cities except one rejected the Liberals more strongly than the rural communities. That one, the upper-class Quebec suburb of Sainte Foy, was sufficient to change the over-all balance so that the Liberals lost 15.6 per cent in the urban part and 19.3 per cent in the rural.

Liberal strength in Quebec in 1962 was thus a compound of Anglo-Saxons and some low-status rural French Canadians in more remote constituencies of the Gaspe region. It is not misleading to say that the Liberal party had been rejected by French-Canadian opinion, both rural and urban. This rejection was less pronounced in lower-status rural areas where tradition was strongest and where Social Credit television broadcasts found a smaller audience. It was strongest in those constituencies of the Quebec North shore where an increasing and highly transient population had fewer established political ties.

III. THE PROGRESSIVE CONSERVATIVES

In 1958, it seemed that John Diefenbaker (and Maurice

Liberals among better educated constituencies less than 85% French. For ten constituencies, the median shift was a gain of 7.2%. This is discussed in greater detail in William P. Irvine, "The Federal Liberal Party and the New Quebec: A Study in National Unity," unpublished MA thesis submitted to the Department of Political Science, Queen's University.

10. The gap is even larger if we ignore the eight constituencies over 15% non-French. The corresponding median loss figures become -15.3% and -9.3% for the other twenty-five constituencies.

Duplessis) had performed the impossible for the federal Conservatives in Quebec. He came within four-tenths of a percentage point of capturing a majority of the popular vote, and won fifty seats – twenty-four of them by a margin of more than 10 percentage points. Over the next four years, however, he proved unable or unwilling to formulate policies and find lieutenants enabling him to forge this support into a permanent Conservative coaliton. This neglect cost him and his candidates support in every seat. In only two ridings did he lose less than 5 per cent of the vote as compared to 1958, In losing to all opponents, the PC shift blurred any broad trends such as those identified for Liberals and Social Credit. For example, the twelve constituencies where Conservatives lost between 20.0 and 24.9 per cent included such diverse constituencies as Champlain, Kamouraska, Sherbrooke, Mount Royal, and Notre-Dame-de-Grâce. In some of these, Social Credit was attracting most of the former Conservatives, in others, most shifted to the Liberals and NDP.

Looking at Table V, we see that trends are disrupted in the 15.0 to 19.9 per cent range of Conservative losses. This range includes some upper-status Montreal constituencies shifting to Liberal and NDP, Anglo-Saxon rural constituencies shifting to Liberals and Social Credit, and rural French constituencies shifting to Social Credit. The fact that all ranges of Conservative loss up to 25 per cent included some constituencies where the Liberals were the principal gainers accounts for the presence of "highly educated" constituencies throughout all of these ranges. The mixture of Liberal and Social Credit gains up to 20.0 per cent Conservative loss accounts for the relatively stable proportion of French-Canadians in all of these ranges.

Conservatives lost to all three opponents in fourteen constituencies. These numbers are too small to justify tabulation, but the trend of PC losses is from generally low losses in French lower-status constituencies to high losses in upper-status English ridings. Conservatives lost least to the Liberals in Isles-de-la-Madeleine, Châteauguay-Huntingdon-Laprairie, and Laval, and most in St. Lawrence-St. George, Mount Royal, and Notre-Dame-de-Grâce Conservative losses to Social Credit showed the same ambiguity with respect to educational and economic status as did Liberal losses. More heavily French constituencies deserted the Conservatives to a greater degree than "less French" constituencies, and the presence of a large middle class in the constituency produced a greater loss in favour of Social Credit than either the virtual absence of such a middle class, or the existence of an entrenched upper class.

The median Conservative loss in the thirteen completely rural constituencies was 16.8 per cent; in the twenty-five urban constituencies, 13 per cent. This slight preference for the Conservatives in the cities is carried into the mixed constituencies, where the PC's lost 22.2 per cent in urban sections, and 23.8 per cent in rural sections. Eliminating the eight constituencies less than 85 per cent French sharpens the contrast: -23.3 per cent in urban areas, -26.7 per

Table V
Conservative Loss and Population Characteristics
(in Median Values)

% PC loss	0.0 to 9.9	10.0 to 14.9	15.0 to 19.9	20.0 to 24.9	25.0 to 29.9	Over 30.0
Turnout (1962 cf. 1958)	-1.0	-3.05	-0.85	-2.5	+1.8	-1.15
% Anglo-Saxon	8.8	4.35	12.0	6.9	2.05	2.45
% French	79.4	77.85	77.55	90.4	97.05	96.35
% Pop. growth	8.0	2.0	9.8	7.7	7.4	5.85
Median earnings ($)	3,473	3,229	3,115	3,066	3,212	3,032
% No schooling	5.7	5.8	6.45	7.15	7.95	8.4
% University	2.9	3.15	3.95	2.85	2.8	3.1
N low education (N=24)	1	4	2	5	6	4
N medium education (N=31)	5	6	7	4	5	4
N high education (N=22)	3	8	5	3	1	2
Total no. of constituencies	9	18	14	12	12	10

cent in the rural areas.   Initially, this is somewhat surprising.
Given the urban character of the Social Credit movement, we might
have expected the reverse to be true, as it was for the Liberals.
That it was not the case testifies to the lingering doubts and prejudices towards the Conservatives in French-Canadian rural areas.

One interpretation of the results suggests that the voters who
had been dissatisfied with the Liberals in 1957-58 and deserted them
for the Conservatives, came to be dissatisfied with both old parties,
and therefore voted Social Credit in 1962.   There is little evidence
that this was precisely the case.   The Conservative percentage in
1962 was within 2 per cent of the 1953 percentage in only five constituencies, and within 5 per cent in only seventeen constituencies
out of seventy-three. (11)   A possible refinement of this hypothesis
would be that those who voted most heavily against tradition in 1958
(i.e., against the Liberals) would be most likely to vote against the
two-party system in 1962.   Again, the evidence is inconclusive.
The fifteen constituencies outside Montreal shifting most heavily
against the Liberals in 1958 include five of the fifteen most heavily
Social Credit constituencies but also three of the fifteen least Social
Credit constituencies in 1962.   While the Conservatives proved unable, in 1962, to hold on to their 1958 supporters, they improved
their position in Quebec as compared with their strength in the St.
Laurent era.   In 1962, without the help of any provincial machine,
the Conservatives still were ahead of their 1953 vote in thirty-seven
constituencies. (12)   Of the twenty-one where the gain was more
than 10 per cent, ten were in Montreal.   Seven of these ten constituencies were in areas less than 10 per cent Anglo-Saxon despite

11. St. Hyacinthe and Terrebonne are omitted because they
returned Liberals by acclamation in 1953.

12. The rank correlation between increasing PC gain 1953-62
and increasing percentage French-Canadian is 0.498, significant at
the 5 per cent level.

the Conservatives' previous strength among the English business elements. Six more were in the Montreal region, two others in the Three Rivers region, and the remaining three were Chicoutimi, Brome-Missisquoi, and Kamouraska. Of the sixteen other constituencies where the Conservatives were ahead by less than 10.0 per cent, seven were on Montreal Island, two in the Montreal region, two in the Eastern Townships, three in the Quebec city region, and one each in Gatineau and Lapointe. The Conservatives thus improved their vote in seventeen of twenty-one constituencies on Montreal Island, and eight of twelve in the Montreal region. The Conservatives found themselves over 10 per cent below their 1953 position in twenty constituencies, but these were dispersed through every region in the province. Except for losses in two high-status Montreal constituencies and in two low-status Quebec city constituencies, most of their heavy losses were on the fringe areas of each region. This tends to confirm the finding that Conservatives did better in urban than rural areas. This is understandable in view of the strong rural prejudices against the "conscriptionists."

IV. THE "OTHERS"

Neither the New Democratic party candidates nor independents managed to win a seat in Quebec in 1962. This is no measure of their importance or effectiveness, however. Of the forty-one seats which it contested, the NDP increased its vote in thirty-six, including all twenty-one Montreal constituencies. (13) Independents gained in eleven seats. The NDP gained 15.1 per cent in St.Jean-Iberville-Napierville and 14.6 per cent in Outremont-St. Jean. In all, the NDP vote increased by more than 5 percentage points in sixteen constituencies, all on Montreal Island or in the Montreal region. The increments in the shift are so small that the data in Table VI can be grouped in only three categories. One is thus forced to speak not of "trends" but of "differences."

The differences are striking, however. The constituencies where "Others" gained most heavily are more Anglo-Saxon, higher-status, and much better educated than those in which they lost. They are also more heavily populated with non-French, non-Anglo-Saxon people, principally Jewish and Italian. Eight of fourteen constituencies with high gains were "highly educated," only one was "poorly educated." Where "Others" lost, six of sixteen were "poorly educated," only two were "highly educated."

While the "Others" vote is difficult to evaluate statistically, it does provide an important clue to the attitudes of the voters. The politics of the 1962 election in Quebec is the politics of protest - a protest against the two traditional parties if not against the whole federal structure. Such a protest can take three forms at election time - abstaining, voting for Social Credit, or voting for "other" candidates. As has been outlined, the most important form was to vote for Social Credit, but "other" voting was important on Montreal

---

13. The comparison here is with the CCF vote of 1958.

Table VI
"Other" Shift and Population Characteristics
(in Median Values)

% "Other" shift	Loss	0.0 to 4.9	Over 5.0%
Turnout (1962 cf. 1958)	-0.45	-3.1	-2.95
% Anglo-Saxon	4.2	6.6	9.6
% French	93.95	86.1	78.05
% Pop. growth	8.3	6.5	11.2
Median earnings ($)	3,184	3,209	3,752
% No schooling	6.9	6.2	4.25
% University	2.9	3.4	4.05
N low education (N=11)	6	4	1
N medium education (N=23)	8	10	5
N high education (N=19)	2	9	8
Total no. of constituencies	16	23	14

Island, and there were heavy declines in turnout among certain constituencies of the Gaspé and Montreal regions. On the other hand,
there were areas of both increased turnout and strong support for
Social Credit.   People in these areas were not merely opposing,
but also expressing a positive belief in Social Credit as a vehicle
for resolving their national and economic dissatisfaction.

    Table VII illustrates the four major types of shift which occur-
ed.(14)   The constituencies where Social Credit gained from all its
opponents may be considered as areas of positive support for Social Credit.   Twelve of fifty-six constituencies where there were
multi-candidate fights fell into this category.   Median shift to Social
Credit was 50.1 per cent and there was a median increase in
turnout.   Three of the six constituencies in this group where turnout dropped gave comparatively slight support to Social Credit.
Possibly, due to the strength of local machines, the voters, while
exhibiting an affinity for Social Credit, felt that abstention was a more
practicable form of protest.   In Lac-St.-Jean constituency, the turnout dropped by only 0.1 per cent.   As turnout in 1958 was considerably higher than it had been during the "Liberal era," such a
minor decline may simply reflect the difficulty of sustaining a high
degree of interest in an increasingly urbanizing constituency.   The
two other cases of "atypical" turnout declines, Chicoutimi, and
Compton-Frontenac, are more difficult to explain.   Both still registered turnouts of 85 per cent or more, which suggests that the
1958 turnout was inflated for some reason or other.   As indicated
in Table VII, these constituencies were quite French, generally
lower middle status, and moderately "well educated."

    In contrast to these are the constituencies where both Social

---

    14. Three constituencies shifted from Conservative and "Other"
to Liberal and Social Credit.   They were Isles-de-la-Madeleine,
Ste. Anne, and St. Henri.

Table VII
Various Types of Shift and Population Characteristics
(in Median Values)

	PC only party to lose	Socred gain from 3 opponents	Socred gain from trad. parties	Socred + other gain from trad. parties
Turnout (1962 cf. 1958)	-0.4	0.7	-0.8	-2.95
% Anglo-Saxon	22.2	3.45	2.1	4.7
% French	62.5	95.7	97.1	89.05
% Pop. growth	8.0	8.8	3.1	7.35
Median earnings ($)	3,464	3,049	2,469	3,236
% No schooling	4.5	7.55	7.2	6.45
% University	8.0	3.1	2.4	3.4
N low education (N=20)	0	5	!0	5
N medium education (N=30)	5	6	6	13
N high education (N=22)	8	1	3	10
Total no. of constituencies	13	12	!9	28

Credit and "Others" gained.   These areas were protesting against
the traditional parties, without having any consensus as to a solution
of their malaise.   The higher rate of abstention supports this "un-
directed protest" hypothesis.   These were upper-middle-status,
less French and generally better-educated constituencies.   Ten were
on Montreal Island where Social Credit was consistently unable to
canalize all the discontent.   The median earnings for the eighteen
constituencies outside Montreal was $3,049, exactly the same as
where Social Credit gained from all opponents, but the median percentage Anglo-Saxon was 4.95 per cent, appreciably higher.   In
thirteen of the twenty-eight cases, the constituency had not been
contested by "Others" before.   In five of these, the gain was less
than 2 per cent which may be accounted for simply by having the
name on the ballot.   In the other eight cases, as well as the fifteen
where "Others" had run before, it seems obvious that the candidate
did fill a need not met by the Social Credit standard-bearer.
        In the nineteen constituencies where there were no "Other"
candidates, the results are more ambiguous.   Seven saw an increased turnout; in twelve turnout declined.   Table VIII shows the
relevant data.
        The constituencies in this category where turnout increased
shifted more heavily to Social Credit than those where turnout
decreased.   The pattern of lower-middle economic and educational
status combined with a high percentage of French, generally follows
the pattern for constituencies where Social Credit gained at the expense of all three opponents.   The constituencies where turnout fell
are quite clearly constituencies of economic protest.   Median population increase is extremely low.   Population actually fell between
1956 and 1961 in four of the constituencies.   With educational status
so low, the nationalist appeal of Social Credit probably had little

Table VIII
Social Credit Gain from Traditional Parties and Turnout Change

	Turnout Increase	Turnout Decrease
Median Socred gain	46.7	37.1
Median % Anglo-Saxon	2.7	1.9
Median % French	96.3	97.3
Median % population growth	7.7	1.4
Median earnings ($)	3,274	2,039
Median % no schooling	6.7	7.4
Median % university	2.8	1.7
N low education (N=10)	1	9
N medium education (N=6)	4	2
N high education (N=3)	2	1
Total no. of constituencies	7	12

impact. A vote for Social Credit because "on n'a rien à perdre" is not likely to elicit the same response as a vote for a party which can satisfy the claims of nationalism, and which can act as a vehicle for the release of the frustrations of lower middle-class existence.

Finally, there were the thirteen constituencies where the Conservatives lost to Liberals, Social Credit, and "Others." These were strongly Anglo-Saxon, strongly "ethnic" urban constituencies of high economic and educational status. As the upper classes are sufficiently numerous to show up in the shift, their support for the Liberals becomes more obvious here than elsewhere. "Others" probably drew support from the middle classes, and upper-class French, and Social Credit from the lower-middle and lower classes that seemed to comprise its support in Montreal. Even these groups must have been somewhat inhibited by the absence of a general response to Social Credit in these constituencies. Quebec voting in the June 1962 election thus appears to be quite stratified. The very high-status and Anglo-Saxon constituencies, dissatisfied with Mr. Diefenbaker's unconventional Conservatism, and attracted by the urbanity, education, and professionalism of Liberal candidates, shifted from the Conservatives to the Liberals. Some of this status appeal of the Liberals may have had an impact on the French as well, but they tended to be sympathetic to "Others," mainly the NDP rather than to Independents. This reflects the different national aspirations of the better educated French, and their unwillingness to support a party still largely dominated by "old guard," patronage-oriented Liberals.

Support for Social Credit was of two kinds - a protest against continued economic lag in certain areas of the province, and a positive response from lower-middle and lower classes as a vehicle for the release of national and social tensions. The constituencies which responded least to Social Credit are those with a small middle class and remote from any centres with sizable middle-class populations. In the absence of these conditions to sustain a nationalist protest, Social Credit was less successful. An economic protest alone could not be translated into a high degree of Social Credit voting. Conditions for nationalistic protest were present in many Montreal constituencies but were not translated into Social Credit votes because of the "Créditistes'" inability to convey an impression of themselves as a serious and viable protest movement. This lack of communication perhaps reflects the importance of the Anglo-Saxon element and the Montreal press as opinion leaders. The increased Social Credit vote in 1963 in Montreal may be partly explained by the awareness that it was a strong movement.

THE PRESS OF ONTARIO AND THE ELECTION

T.H. Qualter and K.A. MacKirdy

As the press remains the prime source of fact and of opinion, the way in which newspapers handle elections continues to be a matter of interest. It has, however, been a topic something akin to the weather; a good deal of talk about it, but very little attempt to do anything.

Disturbed by the mass of imprecise and unverified charges and countercharges, the authors of this article decided to attempt a process of systematic press analysis. We attempted to classify and analyse all items treating the election which appeared in a selected group of Ontario daily newspapers between April 18 and polling day, June 18. It was, of necessity, primarily a statistical analysis, for, to refer back to the weather analogy, the science of meteorology has been built up on weather data collected over many years, but no such basic material has been collected on the Canadian press.

The statistics which follow were derived by identifying all items relating to the election campaign in the eight designated newspapers, analysing their category (news item, editorial, photograph, paid advertisement, etc.) location in the paper, length, content, and bias. This information was recorded by a numerical code on data cards which were then fed into an electronic computer. (1) The tables published here are but a small sample of those which we have compiled, and barely suggest the possibilities of this technique. A refined version of this technique is being employed on a more thorough analysis of the press coverage of the 1963 election.

II. ALLOCATION OF TOTAL SPACE TO EACH PARTY

Table I provides a breakdown of total election material. Every item having any connection with the election, or any of the parties, is listed here. (Included are all news items, editorials, cartoons, photographs, articles, social notes, letters to the editor, feature material, and advertisements.)

In devising the coding system it was decided that a report of a political meeting would be regarded as space for the party holding the meeting, even if the content were largely an attack on a rival

---

1. The computer program was developed by Professor J.W. Graham of the Department of Mathematics, University of Waterloo. It is outlined in his paper, Statistical Report Generator, available from Professor Graham.

Table I
Allocation of Total Space to Each Party

	Telegram		Toronto Daily Star		Globe and Mail	
	Column inches	%	Column inches	%	Column inches	%
Progressive Conservative	7,373	34.7	8,178	33.4	6,195	33.4
Liberal	3,835	18.1	5,701	23.2	5,036	27.1
New Democratic	1,502	7.0	2,395	9.7	1,617	8.7
Social Credit	634	3.0	686	2.7	1,293	7.0
Other parties and Independents	105	0.5	62	0.3	101	0.5
Combined PC and Liberal	1,859	8.9	992	4.1	748	4.0
" " " NDP	121	0.6	116	0.4	67	0.4
" Liberal " "	162	0.8	131	0.5	75	0.4
Any other two-party combination	246	1.1	51	0.3	133	0.7
Combined PC, Liberal and NDP	1.103	5.3	899	3.6	691	3.8
Combined all four parties	2,611	12.3	1,893	7.7	1,100	5.9
Combined more than four parties	178	0.8	211	0.9	263	1.4
Unspecified parties in general	161	0.6	1,039	4.2	379	2.0
No party content	1,348	6.3	2,230	9.0	863	4.7
	21,238	100.0	24,584	100.0	18,561	100.0

party. Reports of joint party meetings, cartoons featuring two or more party leaders, reports of where the four party leaders were at any particular time, surveys of the prospects of each party in a given riding, and other items of this kind are listed against the combined party headings. Most of the material with "no party content" consisted of items on election law and machinery, historical material and "human interest" stories about voters.

The first point of interest is the relatively wide range in the total amount of attention given to the election, a range which is not directly related to the circulation or size of the papers involved. Even within the metropolitan Toronto area there was a considerable variation in total coverage, with the Toronto Daily Star having over 6000 more inches of election space than the Globe and Mail. Of the total combined space in all eight papers surveyed, 15.9 per cent was in the Star, 13.7 per cent in the Telegram, 13.1 per cent in the Ottawa Citizen, 12.4 per cent in the Kitchener-Waterloo-Record, 12.0 per cent in the Globe and Mail, 11.6 per cent in the Ottawa Journal, 11.2 per cent in the Hamilton Spectator, and 10.1 per cent in the London Free Press.

If the papers are arranged in terms of percentage of the total space (i.e., total number of pages in all papers for the period of

Ottawa Citizen		Ottawa Journal		Kitchener-Waterloo Record		London Free Press		Hamilton Spectator	
Column inches	%	Column inches	%	Column inches	%	Column inches	%	Column inches	%
5,261	30.9	6,152	34.3	5,854	30.5	6,112	39.0	5,801	33.5
5,267	25.9	5,053	28.2	4,452	23.2	4,593	29.3	3,491	20.2
1,672	8.2	1,165	6.5	2,077	10.8	1,187	7.6	1,576	9.1
1,292	6.3	779	4.3	1,317	6.8	523	3.4	353	2.0
10	–	17	0.1	186	1.0	25	0.2	141	0.8
1,176	5.8	671	3.7	522	2.9	289	1.8	549	3.2
81	0.4	34	0.2	65	0.3	34	0.2	96	0.6
32	0.2	24	0.2	29	0.2	35	0.2	47	0.3
51	0.3	31	0.2	162	0.7	50	0.4	33	0.2
452	2.2	189	1.0	288	1.5	180	1.1	737	4.3
2,398	11.8	2,010	11.3	1,824	9.4	1,522	9.7	1,974	11.3
273	1.3	55	0.3	220	1.1	–	–	511	3.0
29	0.1	263	1.4	838	4.4	104	0.7	762	4.4
1,350	6.6	1,474	8.3	1,386	7.2	1,001	6.4	1,224	7.1
20,364	100.0	17,917	100.0	19,250	100.0	15,664	100.0	17,295	100.0

the survey multiplied by the number of column inches per page)
devoted to the election, a somewhat different ordering appears.
The K-W Record then heads the list with 5.2 per cent of its total
space devoted to the election, the Ottawa Citizen ranked second
with 4.9 per cent, the Ottawa Journal and the Globe and Mail both
gave 4.3 per cent of their total space to the election, the Telegram
and the Star both gave 4.0 per cent, and the Spectator and the
Free Press again came at the bottom of the list with 3.3 per cent
and 3.2 per cent respectively.

The second point of interest is the fact that all eight papers
devoted very nearly the same percentage of their total election space
to the Progressive Conservatives. Five of the papers gave between
33.4 and 34.7 per cent of their election coverage to the government
party, and the maximum range was from 30.5 per cent in the
Record to 39.0 per cent in the Free Press. In contrast to this
similarity a marked divergence is apparent in the allocation of space
to the other three parties. These were given a combined total of
only 28.1 per cent of the space in the Telegram (i.e., some 6.5
per cent less than the total for the Progressive Conservatives alone)
and a maximum combined total of 42.8 per cent in the Globe and
Mail.

The Liberals received their poorest coverage (in terms of percentage of space) in the Telegram, which came second highest in its coverage of the Conservatives, and their highest coverage (again in percentage terms) in the London Free Press. It is noteworthy that two pro-Conservative papers, the Globe and Mail and the Ottawa Journal, allocated a higher percentage of their total election coverage to the Liberal party than did the two leading Liberal papers, the Toronto Daily Star and the Ottawa Citizen.

Policy towards the two minor parties varied considerably, especially when these were considered in relation to the two larger parties. In the Free Press for example, the Conservatives and the Liberals together were allocated approximately six times as much space as the New Democrats and the Social Credit party, whereas in the Record the ratio was less than three to one. On the average the two larger parties were allocated between four and five times as much space as the two smaller. On combined figures for all eight papers the New Democratic party received 8.5 per cent of the total space and Social Credit 4.6 per cent. The Telegram and the Free Press allocated significantly less than this average space to both the small parties. The Record allocated to them considerably better than average coverage. The other papers had a mixed approach, with the Star and the Spectator both giving the New Democrats more favoured coverage (in terms of total space) than Social Credit, and the Globe and the Citizen both improving the position of Social Credit relative to the New Democrats. Other parties (mainly the Communists) and independents were virtually ignored in all papers.

In most of the papers the amount of space allocated to the various two and three party combinations was reasonably similar. Only in the Telegram was there an unusually high percentage here - a total of nearly 30 per cent compared with an average of about 17 per cent.

II. BREAKDOWN OF ELECTION COVERAGE FOR EACH MAIN PARTY BY DEGREES OF SUPPORT

Table II takes the figures in the first four lines of Table I, the figures for the four main parties, and analyses these by the degree of support.

The terms "favourable" and "unfavourable" are not as subjective as might have been expected. It is true that in many cases the newspaper report of a speech may have given a different impression than the speech itself. The report would almost certainly be far from complete and in the process of selection the speaker's most telling arguments may have been omitted in favour of some incidental comments. But as our interest was with the image presented in the press and as we were not concerned with the impact of the candidate's oratory on those listening to him, we took each press item as a self-contained unit. From this approach we classified all reports of speeches, if presented without comment, as favourable. Such reports, we feel, provided publicity to the candidate and his party.   Furthermore, the account of his address would normally reflect some ideas which he intended to convey.

Similarly, editorial comment, whether in formal editorials, in headlines or comment within the body of a news item, was taken at its face value.   That is to say, an editorial openly critical of a party was classified as unfavourable even if, in our personal opinion, the criticism was misguided and likely to bring comfort and support to the attacked party.

We were encouraged in this approach to classification by the fact that although at various times several people with different political loyalties were engaged in "coding" there were few disagreements on classification and none that was not easily resolved.

The most interesting point here is the comparative treatment of the different parties by each paper.   The highest degree of partisanship appeared in the Ottawa Citizen where the ratio of favourable to unfavourable comment for the Liberals was in the range of 55:1 compared with a ratio of 4:1 for the Conservatives.   The Toronto Daily Star, as expected, also accorded the Liberals most favoured treatment.   The favourable and unfavourable ratio here exceeded 32:1, while for the Progressive Conservatives the amount of favourable treatment was only very slightly larger than the amount of unfavourable.   In terms of the ratio of favourable to unfavourable, three other papers, the Kitchener-Waterloo Record, the Hamilton Spectator and the London Free Press, also showed pro-Liberal leanings, although not to such a marked extent as the Citizen or the Star (published where other local papers with differing political loaylties were available).   In all three papers, however, the total amount of material, both favourable and unfavourable, allocated to the Conservatives was greater than the amount allocated to the Liberals.

Pro-Conservative support came principally from the Telegram and the Ottawa Journal, although the tables indicate that the pro-Conservatism and the anti-Liberalism of these two papers was less extreme than the pro-Liberalism and anti-Conservatism of their two principal rivals.   Although the Globe and Mail favoured the Progressive Conservatives, the differentiation between all four parties was much less marked than elsewhere.

In terms of total favourable space the New Democrats received their greatest support in the Star and Social Credit its greatest amount of total favourable space in the Citizen.   The greatest volume of anti-New Democrat space appeared in the Globe and Mail and the greatest volume of anti-Social Credit space was in the Record.

In terms of the percentage share of the total favourable coverage the Conservatives, with 58 per cent, received their greatest support from the Telegram.   This figure is in contrast to the 33 per cent of all the favourable material in the Star.   The Liberals, not unsurprisingly, received their greatest share of total favourable material (45.5 per cent), in the Star and a low figure of 27.1 per cent in the Telegram.   The New Democratic party had a high of 17.2 per cent of the total favourable copy in the Star and a low of

Table II
Breakdown of Election Coverage for Each Main Party
(Using "Single Party" items only) by Degrees of Support

	Progressive Conservative Column inches	%	Liberal Column inches	%	New Democratic Column inches	%	Social Credit Column inches	%
Telegram								
Favourable	6,824	92.6	3,195	83.3	1,276	85.0	473	74.6
Neutral	66	0.9	13	0.3	4	0.3	11	1.7
Unfavourable	341	4.6	627	16.4	207	13.8	150	23.7
Mixed	142	1.9	–	–	15	0.9	–	–
	7,373	100.0	3,835	100.0	1,502	100.0	634	100.0
Toronto Daily Star								
Favourable	3,891	47.6	5,361	94.0	2,030	84.8	523	76.2
Neutral	245	3.0	174	3.1	80	3.3	23	3.4
Unfavourable	3,648	44.6	166	2.9	186	7.8	140	20.4
Mixed	394	4.8	–	–	99	4.1	–	–
	8,178	100.0	5,701	100.0	2,395	100.0	686	100.0
Globe and Mail								
Favourable	5,124	82.7	4,243	84.3	1,187	73.4	1,029	79.6
Neutral	60	1.0	38	0.8	65	4.0	30	2.3
Unfavourable	580	9.3	611	12.1	216	13.4	158	12.2
Mixed	431	7.0	144	2.8	149	9.2	76	5.9
	6,195	100.0	5,036	100.0	1,617	100.0	1,293	100.0
Ottawa Citizen								
Favourable	4,838	77.0	4,985	94.7	1,541	92.2	1,292	100.0
Neutral	183	2.9	123	2.3	7	0.4	–	–
Unfavourable	1,091	17.4	91	1.7	124	7.4	–	–
Mixed	169	2.7	68	1.3	–	–	–	–
	6,281	100.0	5,267	100.0	1,672	100.0	1,292	100.0
Ottawa Journal								
Favourable	5,694	92.6	4,236	83.9	1,066	91.5	692	88.8
Neutral	10	0.1	64	1.2	2	0.2	73	9.4
Unfavourable	324	5.3	699	13.8	91	7.8	14	1.8
Mixed	124	2.0	54	1.1	6	0.5	–	–
	6,152	100.0	5,053	100.0	1,165	100.0	779	100.0

Table II (continued)

Kitchener-Waterloo Record								
Favourable	4,645	79.3	4,107	92.3	1,825	87.9	1,105	83.9
Neutral	122	2.1	31	0.7	9	0.4	102	7.7
Unfavourable	630	10.8	201	4.5	207	10.0	46	3.5
Mixed	457	7.8	113	2.5	36	1.7	64	4.9
	5,854	100.0	4,452	100.0	2,077	100.0	1,317	100.0

London Free Press								
Favourable	5,295	86.6	4,173	90.8	932	78.5	394	74.1
Neutral	160	2.6	161	3.5	99	8.3	35	6.6
Unfavourable	450	7.4	215	4.7	156	13.2	32	6.0
Mixed	207	3.4	44	1.0	–	–	71	13.3
	6,112	100.0	4,593	100.0	1,187	100.0	532	100.0

Hamilton Spectator								
Favourable	4,643	80.1	3,150	90.2	1,330	84.4	254	72.0
Neutral	164	2.8	27	0.8	64	4.1	7	2.0
Unfavourable	727	12.5	207	5.9	182	11.5	39	11.0
Mixed	267	4.6	107	3.1	–	–	53	15.0
	5,801	100.0	3,491	100.0	1,576	100.0	353	100.0

8.6 per cent in the Free Press. The comparable figures for Social Credit were 10.2 per cent in the Citizen and 2.7 per cent in the Spectator.

III. COMPARATIVE PARTY BIAS IN NEWS AND IN EDITORIALS

Table III takes two of the most important forms of election items, the news story and the editorial, and compares the support for the four main parties in each. Only the material included in the first four lines of Table I was analysed here, no attempt being made to prorate the items dealing with two or more parties at once. Whereas in Table II a distinction was made between neutral material and material that was a mixture of favourable and unfavourable comment, these two categories are treated as one here, in Table III.

The first curious point to emerge is the astonishingly similar treatment of the Progressive Conservatives in the news columns of the Telegram and the Ottawa Journal. Both had some 2,500 inches of pro-Conservative news (500 inches more than any other paper). Both had less than 100 inches of anti-Conservative news, (less than

Table III
Comparative Party Bias in News, Editorials

		Telegram Column inches	%	Toronto Daily Star Column inches	%	Globe and Mail Column inches	%
News							
PC	Favourable	2,530	92.6	2,080	68.3	1,881	82.5
	Neutral	104	3.8	272	8.9	269	11.8
	Unfavourable	97	3.6	692	22.8	129	5.7
		2,731	100.0	3,044	100.0	2,279	100.0
Lib.	Favourable	1,468	97.3	2,714	93.5	1,665	89.6
	Neutral	13	0.9	87	3.0	100	5.4
	Unfavourable	27	1.8	101	3.5	93	5.0
		1,508	100.0	2,902	100.0	1,858	100.0
NDP	Favourable	808	94.5	1,214	87.2	611	78.5
	Neutral	19	2.2	91	6.5	90	11.6
	Unfavourable	28	3.3	87	6.3	77	9.9
		855	100.0	1,392	100.0	778	100.0
Socred	Favourable	220	68.9	250	81.2	414	74.9
	Neutral	11	3.5	12	3.9	61	11.0
	Unfavourable	88	27.6	46	14.9	78	14.1
		319	100.0	308	100.0	553	100.0
Editorials							
PC	Favourable	664	95.5	23	2.1	196	47.8
	Neutral	20	3.0	77	6.9	83	20.2
	Unfavourable	11	1.5	1,016	91.0	131	32.0
		695	100.0	1,116	100.0	410	100.0
Lib.	Favourable	9	3.7	233	91.4	–	–
	Neutral	–	–	–		31	10.0
	Unfavourable	242	96.4	22	8.6	280	90.0
		251	100.0	255	100.0	311	100.0
NDP	Favourable	10	25.0	20	32.8	–	–
	Neutral	–	–	21	34.4	8	32.0
	Unfavourable	31	75.0	20	32.8	17	68.0
		41	100.0	61	100.0	25	100.0
Socred	Favourable	–	–	–	–	42	52.5
	Neutral	–	–	–	–	9	11.2
	Unfavourable	15	100.0	–	–	29	36.3
		15	100.0	–	–	80	100.0

Ottawa Citizen Column inches	%	Ottawa Journal Column inches	%	Kitchener-Waterloo Record Column inches	%	London Free Press Column inches	%	Hamilton Spectator Column inches	%
2,037	83.5	2,571	93.4	1,716	71.1	1,359	82.1	1,662	83.2
154	6.3	104	3.8	355	14.7	133	8.0	135	6.7
248	10.2	79	2.8	343	14.2	163	9.9	201	10.1
2,439	100.0	2,754	100.0	2,414	100.0	1,655	100.0	1,998	100.0
1,678	88.4	1,929	91.8	1,695	94.1	1,086	90.9	1,148	90.7
183	9.6	67	3.2	68	3.8	73	6.1	72	5.7
38	2.0	106	5.0	39	2.1	36	3.0	46	3.6
1,899	100.0	2,102	100.0	1,802	100.0	1,195	100.0	1,266	100.0
1,132	95.3	690	94.5	1,064	90.3	98	77.8	608	81.7
-	-	6	0.8	39	3.3	70	10.9	22	3.0
56	4.7	34	4.7	75	6.4	72	11.3	114	15.3
1,188	100.0	730	100.0	1,178	100.0	640	100.0	744	100.0
1,026	100.0	589	87.8	694	78.1	259	67.1	174	75.0
-	-	69	10.3	157	17.7	83	21.5	37	15.9
-	-	13	1.9	38	4.2	44	11.4	21	9.1
1,026	100.0	671	100.0	889	100.0	386	100.0	232	100.0
60	14.3	439	98.9	30	18.6	103	47.9	177	40.4
30	7.1	-	-	39	24.2	77	35.8	47	10.7
331	78.6	5	1.1	92	57.2	35	16.3	214	48.9
421	100.0	444	100.0	161	100.0	215	100.0	438	100.0
200	82.6	49	13.4	16	100.0	14	13.0	76	39.6
8	3.4	14	3.8	-	-	4	3.7	17	8.9
34	14.0	303	82.8	-	-	90	83.3	99	51.5
242	100.0	366	100.0	16	100.0	108	100.0	192	100.0
-	-	20	54.1	-	-	8	27.6	-	-
-	-	-	-	6	10.0	-	-	-	-
12	100.0	17	45.9	54	90.0	21	72.4	57	100.0
12	100.0	37	100.0	60	100.0	29	100.0	57	100.0
42	100.0	3	100.0	-	-	31	81.6	-	-
-	-	-	-	9	69.2	-	-	-	-
-	-	-	-	4	30.8	7	18.4	31	100.0
42	100.0	3	100.0	13	100.0	38	100.0	31	100.0

any other paper), in both 3.8 per cent of the Conservative news was neutral (a lower percentage than in any other paper) and in both the ratio of favourable to unfavourable news was considerably higher (26:1 in the Telegram and 33:1 in the Journal) than for the other papers.

Not unexpectedly the greatest amount of anti-Conservative news was in the Toronto Daily Star, but, more surprisingly, the Kitchener-Waterloo Record apparently had more anti-Conservative news space than the Ottawa Citizen.

For the Liberals a point of great interest is the very small amount of anti-Liberal news published. In only three papers did the total exceed fifty inches, compared with an eight-paper average of 240 inches of anti-Conservative news. A surprise of the survey was the discovery that the Journal carried more pro-Liberal news than the Citizen. Furthermore, two other papers, not usually regarded as overwhelmingly pro-Liberal partisans, the Globe and Mail and the K-W Record, had virtually the same amount of pro-Liberal news as the Citizen.

Using total figures for all eight papers it was found that the Progressive Conservatives were allocated 40 per cent of all favourable news space, the Liberals were allocated 34 per cent, the New Democratic party 17 per cent, and Social Credit 9 per cent. Using these averages as a standard it is possible to draw some conclusions about the relative partisanship of the different papers. The Telegram appeared in these terms to be the most partisan. In this paper more than 50 per cent of all favourable news was allocated to the Conservatives, compared with less than 30 per cent for the Liberals. The Star was the most pro-Liberal with 43 per cent of the favourable news being allocated to the Liberals and 33 per cent to the Conservatives. These were the highest figures for the Liberals and the lowest for the Conservatives. Completely unexpected was the fact that in the Citizen the Liberals were allocated less than 29 per cent of the total favourable news, a figure lower even than that in the Telegram. This is in part explained by the very high percentage of favourable news space allocated by the Citizen to the two minor parties. As far as the two larger parties were concerned, the Kitchener-Waterloo Record came closest to impartiality, giving the Conservatives 33 per cent of the favourable news and the Liberals 32.9 per cent.

The two minor parties probably received their poorest news support in the Globe and Mail, for while both the larger parties received a higher than average share of favourable news space, the two small parties received less than average, with the New Democrats faring worst, receiving here a smaller percentage of favourable news than in any other paper. Three papers, the Telegram, the Star, and the Hamilton Spectator, virtually ignored Social Credit in news columns, each paper giving the party less than 5 per cent of the total favourable news space.

In the editorial columns the party biases of the papers were clear and unmistakable. The Telegram declared its unqualified support for the Progressive Conservatives and its equally unqualified opposition to the Liberals, while the Star, in a somewhat larger amount of editorial space, simply reversed the position. Editorially the Globe and Mail was unreservedly opposed to the Liberals, but its support of the Conservatives was, to say the least, mixed, with less than half the editorial space devoted to that party being classi- fied as favourable. The greater condensation of Globe editorial writing is apparent when the totals of column inches devoted to edi- torials in the three metropolitan dailies are compared.

Like its Liberal counterpart in Toronto, the Ottawa Citizen devoted only a small amount of its editorial space to praising the Liberals and concentrated its editorial efforts on attacking the re- cord of the Government. The Journal and, of course, the Tele- gram, defended the Government's record more vigorously than they attacked the opposition. The attitude of the Spectator is peculiar. It devoted more than twice as much space to the Conservatives as to the Liberals, but for each party there was just slightly more unfavourable comment than favourable. The London Free Press, with relatively little editorial material, demonstrated clear pro- Conservative, anti-Liberal leanings. The Record, which had less total editorial space than any other paper devoted only a very small percentage (less than 25) of this space to partisan comment. The stress of this small amount of partisan editorial material was anti-Conservative.

Editorial comment on the two minor parties was, in all papers, insignificant, the Social Credit party being virtually ignored editor- ially.

IV. BREAKDOWN OF TOTAL ELECTION COVERAGE BY POSITION IN THE PAPER

In any study of the press a great deal is always made of the position as a major factor in determining the impact of an item. For the purpose of this study we used a six-fold classification de- fined in the table. The ordering is not one of priority. One of the things which had to be taken into account was the wide variation in what the papers apparently regarded as their most important pages. The main value of Table IV is to serve as a standard when making a more detailed analysis of other material by position. Thus, for example, in the Toronto Daily Star, 18.2 per cent of all election coverage was on Page 1, or was found in stories which originated on that page (continued stories were credited to the page of origin), while 26.6 per cent of items about the Liberal party and only 0.6 per cent of items relating to Social Credit were to be found in this most important position.

It would be quite meaningless to state simply the amount of coverage a party received in a given position without also stating the general practice of the paper. For example, the allocation of 10 per cent of a party's total coverage in, say the Record to Page 1 could indicate a greater degree of partisanship than the allocation of 20 per cent of the same party's total coverage to Page 2 of the Star. Ten per cent in the front page of the Record represents

Table IV
Breakdown of Total Election Coverage by Position in the Paper

	Telegram		Toronto Daily Star		Globe and Mail	
	Column inches	%	Column inches	%	Column inches	%
Position 1 (Page 1)	3,517	16.5	4,473	18.2	2,739	14.8
Position 2 (Front page of any section other than Section 1 – and not also a special election page.)	556	2.6	897	3.7	1,136	6.1
Position 3 (Any one of: Editorial page, other main news page, last page of any section.)	6,452	30.4	6,190	25.0	4,503	24.3
Position 4 (Any page devoted largely to election coverage.)	3,247	15.3	1,840	7.5	5,681	30.6
Position 5 (The front page of any section other than section one, if devoted largely to election coverage.)	281	1.3	5,288	21.6	244	1.3
Position 6 (Any other page)	7,185	33.9	5,896	24.0	4,258	22.9
	21,238	100.0	24,584	100.0	18,561	100.0

nearly three times the average Page 1 treatment, but 20 per cent in the Star is only slightly better than average.

It should be noted that the two papers which gave the smallest amount of total coverage to the election, the London Free Press and the Hamilton Spectator, also made the least use of special pages and scattered the highest proportion of their election material throughout the general news pages of the paper.

V. SPACE GIVEN TO EACH PARTY IN EACH POSITION IN THE PAPER

With Table IV as background, the treatment of the various

Ottawa Citizen Column inches	%	Ottawa Journal Column inches	%	Kitchener-Waterloo Record Column inches	%	London Free Press Column inches	%	Hamilton Spectator Column inches	%
1,182	5.8	1,531	8.5	705	3.7	1,726	11.0	1,477	8.5
213	1.0	901	5.0	1,279	6.6	298	1.9	1,676	9.7
6,807	33.4	2,823	15.8	3,681	19.1	2,631	16.8	4,194	24.2
2,880	14.1	601	3.4	6,122	31.8	2,402	15.3	1,230	7.1
2,623	12.9	5,443	30.4	2,701	14.0	–	–	179	1.0
6,659	32.8	6,618	36.9	4,762	24.8	8,607	54.9	8,539	49.5
20,364	100.0	17,917	100.0	19,250	100.0	15,664	100.0	17,295	100.0

parties is here examined in terms of position in the paper. Any of the positions 1 to 5 can be regarded as more or less "favoured," while position 6 is "unfavoured." A party which received higher than the average percentage in any of the favoured positions (as shown in Table IV) can be regarded as having received preferred treatment by position. A party which received higher than average percentages in position 6 was discriminated against in terms of position. It is in this type of table that the potentiality of analysis by electronic computer becomes fully apparent.

In the Telegram, as might have been expected, the Progressive Conservatives received preferred treatment on page 1. This further strengthened the impact of the ratio between the parties as

Table V

Space Given to Each Party in Each Position of the Paper. (For Position Coding see Table IV)

	Column 1		Column 2		Column 3		Column 4		Column 5		Column 6		Total	
	inches	%	inches	%	inches	%	inches	%	inches	%	inches	%	Column inches	%
Telegram														
PC	1,521	20.6	149	2.0	1,724	24.7	1,193	16.2	88	1.2	2,602	35.3	7,373	100.0
Lib.	638	16.7	91	2.4	855	22.3	688	17.9	47	1.2	1,516	39.5	3,835	100.0
NDP	189	12.5	52	3.4	374	25.3	279	18.5	102	6.7	506	33.6	1,502	100.0
Socred	107	16.9	87	13.7	139	21.9	172	27.1	8	1.3	121	19.1	634	100.0
Other parties & independents	30	28.6	–		14	13.3	26	24.7	5	4.8	30	28.6	105	100.0
Toronto Daily Star														
PC	1,958	23.9	185	2.3	2,675	32.7	389	4.8	1,180	14.3	1,791	22.0	8,178	100.0
Lib.	1,515	26.6	197	3.5	986	17.3	264	4.6	1,358	23.8	1,381	24.2	5,701	100.0
NDP	251	10.5	139	5.8	484	20.2	173	7.2	930	38.8	418	17.5	2,395	100.0
Socred	4	0.6	36	5.2	157	22.9	89	13.0	168	24.5	232	33.8	686	100.0
Other parties & independents	–		–		10	16.1	11	17.7	19	30.7	22	35.5	62	100.0
Globe and Mail														
PC	1,513	24.4	384	6.2	1,063	17.2	1,546	25.0	89	1.4	1,600	25.8	6,195	100.0
Lib.	782	15.5	416	8.3	877	17.4	1,354	26.9	64	1.3	1,543	30.6	5,036	100.0
NDP	101	6.2	107	6.6	310	19.2	794	49.2	46	2.8	259	16.0	1,617	100.0
Socred	81	6.3	–		452	35.0	615	47.4	37	2.9	108	8.4	1,293	100.0
Other parties & independents	–		–		5	5.0	40	39.6	–		56	55.4	101	100.0
Ottawa Citizen														
PC	403	6.4	108	1.7	1,843	29.3	794	12.6	636	10.1	2,497	39.9	6,281	100.0
Lib.	168	3.2	48	0.9	1,299	24.7	954	18.1	600	11.4	2,198	41.7	5,267	100.0
NDP	54	3.2	–		523	31.3	291	17.4	339	20.3	465	27.8	1,672	100.0
Socred	15	1.2	–		339	26.2	196	15.2	537	41.6	205	15.8	1,292	100.0
Other parties & independents	–		–		10	100.0	–		–		–		10	100.0

Table V (continued)

Ottawa Journal														
PC	465	7.6	333	5.4	943	15.3	50	0.8	2,010	32.7	2,351	38.2	6,152	100.0
Lib.	199	3.9	155	3.1	822	16.3	60	1.2	1,516	30.0	2,301	45.5	5,053	100.0
NDP	10	0.9	48	4.1	171	14.7	65	5.5	524	45.0	347	29.8	1,165	100.0
Socred	43	5.5	34	4.4	45	5.8	39	5.0	336	43.1	282	36.2	779	100.0
Other parties & Independents	1	5.9	–		–		–		2	11.8	14	82.3	17	100.0
Kitchener–Waterloo Record														
PC	438	7.5	411	7.0	1,148	19.6	1,486	25.4	631	10.8	1,740	29.7	5,854	100.0
Lib.	112	2.5	328	7.4	484	10.9	1,277	27.6	1,133	25.4	1,168	26.2	4,452	100.0
NDP	46	2.2	53	2.6	329	15.8	888	42.8	230	11.1	531	25.5	2,077	100.0
Socred	41	3.1	–		99	7.5	894	67.9	110	8.4	173	13.1	1,317	100.0
Other parties & Independents	6	3.2	2	1.1	–		26	14.0	17	9.1	135	72.6	186	100.0
London Free Press														
PC	666	10.9	65	1.1	638	10.4	965	15.8	–		3,778	61.8	6,112	100.0
Lib.	284	6.2	103	2.2	849	18.5	845	18.4	–		2,512	54.7	4,593	100.0
NDP	140	11.8	20	1.7	87	7.3	258	21.7	–		682	57.5	1,187	100.0
Socred	14	2.6	2	0.4	95	17.9	191	35.9	–		230	43.2	532	100.0
Other parties & Independents	–		–		–		4	16.0	–		21	84.0	25	100.0
Hamilton Spectator														
PC	920	15.9	499	8.6	1,377	23.7	290	5.0	73	1.3	2,642	45.5	5,801	100.0
Lib.	142	4.1	300	8.6	862	24.7	210	6.0	45	1.3	1,932	55.3	3,491	100.0
NDP	72	4.6	3	0.1	320	20.3	64	4.1	19	1.2	1,098	69.7	1,576	100.0
Socred	2	0.6	27	7.7	101	28.6	10	2.8	11	3.1	202	57.2	353	100.0
Other parties & Independents	5	3.5	–		–		–		–		136	96.5	141	100.0

shown in Table I. In terms of total space the Conservatives had nearly twice as much coverage as the Liberals. In terms of page 1 space they were allocated 2 1/2 times as much. The Liberals and the Social Credit party received a share of page 1 space close to the Telegram's average for the whole election. The New Democrats alone received less than a proportionate share of page 1.

Positions 2 and 5 were not widely used in the Telegram and the figures shown here are not large enough to be meaningful. The only point of interest is that the New Democrats, discriminated against on page 1, received more space, and a higher percentage of their own coverage, in position 5 than any other party. In the other positions all the parties were given remarkably similar treatment. (2)

In the Toronto Daily Star both major parties received higher than average, and surprisingly similar, page 1 treatment. The New Democrats were again at some disadvantage, while Social Credit was virtually ignored as front page news. If the New Democrats did not appear on page 1 as often as they might have liked, they did get a very large share of the front pages of the other sections, nearly half their total coverage being in either position 2 or position 5. In terms of percentage share of their own coverage they received the most preferred treatment on the two pages. The Progressive Conservatives were allocated a disproportionate share of position 3 coverage, much of it in fact being unfavourable editorials and cartoons. A larger than average percentage of Social Credit coverage was scattered in the less important pages.

The importance of position is seen most clearly in the Globe and Mail. Generally this paper, while at all times favouring the Progressive Conservatives, preserved a fairer balance between the two major parties than either of the other Toronto papers. In total space the ratio was 11:9, and in terms of favourable space, very nearly the same, but on page 1 the Progressive Conservatives had a tremendous advantage, receiving in fact more than half of the total page 1 coverage, and very nearly twice as much as the Liberals. The disadvantage of page 1 treatment was carried over to position 6, where the percentage of Liberal material in this unfavoured placing was significantly higher than the Conservative percentage. In all other positions the percentage ratios for the two main parties showed only the slightest variations. The two minor parties also received fairly similar treatment in terms of position, with the exception that the percentage of Social Credit material in position 3 was higher than average. This is to be explained largely

_____

2. A factor in positioning which was not codified in this survey but which might deserve study in the future is the practice of using photographs of shapely females to draw attention to stories about favoured candidates. On May 15th, for instance the Telegram ran stories about two local Conservative candidates around the pictures of members of the Canadettes chorus line. Male coders did not consider that category 6 truly represented this position.

by the appearance, early in the campaign, of a series of articles on the nature of the Social Credit movement.

One usually expects that a paper which normally supports one particular party will reflect that support by giving the favoured party preferred treatment in key positions, especially page 1. In most of the papers surveyed this has been the case, but, for some reason, the Ottawa Citizen proved an exception. For example, 5.8 per cent of all election coverage in the Citizen was on page 1, but 6.4 per cent of the Conservative coverage and only 3.2 per cent of the Liberal coverage was in this favoured position. The second most preferred position would probably be position 5, the front page of another section devoted largely to election news. Here the margin in favour of the Liberals was so slight as to be insignificant and was not, in fact, much greater than the coverage given to the Social Credit party. A greater percentage of the Liberal coverage was scattered on the less important pages of position 6 than was the case with the Progressive Conservatives, although again the difference was not great.

The Ottawa Journal followed much more closely the normal newspaper pattern. As might have been expected, the Conservatives received relatively more favourable treatment on the key positions 1, 5, and 2 while a disproportionate percentage of Liberal coverage was scattered throughout position 6. The minor parties in both capital city papers received most of their coverage in special election pages and were virtually ignored as front page news.

The Kitchener-Waterloo Record resembled the Globe and Mail in that it used page 1 to strengthen a tendency in total election coverage. Reference to Table I will show that in the Record the ratio of total Conservative to Liberal material was roughly 3:2, but, as Table V shows, on page 1 the ratio increased to nearly 4:1. The Conservatives were allocated three times as much total space as the New Democrats, but ten times as much front page space. The mixed leanings of the Record mentioned briefly in the comments on Table II, are quite clearly demonstrated here. The Conservatives undeniably benefited on page 1, but in position 5 - in the Record probably the second most important position - the Liberals had nearly twice as much space as the government party. The special election pages of position 4 showed remarkable impartiality, with the two larger parties receiving quite similar coverage and the two smaller parties, as a group receiving less than the main parties, between themselves were treated identically.

It is difficult to read any pattern or significance into the figures for the London Free Press. The Conservatives were favoured in positions 1 and 4, but discriminated against in positions 2, 3, and 6. Nor do the percentage figures give any clear indication of the paper's political leanings. The only conclusion which one can reach is that the editors did not make any consistent use of positioning to strengthen or emphasize political favouritisms.

The Hamilton Spectator, on the other hand, made effective use of position to favour the Progressive Conservatives. Of all four

parties the Conservatives alone received better than average coverage on page 1. (The Conservatives had six times as much front
page space as the Liberals and thirteen times as much as the New
Democrats.) The Conservatives were also the only party to be
allocated a less than average percentage share of the unfavoured
position 6. The two smaller parties were especially discriminated
against by position, both being virtually ignored on the front pages
and a disproportionate share of their total space being relegated to
the less important pages.

VI. ANALYSES OF THE NEWSPAPERS

The point of this survey was to make a comparative analysis
of how an election campaign would appear to the readers of different
newspapers. In addition to the material presented so far we analysed the treatment accorded the party leaders, the use of headlines,
cartoons and photographs, the differences displayed by the various
papers in describing the same event, and the advertising carried by
them. (Information about this aspect of our work can be obtained
by writing to the authors.) The following conclusions, paper by
paper, may be worth some consideration.

The _Telegram_ was committed to support the Progressive
Conservative party and at no time during the election was there any
doubt about where its sympathies lay. For the _Telegram_ the
election was basically a struggle between a Conservative government and a Liberal opposition, with two minor parties doing little
more than to confuse the issue. The paper relied heavily upon
its own resources and had an effective team of correspondents
travelling with the party leaders. The pro-Conservative material
in the _Telegram_ included more copy critical of the opposition parties than was to be found in any other paper. This paper devoted
more of its formal editorial space to support the Conservatives than
any other paper, but followed both the _Ottawa Journal_ and _Globe
and Mail_ in its anti-Liberal editorial space. In its editorials it
effectively ignored the two smaller parties.
The election was also one of personalities, with the struggle
seen primarily as one between Mr. Diefenbaker and Mr. Pearson.
It was in the _Telegram_ that the greatest proportion of space given to
each of the two main parties was devoted to the activities of the two
party leaders. In fact, in this paper Mr. Diefenbaker was the key
figure in some 80 per cent of all the space given to the Progressive
Conservatives, a figure which should be compared with an average
of some 60 per cent in the other papers.
The issues which concerned the _Telegram_ illustrates its role
not merely as a reporter, but also as a partisan in the campaign.
Together with the _Ottawa Citizen_ it gave an unusual amount of attention to ridiculing the claims of its rivals. It defended at length the
government's policy on unemployment and devaluation and denied that
the opposition parties were competent to solve any of Canada's
problems. In an attempt to gain the support of new voters of non-

British origin, it stressed the government's stand against communism. In short, the Telegram was a strongly partisan supporter of
Mr. Diefenbaker and the Progressive Conservative party and
stressed the issues raised by the Conservatives, minimizing the
coverage of other themes.

The Toronto Daily Star. Like the Telegram, the Toronto
Star was unashamedly partisan, perhaps in many respects even
more so. It gave its backing to the Liberal party and in terms
of the ratio of favourable to unfavourable treatment of the major
parties, it supported its chosen party more enthusiastically than did
the Telegram in its backing of the Conservatives. The Toronto
Daily Star contained more unfavourable material (a total of more
than 4000 inches) than any other paper, with 90 per cent of it
being anti-Conservative. Some three-quarters of this anti-Conservative copy originated in the Star's editorial offices or with its local
reporters. Because the Star was supporting an opposition party,
a somewhat higher than average percentage of the "favourable"
material in the paper consisted of Liberal attacks on the Conservatives, rather than simply praise of the Liberal program. This is
to be expected, for an opposition party will normally campaign on
the failings of the government, while the government party is more
concerned to defend its own record, but the effect was to create
quite a different impression of the election as seen by the pro-Conservative Telegram and the anti-Conservative Star. This critical
or negative approach was seen most strikingly in the editorials
where the Star gave just over 1,000 column inches of editorial space
to attacking the Progressive Conservatives, a figure which should
be compared with the highest total of anti-Liberal editorial space -
300 inches in the Ottawa Journal, and a high of 600 inches pro-
Conservative space in the Telegram.
        One of the most interesting features of the Star was the great
amount of space it devoted to non-partisan election background
material and information on election machinery and law. The reader of the Star could have become better informed than most people
on the mechanics and traditions of Canadian elections. During the
campaign the Star also published a number of articles, not directly
related to the Canadian election, but nevertheless relevant to some
of the issues involved. There was, for example, an informed and
balanced series of articles on the welfare state in Sweden and other
material of a similar kind.
        To conclude, the Star was unequivocally partisan, although
perhaps more inclined to attack the government than to give positive
support to the favoured Liberals. At the same time it seemed to
recognize an obligation to inform the reader, not only of the issues
involved in this election, of what exactly an election meant in Canadian political life. Running through the general pro-Liberal approach
was a relatively sympathetic treatment of the New Democratic party
and its favoured issue of medical insurance. The reader of the
Star was certainly more aware than the reader of the Telegram
that there were more than two parties involved in the election and

that there were issues other than those raised by the Conservatives.

The Globe and Mail has claimed to be Canada's only truly national newspaper. It is interesting to see how its handling of the 1962 federal elections substantiates this claim. In many respects the Globe played a middle role. Out of the eight papers examined in most detail, it ranked fifth in the total amount of space given to the election, and fourth in the percentage of all the space devoted to election material. It ranked fourth also in the amount of space it gave to the Progressive Conservatives, the Liberals, and the New Democrats, although it came second in the amount of space it allotted to the Social Credit.

The Globe did favour the Conservatives, but the partisanship was less marked than in any other metropolitan newspaper. In the Globe the Liberals fared better than they did in the Telegram, and the Conservatives better than in the Star. The New Democrats, however, were not popular with the Globe and received some of their most unsympathetic treatment here.

Editorially the paper showed that it was more anti-Liberal than pro-Conservative. Almost all the editorials dealing with the Liberals were unfavourable, but of the "Conservative" editorials less than half were favourable and nearly one-third were unfavourable.

As befits a paper of the character to which it aspires, the Globe devoted more space than any other to surveys of the situation in the various provinces and the electoral hopes of the parties in the different areas of Canada. It devoted more space than any two other papers to comments on the election in parts of Canada beyond Ontario, this being one of the most valuable and distinctive features of the Globe's election coverage. From the same policy approach the Globe gave less than average attention to the local scene and gave relatively high stress to the national campaign. At the same time, however, it gave disappointingly little attention to information on election machinery and law and, apart from a series of articles on Social Credit, did less than the other papers in providing the background material which would lead to a better understanding of what the election was about.

The issues raised in the Globe reflected the paper's general image of itself. Federal-provincial relations received more than the usual amount of attention. It was the only metropolitan paper to lay any stress on agricultural policy. The issues were national issues, for the election was not going to be decided solely within Metropolitan Toronto, or even within Ontario.

The Ottawa Citizen was another of our partisan papers supporting the Liberals and at the same time it was the most "election-conscious" paper, giving a very high percentage of total space to election material. As was to be expected from a strongly pro-Liberal paper, the Citizen allocated much less than the average percentage of space to the Progressive Conservatives. At the same time, however, it did not give the Liberals as much coverage as might have been expected. But when it came to the ratio of favourable to unfavourable material, the Liberals had nothing to complain about, and, in this category at least, the Citizen showed itself to be the most partisan of the papers studied. As a newspaper favouring the party in opposition, the Citizen devoted a good deal of energy to attacking the government and much of its pro-Liberal copy could just as easily have been classified as anti-Conservative. This negative approach, natural for opposition parties seeking office, was reflected in the editorials, with somewhat more of them concerned with attacking the Conservatives than with praising the Liberals.

The major issues in the Citizen revolved around the general incompetence of the government, its alleged ridiculous and far-fetched claims, and the high hopes of victories with which the Liberals approached the election. It was more concerned than most papers with generalities, with the general party "image" than with specific policy issues, and so turned its attention largely to questions of political ethics, of honest campaigning, of political administrative competence, and of democratic-undemocratic sympathies.

The reader of the Citizen would see the election as one in which a vigorous, imaginative Liberal party was seeking to save Canada from an incompetent, bungling Conservative administration. The principal task was to convince the people that the Conservatives were no longer fit to govern, rather than to praise the Liberals, for in fact, the Liberals were the only possible alternative to the Conservatives. The minor parties were not seen as serious contenders for office and apart from giving their activities reasonably fair news coverage, they did not merit significant editorial attention.

The Ottawa Journal provided a suitable counter to the Citizen for it was as partisan in its loyalty to the Conservatives as the Citizen was to the Liberals. It was, however, less concerned with the election as a whole and carried significantly less election copy than did the Citizen.

For the Journal it was, even more than with most of the other papers, a two-party contest, with the two major parties being allocated some two-thirds of all the election material in the paper, a figure exceeded only by the London Free Press. At the same time the two smaller parties with just under 11 per cent of all the election space the Journal had a smaller share of the space here of any paper except the Telegram.

The Journal had somewhat conservative ideas of what a newspaper was, for it gave rather more than average portions of its total space to news and something less than average to photographs and articles.

The interests of the Journal were provincial rather than national, that is, when compared with the other capital city paper. The most important single election issue for the Journal was that of unemployment and the paper gave a good deal of time to the defence of the government employment record. It also defended at length the government's action in devaluating the dollar, and in general paid a lot of attention to broad financial and economic questions.

Thus for the Journal the election campaign was a question of defending the Conservative government's record, especially on the whole range of economic issues, including unemployment and devaluation. It was less a struggle between personalities than between parties and policies. The election itself was one which would be set primarily in Ontario.

The Kitchener-Waterloo Record. The papers so far studied all had competitors published in the same city. The Record, however, is the only daily published in Kitchener-Waterloo. The editors obviously felt that this placed upon them a different kind of responsibility. A newspaper which is one of several in a big city has a freedom for partisanship which does not properly belong in the sole paper of a smaller town, which must try to represent the interests of very divergent groups.

The Record was perhaps the most election-conscious paper of our survey, with the highest percentage of its total space for the period of the election devoted to election material. It was also the paper which attempted the closest balance among all four parties with less than average coverage to the two larger parties and better than average to the New Democrats and Social Credit.

Editorially the paper was pro-Liberal and perhaps even slightly more emphatically anti-Conservative, an attitude reflected in a relatively high percentage of anti-Conservative news.

Much of the concern of the Record was with local issues, and especially what the various parties might do for Waterloo North. As befits a paper in a riding with a large rural section, it gave to agricultural policy an importance not found in any of the other papers so far discussed.

The Record was thus seen as a pro-Liberal paper which tried, nevertheless, to preserve a reasonable balance between the parties in its news coverage, especially in regard to the local election campaign which was for the Record the most important part of the election. It was not as impartial as total coverage figures would indicate, for it increased its pro-Liberal sympathies by effective positioning, that is, by giving pro-Liberal items more favoured treatment on page 1. At the same time the reader of the Record could be reasonably well informed of the issues of the election, for it carried a great deal of syndicated news of the campaign in all parts of the country.

The London Free Press. From the point of view of election coverage, the Free Press was a disappointing paper. It carried the least amount of election material for the eight papers studied and it allocated the lowest percentage of its total space for the two months of the campaign to the election.

Editorially it supported the Progressive Conservatives who received some 39 per cent of all the election copy in the paper - the highest figure in the survey. Its approach was positive, that is, it supported the Conservatives but did not concern itself with any major attacks on the rival parties.

It was interesting to note that while the Free Press carried the least amount of total election material, and the least amount of election news, it also carried the greatest amount of political advertising. In fact, the Free Press carried more than twice as much advertising copy as was to be found in any one of the Toronto papers. The paper was also very little concerned to fill in the background information to the election through surveys of party prospects in ridings outside the immediate London area or through general information articles. Of all the papers surveyed it was the one which paid the least attention to the national election campaign as distinct from that which concerned primarily the circulation area of the paper.

Although in terms, both of size (number of pages) and circulation, the Free Press was a reasonably large paper, it was more deeply concerned with the affairs of Southern Ontario than with the rest of Canada. The election was not the most important event of May and June 1962 and to a very large extent it interested the Free Press only in so far as it impinged on the interests of the local area. The reader of the Free Press had fewer opportunities than other readers to become fully aware of the complex and involved issues which made up the 1962 elections.

The Hamilton Spectator, like the Free Press, clearly envisaged itself as a local paper. It, too, paid relatively little attention to the election and was more concerned with happenings in the Hamilton area. Its politics were at first rather hard to assess. There was a good deal more news that was pro-Conservative than there was pro-Liberal, but the ratio of total favourable to total unfavourable material showed Liberal leanings. There were more editorials praising the Conservatives but also more critical of them than was the case with the Liberals.

The political partisanship emerged most clearly from the treatment of the party leaders and through most effective use of positioning which enabled the Conservatives to dominate the front page. The ratio of total space between Conservatives and Liberals was in the order of 3:2. On page 1, however, it was better than 6:1. The two smaller parties, and especially Social Credit, were virtually ignored as front page news.

Again, like the London Free Press, the Spectator combined a much smaller amount of news space with a very much higher than average amount of paid political advertising, although, in contrast to the London paper, the Spectator published a whole series of articles reviewing party prospects in each of the ridings of the Hamilton area and the Niagara Peninsula. These surveys, however, were still largely of local interest and strengthened the impact of the paper as one basically of local interest.

In an area with large numbers of new Canadians and where appeals specifically to the "ethnic" vote achieved a prominence ex-

ceeded only in Toronto, the <u>Spectator</u> did accept the responsibility
of informing readers of the mechanics of an election in a democracy.
It devoted more space than any other paper, including the larger
metropolitan dailies specifically to the theme of information on election
law and machinery. (3)   Because so few papers paid sufficient
attention to this point, the <u>Spectator</u> deserves some special mention
for the service it gave to its readers. To conclude, the <u>Spectator</u>
was a mildly pro-Conservative paper, allied to the needs and issues
of the Hamilton area and not as concerned as might have been with
the election campaign outside this area.

VII. CONCLUSION

The main object of our study has been achieved. We have
shown how each paper has its own picture of an election, and this
picture can vary considerably. We have also shown some of the
ways in which a paper's idea of an election and its issues can be
presented and some of the ways in which a newspaper can show
its partisan leanings. We hope that in demonstrating the fact of
partisanship we will not be charged with condemning it, or with
suggesting that all papers could be non-partisan. It is our opinion
that strictly non-partisan papers would be deadly dull and that too
many of them would hinder the development of a lively democratic
community. We would, however, perhaps like to see papers admit
more readily to partisanship and not try to disguise bias as objec-
tivity.

These final remarks were written at a time when work had
already begun on a similar survey of the press coverage of the
1963 election, a survey which this time will cover the whole of
Canada. The main value of the present survey is, thus, unavoid-
ably seen in its contributions to further study. We present this
report, therefore, in part for the interesting but incomplete information it contains, and in part as a guide to the technique of newspaper analysis which we are confident can be developed to produce
most fruitful and valuable results. (4)

---

3. The <u>Hamilton Spectator</u> carried 1,244 column inches.   The
one other paper that showed similar concern with the theme was the
<u>Kitchener-Waterloo Record,</u> with 1,127 inches. Figures for the
other six papers are as follows: <u>Telegram</u>, 370; <u>Toronto Daily
Star</u>, 617; <u>Globe and Mail</u>, 434; <u>Ottawa Citizen</u>, 731; <u>Ottawa
Journal</u>, 732; <u>London Free Press</u>, 761.

4. Research for this chapter was made possible by short-term
grants from the Canada Council and through the co-operation of the
publishers of twenty-seven Ontario newspapers (including all mentioned in this chapter) who provided complimentary subscriptions for
the two-month period preceding polling day.

THE COUNTER-REVOLUTION IN SASKATCHEWAN

Norman Ward

I

Saskatchewan is a landlocked rectangle whose constituency boundaries, like those of the province itself, are almost wholly manmade rather than natural contours. The province's population has grown slowly in recent years (from 831,728 in 1951 to 925,181 in 1961), but urbanization has been proceeding at an accelerating rate; the rural farm population was 48 per cent of the total in 1951 and 33 per cent in 1961, while the urban proportion in the same period grew from 30 per cent to 43 per cent. Only three of the province's seventeen federal constituencies reflect the increased urbanization in a positive sense: the populations of Saskatoon, Regina City, and Moose Jaw-Lake Centre (which includes some of Regina's suburbia) variously grew from 35 to 70 per cent between the last decennial censuses. Seven other predominantly rural seats showed moderate increases, while seven registered declines in population. Ethnically the population is just over 40 per cent of British origin, with those citizens almost equally divided between rural and urban dwellers. The next largest groups (German, 17 per cent; Ukrainian, 9 per cent; Scandinavian, 7 per cent; French, 6 per cent) show a marked preference for rural life, but in a ratio of less than two to one, and so do practically all the smaller groups with two notable exceptions: the Italian and Jewish people are predominantly urban. Though many of these groups in the rural areas live in clearly defined communities with their own political loyalties, the population is sufficiently scattered, and its voting habits sufficiently inconsistent, that it is uncommon in federal elections now for one or more of the groups to hold anything resembling a balance of power in the election or defeat of a particular candidate.

Before the election of 1958, Conservative fortunes in Saskatchewan could hardly have been considered good. Except for the wartime election of 1917, when a Unionist party, seeking the support of an electorate which was frankly gerrymandered against the Liberals, won all the seats in the province, the characteristic federal result in Saskatchewan was always overwhelmingly non-Conservative. Progressives, Liberals, and CCF-ers all took their turns at winning the province's constituencies, but the Conservatives' best showing before 1958 was eight seats (out of twenty-one) in the party's national victory of 1930. On several occasions the party has been represented by Saskatchewan contingents ranging from no members to two, and its share of the popular vote has dropped as low as 12 per cent, and that as recently as 1953. Nor has it fared much better provincially: the Conservative party has formed a provincial administration only once, in 1929-34, with minority support, and except for one member who was elected as a joint Liberal-Conservative in 1953, has not held a provincial seat since.

The phenomenal rise of the Progressive Conservative party in federal constituencies in Saskatchewan since 1953 must be seen in its proper context if the election of 1962 is to be understood. No statistical series could illustrate the party's change in direction more dramatically than those of the party's share of the popular vote in each electoral district, as in Table I.

Against this story of continuing success must be put the records of the other parties. The Labour Progressive party, which occasionally runs a candidate here and there in Saskatchewan, has never polled more than a few hundred votes and can be dismissed as a negligible factor in Saskatchewan politics. The same cannot be said of Social Credit, which elected two provincial members in 1938 and three in 1956, and which (except for the federal election of 1958, when it had only one candidate) has fielded almost full slates for the past several elections, four of its representatives in 1953 outdrawing the Progressive Conservatives. Social Credit is the one party in Saskatchewan whose relative popularity was much the same in 1962 as in 1953. In 1953 its candidates received from 3 per cent to 15 per cent of the popular vote in their constituencies; almost all of them materially improved their standing in 1957 with the strongest among them winning 33 per cent of the vote in Rosthern; and in 1962 they all dropped back to approximately their position in 1953.

Not so the Liberals and the CCF-NDP (the Co-operative Commonwealth Federation, Saskatchewan section of the New Democratic party) whose significant electoral records are shown in Table II. It will be seen that the Liberal decline in its strongest areas was both quicker and less catastrophic than that of the CCF-NDP; the Liberals, indeed, by increasing their share of the popular vote in thirteen of the seventeen constituencies, all but turned a corner in 1962, while the CCF-NDP continued to decline sharply everywhere but in Regina City, where its leader, T.C. Douglas, was the candidate. Thus the Progressive Conservatives, who made poor third or fourth place showings in 1953, in 1962 ended up with sixteen strong firsts and one threatening second; the Liberals in 1962 won one seat (Assiniboia) by a minute margin and came second in eight others; while the CCF-NDP, which ran either first or second in every seat in 1953, in 1962 dropped back to eight seconds and nine thirds. The election of 1962 thus confirmed that the impressive rise of the Progressive Conservative party in federal politics in Saskatchewan was accompanied by a lesser but almost equally striking decline for the CCF-NDP, with the Liberals occupying their customary position in between the two others.

These massive changes in the voting pattern in Saskatchewan

Table I
Percentage of Popular Vote Polled by Progressive Conservative
Candidates in Saskatchewan Constituencies in Federal Ceneral
Elections, 1953-62

Constituency	1953	1957	1958	1962
Assiniboia	9	9	29	35
Humboldt-Melfort	8	23	49*	52*
Kindersley	5	17	42*	41*
Mackenzie	5	18	53*	49*
Meadow Lake	9	19	53*	52*
Melville	6	13	42*	44*
Moose Jaw-Lake Centre	19	33	59*	52*
Moose Mountain	-	18	46*	42*
Prince Albert	44*	53*	72*	71*
Qu'Appelle	27	34*	59*	58*
Regina City	9	26	54*	50*
Rosetown-Biggar	11	25	48*	52*
Rosthern	9	-	46*	53*
Saskatoon	18	38*	61*	56*
Swift Current-Maple Creek	6	16	45*	41*
The Battlefords	7	20	54*	53*
Yorkton	-	10	44*	44*
*Winning candidates	1	3	16	16
Absolute majorities	0	1	8	10

Table II
Percentage of Popular Vote Polled in Saskatchewan Constituencies
in Federal General Elections since 1953 by Parties
Whose Candidates Won in 1953

Constituency	1953	1957	1958	1962
Liberal seats in 1953				
Meadow Lake	43*	32*	25	28
Melville	50*	40*	28	29
Qu'Appelle	38*	30	24	23
Rosthern	45*	36*	25	22
Swift Current-Maple Creek	43*	37*	27	29
CCF seats in 1953				
Assiniboia	52*	47*	42*	24
Humboldt-Melfort	47*	36*	33	23
Kindersley	42*	38*	33	23
Mackenzie	44*	41*	32	23
Moose Jaw-Lake Centre	51*	34*	27	22
Moose Mountain	47*	34*	28	20
Regina City	45*	35*	27	29
Rosetown Biggar	55*	45*	38	24
Saskatoon	48*	36	25	22
The Battlefords	47*	39*	31	23
Yorkton	52*	43*	34	23
*Winning candidates				

have been accompanied by a substantial increase in the turnout of electors on polling day, as is shown in Table III. Several factors indicate that the growing turnout chiefly benefited the Conservatives, and one result was that whereas before the tide started to turn in that party's favour the margin of victory held by a winner over a runner-up tended to be small (less than 10 percentage points in the popular vote in nine instances in 1953), now the Progressive Conservative margins are much larger: all winning Progressive Conservatives led their nearest rival by at least 10 percentage points in 1962, and eleven of them by more than 20.

Table III
Percentage of Electors Who Voted in Saskatchewan Constituencies in Federal General Elections, 1953–62

	1953	1957	1958	1962
Lowest	65	74	73	81
Median	75	81	82	86
Highest	84	86	88	89

The magnitude of these victories in Saskatchewan renders all but useless more refined analyses of the electoral data, though some interesting observations can be made. Seven of the Saskatchewan seats are virtually all rural, with a negligible number of electors in urban polls, and two are equally solidly urban. The eight which contain an appreciable mixture of both rural and urban polling districts in general follow the same pattern: the winning candidate led in both rural and urban areas. The one clear exception is Moose Mountain, where the Progressive Conservatives have consistently done less well in the urban districts than in the rural, and where in 1962 the Liberals carried the city of Estevan but lost the seat in the rural votes.

In Assiniboia the Liberals from 1957 did better in the urban polls than in the rural, while the CCF-NDP were relatively stronger rurally; but when in 1962 the former successful CCF candidate defected and ran as a Liberal, he took with him the rural-urban bias of his former party and was weaker in the city of Weyburn than in the surrounding country. In three seats (Melville, Moose Mountain, and the Battlefords), the Conservatives were appreciably stronger in the rural than in the urban polls, but the reverse was true in Swift Current-Maple Creek. In the last named constituency the Liberals ran more strongly in the rural than in the urban polls, and the CCF-NDP did the same in Yorkton. In the Battlefords and Yorkton the Liberals showed greater urban than rural strength, and in Melville the CCF-NDP in the urban polls came within one percentage point of overtaking the winning candidate. But in none of these seats (except for Moose Mountain) can it be said that the winning candidate was saved, or the runner-up defeated, because of a sharp distinction in rural-urban voting patterns within his constituency.

Nor is any historical pattern evident; i.e., the rural polls did not swing to the Conservatives ahead of the urban, or vice versa. The Conservatives, in short, beginning with 1957 picked up strength everywhere, and the election of 1962 showed no serious signs that they were beginning to sag badly in either rural or urban districts. The only possible development in 1962 that might be considered indicative of a trend turned on the fact that the seats in which the Conservatives held their own or increased their share of the popular vote were predominantly rural, while the group in which Conservative popularity slipped included all the major urban areas.

Clearer distinctions can be found in some aspects of the ethnic vote, though here too the rise of the Conservative party was so general that it is difficult to isolate the voting habits of certain given minorities, particularly since purely local interests can so often be a significant influence. The constituency with the largest concentration of citizens of Ukrainian descent is probably Yorkton, a seat formerly held by a CCF member who was fluent in English and Ukrainian. Yorkton has followed the Conservative swing, but more slowly, and at a lower level. A Conservative candidate ran a poor third in 1957 (the party had no candidate in 1953), but won in 1958 and 1962 with popular votes of 44 per cent. The CCF-NDP vote in Yorkton has declined in all elections since 1953, and the Liberal has followed the provincial pattern of turning upwards slightly in 1962. The seat is one of the weakest of the Conservative holdings, but the government candidate won handily in 1958 and 1962, despite the fact that his name is Clancy, and his Liberal opponent was one Hluchaniuk. An examination of isolated polls known to be predominantly Ukrainian in other districts has in every instance shown the same result: the electors of Ukrainian descent have in varying degree been swept along with the Conservative tide.

The contrary is true of many Roman Catholic communities of both French and German extraction. The largest French-Canadian centre in Saskatchewan, Gravelbourg (in Swift Current-Maple Creek), has remained staunchly Liberal, giving the party 70 per cent of the vote in 1962, a slight increase over 1958. The village of Prud'homme (in Rosthern) was carried by the Conservatives in 1958, but returned to its customary position in the Liberal column in 1962. On the other hand, a number of other French-speaking areas have voted Conservative, and in many instances the reason advanced is the beneficence of the government in providing some needed public work in the vicinity.

German Catholic communities have also shown continuing support for the Liberals, though in all of those examined the Conservatives have none the less made remarkable gains since 1953. Humboldt (in Humboldt-Melfort-Tisdale) went Conservative by a small margin in 1958, but came back to the Liberals in 1962; Muenster has remained Liberal since 1953, though Liberal support has declined from 58 per cent to 49 per cent; in other predominantly German Catholic areas the Liberals held on in the 1958 election, but lost to the Conservatives in 1962. The CCF-NDP was rarely strong in any of the communities examined, often running behind

Social Credit which, in turn, commonly outpolled the Conservatives in 1953 and 1957. But as noted above, none of these ethnic variations, however interesting, occurred in groups large enough or homogeneous enough to upset the general trend towards the Conservative party in all electoral districts. The armed forces vote, it should be added, was overwhelmingly Liberal in every constituency except Prince Albert; the Indian vote was even more solidly Conservative.

    The one seat which perhaps best epitomizes the rise of the Progressive Conservatives is Saskatoon. Saskatoon is neatly bisected by the South Saskatchewan River into a west side and an east side, the former of which (widely regarded as "the other side of the tracks" in the city's general opinion) was invariably the chief factor in delivering the constituency to the CCF from 1945 to 1953 inclusive. The city's population of approximately 100,000 is slightly less than half of British origin, and roughly 15 per cent of German extraction, 10 per cent of Ukrainian, 6 per cent of Scandinavian, and 5 per cent each of French and Netherlands, with an additional dozen or more groups having significant representation. In 1957 the Progressive Conservative candidate carried the seat by a large plurality over his CCF opponent on the east side of the river; on the west side the CCF kept a substantial plurality. In 1958 the Progressive Conservative captured 63 per cent of the votes on each side of the river, carrying all but two of the constituency's 152 polls. In 1962 the Progressive Conservative carried every poll in the constituency, but his share of the popular vote dropped to 56 per cent on the west side, and to 57 per cent on the east. The Liberal candidate, who ran third with 19 per cent of the vote, obtained 56 per cent of the armed services vote.

II

    The chief question to be asked about the election of 1962 in Saskatchewan is obvious: why, when Conservative strength was melting away almost everywhere else in Canada, did the only area in North America governed by a socialist party go more strongly Conservative than ever? The answer is to be found in the exploitation of facts and issues that were unique to Saskatchewan.

    First among these is the curious paradox that makes the Progressive Conservative party so immensely strong in the federal constituencies, but so weak as to be almost non-existent in the provincial. The Liberals and the CCF-NDP have strong provincial organizations, and between them a monopoly of seats in the legislative assembly. Provincially they fight only each other; federally they fight each other also, but share a stronger common enemy whose role as the "third" party in 1962 permitted it to benefit from the antagonism of the other two. While the provincial organizations of both Liberals and CCF-NDP threw themselves into the federal election in 1962, they were at a considerable tactical disadvantage in opposing, without proven federal leadership of their own, a powerful federal organization dominated by powerful federal leaders. None of the issues that developed during the campaign in Saskatchewan could be exploited in such a way as to overcome the Conservatives' initial advantage.   The two fundamental issues on which the election in Saskatchewan turned, indeed, both played into the Conservatives' hands.

Government policy, and nature, worked together to strengthen in a predominantly agricultural community the position of a government whose sales of wheat, especially to China, had already ingratiated it with thousands of electors.   Early in March of 1962 the United Nations conference on wheat, in which Canada was an active participant, cheered the prairie voter by agreeing on a new basic price which was 12.5 cents above the previous one.   Later in the same month the Canadian government announced a record-breaking final payment on the 1960 crop which put approximately eighty million dollars into the hands of Saskatchewan farmers. (1) The Minister of Agriculture followed this up with a request to farmers to grow more grain in 1962, to permit the government to sell it in "hungry markets."   Early in May the devaluation of the Canadian dollar, though loudly decried elsewhere, meant another six cents per bushel increase in the price of wheat. (2)   The Prime Minister later in the month announced that another type of income for farmers, the acreage payment, would from then on be made each year instead of on an "ad hoc" basis. (3)   A general rain soaked most of the province at the end of the month, and a week before the election Saskatchewan newspapers were reporting that crop prospects for 1962 were bright.   The government's own prospects looked so healthy, indeed, that many observers believed that it needed no issues other than agricultural ones - a belief apparently shared by the Conservative candidates, few of whom, judging from the provincial press, were guilty of overwork in their campaigning.

But there was another major issue: the CCF-NDP's provincial medical care plan.   The provincial government had won an election on the medicare issue in 1960, but opposition to the scheme as a whole, and to particular aspects of it, had been growing throughout 1961 and into the spring of 1962, when negotiations between the provincial government and the College of Physicians and Surgeons finally broke down.   By a fortuitous circumstance, and primarily for administrative reasons, the original starting date for the plan was set back from April 1 to July 1; the announcement was made public before that of the federal election date.   The intensity of feeling between various factions over medicare thus continued to grow throughout the entire federal campaign, and medical and federal politics became inextricably involved.   In so far as anybody can be said to have gained anything from the extraordinary confusion that developed, the leading beneficiary was the federal Progressive Conservative party; not in the direct sense that it can be shown to have received many votes because of medicare, but in

---

1. Saskatoon Star-Phoenix, April 4, 1962.   The payment was 31.843 cents per bushel.
2. Ibid., May 3, 1962.
3. Prince Albert Herald, May 23, 1962.

the indirect sense that it was able to remain free of practically all the critical aspects of medicare that involved both the Liberals and the CCF-NDP.

The Progressive Conservative party, as has been suggested, hardly needed help; but where its agricultural policies made their chief appeal in the rural seats, the medicare controversy took up the slack in the towns, reaching its peak in Regina. Even without issues the Progressive Conservative party had two strong federal leaders in the Prime Minister and the Minister of Agriculture, both of them former provincial party leaders who had overcome what seemed like insuperable odds to make their mark in Dominion politics. Mr. Diefenbaker's constituency, Prince Albert, is the key northern seat in the province; Mr. Hamilton's, Qu'Appelle, is a solidly rural seat in the south. Both these men enjoyed in 1962 great personal popularity in Saskatchewan, and their capacity to attract support remains a dominant element in their party's fortunes. (4) By comparison, the other parties were relatively poorly served. Mr. Douglas had been an enormously popular leader, but his departure to the federal scene was undoubtedly regarded by some as a form of defection, and he was inescapably identified with the troublesome medical care plan which he left behind him. He was widely accused of having tried to use medicare as a personal springboard into the federal arena. The only prominent Liberal figure, Hazen Argue, actually was guilty of defection, having been a CCF-NDP member until early in 1962; by June he had neither won the whole-hearted acceptance of his new Liberal colleagues, nor outlived the unfavourable publicity that so often attends the switching of parties. The Social Credit party, though its provincial head was a perennial candidate in both local and federal elections, had no leaders comparable even to Mr. Argue, let alone the giants of the Progressive Conservatives.

The three opposition parties thus all entered the political race in 1962 with varying handicaps not shared by their opponent, a fact which becomes apparent if one looks in more detail at their involvement with the campaign's chief issues. The New Democratic party was making its debut in federal politics, and under peculiarly inauspicious circumstances. Mr. Argue's defection was compounded in May by the resignation of the provincial Minister of Public Works who had, as Minister of Public Health, steered the contentious medical care bill through the assembly. Both Mr. Argue and Mr. Erb had listed prominently among their reasons for leaving the party its connection with unions - a connection which had aroused many misgivings among the party's rural supporters. The misgivings were not allayed by the fact that the Minister of Public Health who took over from Mr. Erb was one of Saskatchewan's most prominent unionists; that the chief provincial ministers concerned in the medicare dispute were all non-farmers; or that large advertisements

---

4. Even in 1963, candidates opposing the Progressive Conservatives found that one line of attack closed to them was that which attempted to cast any reflection on the "Diefenbaker image."

were placed in newspapers by union organizations urging support for the NDP and its medical scheme. Since the party relied increasingly on medicare throughout the campaign, with both its federal and provincial spokesmen paying less and less attention to other issues (though Mr. Douglas did produce a five-point farm program, and from time to time discussed other matters), the several weaknesses of its position in regard to medicare heightened the danger that the party was "putting all its eggs in one basket," and a damaged basket at that. Nevertheless, its advertising and publicity wound up the campaign with a heavy emphasis on the medical plan.

The CCF-NDP at least fought the election in Saskatchewan on a lively local issue. The Liberal party throughout the campaign exhibited a striking ambivalence: while the provincial Liberal organization gave considerable assistance to the federal, many prominent Liberals in the province were active in the anti-government group that became known as the KOD (Keep Our Doctors Committee), and several Liberal candidates were convinced that Liberal supporters were working to secure the election of Progressive Conservatives in order to ensure the defeat of CCF-NDP candidates. At the same time, as a weird obligato to the main themes in Saskatchewan, the publicity employed in the province by the national Liberal organization was clearly prepared to appeal to other parts of Canada, and by virtually ignoring agriculture and medicare had no more relevance to the campaign in Saskatchewan than if it had emanated from Texas or South Carolina. One advertisement used in the province was critical of the devaluation of the dollar which, as noted above, had meant to prairie farmers another increase in the price of wheat.

The Liberals in Saskatchewan did attempt to counter the Conservatives' success among the farmers by offering a still higher price for wheat, but as a promise this could not compete with the hard facts of crop sales arranged by the government. On the medicare issue, however, the Liberal party as a whole was divided several ways. The party as an organization had no connection with the KOD, which as a pressure group was extremely busy pushing petitions, organizing cavalcades to Regina, and generally opposing the CCF-NDP medical plan in every conceivable way; the KOD always insisted it was non-partisan, and in its publicity scrupulously avoided involvement in the federal election campaign. It inevitably attracted the attention and support of others interested in opposing the CCF-NDP, many more of whom appeared to be Liberal than Conservative. Ultimately Liberals included several identifiable groups; those primarily interested in the federal field as such, who presumably voted Liberal; those primarily interested in the provincial field, who thought that a trouncing of the CCF-NDP in the federal campaign would be a good thing on principle, many of whom were believed to have voted Conservative; and those primarily interested in the provincial field who saw in a potential Conservative sweep of the federal seats the danger of contributing to a rejuvenation of the provincial Conservative organization which in turn, by dividing the anti-CCF-NDP forces in the next provincial election, could undermine the Liberals' chance of winning them. The provincial party officially took the last position; but certainly in the major cities there were many Liberals in the other two groups, and in Regina the local association was so anxious to ensure the defeat of Mr. Douglas that it was reluctant to nominate a candidate and had to be persuaded to do so. (5)

With the Conservatives in an initially strong position, fielding a stable of generally inoffensive candidates who had already won at least once, the CCF-NDP caught up in the consequences of its provincial medical plan, and the Liberals divided, the activities of the small and impoverished Social Credit party hardly mattered. Although, like the federal Liberal organization, Social Credit produced a medical plan of its own, the CCF-NDP plan and its critics were too far in the ascendant in Saskatchewan for alternative health schemes to attract much serious attention. The provincial leader, Mr. Kelln, early expressed the opinion that the medical profession was becoming a tool of the Liberal party, and made the point that it was just as wrong for the profession to use a political party to protect it as it was for labour to use the CCF-NDP. (6) The national leader, Mr. Thompson, late in the campaign said that Canadian sales of wheat to Communist China were hurting countries friendly to western powers. (7) Neither of these views was likely to win votes in Saskatchewan, and Social Credit made little headway; in only one seat, Assiniboia, did it have enough support (5 per cent of the popular vote) conceivably to have affected the close result there. The Labour Progressive party ran a single candidate in the province; he received 317 votes.

Far above the sea of troubles in which other parties floundered in Saskatchewan in 1962 rode the Progressive Conservatives, so serene and confident that leading figures among them occasionally expressed concern that the party's candidates were not working hard enough. The party's strength in agricultural matters has already been indicated; its publicity in 1962 in the province shrewdly concentrated on Mr. Diefenbaker and the Diefenbaker party's agricultural policies, and studiously avoided medicare. The party was able to keep remarkably free of that bitter issue, for having no members in the provincial assembly, and no immediate hopes of getting any, it had no need to back any side in the medicare controversy because of its potential effect on future provincial elections. At the national level the government had appointed the Royal Commission on Health in June of 1961, with the Chief Justice of Saskatchewan as its chairman, and this impressively far-sighted move allowed the party a year later to avoid all commitments on health policy pending the receipt of the commission's report.

Even casual references to the medicare dispute by Progressive Conservatives in Saskatchewan are exceedingly hard to find.

5. Letter from Mr. Ross Thatcher, March 20, 1963.
6. Regina Leader-Post, Feb. 26, 1962.
7. Saskatoon Star-Phoenix, June 14, 1962.

In April of 1962 the Saskatchewan Young Progressive Conservatives in convention, after a "stormy one-hour session," voted in favour of delaying implementation of the provincial plan until agreement between the government and the doctors had been reached (8); on the same day the senior provincial association of the party elected a doctor as its president. (9)   (Only one doctor, the Liberal candidate in Qu'Appelle, was nominated by any of the parties in 1962.)   On June 6 the Minister of National Health and Welfare said in a Dominion-wide broadcast that the government sought to provide adequate health services without such disputation as had developed in Saskatchewan. (10)   These references constitute virtually all the overt moves made by the Progressive Conservatives in regard to the hottest issue in the campaign in Saskatchewan.

Between rural satisfaction, and urban confusion over a provincial policy that almost solely involved other parties, the Progressive Conservative position in the province was thus impregnable. It was bolstered yet further by the progress of the South Saskatchewan dam, commonly referred to by Conservative candidates as the Diefenbaker Dam, and of course the vast appeal of Mr. Diefenbaker himself, already referred to.   No other issues were of sufficient interest to be counted as significant.   Nuclear arms, unemployment, governmental indecision, and allied topics were, of course, brought up from time to time by the other parties, but they rarely received a reception which the parties considered encouraging enough to justify concentrating on them.   Charges that governmental policies were vague and confusing, however effective elsewhere, fell on deaf ears in Saskatchewan, where the government's stand on vital matters was perfectly clear.   It was impossible to convince electors that the government was indecisive, when in fact years' accumulations of previously unsold grain were visibly dwindling, thanks to decisions for which the governing party received all the credit.

Issues and personalities apart, the Progressive Conservatives were the beneficiary of one more fortuitous circumstance: the uncommitted voter dismayed or alarmed or disgusted by the intensity of the fracas over medical care could find a haven only in the Diefenbaker party.   To the other main parties the election was clearly a hurdle to be surmounted before they could get on with the medical care dispute: a leading member of the medical profession predicted in mid-May that no action to settle the dispute between the provincial government and the doctors could be expected until after the election (11), and this view was widely accepted.   The provincial Liberal leader, Mr. Thatcher, said late in May that an emergency session of the legislature should be held after the

---

8. Moose Jaw Times-Herald, April 27, 1962.   The day before, the Conservative candidate in Saskatoon reportedly said that medicare would not be an issue in the campaign.

9. Regina Leader-Post, April 27, 1962.

10. Moose Jaw Times Herald, June 6, 1962.

11. Prince Albert Herald, May 18, 1962.

election. (12)   On June 7 the national leader of the CCF-NDP, Mr. Douglas, predicted a solution to the dispute would follow the election. (13)   On the following day the Saskatoon Star-Phoenix suggested editorially that discussion of holding a plebiscite on medicare should be postponed until after the election. (14)   The election itself was freely interpreted as a plebiscite on medicare.

It is difficult to see the election results in that light.   Certainly the CCF-NDP encountered a severe defeat; but in the one constituency where the most concerted attempt to "get" the party's candidate was made, Regina (15), the party's share of the popular vote actually increased slightly over 1958, while both the Liberals' and the Progressive Conservatives' declined.   If the anti-medicare forces of all origins had been sweepingly successful in shifting votes to the Progressive Conservatives, one would have expected the Progressive Conservative vote to increase where the forces were most active; in fact it was in those very areas that it slipped downward.   Similarly one would have expected the Liberal vote to decline, but it increased in most constituencies, dropping slightly, though measurably, only in Regina, Rosthern, and Qu'Appelle (where its lone doctor candidate ran.)   It is impossible, in short, to find in the election results any specific evidence that the medicare dispute either seriously hurt the Liberals or materially helped the Conservatives; it appears to have hurt the CCF-NDP, but that combination had been declining steadily almost everywhere since the election of 1953 anyway.

The surest conclusion, considering the nature of the campaign, the issues and the leaders offered by the parties, and the predominantly rural bias of Saskatchewan constituencies, is that without the medicare dispute the election results would have been substantially the same.   The really surprising element, indeed, is not that the Conservatives won sixteen of the province's seats, but that they failed to carry the seventeenth.

---

12. Regina Leader-Post, May 31, 1962.
13. Moose Jaw Times Herald, June 7, 1962.
14. Saskatoon Star-Phoenix, June 8, 1962.
15. The only daily newspaper in Regina, the Leader-Post, though normally Liberal, appears to have given its blessing to Liberals to vote Progressive Conservative.   In editorials on June 13 and 16, 1962, though they are both rather ambiguous, the journal deplored that "normal political appeals are falling on deaf ears," but pointedly referred to the election as a "matter for electors to decide in terms of their desire to elect or defeat Mr. Douglas."

THE NDP: BRITISH COLUMBIA'S LABOUR PARTY

Walter D. Young

If the 1962 general election proved anything at all, it proved what many had suspected for some time: the New Democratic party is an urban working-class party. (1) It also showed that NDP support in BC is derived from essentially the same areas that favoured its predecessor, and further, that the important people in the party - the successful candidates - tend to be mostly of good CCF stock.

In British Columbia the NDP was the victorious party. It won ten of the province's twenty-two seats and of these ten all but one had been areas of traditional CCF strength. All ten of the elected MP's had been active supporters of the CCF at either, or both, the provincial and federal levels of government and had sought public office before - with varying degrees of success. The chief difference between the New Democratic party and the Co-operative Commonwealth Federation, in British Columbia at any rate, seems to be one of the degree and kind of trade union assistance and co-operation.

The Conservative defeat in BC was by any standard crushing but not surprising. The Conservative victory in the previous election was really an exploratory gesture on the part of the electorate to see if the Diefenbaker of the platform and television screen was the leader sought to infuse new direction into a bewildered and aimless nation. (2) The return to the province's unmistakable leftist proclivities was not unexpected, although most observers did not envisage as decisive a return.

The Conservative party held eighteen of the province's twenty-two seats at dissolution; it lost twelve of these in the elections: four fell to Liberals, two to Social Crediters, and six to New Democrats. Their share of the popular vote in the province fell from 49 to 27.4 per cent. The Liberal popular vote rose from 16 to 27.4 per cent, while the New Democrats added 7 percentage points to the CCF's popular vote in the 1958 election for a total of 31 per cent. In ten

---

1. Working class in the broad sense including wage earners and salary earners whose income is low enough and insecure enough to place them on the outer fringes of those enjoying the benefits of an affluent society.

2. See the discussion of this matter in Beck & Dooley, "Party Images in Canada," Queen's Quarterly, LXVII, no. 5, autumn, 1960.

of the twelve ridings which they lost the Conservatives ran third, behind Liberals and New Democrats in eight of these, Social Credit and Liberal in one and Social Credit and NDP in the other. There can be little doubt about the magnitude of the Conservative defeat.

At first sight the Liberal resurgence seems dramatic and more significant than the slight NDP gains. But at the height of Liberal success in BC in 1949, that party polled no more than 34.5 per cent of the popular vote; nor does ·there seem to be any indication that any of the Liberal seats in the province could be considered "safe" seats while there is little doubt that, on the basis of past performance, at least eight of the NDP seats can be so considered. The New Democrats have a strong base in this province: in none of the ten seats they won did they poll less than 35 per cent of the vote.

It is not surprising that this should be the case, although it is interesting that British Columbia and not Ontario should be the strongest province for the new party. BC returned half the party's members in the Twenty-fifth Parliament and provided 20 per cent of the party's total national vote. Ontario provided 44 per cent of the vote but there are eighty-four constituencies in Ontario to British Columbia's twenty-two; in addition, BC's electorate is a mere one third the size of Ontario's. It is also interesting that this strength should be growing. The electorate in the province has increased by 10 per cent since 1957 while the NDP-CCF vote increased by 61 per cent over the 1957 election. (3) This increase could not be attributed either wholly or in part to any great increase in voter turnout for the difference in turnout between 1957 and 1958 was only 4 percentage points and between 1958 and 1962 only one. The reasons for the sucess of the New Democratic party lie elsewhere.

While it is difficult to single out any one factor as being primarily responsible for the strength of the party in BC, the most obvious is the urban nature of British Columbia and the urban orientation of the New Democratic party – an orientation which, despite general opinion to the contrary, it shares with its immediate predecessor, the CCF. Although it achieved its most dazzling success in Saskatchewan, both provincially and federally, the CCF was led by men with urban-labour backgrounds: J.S. Woodsworth, – a man clearly more the product of labour politics than agrarian protest; M.J. Coldwell, whose socialism is Fabian socialism; David Lewis, Stanley Knowles, F.R. Scott, all from urban centres, all with urban backgrounds and all with an urban orientation or outlook. At the national level, at least, and certainly in BC the CCF was an urban working-class party which paradoxically, at its height in the forties and early fifties, had more appeal for the farmer than the

_____

3. All population figures and election results are from the preliminary reports of the 1961 Census published by the Dominion Bureau of Statistics and the Reports of the Chief Electoral Officer. Percentages are from Howard Scarrow, Canada Votes (New Orleans, 1962) and from my own calculations.

worker who may, at that time, have seen his trade union as a more viable source of succour. As Professor McNaught points out: "The urban socialist leadership and ideology in the background of the CCF is too obvious to deny. The fact is that the movement sprang from urban labour, the Christian social gospel of the Protestant churches and, importantly, from radical urban intellectuals - as well as from the soil of the wheat belt." (4) It was Woodsworth himself who said that the origins of the party could only be understood if one first understood the Winnipeg General Strike. (5)

The socialist or left-wing tradition in BC can be traced back to the turn of the century (6) but for purposes of this paper it is not necessary to go beyond the 1945 federal general election. Since that election the CCF-NDP never had less than 20 per cent of the popular vote, its median popular support standing at 27.5 per cent for the six general elections in the period 1945-62. The comparable Liberal party median support is 26 per cent and the Progressive Conservative's 28.2 per cent. The most significant figures in this respect, however, are those which indicate the range or fluctuation in support. Liberal support expressed as a percentage of the popular vote has fluctuated between 34.5 and 16.2 per cent showing a range of 18. Conservative support has fluctuated between 14 and 49 per cent, a range of 35; while the CCF-NDP support has a range of 8, between 22.5 and 30.9 per cent. While this simply illustrates what is almost a truism - that support for an ideologically oriented party involves a degree of commitment that precludes shifting allegiance freely - it does demonstrate that in British Columbia, since 1945 at least, there is a solid core of left-wing support. It is a core clearly more solid than any that ever existed in Saskatchewan. Provincially in BC the CCF-NDP has never had less than 28 per cent of the vote with a range of 9 and a median support over the nine elections from 1933 to 1960 of 32.2 per cent of the popular vote. The party has formed the official opposition in the province since 1952.

The strength of the NDP support in the 1962 election was clear and unmistakable. With the exception of Vancouver Burrard where the provincial president, Tom Berger, won by 94 votes, the New Democratic margin of victory was more than adequate. At its lowest in Kootenay East it was 2,088 and at its highest in New Westminster it was 9,902. The average NDP margin of victory was slightly more than 7,000 votes. The party's candidates also ran second in four ridings and in each case by margins of less than 1,500 votes.

In addition to the reasons already given, this consistent support

---

4. K.W. McNaught "C.C.F. Town and Country," Queen's Quarterly, LXI, no. 2, summer, 1954, p. 212.

5. Correspondence (unclassified) CCF Collection, Dominion Archives. See also the transcript of an interview with Fred White, in possession of Professor Paul Fox, University of Toronto.

6. See, for example, D.G. Steeves The Compassionate Rebel (Vancouver, 1960), chapters II and III, passim.

for the NDP is the result of the fact that British Columbia is an urban-industrial province the economy of which is particularly sensitive to changing market conditions since it is based on primary production and is very dependent on export trade. It is perhaps best described as a frontier economy and consequently the clear class differentiation which that implies provides the conditions in which left-wing parties flourish. The dependence of the province's major resources upon international market conditions and the concomitant sensitivity of management to costs contributes to the hostility in what are traditionally rancorous labour-management relations. In addition the province's main industries - fishing, logging, mining, and the related industries of packing, pulp, paper, millwork, and smelting - are all highly unionized. It is generally agreed that British Columbia is the most highly unionized province in Canada with approximately one half the labour force in unions. (7)   The high wages paid in these basic industries squeeze the secondary industries in the Vancouver area and consequently exacerbate labour-management relations there. Thus the provincial economy is one which lends both cause and solidarity to the left-wing party with either labour sympathy or labour support.

It is also necessary to mention the labour legislation of the Social Credit provincial government which, in the view of organized labour, indicates that the Social Credit administration is making common cause with management. This has tended to solidify the labour movement and add considerable weight to the arguments in the unions for more vigorous political action.

The labour situation in the province is further complicated by the existence of small but powerful and vocal communist minorities in several of the larger unions - in two of them the communists are actually in positions of leadership. The presence of these groups compels the non-communist leaders to make a virtue of a sometimes excessive militance in order to maintain their positions. This contributes to the strife and increases both union solidarity and the class consciousness of the rank-and-file unionist and non-union working man. In addition, the spokesmen for management have on occasion displayed even less tact and diplomacy in these matters than Jay Gould or any of the "Robber Barons". In BC it is Big Labour versus Big Business.

The BC Federation of Labour had traditionally lent its support to the CCF and unions in the Federation frequently contributed both funds and personnel to party campaigns. In short, organized labour and the CCF had made common cause long before the genesis of the New Democratic party. The formation of the new party in BC simply made the relationship formal and explicit and, it was thought, would provide for regular monthly contributions from the members of affiliated locals and unions. Unlike Ontario where three distinct groups merged to form the new party - the CCF, the On-

---

7. Canada, Department of Labour, Labour Organization in Canada, (Ottawa, 1960) and British Columbia, Labour Department, Annual Report (Victoria, 1961).

tario Federation of Labour, and the numerically smaller New Party clubs – the NDP in British Columbia was exclusively the creature of the BCFL and the CCF. The element of "Liberally-minded" middle-class people present in Ontario was largely absent in BC where the New Democratic party became the official party of organized labour.

It would be natural to expect the two elements in the party to work in close co-operation, the labour movement placing at the disposal of the party its own network of communications for the dissemination of party election propaganda. This did indeed occur in the 1962 election, but the resulting campaign structure was of a special sort as a direct result of legislation passed by the provincial government, ostensibly to protect the rights of union members who did not wish to support the New Democrats but in fact, and quite obviously, to cut off the official opposition party from its chief supply of funds.

The statute, passed in 1961 and known generally as "Bill 42," prevents trade unions from using membership dues, however collected, to support a political party. It provides employers with the right to refuse to check off union dues in the absence of a statutory declaration from the union to the effect that moneys collected or any part of them are not being and will not be used to support a political party. (8) This effectively denied the party its major source of income both for normal operations and electioneering.

There was no question about the effect this legislation had on the conduct of the campaign. The New Democrats were limited by a shortage of funds. There was thus no compensating advantage to offset a probable loss of middle-class support resulting from the close connection between organized labour and the party. And in a province where labour-management antipathy is intense, the middle-class anti-labour bias is also pronounced. Nor indeed had the development of the new party proceeded far enough to result in any significant increase in trade union rank and file participation in the operation of the campaign. Consequently help from the unions was to some extent overcome by an effective but necessarily "ad hoc" series of arrangements between the party, the BC Federation of Labour, and the various unions. But party officials all agreed that these arrangements were not effective enough to offset the damage done by Bill 42 and by the negative image of trade unions amongst the middle classes.

---

8. British Columbia, Statutes, an Act to Amend the Labour Relations Act, 9-10 Eliz. II (1961) c. 31 s. 5: "No trade-union and no person acting on behalf of a trade-union shall directly or indirectly contribute to or expend on behalf of any political party or to or on behalf of any candidates for political office any money deducted from an employees' wages under subsection (1) or a collective agreement, or paid as a condition of membership in the trade union." And clause (d) which provides for a statutory declaration to the employer that the union is complying with this provision, in the absence of which the employer may cease to "check-off" union dues.

The campaign organization was accordingly based on the twin foundations of the BC Federation of Labour and the Provincial New Democratic party. Officials of the Federation and officers of several of the key unions met daily with party officers during the latter stages of the campaign to assess progress and tactics. The main burden of the campaign in the urban areas was carried by the Lower Mainland Campaign Committee which consisted of an NDP MLA, the assistant secretary of the BCFL, and an official of the International Woodworkers of America. The staff of the committee was joint NDP-BCFL. The over-all supervision of the campaign in the province and the link with the party's national headquarters was the responsibility of a provincial campaign committee which was under the direction of Mrs. Jessie Mendels, party secretary, and three party officers, including the provincial president, Tom Berger.

The Lower Mainland Campaign Committee was responsible for eleven of the provinces' twenty-two ridings and confined itself primarily to providing television and radio coverage for the area, and the co-ordination and supervision of the constituency campaigns generally. It was, in addition, to act as a general advisory body. In this capacity a number of its members visited several of the out-of-town ridings, but a shortage of funds prevented either the Lower Mainland Campaign Committee or the provincial campaign committee from travelling extensively in the province. In Vancouver the activities of the lower mainland committee consisted primarily of collecting funds from the eleven ridings to buy television time, and the production and advertising of the programs. On occasion large meetings were organized where more than one riding was involved but little emphasis was placed on this aspect of campaigning. An important function of the committee was, of course, to act as a channel of communication to and from the unions and the constituency organizations. Services the unions could provide were made available in several instances through this committee.

The provincial committee had relatively less to do since the interior ridings ran their own campaigns. Frank Howard in Skeena and H.W. Herridge in Kootenay West, for example, were neither given nor did they seek any advice or assistance. The assistance offered the up-country ridings was essentially the supplying of literature provided by the national headquarters, printing for some, speakers for as many as the party could afford to send - which was very few - and the provision for most ridings, lower mainland and interior, of a special issue of the party newspaper, the Democrat, the front page of which was devoted to the candidate concerned. But as seems to be the case with most parties, apart from the tours of the national leader and the rallies connected with such visits, local campaigns are run pretty much without contact of any continuing or formal nature with the party headquarters. Constituency parties make their own plans for posters, meetings, leaflets, and the like.

The participation of the trade unions in the election was, of necessity, oblique and through the Lower Mainland Campaign Com-

mittee or the constituency organization. Such services as the printing of leaflets at cost or providing the use of office machinery and
the seconding of stenographic and other personnel to constituencies
or committee offices was the most common form of assistance. The
legality of such participation is perhaps tenuous in some respects,
but in the heat of an election campaign perfect records are kept by
few candidates and fewer committees. And it seems traditional to
Canada that no one questions twilight procedures of this nature at
election time.

Not all the assistance given was of such a simple and direct
nature. In one instance a union hired a candidate in order that he
would not be prevented by his job – which was shift work – from
campaigning effectively. It was not coincidental that the job he was
given in the union was one which involved frequent travel to the
union locals in the riding and provided considerable opportunity for
contact with the union members who made up a large percentage of
the riding's electorate. Union notice boards were used for posting
party election material and notices of meetings. It was not unusual
for the union official in a logging camp to act as campaign agent for
the candidate. Space was made available to the party and its candidates in the union and local publications. This in itself was an
asset since, for example, the IWA organ, the Western Canadian
Lumberworker, is published twice monthly and has a circulation of
27,500 and the BCFL journal, B.C. Labor, published monthly,
has a circulation of 140,000. This clearly gave the New Democratic candidates an advantage for, amongst other more obvious
reasons, it stressed the union endorsation of the party and the individual candidate. The close co-operation between unions and party
meant in addition that trained organizers were available and active
while the candidate was elsewhere. Hence Frank Howard could
carry his campaign to the northern reaches of his vast constituency,
secure in the knowledge that the USWA officials at the Alcan Smelter in Kitimat were busy on his behalf.

But there were services which the unions could not provide and
which only money could buy. The party could not afford to buy as
much television time as it would have liked nor did it advertise in
the newspapers apart from "last day" advertisements and small notices announcing television programs and the Douglas rallies. In
addition the amount and quality of campaign literature suffered as a
result of the shortage of funds at the provincial and the local constituency level. A lower mainland constituency association paid
approximately $1,000 as its share of the television campaign, money
which the riding association could have used to good effect in local
campaigning. The lack of adequate funds was responsible for pre-
venting campaign directors, leading provincial figures, and sitting
members from touring as extensively as the organizers would have
liked.

In addition to lack of funds – a complaint echoed by all associated with the campaign – the party's provincial secretary felt that
the absence of a good slogan made a difference. Yet it is difficult
to see what difference an increase in the funds available and the

presence of a snappy slogan would have had in the campaign. The Liberal and Conservative parties spent far more on their campaign in the province with much less to show for it. It may be, however, that the NDP would be able to improve it's image in the middle-class voter's mind by a more polished and hence expensive campaign, and it may be that reliance upon shop stewards and union journals tends to confine the party's appeal to union members and the working class generally. All this notwithstanding, it is never-theless true that twice the amount of money in the party coffers would have made little difference in such ridings as Vancouver Quadra, Coast Capilano, or Vancouver Centre. The availability of sufficient money counts not so much during the campaign as between campaigns in keeping the party's name, personalities, and activities before the public in the best possible light. The only party to re-cognize this fact seems to be the Social Credit party, Quebec branch. (9) During the campaign the party's work is done most effectively through careful and assiduous constituency organization.

Assistance provided by the national campaign committee was slight, apart from the tours of the party leader. It consisted in the main of large, rather uninspired and uninspiring posters bearing the leader's photograph but, according to the provincial secretary, they were too late in coming to be of much use. A well-drafted and carefully researched set of speakers' notes was also provided for candidates and managers from the national office, but again these were rather late in coming and the tendency of most candidates to concentrate less and less on public meetings raises questions about the value of such an expensive project. There were three national leaflets, all with space for the addition of the local candidate's picture, one dealing with medicare and two with the national program. These were not, however, provided without charge. In all cases the can-didate had to buy these at cost and pay shipping charges.

The campaign was in BC very much a locally run affair. The party was early enough into the fray. A candidates and managers school was held in February at which the national organizer Stephen Lewis instructed in basic electoral techniques. The New Democrats were first in the field in this respect.

In addition to the national leaflets, many of the province's NDP candidates made use of the special issue of the Democrat referred to above. The standard newspaper format was followed with the front page reserved for copy submitted by the candidate concerned. A typical edition was that of H.A.L. Fanthorpe, NDP nominee in Victoria. The front page carried an "Open Letter to ALL Voters" which outlined the philosophy of the NDP and its policies: "The New Democratic Party has been founded to unite for democratic action, all Canadians who put human rights and human dignity above the pursuit of wealth; and public welfare before corporate power." A biographical sketch of the candidate, a large picture and smaller

---

9. See S. Trenaman and D. McQuail, Television and the Political Image (London, 1961), p. 226; and this essay, infra. p. 192.

one of his family and mention of some local issues completed the page. The following two pages were standard for all candidates and outlined the party platform on nuclear weapons, full employment, medicare, and trade union support, and included a biographical sketch of T.C. Douglas. The last page was devoted entirely to the party platform on consumer protection entitled "A Consumers Bill of Rights."

But the main emphasis, at least where coverage was available, was on television. In the lower mainland area there were thirty-one party broadcasts on television in the period June 1 - June 16, not including the free-time broadcasts over the CBC network. For the same period only thirty minutes of radio time was purchased by the lower mainland committee. Party officials insist that there is great wisdom in this form of campaigning and regretted not being able to do more. But it is interesting to note that several of the candidates felt that newspaper advertising was as important as television; indeed some felt it was more important. (10)

The platform which the party advanced through television and other media during the campaign was, of all the party platforms, the most specific and the most inclusive. A survey of the major newspapers in the province indicates that all aspects of the party's program were put forward with the greatest emphasis placed on those dealing with employment and nuclear arms. The successful candidates in the three ridings of Vancouver East, Vancouver Kingsway, and New Westminster, for example, indicated in replies to a questionnaire that unemployment, medicare, economic planning, and opposition to nuclear weapons were the issues they stressed most. Mrs. Jessie Mendels thought that the party's promise to provide jobs for everyone within a year of taking office may have been rather rash and a cause of lost support.

But apart from her statement and the personal observations of various observers, there is no conclusive evidence on this question. In his major speech of the BC campaign, the party leader, T.C. Douglas, outlined as the party platform: jobs for all within twelve months of an NDP government assuming office, old age pensions of $75 at 65 years of age, retirement allowance, subsidized housing and medicare. (11) The one plank which might have brought the party more support from the middle class had it been given greater prominence was the "consumer's bill of rights." This is an issue of considerable importance with a broad and virtually non-partisan appeal. It was also a plank which no other party included in its platform.

While there may have been some slight disagreement about the importance of the issues or the value of television and newspaper advertising, there was complete agreement about the value of T.C. Douglas as the party leader. All campaign officials agreed that

---

10. This was learned through interviews and questionnaires involving candidates and managers.

11. Reports of the "Douglas Rally," Vancouver Sun and Vancouver Province, July 14, 1962.

Mr. Douglas was the key factor in the party's success in BC. Described frequently as a formidable platform orator and as "the most effective party leader" (12), his Vancouver rally attracted more listeners than either Mr. Pearson's or Mr. Diefenbaker's. Over ten thousand people filled the Vancouver Forum and an adjoining building and with the aid of a public address system, listened on the lawns outside the buildings on the evening of June 14. (13)

Attendance at rallies is not a reliable indicator of the strength of a party's support at the best of times. Party managers will agree that an "overflow crowd" is valuable for publicity purposes and for promoting a band-wagon appeal and it is for these purposes that rallies are carefully planned beforehand. And the Douglas rally was no exception. The organization was in the hands of the BCFL and the Lower Mainland Campaigning Committee, who managed to produce not only the largest and most enthusiastic crowd of the three major rallies, but also the longest and most successful motorcade. There can be little doubt that the collapse of the Prime Minister's rally did him some harm although it has been argued that his handling of the organized hecklers did him credit. It is also clear that the success of the Douglas rally in Vancouver did some good for the cause of the New Democrats in the city since it recaptured the image the party had established for itself at its highly successful founding convention in the summer of 1961 but which it had lost some time between the convention and the election.

It is also true that the attention Mr. Douglas as a personality brought the party and the generally favourable, if not laudatory, attitude of the press towards him plus his ability as an orator helped to increase the party's strength and bring some of the floating votes ashore at the New Democrat's camp. But attendance at the rally was probably more an indication of the organizational ability of the unions than of any spontaneous outburst of support for the NDP. Nor can one discount the fact that the Vancouver Forum is in the east end of the city, closer to the traditional left-wing strongholds than any other area. It would seem clear that Mr. Douglas as a leader and as a personality was a factor, but it is doubtful if he was as significant a factor as his supporters insist, although the party did increase its poll in the metropolitan Vancouver area by close to 200,000 votes. The lack of survey data makes it virtually impossible to assess the impact of the individual leader on an area and party organizers are not the best judges of these matters.

Certainly Mr. Douglas' image as a man of the people did him no harm. His always travelling economy class on regularly

12. John Saywell, "Two Views of the Election: (1) Return to Reality," Canadian Forum, XLII, no. 498, July, 1962, p. 74.

13. The figures are from reports of the rally in the Vancouver Sun and Province and are based on the legal capacity of the two buildings which was strictly enforced as a result of the fiasco at the Conservative rally in the same building two weeks earlier.

scheduled flights, carrying his own luggage with an entourage of at
the most two or three advisers, did establish his identity in this
respect. New Democratic party organizers insist that one weakness in the campaigns of the Liberals and Conservatives was over-
expenditure, a view apparently shared by the Liberal organizer, at
least, who pointed out in his report of July 15, 1962, that aspects
of the campaign were "too fancy." (14) Nor can one entirely discount the explicit nature of the NDP program, at least with respect
to the programs of the Liberal and Conservative party. Even the
Liberal organizer felt that the Liberal campaigning was "too general" and that it should have been more specific and down-to-earth.
How much support the NDP picked up because of its leader's personality, policy on nuclear weapons, economic planning, medicare,
and unemployment, it is difficult, if not impossible, to say; particularly since there is no information on the proclivity of the Canadian
voter - or the BC voter - to vote for parties not candidates, or
leaders not candidates, to say nothing of specific issues in platforms.

Nor is the standard explanation of third-party strength as indicative of social or general protest valid here - or anywhere else
for that matter. A protest vote, after all, need not register funda-
mental disagreement but merely a passing pique. It may involve no
more than a transfer of support from one party to another; e.g.,
an explanation of the 1957 and 1958 Conservative renaissance could
be given on this basis, though it would be somewhat superficial.
Protest, after all, assumes that the protestant will probably return
once the disease is remedied.

A vote for the NDP is more than protest in this sense. The
nature of the party and its image in society involve a degree of
commitment rare among supporters of the Liberal or Conservative
parties. There is no reason to dispute the conclusion of Professor
Meisel that "most N.D.P. votes are not cast as a consequence of
a momentary decision by the voter about the current appeal of a
given party, but as the result of his commitment to a seriously held
view about the nature of society and government." (15) On this
basis Mr. Douglas on the hustings as late as two or three weeks
before the election would not really make that much difference since
it is highly unlikely that the voter is going to swing all the way from
supporting Mr. Diefenbaker to supporting Mr. Douglas in the last
three weeks of the campaign - or, indeed, at any time throughout
the campaign. It would be a mistake to discount what may have been
the chief asset of the NDP in increasing its support: the party's
founding convention in the previous summer. And of course the
greatest impact of the convention must have been on the urban areas
reached by television and the large dailies which gave the event such

_____

14. I was unable to see a copy of this report, but this information was provided by a reliable source with access to this document.

15. John Meisel, "The June 1962 Election: Break-Up of Our
Party System?" Queen's Quarterly, LXIX, no. 3, autumn, 1962,
p. 343.

wide coverage.

It may be a paradox of political campaigns that successful rallies in the final weeks of the campaign do not effect any last minute
conversions although their absence will tend to discourage the marginal and less enthusiastic supporters from voting or working to get
out the vote.   Their chief effect seems to be on the already committed, stimulating them to get out and vote.   In fact it is likely that
the bulk of the campaign does little else than this, although while
studies of voting behaviour in Britain and the United States would
corroborate this, the lack of any similar studies in Canada leaves
this as simply a guess. (16)

A constituency-by-constituency analysis of the New Democratic
party's support is perhaps the best way of illustrating what seems to
be the basic reason for the success of the party in British Columbia
by indicating the urban basis of the party's support and the traditional
strength and relative consistency of this support.   The one riding
which was least typical and which no pundit even suggested as a
possible NDP seat was Vancouver Burrard.   And it provides a
picture of organization and union participation which, if not typical,
is the party ideal.

If ever a seat was out of reach, party officials felt this was it.
It was a riding in which the party had received only 13 per cent of
the vote in 1957 - trailing even the Social Credit candidate, and
only 17 per cent in 1958.   The candidate was, however, a good
one.   Tom Berger was president of the provincial NDP, a young
and successful lawyer - albeit a labour lawyer; this was a happy
combination for a riding which runs east and west across the heart
of the city's older residential area including the traditionally CCF
east end and the middle to upper-middle-class areas of Kerrisdale
and Kitsilano.   While not a "new party" man, having contested
Vancouver Centre for the provincial CCF in 1960, Mr. Berger was
young enough to be associated with the New Democratic party more
than with the old CCF, an important factor in the west end of the
riding. (17)

In April Mr. Berger met with several key people from the

---

16. See, for example, David Butler, The British General
Election of 1951, (London, 1952), B.R. Berelson, P.F. Lazarsfeld, W.M. McPhee, Voting (Chicago, 1954).   Professor Meisel in
his Canadian General Election of 1957 (Toronto, 1962) argues that
on the basis of surveys by the Canadian Institute of Public Opinion
the campaign was of considerable importance in influencing voters'
decisions.   (See p. 190 ff.)   It would appear that the wide swing
toward and again away from the Conservative party between 1953
and 1962 indicates a sizeable floating vote that may be highly susceptible to political campaigns.   How much and by which elements of
the campaign remain as matters for further research.

17. In the opinion of the provincial secretary the existence of the
NDP has helped "cleanse" the old CCF image of its "red tinge."
This, she felt, was important in Vancouver Burrard.   In addition
she felt that the NDP gave the party an aspect of "practicability"
which, apparently, voters felt the CCF lacked.

BCFL, including Pat O'Neal, the secretary, officials of the Vancouver local of the IWA, and the national organizer, Stephen Lewis.
The unions were particularly anxious to see Mr. Berger elected
and they promised close support. It was decided to conduct the
standard CCF campaign: one based on intensive canvassing by able
and trained canvassers who would not merely fill mail boxes with
propaganda but would actively solicit support on the doorstep.

    With trade union assistance it was possible for the Vancouver
Burrard NDP constituency association to undertake what amounted
to a saturation campaign. It opened with the mailing to every address in the riding of a pamphlet introducing the candidate. This
was handled completely by the unions. The pamphlet was elaborate
and effective and included a perforated section to be filled out and
returned, postage paid, by any recipients interested in helping the
party. (18) This was followed by a canvass of roughly 90 per
cent of the riding by "trained" canvassers: individuals familiar enough
with party policy and objectives to proselytize on the door-step.
During this canvass a second leaflet prepared by the constituency
association was distributed which presented further information about
the candidate and introduced his election manifesto. Canvassers
were also supplied with the national program leaflet "New Dimensions" and a medicare folder for distribution to interested voters. A
second canvass covered half the riding and the national leaflet "New
Leadership" was distributed. This leaflet also included a picture of
Mr. Berger and a brief biographical statement. The second canvass was based on the results of the first indicating where further
canvassing would possibly increase party support. The final distribution was the mailing to every voter of a poll-card indicating the
voter's polling station and listing the party telephone number for transportation. With the exception of the addressing of the envelopes,
this was carried out entirely by the trade unions. In addition one
union seconded a member of its office staff to the constituency headquarters for six weeks.

    It was on canvassing that the energy of the party was expended.
Public meetings were kept to a minimum and confined almost entirely
to all-candidate meetings where it was felt that Mr. Berger showed
to good advantage. Some use was made of spot announcements on
the radio stations and advertisements were placed in the small district "newspapers" or weekly advertising sheets in the riding. The
candidate also appeared frequently in the party television broadcasts
arranged by the Lower Mainland Campaign Committee. But the
credit for victory was given by Fred Vulliamy, the campaign manager, to successful canvassing. The party organization in the riding
was well staffed by, as one newspaper put it, " ...a hard core of
professional people ... social workers, teachers, engineers, two
economists, UBC professors, a former British Labour party or-

---

18. A number of NDP candidates across the country used
these on their introductory leaflets with generally disappointing results. In Vancouver Burrard approximately 100 of the slips were
returned and some 75 proved to be useful. Tom Berger's campaign
manager felt that this hardly justified the expense.

ganizer and only one union official. (19)   The value of union assistance lay elsewhere than in the more mundane and straightforward
tasks of doorstep electioneering.

The result was a narrow win by a margin of 94 votes over
the Liberal candidate.   In winning Mr. Berger doubled the previous
CCF poll, getting 31.4 per cent of the votes.   The NDP carried
every poll but one in the eastern half of the riding – an area predominantly working class – and shared most of the polls in the
western half with the Liberals with the exception of those polls in
the obviously wealthier sections which went, almost without exception, Conservative.   There was an unmistakable correlation between
the character of the area and NDP support, in that virtually all
polls in what are clearly working-class districts, districts afflicted
with urban blight, and those bordering on the False Creek industrial
area, were won by the NDP.   Where the houses and apartments
are large and obviously inhabited by those in the upper-income
brackets the Conservative candidate was most successful.   In the
predominantly middle-class districts of Kerrisdale and Kitsilano the
NDP and Liberals shared the polls indicating that the NDP can
make significant inroads in such areas given a personable candidate
with a satisfactory middle-class image such as, apparently, Mr.
Berger had.

It may be significant that Vancouver Burrard is a riding with
a stable population – it increased by only 485 over 1956 – and a
declining electorate – it fell by roughly 6 per cent from 42,155 in
1958 to 39,599 in 1962.   While this may indicate nothing more than
the fact that it is a fully developed urban riding with no further room
for expansion, it could also mean that it is a riding which, in parts
at least, is deteriorating with consequent depopulation; or that it is
one in which social mobility is relatively static in that those improving their status move elsewhere, buying new homes in the suburbs.
The phenomenon of a declining electorate in a constituency which is
in a city that has an over-all increase in population as is the case in
Vancouver, is one that merits further investigation.   If it is true
that the possibility of upward social mobility provides a basis for
support for the traditional elite parties, then a lack of such mobility
or frustrated social ambition would provide a basis for support for
the radical party.   In Vancouver Burrard those polls which included
the larger "high-rise" apartments in which, it would seem, the
young, ambitious and successful tend to live, were among the weakest for the NDP.   On the other hand the party did well in the "re-
spectable" districts where large houses have become rooming houses,
where rents and prices have tended to slip. (20)

What does seem clear is that the NDP is a class party.   This
is not inimical to democracy since society is class-structured and
parties do have different appeal for different classes.   The apolo-
gists for liberal democracy have mistaken social mobility for class-

---

19. Vancouver _Province_, June 16, 1962.

20. See D.V. Smiley, "Canada's Poujadists: A New Look at
Social Credit," _Canadian Forum_, XLII, no. 500, Sept., 1962.

lessness. The urban working-class or lower-middle-class voter will support the traditional parties of the middle class if he is able to see the prospect of realizing his ambition to enjoy the perquisites of middle-class existence; in other words, if there is upward social mobility. The lack of such mobility invariably turns the elector towards those parties which offer other means of realizing the essentially bourgeois ambitions of the working class. If the traditional parties are unable to alleviate the problems of the Canadian who finds himself surrounded by articles he cannot afford but which he has nevertheless bought, and who has a job that is not secure, he will naturally turn to support a party which offers some other way out. (21) In Vancouver Burrard - in fact in all the ridings in British Columbia with a concentration of such people - the NDP was successful. In Quebec essentially the same pressures produced support for the Social Credit party.

In the other ridings in the Vancouver area it would have been remarkable had the New Democrats not won in view of the flight from the Conservative party. In Vancouver East the party has as safe a seat as any party in Canada ever had. Angus MacInnis held the seat for the CCF from 1935 until 1952 when the riding was made into two ridings, Vancouver East and Vancouver Kingsway. Harold Winch of the CCF has held the seat since then with never less than 48 per cent of the vote. In 1962 he carried every poll in the riding. MacInnis contested and won Vancouver Kingsway in the 1953 election. Alex Macdonald held this seat for the CCF in 1957 only to be defeated in 1958 by 204 votes. The seat returned to the earlier pattern in 1962 when Arnold Webster, a high school principal, respected member of the city parks board, and former provincial CCF president, won easily with 48 per cent of the vote and a comfortable margin of 8,200 votes. Both ridings encompass Vancouver's east end, an area predominantly working or lower middle class.

Burnaby Richmond and Burnaby Coquitlam, the latter as safe a seat as Vancouver East, were both part of New Westminster constituency prior to the 1947 and 1952 redistributions. New Westminster, which went solidly NDP in 1962, has never been held by the CCF although that party managed to win at least 24 per cent of the vote in every election since 1945. Burnaby Richmond was first contested in 1949 when the CCF narrowly missed winning through the intervention of an LPP candidate. In the elections of 1953,

---

21. Lipset, Lazarsfeld, Barton, and Linz argue in "The Psychology of Voting: an Analysis of Political Behaviour," in G. Lindzey, ed., Handbook of Social Psychology (Cambridge, Mass., 1954), II, that hope of occupational and social mobility creates "an ambiguity of class position and interest that would lead to cross pressures and withdrawal from political choice" (p. 1134). There seems no evidence for this in BC; in fact the ambiguity of the voter's position in this respect may tend to make him act in defense or desperation, thus his support of either the NDP or the Social Credit party can best be seen as a response to the apparent disregard of his plight by the two "old-line" parties. In a multi-party situation cross pressures are less likely to result in non-voting.

1957 and 1958 its support slipped from 38 per cent of the poll in 1949 to 29 per cent in 1958. In 1963 however, the same candidate who contested the riding for the CCF in the general elections of 1957 and 1958 won the seat for the NDP with 38.5 per cent of the poll. Between 1956 and 1961 the population of the riding increased by 23,800 and the electorate increased between 1958 and 1962 by 8,710. Much of this growth has taken place in the large "dormitory" suburbs which offer low rental housing or low down-payment homes for working-class or lower-middle-class families. And, typically, the figures indicate a relatively larger number of children compared with similar figures for a riding such as Coast Capilano, the residential areas of which are typically high-income. Thus in Burnaby-Richmond the population increase would seem to include some 15,000 children in a total increase of 23,800. In Coast-Capilano where the electorate rose by 9,080 and the population by 22,683 there was an increase in the under-21 population of only 13,603.

Burnaby Coquitlam is another safe seat for the NDP. When first contested in 1953 Erhart Regier won it for the CCF with 37.6 per cent of the vote, a proportion which he increased at each successive election despite the Conservative renaissance. He won the seat in 1962 with 49.9 per cent of the vote only to resign shortly after to make room for the party's defeated leader. In the by-election, held in October, 1962, Mr. Douglas carried the seat with a majority of 8,114, getting just under 50 per cent of the vote. And this despite an apparent breakdown of party organization in the riding.

The parent riding of these two, New Westminster, has been less happy for the CCF-NDP. It does not include the industrial upper reaches of Burrard Inlet - these are within Burnaby Coquitlam - but contains the downtown and residential area of the city of New Westminster and a large portion of the lower Fraser valley between the city and the American border. The population of the riding has increased remarkably since 1956 and the electorate has shown a corresponding rise of 14,508 since the 1957 election - the greatest increase in any of the constituencies in the province. The municipalities surrounding New Westminster have shown the greatest expansion, noticeably Surrey, the largest suburban municipality in BC. The increase in the city of New Westminster itself was only 2,000 out of a total expansion of 38,000.

The NDP candidate in the 1962 election was Barry Mather, a popular humorous columnist for the Vancouver _Sun_. His campaign was further aided by the fact that his wife, Camille Mather, was a well-liked CCF-NDP MLA for the constituency of Delta which is wholly included in the federal riding of New Westminster. Mr. Mather won the seat easily with 39 per cent of the vote and support evenly distributed throughout the riding except, interestingly enough, in the areas which had a strong concentration of older retired people and, according to the candidate, civil servants notably in the White Rock-Crescent Beach area. This is the reverse of the experience of the British Labour party in the 1959 general election where the young people and those with young families voted Conservative while the elderly and retired voted Labour. (22)

This is further illustrated by the relative lack of NDP success in the two adjoining ridings of Victoria and Esquimalt Saanich on Vancouver Island, both of which have large pockets of the elderly, the retired, and civil servants – Victoria being the seat of the provincial government. The census report (23) indicates that the city of Victoria has more people in the "70 plus" age category than in any other and that over 30 per cent of the city's population is over 55 years of age. The same figure for Vancouver city is 23 per cent. In Victoria the NDP polled only 13.8 per cent and in Saanich Esquimalt only 18.6 per cent of the vote. It is interesting to note that slightly under one third of the population of Victoria is Anglican while, for example, less than one sixth of the census respondents in New Westminster declared this faith. (24)   Roughly 75 per cent of the inhabitants of Victoria are of British extraction compared with 60 per cent for New Westminster and Vancouver city. (25)   And while there is no relevant data for any comparison nor any study of ethnicity, age, and voting behaviour in Victoria, the conclusions of Professor Meisel in his study of Kingston are not irrelevant. (26)   The study made by Professor Jewett of the Peterborough and Niagara Falls by-elections indicates, at least in the case of Peterborough, that the NDP draws more strength from the younger than the older voters. (27)   It is possible that the older citizens would naturally tend to identify the NDP with the CCF which they knew during the thirties and forties and which for many was successfully denigrated by the campaigns of B.A. Trestrail and Gladstone Murray.   And, of course, one can equate age with establishment and hence no proclivity for radical voting.

Skeena, held by Frank Howard since 1957, is a "marginal" safe seat for the NDP. The CCF won it from the Liberals in 1945 by a margin of 746 votes but lost it to the same party in 1949 and 1953, each time by a margin of some 1,500 votes. Frank Howard defeated the incumbent Liberal, E.T. Applewhaite in 1957 in a close contest and has held it since. The apparently one-sided outcome of the 1962 election with Mr. Howard winning 59.7 per

22. See D.E. Butler and Richard Rose, The British General Election of 1959, (London, 1960), p. 193 ff. and Mark Abrams and Richard Rose, Must Labour Lose? (London, 1960), p. 58 and passim.

23. Dominion Bureau of Statistics, Census of Canada, 1961; Advance Report, no. AP - 5.

24. Ibid., no. AP - 8.   New Westminster has some 22,000 fewer inhabitants and is the third largest city in the province.

25. Ibid., no. AP - 7.

26. John Meisel, "Religious Affiliation and Electoral Behaviour: A Case Study," Canadian Journal of Economics and Political Science, XXII, no. 2, Nov., 1956, pp. 495-96.

27. Pauline Jewett, "Voting in the 1960 Federal By-Elections at Peterborough and Niagara Falls: Who Voted New Party and Why?" ibid., XXVIII, no. 1, Feb., 1962, p. 39.

cent of the votes resulted from the failure of the Liberal nominee to file his papers properly necessitating his withdrawal from the contest. In 1958 Mr. Howard had 39.8 per cent of the vote. The Liberal vote, or a fair portion of it, does, in Skeena at least, swing to the NDP in the absence of a Liberal candidate.

Union assistance in the form of personnel and access to the rank and file is extremely important in a riding of this size. While visiting the fishing camps and canneries by chartered boat during the campaign Mr. Howard could rely on continuing assistance at such centres as Kitimat, Ocean Falls, or Port Edwards by representatives of the unions in each town. And in cities such as these, which are all company towns, the union is important. What urban middle class there is in the riding is in the city of Prince Rupert, a port with a population of 12,000. Even here, in the Conservative sweep of 1958, Mr. Howard won every poll but nine, although the result was very close, 156 votes separating the CCF and Conservative candidates.

Nanaimo-Cowichan-the Islands returned a CCF member in 1953 and 1957. The riding would have returned a CCF member in 1945 had it not been for the intervention of the LPP whose candidate drew sufficient left-wing support to ensure the election of the Convervative, George Pearkes. Colin Cameron, who had been leader of the provincial CCF, won the seat in 1953 with 39 per cent of the vote, held it in 1957 but lost to the Conservative in 1958 by 705 votes although he had increased his share of the poll to 41 per cent. In 1962 his majority was more than 3000 votes for 42 per cent of the poll. Since the turnout was virtually optimum - 80 per cent of the registered voters - it is likely that this provides a fairly accurate picture of the division of party support in the riding. Mr. Cameron is a docrinaire socialist, in no way typical of the "new" party. His campaign was vigorous and personal, relying more upon public meetings and personal contact than most of the party's campaigns in the province. .There is no certainty that this support would accrue to his successor. With the exception of the 1953 election (when the Liberal candidate was a Mowat, a name of some prestige in the Islands and Cowichan area of the riding) the fight has always been, since 1945, between left and right in the constituency. This is largely the result of the relatively high concentration of retired expatriate gentry in the area around Duncan in the Cowichan valley and on the Gulf Islands where a social stratification based on name and family is still much in evidence.

A riding less difficult to assess is Kootenay West, since 1945 held by Mr. H.W. Herridge. His is unquestionably a personal success dating from his first victory when he contested the seat as an Independent CCF candidate, opposed by an official CCF candidate - who lost his deposit. Since then there has been little doubt in and out of the party that H.W. Herridge has remained Independent CCF. This has assisted the party, particularly in view of the fact that the key union in the riding is the Mine Mill and Smelter Workers local at Trail - a union with little love for the CLC and less for the United Steelworkers, a prominent NDP ally. But Mr. Herridge's support has been shrinking perceptibly since 1940 when he had 54 per cent of the vote to 1962 when he managed to win only 36.7 per cent. The absence of any organization in the riding has led party officials virtually to write it off once Herridge retires.

Comox-Alberni is a riding with its urban population concentrated in the cities of Alberni, Port Alberni, and Courtenay on Vancouver Island. It includes roughly half the province's coast-line and some of the major logging and milling operations. From the NDP point of view it is IWA territory and this union was of great assistance to the successful candidate Thomas Barnett. As an employee of the union he had valuable access to all the locals plus, of course, the assistance of the union in a number of other ways. Mr. Barnett had contested the seat in 1945 but was, like so many of his colleagues, a victim of the LPP intrusion. Between them the CCF and LPP shared 57 per cent of the vote in the constituency. The Liberal incumbent ran as an Independent in 1949 and retained the seat, the CCF candidate, J.H. Cameron, coming second with 40 per cent of the poll. In 1953 Mr. Barnett returned, won the seat, and held it until the Conservative victory in 1958 when he lost by 1,800 votes. His majority in 1962 over the Liberal was 2,800 and his share of the vote 37.5 per cent.

From this hasty analysis of the seats won by the New Democrats it is clear that with the exception of Vancouver Burrard and, possibly Kootenay West, there seems to be evidence of a strong leftist element in the BC electorate. All, except Vancouver Burrard, are constituencies in which the CCF has done well in the past and without exception all were won by candidates who were clearly identified with the old CCF, although here Barry Mather might be an exception since he was not a party member from 1940 to 1961. He was, however, an active supporter of the CCF from 1933-40 and his wife was elected to the provincial Legislature as a CCF MLA in 1960.

There does not seem to be any reason to believe that the party has done that much better than it might have because it was the NDP and not the CCF. At the same time there seems to be little doubt that the image of the NDP was a more happy one in the minds of some than that of the old CCF and this goes some way toward explaining Tom Berger's victory in Vancouver Burrard. The party program was generally in keeping with the new image although in substance it differed little from the CCF program of 1958. The party leader was identified as NDP and not CCF and the literature used was an improvement over the standard CCF material that had often been too tawdry in appearance to be effective. But, again, in the absence of more specific data, it is virtually impossible to sort out the advantages and disadvantages in this area.

There is no conclusive evidence, apart from the success in Vancouver Burrard, that the party has managed to make serious inroads into the ranks of the "other liberally minded persons" appealed to at the founding of the new party. Most critics of the party's development cite the failure to cultivate this area more assiduously as

a serious mistake.   Nevertheless the basic appeal of the party is,
to quote Arnold Webster, the victorious NDP candidate in Vancouver
Kingsway, "along CCF lines."   And Harold Winch campaigned in
Vancouver East as a "CCF-NDP" candidate.

The most important factor, in British Columbia at any rate,
was the close co-operation and assistance of the trade unions.   This
provided the party with a ready-made network of communications
and contact that was unquestionably important in keeping the party
before those voters most likely to support it.   Before the NDP
came into existence there was, it is true, close co-operation between the CCF and organized labour; but the unions and their locals were not directly involved in the party.   The creation of the
New Democratic party in 1961 meant that the trade union movement
had assumed direct responsibility for a political party.   The BC
Federation of Labour is, in a real sense, a wing of the provincial
NDP - or, as some have argued, vice versa.   This involvement
has been heightened by the generally anti-labour attitude of the provincial government and the state of labour-management relations in
the province.   The effort and expense devoted to political education
through the BCFL and the individual unions is unquestionably another
factor in favour of NDP strength.   The federation, its member
unions and their locals had, with the creation of the new party, become directly involved in the affairs of the party and consequently
provided much more assistance than had been the case with the
CCF.   And, what is probably more important, members of the
unions felt an obligation to at least vote for "their" party.

The New Democratic party success was not in the nature of
an upset.   It was in many ways indicative of the solid support the
CCF had managed to build in the province and which the New
Democrats had, through the official entry of unions into politics,
managed to consolidate.   Since it would seem that workers who
belong to unions have a much higher voting turnout than those who
are not organized, (28) it is reasonable to argue that workers who
are members of a union that has endorsed a particular political
party will have a higher turnout and will generally vote for their
union's party   It is only a step from this point to the provision of
support for the party in the shape of poll captains and canvassers.
The unions in BC are highly organized and militant.   The core of
support they provide is vital and significant.   The New Democratic
party in British Columbia is a labour party - and is likely to maintain its strength as long as it remains so.

―――――――
     28. Lipset et al., in Lindzey, ed., Handbook of Social Psy-
chology, II, pp. 1132, 1134.

PART THREE:

NATIONAL STUDIES

THE SOCIAL BASES OF POLITICAL CLEAVAGE IN 1962[*]

Robert R. Alford

The classic studies of voting behaviour have usually examined the way in which workers differ from businessmen, Protestants from Catholics, rural residents from urban ones, young persons from old persons, males from females. Numerous generalizations have been erected, which have seemed to hold for most American elections, and a number of British ones. Workers are more likely to vote for a left-wing party than are businessmen; so are Catholics, urban residents, youth, and men. (1) No detailed surveys of the social bases of Canadian voting behaviour have been done (2), and this paper is an attempt to fill one small hole of the many that exist.

An association between such characteristics of individuals and their party choice implies two conditions: 1) social characteristics of individuals (as determined by a survey) must be connected with some collective experience of a social group or some common experience of individuals of which the social characteristic is an indicator; 2) political parties must have some consistent appeal to certain groups of persons, or to persons with common experiences. Clearly either, both, or none of these factors may be present in a particular political system. These requirements have been more or less taken for granted in political behaviour research in Britain and the United States, because integration of the social structure and the party system is at a high enough level to produce "visible" correlations of the two.

Are these two conditions of an association of social characteristics with voting likely to be found in Canada? A priori, we may answer that this is less likely in Canada than in either Britain or the US, for two reasons corresponding to the above points: 1) Canadian society is more fragmented than either American or British society. There are few "national experiences" to which most social

_____

[*]I am indebted to Miss Byrne Hope Sanders, Director of the Canadian Institute of Public Opinion, for generously allowing access to the CIPO survey analysed here.

1. See S.M. Lipset, _Political Man_ (New York, 1960), chapters 6,7 and 8 for a summary of the evidence of these generalizations.

2. A recently published study of the 1957 Canadian election noted that the "greatest lacuna in the raw material out of which this volume was fashioned ... resulted from the dearth of attitude studies of the electorate based on adequate sample surveys." John Meisel, _The Canadian General Election of 1957_ (Toronto, 1962), p. VIII.

groups have reacted in common. There is not the pressure for assimilation into a national political culture that there is in the United States. Within provinces, among various ethnic groups, such common experiences of persons undoubtedly exist, but may not be visible from gross survey data. 2) The Canadian party system is more fragmented than either American or the British party system. Localism dominates in the selection of candidates and probably in voting, and there is little correspondence of provincial and federal voting patterns. As a result, parties may not have achieved consistent images which could draw to them the support of distinctive social groupings or individuals with common experiences. (3)

Thus, gross survey data giving the relationship between social characteristics of Canadian voters and their party choice may not reveal patterns which actually exist, for example, within ethnic groups in certain provinces. (4)

This paper does not attempt to elaborate a theory of Canadian voting behaviour, but is a descriptive account of the social and demographic bases of support for the four Canadian parties as they were exhibited in the 1962 general election. In one respect this paper may be regarded as a baseline from which changes in future elections may be compared, in another as a presentation of empirical materials on the social bases of party support simply as a way of describing what has never been described before. Speculations on "public opinion" and on the "issues" in elections may afford some insight into the dynamics of Canadian politics, but are no substitute for data upon the actual cleavages dividing the parties.

---

3. See J.M. Beck and D.J. Dooley, "Party Images in Canada," Queen's Quarterly, LXVII, autumn, 1960, pp. 431-88 for a discussion of this point. See also Howard M. Scarrow, "Federal-Provincial Voting Patterns in Canada," Canadian Journal of Economics and Political Science, XXVI, no. 2, May, 1960, pp. 289-98, for a discussion of possible misinterpretations of this pattern of provincial-national voting.

4. The same difficulty may be encountered when computing ecological correlations of social characteristics of an electoral district (income, ethnic composition, etc.) with levels of voting for particular parties. The unit of analysis may be too crude, because of the heterogeneity of Canadian society, and the other reasons given, to discern association which actually exists at a "finer" level. A pioneering attempt to apply statistical methods to Canadian voting, John Meisel and Gilles Paquet, "Some Quantitative Analyses of Canadian Election Results" (paper given at the Canadian Political Science Association Conference on Statistics, June 10-11, 1962), undoubtedly suffered because the unit of analysis had to be, for reasons of the available data, "economic regions," or several constituencies. If a prediction to individual voting behaviour is desired (and this may not always be the most significant goal), smaller political units probably must be used.

The order of presenting the data will be as follows. First, a number of social and demographic characteristics associated (or not associated) with party support will be discussed, for Canada as a whole. Then, within the provinces, other characteristics of voters will be examined in relation to party preferences. Whether, for example, businessmen in Ontario were more Liberal than businessmen in British Columbia, or whether Catholics in Quebec were more likely to vote Social Credit than Catholics in Ontario can be discerned from such a presentation of the data. The limitation on the number of interviews prevents any more detailed treatment such as a simultaneous examination of both province and religion as they affect the relation of other factors to voting. Some speculative discussion of the causes behind these varying patterns will be presented, but it must be emphasized at the outset that detailed studies of the politics of each religious group and each province would be necessary to verify (or disprove) them. Finally a note will be given on Quebec political distinctiveness, and a brief analysis of the level of political interest of party supporters in the various provinces.

SURVEY DATA ON THE ELECTION

The Canadian Institute of Public Opinion survey (#297) which is reanalysed here included 2,129 interviews with Canadian residents plus 571 "weighted" duplications. Of the total of 2,700, 2,604 were eligible to vote. The question was asked of them: "If a Federal election were held today, which Party's candidate do you think you would favour?" The secret ballot method was used. If the respondent did not check one of the ballots after that question, the further question was asked: "Will you please mark the ballot to show the way you are leaning at the present time?" The 2,190 Canadian citizens who answered one of these questions by naming one of Canada's four national parties are the subjects of this analysis of Canadian voting behaviour.

The size of this sample is almost four times that of the normal CIPO one of 690. The interviewing staff of Canadian Facts, Limited, in Toronto, was used, and the interviews were gathered from June 9 to 13, ending only five days before the election on June 18. In order to approximate the actual voting electorate, the tables exclude all those who refused to answer the question on voting (280), those who continued to be undecided after the second question about which way they were "leaning" (83), and those who chose parties other than the four major parties, or who had no preference (the remainder - 51 persons).

This procedure embodies the assumption that these 2,190 persons are a fair sample of the actual electorate on June 18, and that those who were undecided or refused actually split their votes in the same way as those who finally marked their sample ballot for the importunate Gallup interviewer.

Each respondent was also asked his occupation, educational

attainment, age, religion, mother tongue, and whether any member of his family belonged to a trade union. Sex and apparent socio-economic status (home and standard of living) were noted by the interviewer. These social and demographic characteristics as related to patterns of party support form the empirical basis for this paper. A number of other questions were asked concerning political and social attitudes which will not be dealt with here because of space limitations.

The Canadian Institute of Public Opinion uses an "area probability" sample which is not quite a true probability sample of the electorate because the interviewers are given some discretion. In rural areas, respondents are selected on a crude geographical basis by the interviewer. Within urban areas of each province, census tracts are randomly selected after being stratified by income, and a sample of blocks is randomly taken within each tract. Interviewers are sent to these selected blocks, and are allowed to select any house as a starting place.. Once a house is selected, then they go to every second house for subsequent interviews. Within each household, those persons over 21 years of age who are at home at the moment are listed, and respondents are randomly selected from those listed. If no one is at home, or the selected respondent refuses, the interviewer goes to the second house and repeats the procedure until her quota of interviews is filled. The resulting interviews for each province are weighted by age in the office (by simply duplicating the IBM cards for persons in age-groups which are underrepresented).

The sample which results is likely to be biased against people who are not at home, and probably against men, for the same reason, because the CIPO budget does not allow for unlimited "callbacks." The effect of this upon the political figures is difficult to estimate. If people who are not at home as much as others are more likely to be in working-class occupations, and more likely to be men, then, some bias will appear when voting is correlated with class and with sex.

Although the questions from the survey cannot be matched exactly to those asked in the 1961 Canadian Census, the final results of the weighted CIPO sample vary from those of the Census by no more than one or two percentage points for any category of selected variables (age, sex, Roman Catholic proportion, age, mother tongue, rural-urban residence, and province).

The striking accuracy of the voting results of the Gallup Poll in this election is indicated by Table I, which compares the percentage preferring each party in the last pre-election poll with the actual results, for each province except Newfoundland and Prince Edward Island (omitted because of a lack of cases). Even the provincial results are remarkably close, considering the relatively small numbers of persons interviewed, and the liability of a quota sample to error. Only British Columbia is off to any degree, with the NDP getting 11 per cent more votes and Social Credit 12 per cent less in the election than was predicted by the survey one week before.

Before the data are presented and discussed, one qualification

Table I

A Comparison of the Percentage Preferring Each Party in the
Last Gallup Pre-Election Survey with the Actual Percentage Voting
for Each Party, by Province*

Area Poll and Vote	PC	Liberal	NDP	Socred	(100%)
Canada					
Poll	36%	38%	12%	14%	2190
Vote	37	37	14	12	7690
New Brunswick					
Poll	49	41	6	4	69
Vote	47	44	5	4	250
Nova Scotia					
Poll	46	42	12	0	110
Vote	47	42	9	1	421
Quebec					
Poll	25	45	2	28	550
Vote	30	39	4	26	2090
Ontario					
Poll	40	40	16	4	805
Vote	39	42	17	2	2688
Manitoba					
Poll	42	35	14	9	115
Vote	42	31	20	7	389
Saskatchewan					
Poll	46	22	24	8	131
Vote	50	23	22	5	423
Alberta					
Poll	42	19	5	34	149
Vote	43	19	8	29	502
British Columbia					
Poll	22	31	20	27	201
Vote	27	27	31	14	686

*The survey was the Canadian Institute of Public Opinion's
Survey No. 297, which was in the field from June 9 to 13,
1962.   The election was June 18, 1962.   The totals in the
above table for the poll represent actual number of interviews,
for the vote the actual number of voters, in thousands.   Total
election figures exclude the Yukon and Northwest Territories.
Survey figures exclude those preferring minor parties or those
with no preference.   Election figures do not all add to 100 per
cent because of votes for minor parties.   These figures may
differ somewhat from those given in published CIPO reports,
because these data are weighted by age.   The published data,
due to pressure of time, were not so weighted.   Newfoundland and Prince Edward Island are excluded because of a
lack of cases (48 and 12) respectively.   In some subsequent
tables all four "Atlantic" provinces are considered together.
The source of Tables I to IX is the CIPO Survey No. 297.
All the grand totals refer to the 2190 persons answering the
questions on party preference.   Column totals therefore do not
always add to the grand total.

must be inserted.   No attempt is made here to deal with the <u>abso-</u>
<u>lute</u> level of support for a given party.   Generalizations are based
upon <u>differences</u> in the <u>pattern</u> of support given by a number of social and demographic groupings in Canadian society to various parties.   Thus, if the middle class was more likely to vote Conservative than were workers, in both Quebec and Ontario, these are
treated as similar findings, even though the absolute level of vote
for that party may have differed as much as 20 or 30 per cent
from one province to another.   No inferences of the kind: "rich
people voted Conservative" are intended, therefore, because in fact
the more well-to-do in a given province may have voted much more
heavily for the Liberals than they did for the Conservatives.   "Rich
people were more likely to vote Conservative than were poor
people" is the kind of statement that is intended in all cases, even
where the requirements of passable prose have dictated the elimin-
ation of complete statements of the comparison in all instances.
     Because of the impossibility of computing any tests of signifi-
cance for the sample, no statistical tests have been applied to the
data.   Showing confidence intervals or chi-square measures would
give the data a spurious appearance of statistical accuracy.   Giving
the tables in detail allows the reader to draw his own conclusions
about the probable validity of any given statement.
     The possibility always exists that some factor not possible to
examine here (aside from the question of statistical probability)
accounts for a given result.   For example, the great differences
between Catholic and Protestant political behaviour in Canada may
account for the <u>lack</u> of results in some of these tables.   If the effect
of age upon political behaviour, for example, is different for Catholics than for Protestants, then the consequences of age may not be
seen unless the effect of religion is taken into account simultaneously.
The data do not allow such detailed exploration of relationships between a number of factors.
     In general, the findings presented here for one 1962 Canadian
survey must be regarded as hypotheses to be tested by systematic
probability samples of the Canadian electorate, not as definitive results.

SOCIAL CHARACTERISTICS AND CANADIAN VOTING
IN 1962

     As a first step in the presentation of the survey results, we
will show the distribution of party support among various demographic groupings ordinarily considered in the analysis of voting behaviour: social class (here measured by occupation, education, and
general standard of living - the latter as judged by the interviewer),
age, sex, trade union membership, and religion (as well as mother
tongue).   Since this is a secondary analysis of an available survey,
and not an analysis of data collected especially for the present purposes, the categories available are not ideal, and their limitations
must be kept in mind.
     The most striking general conclusion which may be drawn from

Tables I to X is that social class characteristics did not differentiate party supporters consistently, and that regional and religious variations were far more important. (5)   Only between religious groups and provinces did differences of as much as 20 per cent in the support of different parties appear.   The Liberals drew almost identical support in all social class groupings.   The differences that did appear were in the PC and NDP vote.   Age and sex differences were not sharp, nor were rural-urban differences.   The details in those tables will be discussed and then voting patterns within the various provinces.   Finally, within the various provinces the social "profile" of party supporters will be examined.

The tremendous variation of the support given to political parties from province to province is one of the commonplaces of Canadian politics, and a detailed examination of these variations in a number of demographic groupings will be a major focus of this paper.   Table I indicates this great variation.   The Progressive Conservative party in 1962 was strongest in Saskatchewan and Alberta.   The Liberals received more votes than any other party in Quebec and Ontario.   The New Democratic party, nowhere the leading party, drew its greatest support from British Columbia and Saskatchewan.   Social Credit was the second party in Alberta, a strong third in Quebec.   In no province did a given party receive more than 51 per cent of the popular vote.

One striking regularity evident from Tables I to X was the consistency of the vote for the Liberals.   What variation occurred in the vote seemed to see-saw around the constant fulcrum of a 36 to 40 per cent Liberal vote.   Where the Conservatives dropped, the minor parties went up, and vice versa, but seldom did the Liberals budge from their solid vote in every grouping in Canadian society. The two exceptions, of course, were the major cleavages in Canadian politics: the regional and religious factors.   As Tables I and IX show, the Liberal vote was considerably lower among Protestants and in the western provinces than its national average.   The problem of the social sources of these regional and religious variations will be taken up later, in connection with a discussion of Tables XI to XIX.

The lack of any significant class basis for Canadian politics in 1962 is clearly seen in Tables II, III, IV, which show the voting preferences of persons with different occupational, educational, and socio-economic statuses.   There was a slight tendency for skilled and unskilled workers, persons in lower socio-economic positions, and persons with less than a high school education to prefer (more than persons in higher positions) the New Democratic party and the Social Credit party, and less for the Progressive Conservative party, but the picture was by no means consistent.

_____

5. For a comparison of Canada with the United States, Britain, and Australia, which documents the conclusion that social class is far less important for voting behaviour in Canada than in any of the other Anglo-American countries, see R. Alford, Party and Society (Chicago, 1963).

Table II
Party Support by Occupation*
(percentages)

Party	Professional	Owner, manager	Sales	Clerical, other white-collar	Skilled worker	Un-skilled worker	Farming	Total
PC	40	42	47	35	30	30	41	36
Liberal	46	38	34	39	38	39	35	38
NDP	8	8	3	12	18	11	7	12
Socred	6	12	16	14	14	20	16	14
100% =	(109)	(227)	(73)	(190)	(650)	(320)	(329)	(2190)

*Widowed women, retired persons, persons in the military, unemployed persons, and those who refused to answer this question, or who did not give a party preference are excluded. "Occupation" refers to the occupation of the head of the family. The total number of persons giving both their occupation and their party preference was 1,898, but only the grand total of 2,190 is given in this and subsequent tables.

Table III
Party Support by Socio-Economic Status*

Party	A(high)	B	C	D(low)	Total
PC	39%	45%	33%	33%	36%
Liberal	37	37	38	40	38
NDP	8	7	14	10	12
Socred	16	11	15	17	14
100% =	(51)	(516)	(1327)	(296)	(2190)

*Socio-economic status was judged by the interviewer according to the home, and apparent standard of living, on the four-point scale indicated.

Table IV
Party Support by Education*

Party	Public		High		Technical		University		Total
	Some	Grad.	Some	Grad.	Some	Grad.	Some	Grad.	
PC	33%	35%	36%	37%	47%	45%	46%	31%	36%
Liberal	40	41	33	38	37	30	36	57	38
NDP	7	13	15	9	6	22	16	5	12
Socred	20	11	16	16	10	3	2	7	14
100% =	(405)	(454)	(674)	(363)	(30)	(40)	(119)	(94)	(2190)

*Seven persons with no education are excluded.

Table V
Party Support by Trade Union Membership

Party	Union member in the family?		Total
	Yes	No	
PC	26%	40%	36%
Liberal	38	38	38
NDP	22	8	12
Socred	14	14	14
100% =	(578)	(1612)	(2190)

Table VI
Party Support by Age

Party	Age 21-29	30-39	40-49	50 and over	Total
PC	29%	35%	35%	43%	36%
Liberal	40	37	39	36	38
NDP	11	12	15	10	12
Socred	20	16	11	11	14
100% =	(488)	(559)	(463)	(680)	(2190)

Table VII
Party Support by Sex

Party	Sex Male	Female	Total
PC	34%	38%	36%
Liberal	37	38	38
NDP	14	10	12
Socred	15	14	14
100% =	(1100)	(1090)	(2190)

Table VIII
Party Support by Size of Community

Party	Size of Community Farm	Rural non-farm	1- 10,000	10- 30,000	30- 100,000	100,000 and over	Total
PC	43%	42%	38%	39%	33%	31%	36%
Liberal	35	33	33	35	43	42	38
NDP	7	11	9	7	15	14	12
Socred	15	14	20	19	9	13	14
100% =	(341)	(375)	(264)	(138)	(194)	(878)	(2190)

Table IX
Party Support by Religion

| Party | Religion | | | | |
	Protestant	Jewish	Catholic	Other*	Total
PC	47%	19%	24%	27%	36%
Liberal	29	58	49	17	38
NDP	13	23	8	27	12
Socred	11	--	19	29	14
100% =	(1187)	(47)	(915)	(41)	(2190)

*"Other" includes those not answering the question on religion.

Table X
Party Support by "Mother Tongue"*

| Party | "Mother Tongue" | | | |
	English	French	Other	Total
PC	44%	23%	26%	36%
Liberal	35	45	36	38
NDP	13	4	19	12
Socred	8	28	19	14
100% =	(1342)	(572)	(276)	(2190)

*"Mother tongue" means the language the respondent first spoke and still understood.

Some disproportionate voting patterns by different status groups may be singled out for brief comment. The unskilled seemed to be more likely to support Social Credit; the skilled workers the NDP; the professionals the Liberals; and owners, managers, and salesmen the Progressive Conservatives. No consistent pattern appears when either socio-economic status (as judged by the interviewer) or education is examined in relation to party support (Tables III and IV). Social Credit appeared to draw distinctly less support from the better educated than from the less well educated, but this was not true for the New Democratic party. If it were not for the university graduates, who were disproportionately Liberal, a clear relation would appear between education and Conservative voting. It may be noted that farmers' choices were much like those of owners and managers.

Union membership is an aspect of social class status which had a definite relationship to party choice in Canada, as Table V shows. Again, the vote "swung" around a stable Liberal vote among both members and non-members of trade unions, with members distinctly less likely to have voted PC and more likely to have voted NDP than non-members. There was no difference in Social Credit support.

Turning to the two demographic factors of age and sex, as shown in Tables VI and VII, there seemed to be little difference in the political behaviour of men and women in Canada. Younger voters were more likely to vote Social Credit than their elders, and less likely to vote Progressive Conservative.

The rural-urban factor in Canadian politics is portrayed by Table VIII, although clearly the provinces must be examined separately and will be in Table XIX. In general, however, it appears that the Conservatives were strongest in rural areas, the Liberals in larger cities, with no particular strength of the smaller parties in any given size of community. Social Credit seemed slightly stronger in small cities; the New Democratic party in larger cities: whether this was true in all provinces will be seen later.

Unfortunately, no information was available on this survey concerning the ethnic origins of Canadian voters. Respondents were asked their religious preference and their mother tongue, and the association of these two factors with party support is shown in Tables IX and X. Since a high proportion of persons with French as a mother tongue are Catholic, the results may be expected to be very similar. By either indicator, the ethnic-religious factor in Canadian politics remained strong in 1962. Catholics (or persons of French origin) were heavily Liberal and Social Credit; Protestants (or persons of English origin) the opposite. Jews were heavily Liberal.

THE PROVINCIAL EFFECT

The concern now is to see whether the same patterns of political cleavage appeared within the provinces. Were younger voters more likely to vote Social Credit in all provinces (where Social Credit got got any support at all) than older voters? Were trade unionists more drawn to the New Democratic party everywhere? Was tne Conservative party stronger in rural areas in Alberta as well as in Ontario? These and other such questions can be answered tentatively from Tables XI to XIX.

Finding a religious factor in Canadian politics is nothing striking; the Liberal and Social Credit predominance in Catholic Quebec was shown by the election returns. Whether Protestants in Quebec also voted for those parties, and whether Catholics outside of Quebec did is a matter of some interest, which later discussion will take up. Did Catholics in all provinces have a common reaction to political stimuli, thus indicating a more-or-less universal "religious factor" in Canadian politics? Or, did the idiosyncratic character of Social Credit in Alberta as compared to Social Credit in Quebec alter this connection? Table XI gives some preliminary answer to this question.

Religious differences in party support were strong in 1962 in Canada, as Table IX has already shown. The provinces differed considerably in the degree and direction of the religious factor, but it was always present.

For all of Canada, it will be recalled from Table IV, Protestants were considerably more likely to vote Progressive Conservative

Table XI
Party Support by Province and Religion*

Province and Religion	PC	Liberal	NDP	Socred	(100%)
Nova Scotia					
Protestant	53%	46%	1%	–	(77)
Catholic	31	34	35	–	(32)
New Brunswick					
Protestant	72	28	–	–	(32)
Catholic	31	54	6	9	(35)
Quebec					
Protestant	51	46	3	–	(37)
Catholic	24	43	2	31	(493)
Ontario					
Protestant	51	30	14	5	(574)
Catholic	10	70	20	–	(193)
Manitoba					
Protestant	48	25	20	7	(56)
Catholic	35	51	4	10	(49)
Saskatchewan					
Protestant	47	16	28	9	(104)
Catholic	43	43	9	5	(23)
Alberta					
Protestant	45	14	4	37	(106)
Catholic	42	36	3	19	(36)
British Columbia					
Protestant	24	26	22	28	(157)
Catholic	8	54	16	22	(37)
Total	36	38	12	14	(2190)

*The question was: "Now for a question on religion. What is your religious preference – Protestant, Roman Catholic, or Jewish?" The Jews and persons giving other religions or none are excluded here because of too few cases, but are included in the grand total of 2,190.

than Catholics, and vice versa for the Liberals. This was by no means true in all provinces. In the two Atlantic Provinces for which barely enough cases are available, Nova Scotia and New Brunswick, and in Quebec (due in the latter case to the swing to Social Credit) the usual Protestant Conservative connection remained. In both Nova Scotia and New Brunswick, a tendency of Catholics to have voted NDP more than Protestants can be noted. Possibly the NDP fulfilled the same function of a protest third party for Catholics in those provinces that Social Credit did in Quebec. In none of these provinces did Social Credit draw any support from Protestants; it was supported entirely by Catholics. Social Credit thus was not a "regional" phenomenon in the strict sense. Quebeckers did not vote for it across all social lines, but rather according to their religion. In Ontario, the small Social Credit vote came entirely (in the sample) from Protestants. However, even in Ontario, the Catholics were more likely to vote NDP than were Protestants.

Among Protestants, in all provinces except British Columbia, the Progressive Conservative vote was almost the same, ranging only from 54 to 47 per cent. It may be that the social groups likely to be Protestant Conservatives are more definitely stamped with a social class character which is above regional lines in politics, and that they are also more likely to vote in accordance with a national pattern. The income, educational, and occupational composition of the Protestant Conservatives bears this out. This group is the highest-status group of any in Canada, comprising a high proportion of businessmen, professionals and of people largely English in background. It is likely that their vote is far less determined by parochial considerations of religion than by economic and ideological factors, probably having a national rather than a local relevance.

A rough measure of the extent of religious differences in voting from one province to another is gained by subtracting the percentage preferring each party among the Protestants from the percentage preferring the same party among the Catholics, for each province, and then adding without regard to sign. Applying this procedure to Table XI, the rank order of "religious voting" resulting is: Alberta (low), Saskatchewan, British Columbia, Manitoba, Quebec, Nova Scotia, New Brunswick, and Ontario (high). It is worthy of note that the progression is almost from west to east. The religious factor in 1962 decreased in importance as we move away from the older provinces with their history of religious cleavages. Religion was most important in the centre of Canadian Protestantism: Ontario.

Interestingly, very little difference appeared between Protestants and Catholics in Liberal support in Quebec. Whether normally Liberal Catholics went over to Social Credit or not can be answered at least tentatively by examining the sources of the Social Credit vote. Although the table will not be given, the evidence indicates that Social Crediters in Quebec were slightly more likely to come from 1958 Conservative voters than from Liberals. It is possible, of course, that the Catholics who voted Conservative in its victory year of 1958 were former Liberals who, in 1962, instead of swinging back to the Liberals, went Social Credit instead. Such Quebeckers who are disengaged from traditional party allegiances may have distinctive social characteristics and attitudes, but the data available are not adequate to discover them if they exist. (6)

Table XII shows that the effect of religion upon the Liberal vote in particular was marked in every province even with socioeconomic status held constant, except in Quebec, where Social Credit probably drew off much of the Liberal vote.

If social class had any consistent association with party support in Canada, probably a composite picture could be drawn from Tables XIII, XIV, and XV, giving the relationships of party and province to occupation, socio-economic status (as judged by the interviewer), and education, respectively. Unfortunately, the data do not allow the effect of each of these class factors to be examined with the

_____

6. See the papers by Lemieux and Irvine in this volume.

Table XII
Percentage That Catholic Liberal Voting Exceeds Protestant
Liberal Voting, within Different Socio-economic Levels

Province or region	Status-level		
	B	C	D
Maritimes	+15	+14	-12
Quebec	+ 3	0	-*
Ontario	+37	+40	-*
Prairies	+26	+23	+15
British Columbia	-*	+28	-*

*A dash indicates that not enough cases were available, either among Protestants or Catholics, or in a particular status-level, to warrant the computation. Socio-economic status was judged by the interviewer as a four-point scale, three of which are given here. "D" indicates low socio-economic status.

others held constant. It is impossible, therefore, to see whether, for example, Ontario skilled workers with high school education were more likely to vote NDP than skilled workers with only public school education, or whether Quebec businessmen with low incomes were more likely to vote Social Credit than businessmen with high incomes. It is fairly clear from the thoroughly mixed picture which these tables give us that, first, probably the connection between occupation, income, and education was not terribly close; second, that whatever influence these class factors had upon voting patterns, the influence varied sharply from province to province, and, third, that we cannot infer from a finding that manual workers in Ontario were more likely than businessmen to vote Social Credit, that this would also be true for a comparison of poorly educated persons with better educated ones. In this respect, Canada is unlike any other country which has suffered the unkind fate of having pollsters descend upon it; voting patterns cannot easily be predicted from a knowledge of the class status of the voter. This does not mean, of course, that in a given area, say the Peterborough constituency of Ontario, there is not a long-held loyalty of workers to the Liberal party, or businessmen to the Conservatives. Such loyalties are local in character, however, and do not have national relevance.

It may be recalled from Table II that although no sharp differences between the political choices of different occupational groups were found, there was a slight tendency in 1962 for unskilled workers to prefer Social Credit, skilled workers the New Democrats, professionals the Liberals, and managers and salesmen the Conservatives (in each case relative to other groups). The party preferences of occupational groups cannot be examined in such detail for the various provinces, but at least a division into manual workers, persons in non-manual occupations, and farmers is possible. (Table XIII)

Manual workers were clearly more likely to vote NDP in at least six provinces, all (of the eight for which data can be presented)

Table XIII
Party Support by Province and Occupation*

Province and Occupation	PC	Liberal	NDP	Socred	(100%)
Nova Scotia					
Non-manual	48%	43%	9%	–	(21)
Manual	51	30	19	–	(53)
Farming	27	73	–	–	(15)
New Brunswick					
Non-manual	61	33	–	6	(18)
Manual	40	46	8	6	(35)
Farming	–	–	–	–	(10)
Quebec					
Non-manual	25	47	5	23	(162)
Manual	23	41	2	34	(251)
Farming	21	52	1	26	(75)
Ontario					
Non-manual	50	39	9	2	(243)
Manual	29	42	24	5	(371)
Farming	47	39	8	6	(79)
Manitoba					
Non-manual	59	31	3	7	(29)
Manual	21	40	29	10	(48)
Farming	65	23	–	12	(26)
Saskatchewan					
Non-manual	38	24	26	12	(34)
Manual	43	22	22	13	(23)
Farming	55	22	18	5	(55)
Alberta					
Non-manual	32	39	–	29	(28)
Manual	47	13	5	35	(55)
Farming	42	14	5	39	(43)
British Columbia					
Non-manual	20	34	18	28	(50)
Manual	17	34	28	21	(98)
Farming	19	38	14	29	(21)
Total	36	38	12	14	(2190)

*The occupations given in detail in Table II are combined as follows: professionals, owners and managers of businesses, salesmen, clerical and other white collar workers are combined into "non-manual" occupations; skilled and unskilled workers are combined into "manual" occupations.

except Saskatchewan and Quebec. In Saskatchewan, farmers were actually less likely to vote NDP than either manual or non-manual occupational groups. The farmers in Saskatchewan were more Conservative than the other occupations.

Persons in non-manual occupations - professionals, managers, clerks, salesmen - were more likely to vote Conservative than manual workers in only two provinces, New Brunswick and Ontario. In Alberta, manual workers were actually more Conservative than the middle class, and there was no difference in several provinces. Social Credit drew more from the workers than from the middle class in Quebec and Ontario, but the pattern was just the opposite in British Columbia.

A second characteristic related to social class is socio-economic status, the relation of which to voting patterns in 1962 has already been summarized in Table III. Generally, more well-off persons were slightly more likely to vote Progressive Conservative, but otherwise no sharp differences were found, in line with the general absence of class factors in Canadian voting behaviour. Table XIV shows the extent to which this was true within each province.

Contradictory patterns within the provinces actually produced a rather close connection between status and voting in a number of provinces. The Conservatives clearly drew more support from high-status persons than lower-status persons in five provinces, those from the East to and including Manitoba, but drew less support from such persons in Saskatchewan and British Columbia. There was no difference in Alberta. The Liberals showed almost the opposite pattern, with the exception of Quebec. Both Liberals and Conservatives drew more support from better-off persons than poorer persons in Quebec, because the emerging Social Credit party took over the votes of the poorer Quebeckers. No distinct pattern of relationship of status to the vote was evident for the New Democratic party, since only in Ontario and Manitoba were less well-off persons more likely to support it, and this situation was actually reversed in Nova Scotia.

The three provinces farthest west seemed to be the main exception to the generalization that the Conservatives benefited from the votes of the well-to-do more than they did from those of the poor, but otherwise no Canada-wide inferences seem justified.

The third component of social class status – educational achievement – has some relation to voting patterns, as Table IV has already shown. The better educated (except for college graduates) were more likely to vote Conservative in 1962, and the poorly educated Social Credit, but there was no connection between the education of a voter and whether he voted New Democrat or Liberal. Table XV gives the same data for each of eight provinces.

Better-educated Canadians were more likely to vote Conservative in only three provinces: Ontario, Manitoba, and Saskatchewan. In Quebec, Alberta, and British Columbia the reverse was true, and in the two Atlantic provinces there was no difference in the Conservative vote among the better and the poorly educated. The other parties fared in an equally mixed way.

In all of the provinces where Social Credit got appreciable support, Quebec, Alberta, and British Columbia, it was the less educated that provided a disproportionate part. In Manitoba, however, the better educated were slightly more likely to support the Social Crediters than the less educated. The Liberals drew more

Table XIV
Party Support by Province and Socio-economic Status (SES)*

Province and SES	PC	Liberal	NDP	Socred	(100%)
Nova Scotia					
B	68%	16%	16%	–	(25)
C	40	47	13	–	(55)
D	43	50	7	–	(28)
New Brunswick					
B	58	32	5	5	(19)
C	45	45	5	5	(40)
D	–	–	–	–	–
Quebec					
B	28	51	1	20	(122)
C	25	43	3	29	(339)
D	20	42	–	38	(69)
Ontario					
B	55	34	11	–	(194)
C	36	41	18	5	(499)
D	31	45	17	7	(94)
Manitoba					
B	50	43	–	7	(28)
C	46	28	16	10	(68)
D	16	47	26	11	(19)
Saskatchewan					
B	42	32	16	10	(31)
C	47	21	27	5	(78)
D	53	11	18	18	(17)
Alberta					
B	49	15	2	34	(47)
C	38	19	7	36	(74)
D	44	26	4	26	(27)
British Columbia					
B	18	40	15	27	(33)
C	22	27	24	27	(140)
D	29	42	8	21	(24)
Total	36	38	12	14	(2190)

*Socio-economic status was judged by the interviewer on a
four-point scale, ranging from A(highest) to D(lowest),
based on apparent standard of living, residence, and neighbourhood. There were too few cases in most provinces for
the "A" category to be included in the tables. The voting
pattern of the highest socio-economic group in Quebec and
Ontario is discussed in the text.

from the better educated in Quebec, Alberta, and British Columbia,
but more from the poorly educated in Ontario, Manitoba, and Saskatchewan. Similarly, the New Democrats were supported more by
better-educated Canadians in Manitoba and Saskatchewan, more by

Table XV
Party Support by Province and Education*

Province and Education	PC	Liberal	NDP	Socred	(100%)
Nova Scotia					
Low	42%	40%	18%	–	(50)
Middle	49	45	6	–	(47)
High	–	–	–	–	(9)
New Brunswick					
Low	52	41	–	7	(27)
Middle	48	37	11	4	(27)
High	–	–	–	–	(11)
Quebec					
Low	28	41	1	30	(278)
Middle	22	45	4	29	(246)
High	16	80	–	4	(25)
Ontario					
Low	32	47	16	5	(266)
Middle	44	36	16	4	(436)
High	47	40	13	–	(103)
Manitoba					
Low	36	48	12	4	(50)
Middle	45	25	17	13	(53)
High	–	–	–	–	(10)
Saskatchewan					
Low	42	25	25	8	(57)
Middle	53	19	20	8	(64)
High	–	–	–	–	(10)
Alberta					
Low	44	22	6	28	(54)
Middle	41	12	6	41	(78)
High	37	44	–	19	(16)
British Columbia					
Low	27	28	18	27	(49)
Middle	21	27	22	30	(128)
High	17	54	17	12	(24)
Total	36	38	12	14	(2190)

*The attained years of education given in Table IV are combined as follows: some education between 1 and 8 years, and public school graduation are combined into "Low," some high school graduation, and some technical school or graduation are combined into "Middle," and either some university attendance or a university degree are combined into "High."

poorly educated ones in Nova Scotia.

The over-all relationship between trade union membership and party support was not found in all provinces, as Table XVI shows. It will be recalled from Table V that the Liberal vote was about equal among both trade union members and non-members (or, more

Table XVI
Party Support by Province and Trade Union Membership*

Province and Membership	PC	Liberal	NDP	Socred	(100%)
Nova Scotia					
Yes	46%	29%	25%	–	(28)
No	46	46	8	–	(82)
New Brunswick					
Yes	33	55	6	6	(18)
No	56	36	4	4	(50)
Quebec					
Yes	15	41	3	41	(138)
No	28	46	2	24	(412)
Ontario					
Yes	29	41	27	3	(244)
No	45	40	11	4	(561)
Manitoba					
Yes	18	39	39	4	(28)
No	49	33	6	12	(87)
Saskatchewan					
Yes	33	10	57	–	(21)
No	49	25	17	9	(110)
Alberta					
Yes	72	11	–	17	(18)
No	38	20	6	36	(131)
British Columbia					
Yes	11	35	35	19	(69)
No	27	29	13	31	(132)
Total	36	38	12	14	(2190)

*The question asked whether there was any trade union member in the family.

precisely, among persons with or without a trade union member in the same family) but that members were considerably less likely to vote Conservative, and more likely to vote New Democrat. The Liberal and Social Credit vote was not affected by trade union membership. Table XVI allows a more detailed examination of the effect of trade union membership upon Canadian voting patterns.

Those provinces which generally followed the over-all pattern in 1962 were: Ontario, Manitoba, Saskatchewan (not quite so closely), and British Columbia. Here the centre party (the Liberals) was "classless" in its support, and the New Democratic party cut down the Conservative support among trade unionists. In Ontario, for example, over one quarter of the persons from trade union families voted New Democratic, while only ten per cent of those from non-trade union families did so. In Saskatchewan, NDP support was even more striking among trade unionists (57 per cent), cutting down the Liberal vote considerably (to 10 per cent).

The trade union:non-trade union differential was quite diverse in other provinces. In Nova Scotia, the Conservative vote was equal in the two groups, and the New Democratic party weakened the Liberals (among the trade unionists). In New Brunswick, where there is more of a two-party system, the smaller parties especially got little support, and trade union support went to the Liberals. In Quebec, the trade unionists were much more likely to support Social Credit than were non-unionists, and somewhat less likely to support the Conservatives. In Alberta, the trade unionists were far more likely to vote Conservative than the non-unionists, and much less likely to support Social Credit. (Again, it must be repeated that the number of cases upon which these descriptive generalizations are based is extremely small.)

To summarize, where there were two parties, the Liberals usually benefited from trade union support. Where there were more than two parties, the third party (whether New Democratic or Social Credit) usually drew off trade union support from the Conservatives, rather than from the Liberals. Whether the endorsements by labour of various parties or the association of a party with economic liberalism in certain provinces and not in others accounted for these patterns could be discovered by analysis of party and interest group strategy in the various provinces.

The over-all findings on generational differences in party support were that younger voters were less likely to vote Progressive Conservative than their elders, but that there was no difference in Liberal support, and no distinct trend in NDP voting among different age-groups. Social Credit, however, benefited from extra support from younger people. Table XVII enables us to see whether these patterns remained true for all provinces.

With only minor exceptions, younger voters were less likely than older voters to vote Conservative in 1962 in four provinces: Nova Scotia, Quebec, Ontario, and Manitoba. This was not found in Saskatchewan, Alberta, and British Columbia. Younger voters were more likely to vote Social Credit in Quebec, Ontario, Manitoba, and Saskatchewan. In the other provinces, and for the other parties, the results were mixed, or no definite trends could be discerned. In most cases, there was no relationship at all between age and party choice.

It must be emphasized that these results do not mean that younger voters swung from the Conservative party to the Social Credit party; as a matter of fact (from data not given here in detail) a higher proportion of 1958 Liberals under 30 swung Social Credit than did Conservatives of the same age. These results are characterizations of the over-all patterns of certain social and demographic groups, not estimates of individual political behaviour.

The hypothesis that women are more likely to vote for a conservative party because of their greater traditionalism is weakly supported by the over-all figures relating sex to voting patterns (Table VII). Women were found to have been slightly more likely to vote Conservative, and less likely to have voted NDP with no difference in their Liberal or Social Credit vote. Does the sex

<u>Table XVII</u>
Party Support by Province and Age

Province	Age	PC	Liberal	NDP	Socred	(100%)
<u>NS</u>	21-29	29%	43%	28%	–	(21)
	30-39	45	45	10	–	(33)
	40-49	41	41	18	–	(17)
	50 & over	59	38	3	–	(39)
<u>NB</u>	21-29	56	31	13	–	(16)
	30-39	47	41	6	6	(17)
	40-49	35	53	–	12	(17)
	50 & over	61	39	–	–	(18)
<u>Quebec</u>	21-29	17	44	4	35	(145)
	30-39	28	37	1	34	(131)
	40-49	23	55	2	20	(117)
	50 & over	32	43	3	22	(157)
<u>Ontario</u>	21-29	34	46	13	7	(164)
	30-39	35	39	21	5	(208)
	40-49	40	39	20	1	(166)
	50 & over	48	38	11	3	(267)
<u>Manitoba</u>	21-29	28	38	10	24	(29)
	30-39	47	41	12	–	(17)
	40-49	43	32	18	7	(28)
	50 & over	49	32	14	5	(41)
<u>Sask.</u>	21-29	50	17	17	16	(24)
	30-39	36	24	22	18	(33)
	40-49	56	24	20	–	(34)
	50 & over	45	22	33	–	(40)
<u>Alberta</u>	21-29	41	10	11	38	(29)
	30-39	42	24	3	31	(55)
	40-49	35	19	8	38	(26)
	50 & over	49	18	2	31	(39)
<u>BC</u>	21-29	16	35	16	33	(43)
	30-39	23	45	16	16	(49)
	40-49	17	23	35	25	(48)
	50 & over	29	23	15	33	(61)
Total		36	38	12	14	(2190)

differential hold when the various provinces are examined separately? Not entirely, as Table XVIII indicates. In six of the eight provinces (all except Saskatchewan and British Columbia) for which barely enough cases are available, women were more Conservative than men. But, in only three (Nova Scotia, Ontario, and British Columbia) were males more likely to vote NDP than women. Women actually voted more heavily for the New Democratic party in Saskatchewan than men; in the others there was no difference. In general the results indicate that the sex of the Canadian voter did not affect his or her party choice.

Table XVIII
Party Support by Province and Sex

Province and Sex	PC	Liberal	NDP	Socred	(100%)
Nova Scotia					
Male	44%	40%	16%	–	(57)
Female	49	43	8	–	(53)
New Brunswick					
Male	45	45	4	6	(31)
Female	54	38	5	3	(37)
Quebec					
Male	23	44	3	30	(269)
Female	27	45	2	26	(281)
Ontario					
Male	37	38	20	5	(397)
Female	43	42	12	3	(408)
Manitoba					
Male	37	42	14	7	(57)
Female	46	28	14	12	(58)
Saskatchewan					
Male	49	26	17	8	(73)
Female	43	17	33	7	(58)
Alberta					
Male	34	21	6	39	(77)
Female	51	17	4	28	(72)
British Columbia					
Male	24	33	25	18	(109)
Female	20	28	15	37	(92)
Total	36	38	12	14	(2190)

Before this result is accepted, however, we must hold constant the other chief social basis of party choice in Canada: religion,
which may help to establish more securely the absence of any systematic sex differences in voting. Assuming that the selected parties
reflect the "conservative-liberal" dimension, it can be said that there
were in 1962 no regular voting patterns differentiating men and women among Protestants and Catholics in the various provinces.
Protestant women were more likely to vote Conservative than Protestant men in the Atlantic provinces, Ontario, the Prairie provinces,
but not in Quebec or British Columbia. Catholic women, on the
other hand, were less likely than Catholic men to vote Conservative
in the Atlantic provinces and Ontario, but more likely in the Prairies
and British Columbia. Catholic men and women were no different
in their Conservative vote in Quebec. The New Democratic vote
shows the same irregularities. In short, no distinctive sex differences are found which hold for most of Canada. This is not to say,
of course, that within particular provinces or religious groups women may not have some distinctive values or perspectives which produce particular political attitudes. Such distinctive values did not

produce, in 1962 at least, any greater over-all attraction to a Canadian party.

The effect of rural versus urban residence upon the party's relative strength in various provinces is given in Table XIX. This table provides a further check upon the validity of the survey, since such data can be directly compared with the election results. The present author offers these data, therefore, only as a provisional estimate of the rural-urban factor in 1962 in Canadian politics. (7)

It will be recalled from Table VIII that the Conservative vote dropped from rural to urban areas, that the Liberals and New Democrats were slightly stronger in large cities, and that Social Credit was stronger in small cities. The provincial figures are by no means consistent with this over-all finding. The Conservatives were only stronger in rural areas (as compared to the cities) in New Brunswick, Ontario, and Manitoba; there were no rural-urban differences in Conservative support in Quebec, Saskatchewan, and British Columbia. The Liberals were stronger in large cities only in New Brunswick and Alberta; no rural-urban difference appeared in Ontario, Saskatchewan, and British Columbia. The New Democratic party was stronger in large cities of Ontario and Manitoba only, and Social Credit was indeed stronger in the small cities of Ontario, Manitoba, and Quebec. In Alberta, Social Credit strength was mainly in the rural areas as compared to the cities. None of the over-all patterns appeared in Nova Scotia. The uneven effect of such a crude indicator of the social bases of party support as rural-urban residence is clear.

OTHER REGIONAL AND PARTY DIFFERENCES

More detailed analyses of the various provinces and the parties within them would be necessary really to see the interaction of the various social factors related to voting, but they are not possible given the scope of this paper. As examples of the type of analysis which is possible using survey data and which casts some light, hopefully, upon important features of Canadian political and social life, we may consider Quebec's political distinctiveness and the problem of the relative degree of political interest displayed by the social base of the parties in various provinces. Only historical information about the parties and social groups in the provinces could tell us whether the patterns found are stable or transitory.

When repeated patterns are found in a series of public opinion polls, taken with different samples of persons at different times, then the presumption is extremely strong that a real difference in the social structure exists, not merely a passing or transitory pattern of opinion. When a pattern appears on issue after issue, over a period of years, then we may infer that some systematic difference exists.

---

7. Another paper in this volume deals with the same question using election returns. See Meisel, concluding paper in this volume.

Table XIX
Party Support by Province and Size of Community*

Province and Community Size	PC	Liberal	NDP	Socred	(100%)
Nova Scotia					
Rural	46%	35%	19%	–	(48)
Smaller cities	64	36	–	–	(25)
Larger cities	35	54	11	–	(37)
New Brunswick					
Rural	62	26	6	6	(34)
Smaller cities	50	50	–	–	(12)
Larger cities	32	59	5	4	(22)
Quebec					
Rural	24	49	1	26	(157)
Smaller cities	26	32	2	40	(99)
Larger cities	25	46	4	25	(294)
Ontario					
Rural	47	36	10	7	(191)
Smaller cities	47	39	9	5	(157)
Larger cities	35	42	21	2	(457)
Manitoba					
Rural	54	39	–	7	(46)
Smaller cities	–	–	–	–	–
Larger cities	33	32	23	12	(69)
Saskatchewan					
Rural	46	22	27	5	(82)
Smaller cities	48	21	17	14	(29)
Larger cities	45	25	20	10	(20)
Alberta					
Rural	44	17	4	35	(66)
Smaller cities	28	8	6	58	(36)
Larger cities	51	30	6	13	(47)
British Columbia					
Rural	23	27	17	33	(52)
Smaller cities	17	34	29	20	(35)
Larger cities	23	32	19	26	(114)
Total	36	38	12	14	(2190)

*For this table, the classifications of Table VIII are condensed
as follows: "Farm" and "rural nonfarm" are termed here
"Rural"; communities from 1 to 10 and from 10 to 30,000
population are termed "Small cities," and communities from
30 to 100,000 and over 100,000 population are termed
"Larger cities."

The political distinctiveness of Quebec, for example, may be
shown in many ways. From the point of view of concern here,
that of the social bases of the parties, one striking fact which appears from the many public opinion polls conducted by the Canadian

Institute of Public Opinion is the high percentage of Quebec residents who have "no opinion" when asked a question about political issues. This reflects the history of traditionalism in the province, the reliance upon an elite of clerical-professional groups for political action and leadership, and the weakness of a tradition of popular activity in government. Table XX shows the ratio of persons in Quebec who have no opinion when asked certain questions concerning their political opinions to the persons in all of Canada who had no opinion on the same question. (8) A brief summary of the question asked is given, together with the actual percentage of persons answering "don't know' in Quebec, together with the ratio. Thus, on May 4, 1960, a national representative sample of Canadian residents was asked: "Do you happen to have heard or read anything about the population explosion?" Nationally, 51 per cent of Canadians answered that they had not heard of it. Of Quebec residents, 68 per cent answered that they had not. The ratio of these two per cents is 68/51 = 1.3. This ratio appears in the table for each question. (Those questions are given first on which Quebec differs the least. Not all results are consistent with the following interpretations).

Several patterns of distinctiveness emerge from this tabulation of Quebec "don't knows" as compared to other provinces. On almost all questions, no matter what their nature, fewer people in Quebec have an opinion. On certain questions, not only do fewer people in Quebec have an opinion, but this amounts to an extraordinarily high percentage of the population. Sixty-eight per cent of Quebec residents had not heard of the "population explosion," and in the order of the proportion of "don't knows," follow questions on free trade between Canada and the United Kingdom, disarmament, Canadian defence policies, the way the federal government handled financial matters, and the justification for the UN's existence. Note that all of these deal with the position of Canada in the world or with an over-all evaluation of the performance of the nation. These are only of concern to persons interested in, or identified with, Canada as a nation, to whom the position and power and economic stability of Canada is a valued thing.

Now, on certain international issues, Quebec residents did have opinions (what they were is not now of concern), although in most cases fewer of them than residents of other provinces. Asked whether Red China should be admitted to the UN, only 14 per cent of Quebec residents did not have an opinion, asked about the UN supplying birth control information to nations which request it, only 17 per cent did not have an opinion, and this was not strikingly different from the opinion level of the rest of the Canadian population. These are "international" questions which relate to Catholic values, not to the particular position of the Canadian nation, and therefore Quebec residents had opinions. What this shows is that questions

---

8. The ratio would obviously be considerably higher if Quebec residents were compared to all other Canadians, since Quebec is included in the national figure, but for comparative purposes this procedure indicates their distinctiveness.

Table XX

Persons with No Opinions on Political Issues in Quebec as Compared with all Canadians*

Ratio	Quebec %	Release Date	Question
.7	4	6/29/60	Favour requiring each community to build public bomb shelters
.7	6	2/28/59	Name of national anthem
.8	7	9/27/58	Expect to stay in same residence for the rest of your life
.8	15	1/15/58	Appoint a Canadian or British governor-general, or abolish it
.8	7	4/29/56	Canadian or US, government or private, investment in pipeline
1.1	30	10/2/57	Which influences vote more, party or candidate
1.2	42	3/12/58	Satisfaction with present Canadian defence policies
1.2	17	3/21/56	Canadian prison system: good, fair, or poor
1.3	17	5/7/60	Should UN supply birth control information to nations which want it
1.3	68	5/4/60	Heard or read anything about population explosion
1.3	40	7/17/59	Approve of way federal government is handling economic and financial matters
1.4	28	12/13/58	Unions wisely led (percentage "undecided")
1.4	13	2/8/58	Labour entitled to higher wages they are demanding
1.4	46	12/14/57	Should there be free trade between Canada and the United Kingdom
1.4	24	9/11/57	Would you like to see another election in a year
1.4	33	6/9/56	Prefer two- or multi-party system
1.5	23	6/17/59	Should Canada trade with Russia
1.5	21	11/5/58	Is Eisenhower's leadership excellent, fair, or disappointing
1.5	37	10/8/58	Has the UN justified its existence
1.5	14	9/27/58	Should Red China be admitted to the UN
1.6	26	11/30/57	Government or private development of Canadian natural resources
1.6	28	11/6/57	Should there be an election to give the Conservatives a clear majority
1.6	34	6/29/57	Is there too much US influence in Canada
1.8	33	6/3/59	Should "dew line" defences be paid for by US or Canada
1.8	11	7/14/56	Should Canada continue in Commonwealth, join the US, or remain independent
1.9	42	1/25/56	Will disarmament work

*Canadian Institute of Public Opinion, releases, January, 1956 - July, 1960. This table includes all questions asked by the Canadian Institute of Public Opinion between January, 1956, and July, 1960, where results are given for different provinces, and where the question can be considered to be politically relevant, or would indicate traditionalism, local attachment or national identification.

relating to values which are important to Quebeckers evoke knowledge and opinions, but that questions relating to <u>national</u> issues, parties, and events, or to the role of Canada as a <u>nation</u>, find less response in Quebec.

Similarly on national issues, those questions relating to the position of the provinces, or to possible changes in provincial autonomy, find Quebeckers with opinions. Asked whether Canada should stay in the Commonwealth or join the United States, or remain independent, few Quebec residents did not have an opinion (although many more of them as compared to residents of other provinces did not have an opinion). On a similar question, asked two years later, concerning whether the office of governor-general should be abolished, or whether a Canadian or Britisher should be appointed, most Quebec residents had an opinion, and did not differ much from other provinces.

Table XXI
Interest in Coming Election, by Party*

| Party | Index of political interest | Percentage | | | | (N) |
		Very interested	Moderate interest	Little interest	No interest	
PC	30	40%	50%	6%	4%	(794)
Liberal	23	38	47	11	4	(827)
NDP	36	45	46	4	5	(255)
Socred	2	26	50	14	10	(314)

*The questions upon which this table is based are: "Are you interested in the coming election?" If the respondent answered "Yes," he was then asked, "About how much are you interested in it, would you say -- very interested, moderately interested, or only interested a little?" Such a simple question has been found, in United States voting studies at least, to be as good an indication of political involvement and of the likelihood that the person will engage in political activity as more complicated and subtle questions. The "index of political interest" is computed simply by subtracting the proportion answering "no interest" or "little interest" from the proportion answering "very interested."

To turn to another aspect of regional and party differences, the relative degree of political interest exhibited in 1962 by supporters of the various parties is shown in Table XXI. Of particular note is the apparent lack of political interest shown by Social Credit supporters. Whether this is a phenomenon associated with the generally apolitical character of Quebec voters, or to the Social Credit party can be seen from Table XXII, where the same "index of political interest" shown in Table XXI is given for each province. In general, Social Credit did not apparently draw upon voters who are particularly interested in politics, and was sharply unlike the other minor party in this respect. The NDP apparently has a more political social base than any other party. It may be noted that the modal response was a "moderate" degree of interest, given by supporters of all four

parties.   The parties varied in the proportion of persons saying
"very" or "not" interested, but a majority of persons did not give
either of the extreme answers.

As shown in Table XXII, Social Credit supporters had the
lowest level of interest in all provinces.   It was closest to the other
parties in Ontario.   New Democratic supporters were sharply different from those of the other minority party, and their uniformity of
interest across Canada suggests that this party is close to a "national" one in terms of drawing support from the same kinds of people
all over the country.   Political interest, in Quebec, except for the
few New Democrats, was uniformly low, as might be expected. (9)

Table XXII
Index of Political Interest, by Party and Province

Party	NS	NB	Que.	Ont.	Alta.	Man.	Sask.	BC	Total
PC	43	20	2	38	27	6	37	39	30
Liberal	13	22	5	28	32	20	34	45	23
NDP	38	-*	31	37	-	69	29	39	36
Socred	-	-	3	25	0	-10	-20	1	2

*Dashes indicate that not enough cases were available to allow
the computation of the index of political interest, defined in
Table XX.   The higher the number, the higher the level of
interest in the election.   Although there were only 13 New
Democratic supporters in Quebec, they differed so sharply
from the other parties that the result is given.

Lack of interest in the general election may not indicate the
apolitical character of Quebec, because Quebeckers may feel alien-
ated from the nation to the point where elections to a national parliament have less importance for them than for other Canadians.
Additional evidence on the possible political distinctiveness of Quebec
in this respect has already been given.

It may also be possible to discern whether the party differences
in level of political interest were due to generally lower levels of interest of Canadian Catholics in national elections. (10)

Table XXIII shows the "index of political interest" for Protestants and Catholics who voted for each party in each province or
region.   Catholics as a group seemed generally to be less interested
in "the coming election" than Protestants, most markedly in Quebec,
where the few Protestants were as interested in the election as their

---

9. Interpretations of particular differences in Table XXII are
not warranted, because of the high sampling error and the peculiar-
ities of such an index.   No difference of less than 20 is worth noting.

10. In some cases, of course, there were so few Protestants
and Catholics voting for a given party (in this sample) that it is
impossible to tell whether in reality there was a difference in the
voting patterns of the religious groups in a given province.

counterparts in other provinces. This may be another indication of the "nationalization" of the bases of support for the Conservative and Liberal parties among Protestants. The failure of the Social Credit party to draw Catholic support in Ontario was matched by the higher level of interest displayed by its Protestant voters in that province. Unfortunately, a direct comparison of Protestant and Catholic Social Credit voters was possible only in the Prairies, and even here there were only thirteen Catholic Social Crediters in the sample. Their level of interest was considerably lower than the Protestants, but Social Credit in both religions commanded the support of less interested voters than did the other parties.

Table XXIII
Index of Political Interest, by Party, Religion and Region

Region:	Atlantic		Quebec		Ontario		Prairies		BC	
Religion:	Prot.	RC	Prot.	RC	Prot.	RC	Prot.	RC	Prot.	RC
PC	44	40	47	−5	39	20	26	23	42	−
Liberal	33	21	35	−2	26	32	32	22	52	30
NDP	−	46*	−	25*	37	34	34	−	35	−
Socred	−	−	−	4	31	−	−2	−31*	2	−

*See Table XX for a discussion of the index. Asterisks denote figures based on only 11 to 13 cases.

DISCUSSION

It may be that there are literally no stable social bases for the Canadian parties, except possibly certain agrarian support for the NDP and Social Credit, and certain trade union support for the NDP, and except on a very local basis. Canada may be close to that state of affairs where the political parties all circle tentatively around a middle position, like fighters gauging the opposition, wondering how far they have to go toward the centre before they get hit. The political parties in Canada may approximate more closely than those in other countries to the classic description of parties as men temporarily associated because of the necessities of the strategy of power.

Canadian politics also indicates the inadequacy of a simple notion of the "determinants" of voting behaviour, particularly the idea of cross-pressures. This concept, developed in a study of voting in Erie County, Ohio, is a very useful one, but an over simple conceptualization. Essentially, it conceives of a "push-pull" process of presumed opposite political pressures. In Erie County, being a Protestant or a Catholic, a manual worker or in the middle class, a rural or an urban resident, turned out to be the three social characteristics which together allowed for the best prediction of party choice. Also, having "contradictory" characteristics produced certain consequences: lack of interest in the election and a late decision, for example. (11)

---

11. Paul F. Lazarsfeld et al., The People's Choice (New York, 1944).

Note, however, that the empirical data in this United States study allowed for a rather simple dichotomy of each of three characteristics. Whether the complex pattern of social and political cleavages allows for the empirical application of the notion of cross-pressures to Canada is a question which the crude data available here cannot answer.

On the one hand, the very notion of cross-pressures may be inapplicable because of the ambiguity of party imagery and the lack of homogeneity of political experience and socialization among various groups. Cross pressures can only operate under those conditions - suggested at the beginning of this paper - where images of a party are associated with some collective experience of a group. By definition, a social characteristic such as being a Catholic or a worker cannot become a source of "pressure" forming political predispositions unless the connections between a group membership and its "normal" political affiliations are clearly perceived by individuals. Nothing about Canadian politics would lead us to predict such a connection, at least for social class.

It is possible, on the other hand, that the cross-pressures notion would be applicable, using different bases, such as region, replacing class. Assuming that region, religion, and rural-urban residence fulfil these requirements, then we might expect to find that Protestants in Quebec are less likely to vote than Catholics, when social class (which has an independent effect upon political interest and participation) is controlled. Even formulating such a hypothesis, however, raises so many other questions that the usefulness of the cross-pressures notion is cast into doubt. The American voting studies in general have made assumptions about a high level of political consensus and homogeneity of political symbolism which may not apply as clearly to Canada as they do to the United States.

This paper has examined only one aspect of the association of various social factors to party support - the aspect determined by the way the tables were percentaged. That is, the proportion of young voters, Catholics, workers preferring a given party was contrasted with the behaviour of older voters, Protestants, or professionals. This approach is a peculiarly sociological one, because it implicitly assumes that the behaviour of social collectivities or aggregates, variously defined, is the most important way to examine the social bases of support for political parties. The other aspect of this association of social factors with party support has more affinity with political science - to examine the social composition of a party's support: to ask the question, that is, what proportion of Social Credit's supporters in a given province are Catholic as compared with the proportion of New Democratic supporters who are Catholic? This approach implicitly raises the problem of the effect of the social composition of a party upon the types of issues it is likely to take a stand upon, the behaviour of its legislative representatives, its willingness to compromise with other parties or to ally itself with political groups in other provinces. That the Progressive Conservative party's social base is 84 per cent Catholic in Quebec and 84 per cent Protestant in Saskatchewan must surely have implications for the strategies and alliances of the party. The problem of the impact of a given social base upon party behaviour cannot be discussed further here, and is merely mentioned to indicate other ways in which survey data may be used to shed light upon political and social processes.

GROUP PERCEPTIONS AND THE VOTE:
SOME AVENUES OF OPINION FORMATION
IN THE 1962 CAMPAIGN

S. Peter Regenstreif

The factors underlying electoral motivation are many and complex.
Basic attitudes, group identifications, tradition, historic considerations, and momentary events are important elements among many
which interact in an intricate relationship to bring an electorate to a
voting decision. While all these components must be taken into
account, it is often useful for the purposes of analysis to isolate
several or even one of these elements in order to examine them
more carefully and therefore better to understand the mechanisms
of the voting process as they operate in Canada.

It is the intention of this paper to concentrate upon the group
factor because it seems to provide a handy tool with which to explain some of the significant patterns in the federal election of 1962.
The underlying assumption of this approach is the simple one that
"any society, even one employing the simplest and most primitive
techniques, is a mosaic of overlapping groups of various specialized
sorts." (1) Attention will not, however, be focused on an individual's membership in the many voluntary associations, such as fra-
ternal, service and "pressure" organizations, in Canadian life.
This is of only limited significance in the larger consideration of influence on the total vote in an election. (2) Rather, reference group
forces as determinants of voting behaviour will be emphasized. (3)
In this view, the familial as well as the extended social environment
of individuals (their religious and ethnic affiliations, their area or
place of residence, their economic status) is a crucial influencing
factor despite most of these affiliations not necessarily being perceived

---

1. David B. Truman, The Governmental Process (New York,
1959), p. 43.

2. That a relatively insignificant although "influential" number of
people participate in formally organized associations has been demonstrated in a large number of studies in the United States. Extensive
participation is associated with high income and educational levels.
The most recent study is C.R. Wright and H.H. Hyman, "Voluntary
Association Memberships of American Adults: Evidence From National Sample Surveys," American Sociological Review, XXIII,
June, 1958, pp. 284-94.

3. For a general analysis of this concept, see R.K. Merton,
Social Theory and Social Structure, rev. ed. (Glencoe, 1957),
pp. 225-386.

as such by the individuals affected by them. It is worth emphasizing, however, that the placing of people within categories and classes such as ethnic origin, religion and age does not by any means imply that there is such a thing as a "group mind" or that the totality of an individual's behaviour is explainable exclusively through the use of such categories. Furthermore, the impact of these reference affiliations is not equal in intensity or importance. Nevertheless, they all have some role to play.

The remarks made here will concentrate upon the interplay of the components of age, ethnicity, income, region, religion, and residence as they appeared to affect the vote in 1962. Much of the evidence for these observations is based upon a coast-to-coast tour of over 10,000 miles made by the author during the campaign. Three hundred and seventy-five detailed interviews were recorded in eleven key areas.

The areas chosen conform to the major regions of the country. Within these key areas, four variables, religion, income, ethnicity, and residence (i.e. rural, suburban, or urban) govern the sample selection. Once this has been done, sampling is carried out randomly. Interviewing was based on a schedule of thirty-two items which covered such subjects as mass media consumption, previous voting behaviour, parental voting, perception of parties, issues and candidates, the usual socio-economic elements, and vote intention. Several of the questions were open-ended to provide respondents with the opportunity to express themselves as fully as the situation demanded.

While this sample is by no means representative, the use of data arising out of it, when combined, as it is here, with other material from such sources as the Canadian Institute of Public Opinion and the Office of the Chief Electoral Officer can provide enlightening illustrative information which, if nothing else, may have the effect of breathing life into what might otherwise be a dry exposition of election statistics and sample survey tabulations. In general, while this paper may tend to be impressionistic, the author bases his findings on what should by now be an accepted axiom: namely, that while people in casting a ballot are engaged in an individual act, voting is not an isolated incident taking place in a vacuum, but part of a never-ending chain of social events which have deep roots in history and which are continuous in their implications. (4)

I

One of the most noteworthy features of the vote was the pronounced disparity in party strength between urban and rural sectors

---

4. Some of what follows has appeared (in somewhat different form) in the Montreal Star, May 9 - June 16, 1962, passim. The author wishes to thank the Star for permission to use this material and to take this opportunity to express his gratitude to the University of Rochester for its generosity in defraying some expenses and in allowing him the necessary leave.

of the country. The findings of the Gallup poll final pre-election survey conducted during the week preceding election day are instructive:
the Conservatives were strongest in the rural areas and grew pro-
gressively weaker as the size of the community increased. On the
other hand, the Liberal and NDP vote was directly correlated with
community size: i.e. the greater the population density, the larger
was their share of support (see Table I). It is in the fifty-five constituencies of the four major metropolitan centres of Montreal, Toronto, Winnipeg, and Vancouver that the government received its
severest rebuke from the electorate. Here, in 1958, the Conservatives captured forty-one, leaving the Liberals with twelve and the
CCF with two. Four years later, thirty-three of these Conservative seats had fallen to the opposition. Of the fifty-five, the Liberals
now held thirty-seven and the NDP ten. The Conservatives polled
a bare one-third of the vote while the Liberals won two-fifths and
the NDP one-fifth.

Table I

Party Breakdown of Support by Community Size (percentages)

Community Size	PC	Lib.	NDP	Socred	Other
Over 100,000	31.4	39.9	15.0	12.0	1.7
10 - 30,000	36.1	37.5	12.8	12.1	1.5
1 - 10,000	38.3	35.1	8.6	17.6	0.4
Rural	44.7	32.7	9.5	11.6	1.5

One may account for this opposition to the government on the
part of the denizens of metropolitan Canada as evidence of their
superior sophistication compared to their country cousins. (5)
While this is a partial explanation, it is by no means the whole story,
A more all-inclusive explanation would have to consider the difference
in the environments of these areas as well.

As the studies of American voters have shown, residents of
cities belong to more organizations than do rural people and therefore have increased contact with people of similar inclination. This
contact together with the fact that they live in denser population areas
increases the likelihood of political discussion outside the primary
environment of the family. City dwellers are therefore more susceptible to change if it is in the air. There is also some evidence
that, particularly in metropolitan areas, urbanites enjoy greater contact with the media, in part because of competition in the press and
among radio and television stations. As a result, if there are any
issues of a personal or group variety which are at stake in an
election, these may more likely be perceived here. (6)

---

5. For example, see Peter C. Newman, "Why Diefenbaker
Lost Canada," Maclean's Magazine, LXXV, (July 28, 1962), pp. 10,
45-8.

6. Some interesting figures in this connection are presented in
A. Campbell, G. Gurin, and W. Miller, The Voter Decides (Evanston,
1954), pp. 193, 197. A brief summary of American urban-rural differences is provided in R.E. Lane, Political Life (New York, 1959),
pp. 265-7.

All this would be of some interest but of little relevance to an understanding of the phenomenon of the big-city breakaway from the Conservatives were it not for the fact that the government was experiencing pronounced difficulties with another important sector of the 1958 constituency. The disaffection of many dyed-in-the-wool upper-middle- and upper-income Conservatives with the policies of their government was noticeable from coast to coast. This was added to the strong pro-Liberal sentiments among many others in these groups because of what they regarded as disgracefully high deficits run up by the government and the Conservative record of poor management.

The wife of an Eglinton lawyer put the case succinctly: "I think we ought to pull in our ears on the taxation idea. It's bothering me considerably. I think they're giving away too much. Everybody's going toward socialism. I'd like people sinking or swimming on their own." The higher the income, the more strident the criticism, or so it seemed. An insurance office manager earning $13,000 yearly in the Hamilton suburban community of Waterdown was vehement: "I pay taxes for that man down there and he throws the money around. Diefenbaker has spent a lot of money and he hasn't done a good job."

In many ways, this is the greatest paradox of the election and represents a reversal of roles. Traditionally, the Conservatives have been the party of the "rich" in Canada, while the Liberals, at least under Mackenzie King, attempted to foster a public image that they were the party of the common man. Now the upper-middle and upper-income groups were looking to the Liberals as the only "responsible" party on the scene. And the allusions to Diefenbaker by many as "that man" is reminiscent of the attitudes of similar people in the United States who made like references to Franklin D. Roosevelt when he held sway as chief executive.

One of the most vivid illustrations of this interesting "reversal" is provided by the Montreal constituency of St. Antoine-Westmount which juxtaposes lower-income voters against the upper-income élite (some of which is national in influence). The traditional pattern here was for Liberal candidates (such notables as Douglas Abbott and George Marler) barely to hold their own or to even lose in Westmount while they swept the poorer districts of St. André, St. Antoine, and St. Henri. The most recent example of this state of affairs was the election of 1957 in which Marler ran up an over-2,000 edge over his Conservative opponent in the lower income sections only to lose one-quarter of this margin back to him in Westmount. In 1958, when Conservative Ross Webster won the seat, he carried all districts except St. Henri, although he did cut Marler's previous 1,621 margin here by close to 1,000. Four years later, however, former Deputy Minister of National Defence, Liberal C.M. Drury, lost another 500 votes in St. Henri and barely held his party's 1958 vote in St. Antoine. But in Westmount, he turned a 2,302 deficit in 1958 into a 1517 margin in his favour, polling 57 per cent of that area's vote in the process.

Unhappiness with the Conservatives among this "upper class" segment of the electorate was often expressed in personal terms. A

normally Conservative Halifax housewife mused: "I have a feeling Diefenbaker's going out. I just don't like his attitude. He's too sure of
himself. To me, he's not the man I thought he was. In 1958, he
made quite an impression on people out here, you know. I think
he's let them down." This attitude, reflected elsewhere among
upper-income voters, underlines the growing inacceptability of Mr.
Diefenbaker in terms of his religion, ethnic background, and region.
it served as yet another element to fan the smouldering embers of
discontent.

The importance of these high-status groups cannot be overestimated, for while their members are relatively few in number in
comparison with the entire electorate they are the "opinion leaders"
in their communities. The process of information-flow in public
affairs is usually downward. Persons looking for advice on political matters tend to look to those of higher status for guidance. (7)
When the ideology of an open class system prevails, as it does in
these areas (and as it does in most of Canada), then this is yet
another factor turning all eyes toward them and acting to reinforce
aspirations of upward mobility. (8) In an atmosphere in which
questions of "status" and economics loomed large, this "opinion leadership" was significant.

A Vancouver housewife spoke for fully one-third of the
"sample": "I'm becoming ashamed of this country. I used to be
proud of Canada. Now people ask me when I travel 'What's wrong
with Canada?' I don't like to apologize for my country. I want to
be proud."

A salesman in suburban Toronto, a Diefenbaker supporter
four years before, echoed her remarks and was more specific:
"I'm not a party member and I feel free to vote in a different way
every time. I feel some sort of protest is in order. You know,
in some ways, Diefenbaker sold a vision and I don't think it quite
jelled. I've been a bit hurt about the last two years. I know you
pay a price for being Canadian, but the high cost of living and the
high unemployment have made me a bit concerned for Canada. And
the dollar and the Common Market thing. I'm becoming ashamed of
this country."

It must be pointed out that while it is no doubt true that the
"intellectual" community disliked Mr. Diefenbaker's politics and style
almost from the first, it is not this group that is being focused upon

---

7. See E. Katz and P.F. Lazarsfeld, Personal Influence
(Glencoe, 1955), p.330; also B. Berelson, P.F. Lazarsfeld,
W.N. McPhee, Voting (Chicago, 1954), p. 104.

8. See, for example, Lane, Political Life, pp.233-4. It does
not matter that the reality does not conform to belief as John Porter's
myriad investigations attest. (See his "Concentration of Economic
Power and the Economic Elite in Canada," Canadian Journal of
Economics and Political Science, XXII, May, 1956, pp.199-220,
and "The Economic Elite and the Social Structure in Canada," ibid,
XXIII, Aug. 1957, pp. 376-94.) It seems clear that Canada's "upper
class" is a difficult one to crash. What matters is that this is the
belief system and that it has specific effects.

here. Whatever the status of the Canadian intelligentsia (such as it is), it remains a relatively unknown quantity. This group's un-happiness with the national government probably had some popular effect. However, what is of interest here is the urban opinion-leadership which is not necessarily part of the intellectual community. This "leadership" derives its significance from its placement in the work-world as well as from its social position. The same cannot be said for the intellectual community and this is why this upper-income opinion is of importance. In part, these statements suggest that Canadians seem to be more deferential than, say, Americans. In view of the different political ethos of Canada, this does not seem to be a particularly outlandish suggestion.

Finally, the role of the press must be mentioned. In these four metropolitan areas, it was always the newspaper with the high-est circulation that advocated support of the Liberals.

The influences just described directed the voters towards the Liberals. Nevertheless, a substantial number of voters resisted these pressures and while defecting from the Conservatives, did so in favour of the New Democratic party which obtained a vote which exceeded that ever achieved by the old CCF in these areas. For many, this was simply a reversion to their former affiliations: York South, Winnipeg North, and Winnipeg North-Centre once again re-turned socialist candidates. For others, union membership and a sense of working class consciousness were important motivating elements. Again the results of the Gallup poll's final pre-election survey on the distribution of union membership voting are useful in-dicators. The NDP polled close to one-quarter of the union vote. While this was not as high as some past CCF performances across the country in the middle and late 1940's, it was still a factor in victories in constituencies like Vancouver's Burnaby-Richmond, Burrard, and Kingsway (see Table II).

Table II
Breakdown of Union Vote by Party (percentages)

	PC	Lib.	NDP	Socred	Other
Union	24.9	37.7	23.5	12.7	1.2
Non-Union	41.7	36.3	8.0	12.5	1.5

On occasion, trade union affiliation with the NDP was not an unmixed blessing. In some cases this could act as an inducement to vote for one of the major parties against the NDP. For example, in Winnipeg, former CCF voters have been leaving their old areas in the city in the constituencies of North and North Centre and have been moving into the suburbs fringing these ridings. This represen-ted a move upward for them and suddenly they were giving vent to fears of union domination as a rationale for staying Conservative.

More crucial than this organizational support, however, were the subjective feelings of apartness expressed by many first-time NDP voters: "After all, we working people have nothing. How else can working people vote?" This rhetorical question was asked by a Toronto housewife. Economic privation and a sense that a change was needed intensified unhappiness with the "old parties." In Vancouver, a lower-middle-income thirty-seven-year-old housewife who had voted for Mr. Diefenbaker in 1958 said: "I don't know how I'll vote. But I think we're due for a change, I can tell you that! Maybe some of these new parties deserve a chance – the old ones have had theirs. And I'm not a Doukhobor either." Lower-income respondents were characteristically blunt. A middle-aged steamfitter, concerned about unemployment and automation, was bitter: "They say they're doing this and that. But it's only talk. My boy quit school and he can't get a job. They said 'Follow John' --- sure! To unemployment!"

Urban-rural differences and some of the factors just reviewed are partially accountable for the strange manifestation of Social Credit in Quebec. In the twenty-one Montreal Island constituencies, "Creditiste" candidates could barely manage 41,758 votes, a meagre 6.1 per cent of the 679,457 cast. In what the parties for organizational purposes term the "Quebec district," however, they won twenty-four of their twenty-six province-wide total. In the areas outside Montreal, Caouette's forces obtained a half million votes – an astonishing 35.5 per cent share of the total.

The fact that Caouette confined his use of the television medium to the regions outside Montreal for financial as well as tactical reasons is probably one of the best-known features of his remarkable campaign. There is a strong possibility, however, that even had the Montreal area been accorded the full treatment, there would have been no appreciable increase in Socred support here. All the elements in Metropolitan Montreal were operating overwhelmingly in favour of the Liberals (who won twenty-one of the twenty-three seats): opinion leadership (French as well as English), the fine showing of the Lesage provincial government, and perception of economic difficulties among the general population. It is also clear that while Caouette was able to smash the grip of the traditional élites upon their constituencies in the outlying regions in part because of the failure of the provincial government to mount an effective appeal here, his task would have been close to insurmountable with regard to the metropolitan French-Canadian masses. Assuming that Caouette's appeal would have loosened the hold of Montreal French-Canadian opinion leadership, he would still have had extreme difficulty overcoming the problem posed by the Montreal environment which has few of the "folk" elements of the non-metropolitan areas of the province.

II

The importance of region as a factor in Canadian political life has been one of its commonly accepted elements. The 1962 election proved no exception especially where the Maritimes and the Prairies are concerned. Not unexpectedly, it is difficult to separate economic considerations from purely regional ones.

On the Prairies, government losses were insignificant as it

retained all its Saskatchewan seats as well as its rural Manitoba ones. While its share of Alberta support dropped 17 per cent, it lost only two seats in the process. On the other hand, Saskatchewan was the only province in which the Diefenbaker forces increased their vote over their 1958 showing.

The Conservatives did not hold on as well in the Maritimes, but given the extensive nature of their losses elsewhere they did very well nevertheless. Prince Edward Island held firm, but six seats were lost on the mainland, three apiece in New Brunswick and Nova Scotia, although perhaps ethnic and religious factors put most of these losses in the category of special cases.

The wheat deals and Mr. Diefenbaker's western background and political style provide ready explanations for Prairie voting behaviour. A farmer near the village of Parry in South-Central Saskatchewan sang the praises of the local hero in explaining his reasons for staying Conservative: "Johnny's going back!" he exulted. "I was for him last time. I'm for him again." Another farmer near the town of Wilkie pointed out: "Old John has done more for the West in the last four years than anyone in a long time. I'd like to see him go back in." There was also a touch of anti-Eastern feeling in this remark by a Calgary clothing retailer: "The Liberals used to cater to the Eastern part of the country, Quebec especially. Diefenbaker is from the Prairies, the middle of the country. So he should be able to do his best for both East and West."

Local feelings were also important in the Maritimes. A Digby dock-worker moaned: "If we only had something here for the young people. You give 'em an education and just when they get to an age when they can help you, they have to go off to Alberta or the services. We want something here to give work. The tourists don't do us any good. They just go right through." A Cape-Bretoner spoke for many when he claimed: "Canada ends at Quebec for us. We never get anything."

In both areas, the Prairies and the Maritimes, the counsel of prudence is to stay with the government. As a farmer who was switching to Mr. Diefenbaker in the Saskatchewan constituency of Rosetown-Biggar put it: "I vote for someone who can do something for me. What's the point of voting for anyone else?" If anything, many Maritimers were even more hard-headed in appraising their situation. A Yarmouth clerk laid it on the line: "I prefer to support a party that's in power. Besides, at least we get more out of the Conservatives than we ever got out of the Liberals. The thing to do is to go with the majority. That's the way I see it."

These attitudes are rooted in objective conditions. The inhabitants of these areas recognized long ago how necessary government action was to their daily existence. There is, of course, an aspect of the "band-wagon" in this. But in view of the lower living conditions in the Maritimes compared to the rest of the country and the vulnerability of the wheat economy to forces beyond individual or regional control, there is a rationality to this behaviour which cannot be denied. Despite Gallup poll evidence to the contrary, the assumption prevailing in both regions seemed to be that the Tories were going to be returned to office with a reduced majority. What the electoral outcome might have been had the public felt that the issue was by no means settled can only be conjectured upon. It seems clear from the pattern of response, however, that the opposition would have made some substantial inroads had the expectations here been different.

The persistence of a regional ingredient is somewhat anachronistic particularly in the face of heavy inter-provincial migration which has led John Porter to characterize Canada as a "great demographic railway station." (9) The tremendous movement of population might be expected to lessen the force of regionalism as a reference factor. However, as the latest census figures indicate, it is precisely the areas of greatest regional loyalty which, in the last decade, have suffered "net migration" losses, with the province of Saskatchewan leading the way. What seems to be happening is that, while emigrants from these areas (leaving for Central Canada, Alberta, British Columbia, or the United States) leave their old localistic attitudes behind (perhaps in favour of others more in tune with their new surroundings), the people remaining are almost by definition more closely attached to the area and, over time, even experience a reinforcement of sentiments of and for their region. Population growth due to natural increase is politically socialized in the normal manner and thus the feelings for region are maintained and continue to play a role in determining the pattern of political allegiance.

III

Religion continued to play its part in influencing party identification. The normal Canadian patterns in this connection seemed to be unchanged. The Gallup poll national figures show that almost half the Protestant electorate voted Conservative while an almost identical proportion of Catholics supported the Liberals (see Table III). When Quebec is omitted from the calculations, my own admittedly less reliable figures show an even greater preponderance of Catholics expressing Liberal vote intentions. Over 60 per cent of Catholics whom I interviewed outside Quebec stated that they would vote Liberal. Just over half the Anglicans revealed Conservative dispositions. There was not as great a spread in the relative strength of the two major parties among United Churchgoers. Two-fifths could be counted in the Conservative column while 30 per cent expected to vote Liberal. (10) Several other

9. In, for example, his "Some Aspects of Class in Canadian Social Structure," paper delivered at the Institute of Canadian Studies Interdisciplinary Seminar on "Class in Canada," Carleton University, March 16, 1962.

10. The author feels somewhat more confident of his own figures in connection with the subject of religion than in some others because of the close correspondence between them and those of the

studies on the religious background of members of Parliament, voting, and longer-term party support underline that religion has been a constant determining feature of party affiliation and that the above breakdown is not significantly different from observations of past behaviour. (11)

Table III
Breakdown of Religious Vote by Party (percentages)

	PC	Lib.	NDP	Socred	Other
Protestant	48.2	28.8	13.2	9.0	0.8
Catholic	23.0	47.5	9.4	17.5	2.6
Other	24.1	38.5	22.9	14.5	–

Obviously, the religious ingredient is more important in some circumstances than in others. For example, in Nova Scotia, one of the more tradition-oriented provinces, the fact that the population of the constituency of Inverness-Richmond is over three-quarters Roman Catholic is probably the most important reason that the Liberal party enters every election with a decided edge. Only pronounced swings in favour of the Conservatives can bring this riding into the Tory fold and even then by a hair-line margin. This constituency is therefore a key one for the Maritimes on election night. If the Liberals fail to carry it, it is almost certain that all of Nova Scotia is lost to them. To a lesser extent, the religious composition of Antigonish-Guysborough, 60 per cent Roman Catholic, also favours the Liberals.

On the other hand, while religious affiliation does have some influence in suburban communities in Central Canada, its importance is essentially peripheral. Suburbanites seem to be undergoing all sorts of social dislocations from older, more traditional, and established patterns. Generally, they are younger in comparison with the rest of the population and therefore tend to respond more to appeals based on momentary issues and/or personality rather than those directed towards group affiliations. Religion is taking on new and different meaning in the life of these people. It is social and oriented towards secular and neighbourhood values rather than group-identified or personal and therefore its consequences here are mitigated by more powerful forces impinging upon the individual.

It must be emphasized that religious reasons are seldom the ones articulated by respondents when expressing their vote intentions. When pressed on the question, they generally are non-committal or deny even the suggestion that religious considerations

Canadian Institute of Public Opinion nationally.
    11. See J.A. LaPonce, "The Religious Background of Canadian MPs," Political Studies, VI, Oct., 1958, pp.253-8; John Meisel, "Religious Affiliation and Electoral Behaviour: A Case Study," Canadian Journal of Economics and Political Science, XXII, Nov., 1956, pp.481-96; and my "Some Aspects of National Party Support in Canada," ibid., XXIX, Feb., 1963, pp. 59-74.

are meaningful. If there is any mention of this matter, either overt or covert, it is far more likely that it will be the Protestant who will articulate anti-Catholic attitudes rather than vice versa. As well, there is an antagonistic religious undertone as well as the obviously regional element in the remarks of the Calgary retailer quoted above regarding the Liberal party as the party of Quebec. To many Protestants, the Roman Catholic hierarchy and the Liberal party have always worked in close co-operation.

The best that can be ventured in explanation of this phenomenon is to repeat John Meisel's suggestion that Roman Catholics vote Liberal because they have come to accept this as the natural thing to do. (12) The historical and social factors underlying this behaviour are well known, as are those which probably impel Anglicans in the Conservative direction.

IV

The so-called "ethnic vote" has received considerable attention and the euphemism "new Canadian" has by now become a fixture of the jargon of the public platform. As popularly used, ethnic considerations appear to have had relatively little direct bearing on the outcome of the election. Of course, this statement depends on how the term is used. If ethnicity is considered in its broadest meaning, then ethnic factors were extremely important, as they have been since the advent of the British in 1763. However, used in its popular sense, as applicable to the post-1945 immigrant groups who have settled in Canada over 1,500,000 strong, the original assessment must stand.

What analysis there is of the 1958 results points to the fact that Prime Minister Diefenbaker that year received strong support from this segment of the population. There can be no doubt that he was aware of support from this direction and, four years later, some of his campaigning techniques were aimed specifically at these groups. It appears as if they were to no avail. If they were successful, the only groups affected were those Eastern Europeans who were concerned about anti-Communist nationalistic aspirations of the countries which they had recently left behind. Immigrants from Southern Europe were obviously untroubled about such matters.

The major and sometimes only subject of anxiety for all these groups (understandably) was the economic consideration. Poor job opportunities and general unemployment had hit these people hard and first-time voters especially were likely to take their resentment out on the government because of what they conceived of as a cause-and-effect relationship. An unemployed Italian marble-cutter stated his June 18 intentions in halting English: "I vote Mr. Pearson. I not vote in 1958. I come here in 1955. Mr. St. Laurent Prime Minister. I no speak English, nothing. Get good job. Then Mr. Diefenbaker come. Lose job. I got better chance for job with Mr. Pearson." However, second- and third-time voters, even if employed

12. Meisel, "Religious Affiliation and Electoral Behaviour," p.494.

and prospering themselves, were affected by this issue, recognizing that, in spite of their own good fortune, others were not doing as well. In Toronto's York South, the wife of a Greek cabinet-maker said: "I have to think of the working people. Even if I do well and things are good for me, I must think for everybody."

During the campaign, close to a majority of Canadians expressed a belief that the country was more likely to be prosperous when the Liberals are in office than under any other administration. (13) It is not surprising, then, that the Liberals were the ones to gain most from the impact of hard times upon these groups. However, the NDP's share of support from this area, an indication of its strong urban appeal, was almost equal to that accruing to the Conservatives. This fact underlines the sense of disillusionment among these people with the status quo. (14)

V

A large number of observers (among others, Mannheim, Heberle and Neumann, and more recently, Berelson, Harris, and Lazarsfeld) have used the concept of "political generation" in addition to such categories as class or ethnicity to explain political behaviour. The argument is that just as attitudes differ because they are held by those in different positions in the social hierarchy or of various ethnic backgrounds, they also differ as a result of being held by people belonging to different generations. (15)   Thus

---

13. The Gallup poll asked this question: "Looking ahead for the next few years, which political party, the Conservatives or the Liberals --- do you think, if in power, would do the best job of keeping the country prosperous?" It reported the following results:

Conservatives	29%
Liberals	42
Other	7
Either one	1
Undecided	21

These corroborate the author's own findings based on a similar question which showed the Liberals with 47 per cent and the Conservatives with 25 per cent.

14. The final Gallup poll survey showed the following party breakdown on the basis of "Mother Tongue":

	PC	Lib.	NDP	Socred	Other
English	45.5	39.4	13.2	6.4	0.5
French	22.9	42.2	5.1	25.9	3.9
Other	23.3	37.3	20.1	18.1	1.2

The relatively strong showing of Social Credit in the "Other" category was western and overwhelmingly rural.

15. See Rudolph Heberle, "The Problem of Political Generations," Social Movements (New York, 1951). Also see S.M. Lipset, P.F. Lazarsfeld, A.H. Barton, and J. Linz, "The

studies of voting in the United States often show marked differences in party preferences on the basis of age. There are suggestions from these studies that such variations may be products of a situation in which people coming of age during periods of depression or war tend to support the Democratic party while those achieving maturity during prosperous times favour the Republicans.

There is some interesting data on this point implicit in the Gallup poll figures on age-group breakdown by party (see Table IV). The Liberals were strongest among the 21-29 and 40-49 age groups. The NDP's best showing was also in this latter group. There was no difference between the major parties in the 30-39 segment but the Conservatives almost ran away with the over-50 group.

Table IV
Breakdown of Age Groups by Party (percentages)

	PC	Lib.	NDP	Socred	Other
21-29 years	30.5	37.7	11.2	19.4	1.2
30-39 "	36.4	36.4	12.2	14.0	1.0
40-49 "	34.4	39.8	15.6	8.8	1.4
50 and over	44.3	34.0	10.4	9.4	1.9

The figures for the 40-49 age group provide some indication that two earlier developments may be continuing to cast their spell, namely the effect of the war with the Liberals in office and the CCF experiencing an upsurge in the early 'forties. (It will be recalled that the results of a September 1943 Gallup poll showed the CCF with a plurality of national popular support which gave them a 1 per cent edge over the Liberals.) On the other hand, one specific event seems to account for the strength of the Conservatives among the older age group aside from the regional and rural factors involved. The last budget brought down by a Liberal administration prior to the 1957 campaign added "only" six dollars to the old-age pension. Even as late as 1962, the attitude which led to Mr. Diefenbaker's characterization of the Liberals as the "six buck boys" struck a responsive chord, especially in contrast to his own government's action in raising the pension further. The behaviour of this group points to a reversal of sorts too. This age group came to maturity in the 'thirties and after the experience in the early part of that decade with the Bennett administration, the Conservative party's image was that it was "the party of hard times." As a 58-year-old tobacco and cattle grower near the town of Jarvis in the Ontario riding of Norfolk put it: "The working people and the farmers always have it a little better when the Liberals are in." As the figures show, in terms of age-group affiliations, he was definitely in the minority in 1962.

Psychology of Voting: An Analysis of Political Behaviour," in G. Lindzey, ed., Handbook of Social Psychology, vol. II (London, 1954), pp.1147-8 for an elaboration of this concept.

However, this above-quoted attitude in favour of the Liberals, while not holding the above-50 group in line, may have had its effect none the less and may help account for the strength of the Liberals in the youngest age group: people, that is, who were first or, at best, second time voters in 1962. As studies of American voting behaviour show, most people follow the pattern of their families in casting their first vote. (16) In fact, this is one of the most definite generalizations which can be made about electoral behaviour in the United States. In Canada, these first-time voters are the children of voters who themselves first voted in the 1930's. Thus the disposition to favour the Liberals and to feel antipathetic towards the Conservatives on simple grounds of "party identification" was undoubtedly part of the political socialization of the 20-29 group. The so-called "niggardliness" of the Liberals and Mr. Diefenbaker's "generosity" with the pension may have affected their parents, but this issue could not have had anywhere near the same impact on them. From the limited interviewing the author carried among these young voters, it seemed as if the image of the Liberals as "the party of good times" was not an insignificant motivating factor influencing their vote.

CONCLUSION

It must be emphasized that these few remarks concerning the influence of reference affiliation upon the vote are not meant to imply that such portrayals describe an entirely objective reality. Some of the foregoing is an intellectual construct, a special way of looking at the world. It is the contention here that such constructs are useful, however, and this paper has tried to demonstrate how they might be used with some empirical evidence. For if the definition of politics as "the authoritative allocation of values" (17) is accepted, then it is well to underline that these values are largely group-anchored, in the broadest meaning of that term. Thus issues have different connotations according to how they are socially perceived.

One important weakness of the purely sociological explanation is that it tends to underplay the psychology of individual perception. Another way of dealing with voting motivation is by examining

---

16. For example, the Elmira Study of the 1948 Presidential campaign showed 75 per cent of first-time voters siding with their fathers in their political choice. See Berelson et al., Voting, pp.88-9. Also see Campbell, et al., The Voter Decides, pp.97-107, and A. Campbell, P.E. Converse, W.E. Miller, and D.E. Stokes, The American Voter (New York, 1960), pp.154-5. On the role of the family as an agency of political orientation, see H. Hyman, Political Socialization (Glencoe, 1959), pp.69-91.

17. See David Easton's "An Approach to the Analysis of Political Systems," World Politics, IX, April, 1957, pp.383-400.

individual perception. For example, Campbell and his associates structured the factors motivating voters in the 1952 American Presidential campaign in terms of three variables: Party Identification, Issue Orientation, and Candidate Orientation; they claim that this structure provides an analytic device which is applicable not only to that particular election but to all elections. (18) However, the collection of data which such an approach entails requires a resort to sample surveying of a highly specialized and expensive variety. The advantage of the group conceptualization is that it can be readily employed in conjunction with aggregate figures, both from the Census and the Report of the Chief Electoral Officer. As such, it is more within the capabilities of individual observers operating on limited budgets.

A significant feature of Canadian political behaviour is the seeming instability of voter commitment to party over time. It appears as if there are very few constants which can be relied upon in terms of individual party support. One important reason for this state of affairs is the failure of the Liberal party, when it came to power in 1935, to make specific appeals that could be explicitly group-oriented (the one exception being French Canada). While it is true that the decade 1939-1949 saw a substantial program of social legislation enacted, this legislation was not accompanied by the slogans or the display of emblems or indeed by anything resembling the intensity of discussion and even conflict that was so evident in the country to the south. The Liberals avoided such slogans as the "Blue Eagle" and reference to "fat-cats" on Bay and St. James Streets. It seems as if the party had an abhorrence of anything remotely associated with "class" politics and it tried to appeal to the country as a whole. The strategy underlying this social legislation seems to be that it would appeal to the middle and lower economic classes without invoking the charge that the Liberals were not a "national" party because they appealed only to certain specific "classes" in Canadian society instead of "all the people." Of course, this legislation had an implicit appeal and was instrumental in keeping the party in office for close to a generation. This political style, the most significant residue of the King era, has been labelled "managerial" or "governmental" (19) and it remains with the Liberals to this day. Its effect is that there are few groups upon which any party can rely, and all that is left from the Liberal viewpoint is a vague attitude on the part of some above-noted groups that it is in some way "for the common man."

The relative absence of stable group party affiliation may in part account for the comparatively high voting turn-out in Canada in relation to the United States. Normal turn-out in Canada is approximately 75 per cent of those eligible. (The last two elections have

---

18. Campbell et al., The Voter Decides, pp.83-177.

19. See, for example, F.H. Underhill's Presidential Address to the Royal Society "The Revival of Conservatism in North America," Transactions of the Royal Society of Canada, LII, June, 1958, pp.14-16.

seen even higher levels of participation: 79.8 per cent voted in 1958 and 79.3 per cent voted in 1962.) On the other hand, Americans can invariably be counted upon to indulge themselves in outbursts of self-congratulation if 65 per cent of their eligible voters can be induced to come out to the polls in presidential years. However, in the United States, elements of "cross-pressuring" are continuously in operation and affect individuals so substantially that they are unable to come to a vote decision and thus abstain on election day. (20) For example, lower-income urban Catholics might normally be expected to support the Democratic party. When these people move up the income scale or change their residence to suburbia, new surroundings and new status are influences in favour of the Republicans. Occasionally, these influences are so powerful that the party allegiances of these people are changed. Often, however, they are just strong enough to present these people with a situation of conflict to the extent that they cannot make up their minds and thus they stay home.

Part of the differential in turn-out in Canada's favour may, of course, be accounted for in simple institutional terms. It is much easier to vote in Canada than in the United States because the government has the role of enumerating the electorate while Americans must perform a positive act in registering themselves so that they may be eligible. Nevertheless, the relative absence of the "cross-pressure" element in Canada should not be overlooked.

Finally, the entire question of the effectiveness of the Canadian party system as an integrating device for the political process must be considered. (21) The Canadian system has as one of its functional requirements that in any election one party be able to obtain a majority of seats in the House of Commons. Generally, this has happened because one party has been able to "represent" enough of Canada's diversity and thus gain that requisite majority. Ideally, the party system stands at the top of the overlapping reference group layers and acts as an instrument of concensus. This obviously did not happen in 1962 and commentators are now pointing out that Canada may be witnessing a Balkanization of its politics. (22)

The party system "failed" and that failure was probably a compound consisting of historic factors, ideological sets, cowardice, and ignorance. As V.O. Key points out: "The public cannot innovate; it can only acclaim or reject innovation." (23) One of the most

20. See Berelson et al., _Voting_, pp.129-32; also S.M. Lipset, _Political Man_ (New York, 1959), pp.203-19.

21. Talcott Parsons' "'Voting' and the Equilibrium of the American Political System," in E. Burdick and A.J. Brodbeck, eds., _American Voting Behaviour_ (Glencoe, 1959), pp.80-120, is an analysis which employs the "integration" concept to explain the role of parties in the United States.

22. See, for example, John Meisel, "The June 1962 Election: Break-up of Our Party System?" _Queens Quarterly_, LXIX, autumn, 1962, pp.329-60.

23. V.O. Key, Jr., _Public Opinion and American Democracy_ (New York, 1961), p.286.

important avenues of opinion formation is political leadership. This seemed to be lacking in 1962. For of all the manifestations of public opinion noted by observers, one point stands out: that the opinions of the public are aroused in but the slightest degree by most government action. And yet, even before the campaign had begun, all polls, public, and private alike, showed a remarkable falling off of public support from the Conservative government. Six weeks of expensive and tedious campaigning could only produce a stalemate.

One suspects that Canada's politicians overlooked this fact and tended to overestimate the power of some groups to the detriment of the whole. It is an accepted canon of analysis that the most vociferous and attentive groups in a political system are often the least representative. (24) The danger is that political leadership, which tries to be politically responsive and thinks it is succeeding, can mistake the nature of its constituency. Thus, to the Liberals, the upper-income discontent, with its demands for "holding the line," was paramount (forgetting that the distribution of House of Commons seats is not based solely on population but that certain regions, and the rural areas generally, are overweighted). On the other hand, farm satisfaction and rural quiescence were interpreted by the Tories as representative of the country's contentment with the government.

These further remarks by Key provide an apt summation: "The odds are that leadership echelons with a compulsive deference to public opinion become cautious, even to the point of failure to take the initiative on issues of the gravest importance. Politicians so habituated are mightily tempted to avoid disturbing sleeping dogs." (25) The question of leadership was of considerable significance in another connection. It is my own view that one of the major reasons the Liberals did not obtain a plurality (questions of vote distribution aside) was that Mr. Pearson was not seen by the public as an alternative to Prime Minister Diefenbaker. In most areas (Ontario was the exception), the Liberal leader was running behind his party while, if the Diefenbaker coat-tails were not really operating, the Prime Minister was way ahead, not only of his party but of all the other leaders.

In effect, the country seemed to be experiencing an election similar to the one that returned Eisenhower to power in the United States in 1956. At that time, Eisenhower won the presidency easily, but his party lost both Houses of Congress. In other words, if Canada had an electoral and institutional system similar to the American, Diefenbaker would have been the President-Prime Minister while the Liberals would have won the House of Commons. Obviously, this is not the Canadian system and no "ticket-splitting" at this level is possible. However, it was the absence of a positive leadership appeal by the Liberal leader which was at least partially responsible for holding up the break-away from the Conservatives

---

24. See S.M. Lipset's List of social characteristics which correlate with high levels of political participation in Political Man, p.184; also see footnote 2.

25. Key, Public Opinion and American Democracy, p.286.

that was evident everywhere with the exception of the Prairies.

This ingredient underlies the cause of the sudden shift back to the Conservatives towards the end of the campaign.   The Gallup poll had shown the Liberals to be well in the lead with an 8 per cent spread in popular support between them and the Conservatives with just under four weeks to go in the campaign.   Several days before the end, however, a bare 2 per cent separated the two parties.

These statements about the leadership factor are not purely speculative but are based upon answers given by the public to the question: "Forgetting for a moment which party you prefer, which one of the following men (Diefenbaker, Pearson, Douglas, Thompson) do you think would make the best Prime Minister?"   Conservatives hardly ever hesitated in naming Mr. Diefenbaker.   On the other hand, many Liberals replied: "Well, that's a difficult question" or, even, that Mr. Diefenbaker was best.   Minor party supporters were also favourably disposed towards the Conservative leader.   He automatically had the edge, of course, because he was the present incumbent.   Even if this was taken into account, however, the Conservative chieftain remained well in front.

It should not be inferred from this that Mr. Diefenbaker came close to retaining his phenomenal popular appeal of 1958 or that some other leader might have been preferable for the Liberals. There is also no criticism of Liberal campaign techniques or of Mr. Pearson personally implied here either.   These points are concerned solely with the issue of the impact of "leadership" upon the public.   It is clear that Mr. Pearson was the only "available" man for the position of leader of his party in 1958 and he had, in the space of a few short years, reunited a broken party to the point where it was seriously challenging a government with the largest majority in the country's history.   There are many aspects to party leadership and public appeal is only one of these.

POLITICAL BEHAVIOUR AND ETHNIC ORIGIN*

Mildred A. Schwartz

The religious and national battles of preceding generations continue to be fought on the otherwise peaceable electoral front of North American politics. Wasn't Al Smith defeated because he was a Catholic? Didn't those of German origin rally behind Willkie's non-interventionist stand? Didn't normally Republican Catholics swing in favour of Kennedy? Take some examples from recent newspaper headlines in Canada: "Ontario Tories Wooing Metro Newcomers' Votes" (1), "Manning Woos Ukrainian Voters" (2), "Liberals try to Split Socreds on Religion" (3), "Pearson, Douglas Both Blast P.M.'s 'Cruel' Ethnic-Vote Bid" (4), "Quebeckers Cheer as Pearson Advocates Bilingualism for All of Canada" (5), "Tory Ethnic Boss Woos Indians" (6). At first glance these are popular and over-simplified conceptions that have grown up about the connection between ethnic membership and voting behaviour. (7) But they are popular conceptions supported by numerous empirical studies. For both the United States and Canada evidence has been accumulated

---

*I wish to acknowledge all the assistance I received in obtaining data and in the preparation of this article. In particular, I want to thank Professors Donald L. Spence and Henry Zentner of the Department of Sociology and Frederick C. Engelmann of the Department of Political Economy, all at the University of Alberta, Calgary, for their valuable comments. Aubrey Morantz kindly gave me permission to make unreserved use of his Master's thesis for the Department of Political Economy, University of Toronto.

1. Toronto Daily Star, Oct. 26, 1961.
2. Calgary Herald, Oct. 16, 1962.
3. Globe and Mail, May 29, 1962.
4. Toronto Daily Star, June 13, 1962.
5. Globe and Mail, May 14, 1962.
6. Toronto Daily Star, June 13, 1962.
7. By ethnicity is meant origin from a common cultural background based on nationality, language, religion, or race, either singly or combined. See Frank G. Vallee, Mildred Schwartz, Frank Darknell, "Ethnic Assimilation and Differentiation in Canada," Canadian Journal of Economics and Political Science, XXIII, no. 4, Nov., 1957, p.541. Everyone then has an ethnic origin, although it is often difficult to decide what this is as a result of intermarriage or distance from the immigrant generation, nor is it always a salient social characteristic.

indicating the links between ethnic group membership, turnout at elections, and party preference. (8) An analysis of characteristics of voters from a Gallup poll survey taken just prior to the 1962 election indicated that Catholics were almost twice as likely to vote Liberal as were Protestants while the Conservative party had comparatively less appeal to those whose mother tongue was other than English. (9)

   Along with an emphasis on the connection between ethnic origin and party preference has been a recognition of the enduring nature of political loyalties. Here again we have documented material on the stability of preference, not only within an individual's life (10), but over generations. (11) Hyman has recently assembled an inventory of the literature on the socio-psychological processes which lead to the establishment of political loyalties early in life. (12) For

------

8. Among the numerous studies are the following: Alfred de Grazia, "The Limits of External Leadership over a Minority Electorate," Public Opinion Quarterly, XX, 1956, pp.113-28. L.M. Fuchs The Political Behavior of American Jews (Glencoe, 1956). Samuel Lubell, The Future of American Politics (New York, 1956), pp.72-79, 82-84, 224-227. Madge M. McKinney, "Religion and Elections," Public Opinion Quarterly, VIII, 1944, pp.110-14. Bernard R. Berelson, Paul F. Lazarsfeld, and William N. McPhee, Voting (Chicago, 1954), pp.61-73. John Meisel, "Religious Affiliation and Electoral Behaviour: A Case Study," Canadian Journal of Economics and Political Science, XXII, no.4, Nov., 1956, pp. 481-96. S.M. Lipset, Agrarian Socialism (Berkeley and Los Angeles, 1950), pp.183-6, 190-2. S.M. Lipset, P.F. Lazarsfeld, A.H. Barton, J.J. Linz, "The Psychology of Voting: An Analysis of Political Behavior" in Gardner Lindzey, ed., Handbook of Social Psychology, II (Cambridge, 1954), pp.1124-1170. Paul F. Lazarsfeld, Bernard R. Berelson, and Hazel Gaudet, The People's Choice, 2nd ed. (New York, 1948), pp.21-25. Robert R. Alford, Social Class and Voting in Four Anglo-American Democracies (Berkeley, 1961), pp.286-95. Arthur Kornhauser, Albert J. Mayer, Harold L. Sheppard, When Labor Votes (New York, 1956), pp.29-75. Angus Campbell, Philip E. Converse, Warren E. Miller, Donald E. Stokes, The American Voter (New York, 1960), pp.295-332. Robert E. Lane, Political Life (Glencoe, 1959), pp.235-55. Angus Campbell, Gerald Gurin, Warren E. Miller, The Voter Decides (Evanston, 1954), pp.76-9.

9. Canadian Institute of Public Opinion releases, July 11, 1962, and August 1, 1962. See also the paper by R.R. Alford in the present volume.

10. Campbell et al., The American Voter, pp.146-9; Campbell et al., The Voter Decides, p.17.

11. V.O. Key, Jr. and Frank Munger, "Social Determinism and Electoral Decision: the Case of Indiana," in Eugene Burdick and Arthur J. Brodbeck, eds., American Voting Behavior (Glencoe, 1959), pp.281-99; Lazarsfeld et al., The People's Choice, p.142; Lipset et al., "The Psychology of Voting: An Analysis of Political Behavior," pp.1166-8.

12. Herbert H. Hyman, Political Socialization (Glencoe, 1959),

Canada it is possible to get some indication of the continuity of party preference from an examination of Gallup poll data. In fifteen surveys conducted by the Canadian Institute of Public Opinion since 1951, at least half of the electorate said they would vote for the same party in the coming election as in the previous one. (13)

It is often difficult to isolate the factors responsible for the initial attachment of a particular ethnic group to a political party. For this reason the present Canadian political scene presents a unique social laboratory. Since the end of the Second World War, more than two million immigrants have come to Canada and found themselves in a new political setting. Here then we have the opportunity to investigate how groups formulate new attachments to political parties.

In seeking to account for these attachments, we should look at the structural implications which follow from the fact of ethnic identity. For example, age and sex are two variables which are often examined in relation to political attitudes or behaviour, with the finding that women and older persons are more conservative than their opposite numbers. (14) But these findings give us no explanation of why this should be so until we turn to the life situation which is part of age and sex statuses. This life situation is partly made up of historical circumstances and partly of reciprocal expectations inherent in the statuses occupied, with each contributing in varying degrees to the attitudes or behaviour under consideration. (15) Life situations can vary over time, because of shifts both in statuses occupied and in environmental circumstances. Ethnic origin, as an explanatory variable, needs to be treated in a manner analogous to

especially pp. 69-87. See also H.H. Remmers, "Early Socialization of Attitudes," in Burdick and Brodbeck, eds., American Voting Behaviour, pp. 55-67.

13. Percentage of Total Sample with Same Party Preference for Past and Intended Vote

Survey Date	%	Survey Date	%
August, 1951	59	March, 1957	48
May, 1954	58	December, 1957	58
September, 1954	57	August, 1958	68
November, 1954	63	March, 1959	60
July, 1955	62	July, 1960	56
March, 1956	74	July, 1961	47
October, 1956	67	January, 1962	50
		March, 1962	52

Source: Compiled by author from CIPO surveys supplied by the Roper Center for Public Opinion Research.

14. For example, Hans Toch, "Attitudes of the 'Fifty Plus' Age Group: Preliminary Considerations Toward a Longitudinal Survey," Public Opinion Quarterly, XVII, no.3, 1953, pp.391-4; Mark Benney, A.P. Gray, R.H. Pear, How People Vote (London, 1956), pp.106-7.

15. Suggestions of this nature are contained in William M. Evan, "Cohort Analysis of Survey Data: A Procedure for Studying Long-term Opinion Change," Public Opinion Quarterly, XXIII, no.1, 1959, pp.63-72, and Benney et al., How People Vote, pp.108-9.

age and sex.   The questions which need to be raised centre on the consequences of occupying an ethnic status.

An adequate examination of the relation between political behaviour and ethnic origin would begin by examining samples of foreign-born, controlling for national origin and length of residence in Canada, and comparing these to native-born, similar in such respects as socio-economic status.   Such a study has in fact been designed but circumstances have prevented its being carried out at this time. Instead the present article presents a series of hypotheses about the relation between ethnic origin and political behaviour which remain to be tested.   The propositions have been inductively derived from material obtained on the foreign-born resident in three federal ridings in Metropolitan Toronto prior to the 1962 general election. (16) Under each hypothesis I have listed a number of sub-hypotheses which are components of the more general statements, along with some examples of these.   These examples are in no way to be considered proof of the theoretical scheme but rather as illustrations of the kind of information which would constitute evidence.

The following hypotheses are concerned with those features of social life which tend to encourage political participation, either in general or in a partisan direction.   Political participation has been variously defined to include such obvious things as voting or formal membership in a political party and also taking part in political discussions, reading or listening to political news, actively working on behalf of a party or candidate, and so on.   For our purposes we will say that a minimum definition of participation involves voting.   In the case of the foreign-born, this kind of participation requires first the acquisition of citizenship and this step should then be included in our minimal definition.   The hypotheses consist of three major propositions basic to my concept of life situation as it relates to participation.   No attempt is made here to rate the relative importance of these propositions.

In this discussion, ethnic origin is not systematically treated as a differentiated property.   That is, while some mention is made of the fact that ethnic groups differ not only among themselves but also internally (17), this is not specifically the focus of the paper.   An adequate empirical investigation would need to take this differentiation into account. (18)   But even the illustrations used in the following discussion indicate the existence of certain critical differences within and among ethnic groups, for example, in the issues with which they are concerned in their contacts with a politicizing environment, in

---

16. The source material consists of fifty interviews conducted or supervised by the author, a hundred done for a Master's thesis in the Department of Political Economy at the University of Toronto by Aubrey Morantz, and a survey of the relevant literature.   Federal ridings are those with a large proportion of foreign-born voters: Spadina, Davenport, and York South.

17. See below, p.262-3.

18. Vallee et al., "Ethnic Differentiation and Assimilation," p.540.

their utilization of ethnic newspapers, and in their homeland experiences. Many other differences exist as well, in such things as
residential patterns (19) and occupational distribution. (20) Further
study is needed to characterize different types of ethnic groups in
their relation to the political milieu. But for the time being, even
the relatively undifferentiated use of ethnicity employed here points up
the fruitfulness of this concept for research purposes.

I. PARTICIPATION IS ENCOURAGED BY EXPOSURE
TO A POLITICIZING ENVIRONMENT

1.   Where the environment promotes situations increasing political
awareness, participation will also be increased.   This involves such
things as opportunities for hearing about political parties, being able to
discuss them, and being conscious of society as made up of diverse
interest groups with affinities for particular parties.   Those completely apathetic to politics, or who find it uninteresting and uninspiring
are less likely to vote. (21)   For the immigrant, interest may be
affected by comparison with politics in the home country.   Local
politics may then appear less interesting and exciting.   One respondent noted that at home politics was the favoured topic of discussion
while here it was work.   Casual observation often suggests that
native Canadians are more interested in United States presidential
elections than in Canadian ones.   In the face of Canadian indifference,
immigrants may be curtailed in their opportunity to become knowledge-
able about or interested in Canadian politics.   One respondent said
she never discussed politics with her native-born friends, since it
appeared to be one of those socially tabooed subjects like religion or
salaries.

Taking part in any kind of group where voting, collective de-
cision-making, and shared activites are required, all constitute the
makings of a politicized environment.   Some groups have obviously
more political content than others, but membership in any kind of
association helps to make individuals politically conscious. (22)
Among the immigrants who were interviewed for this pilot study

19. City of Toronto Planning Board, Report on Ethnic Origins
of the Population of Toronto, 1960 (Toronto, 1961).

20. Bernard Blishen, "The Construction and Use of an Occupational Class Scale," in Bernard Blishen, Frank Jones, Kaspar
Naegle, and John Porter, Canadian Society (Glencoe, 1961), pp.
477-85.

21. Berelson et al., Voting, pp.31-3, 314.   Lazarsfeld et al.,
The People's Choice, pp.40-51.   Campbell et al., The Voter Decides, pp.33-5.

22. For example, looking at such things as " ... interest in
social issues, voting, and support of community charities - show
that voluntary association participants are more involved civically
than non-members." C.R. Wright and Herbert H. Hyman, "Voluntary Association Memberships of American Adults: Evidence from
National Sample Surveys," American Sociological Review, XXIII,
June, 1958, p.293.

there were clear differences in contacts with politicizing groups. For example, the Italians stand out by the low level of their political environment. Many of these immigrants had been interested in politics in Italy, but undoubtedly there was also a long history of discouragement for this kind of involvement. Coming to Canada they tended to interact with members of their own group, but characteristically this interaction has not become formalized into organizational activities. One exception is the participation of some Italian immigrants in labour unions. Hungarian immigrants by contrast soon joined groups which were often concerned primarily with their homeland, but by extension, also with actions of the Canadian government as these had implications for homeland problems. (23)

2.   The existence of an explicit and positive national identity will promote participation. What is required here is a fairly clear-cut conception of the kind of country Canada is and a willingness to make a wholehearted commitment to this. In determining this national identity, particularly for newcomers, the lack of political symbols in Canada may be a handicap. One immigrant inquired about the number of pictures of the Queen he saw in public places, wondered whether Canadians paid taxes to support the Royal Family, and if there was a strong monarchist party in Canada. He was unimpressed with the suggestion that the Queen acted as a unifying symbol. "If you have your own country you should have your own symbols." Another respondent felt Mr. Diefenbaker had curtailed immigration during a period of heavy unemployment not for this reason but because "He's afraid we'll take away the Queen." Political symbols are a short-hand way of identifying a country, but they are also filled with emotional content, and it is this which may be important in furthering attitudes of political loyalty.

The character of a country may be defined in many ways additional to its symbolic representations, and in some cases particular aspects of this character can deter a sense of identification. For example, this may occur among those immigrants who complain of the lack of "culture" in Canada. The deterrent may arise from the superior rating which is given to the home country in comparison with the new one. Another possible view was expressed by one immigrant who, although he had achieved financial success and ties with his ethnic and the larger community, had little interest in acquiring citizenship. While he was a strong exponent of the ethic that hard work is always rewarded and that immigrants have full opportunities, he believed that immigrants are never completely accepted politically. His feeling was that an immigrant was always a second-class citizen, and unless he was handicapped by not having a passport, there was no particular advantage to becoming a citizen of Canada. Here the reluctance to identify with Canada was associated with the actual or feared rebuff he would receive in the political sphere.

---

23. Compare Oscar Handlin, The Uprooted (Boston, 1951), p.207.

If an explicit Canadian national identity tends to encourage participation, particularly if this is evaluated in favourable terms, strong attitudes of loyalty to another political entity will discourage participation. At the same time, a strong attachment to one's former homeland need not prevent an additional identification with Canada. For example, one Italian immigrant who discussed his love of his home country, acknowledged "living here is much better" and for this reason, he was committed to making a home in Canada, and to raising his children as Canadians. Other individuals or even whole ethnic groups who see their sojourn in Canada as only temporary, may not be willing to make this same kind of commitment. For example, those from Iron Curtain countries who expect shortly to return attempt to sustain a strong attachment to their homeland and may be reluctant to acquire citizenship.

3.   **Participation is encouraged where government and its functions are not seen as unduly complex or remote.** The potential voter should not feel that politics and government are so complicated that they cannot be readily understood, nor should he believe that government is primarily influenced by a strong leader rather than by party politics. Instead, the voter should feel that government is not so difficult to influence that the average citizen cannot make his opinions felt. These are factors contained in what has been termed "a sense of political efficacy." (24) At the same time as the voter sees the political process as within his comprehension and influence, he needs to appraise realistically the forms which this influence can take. For example, several Italian respondents commented that when former Mayor Phillips was approached by ethnic representatives about Sunday movies, he listened sympathetically and, in the resolution of this problem, they were permitted some influence. These respondents were impressed with the efficacy of personal contacts with candidates. Another respondent noted how political party members established direct links with voters when they attended ethnic meetings and said, "Call me whenever you need help." At the organizational level, some groups have discovered the effectiveness of contacts with their members of Parliament, cabinet members, and the prime minister. Influence through voting, especially if this can be delivered as a bloc, is always the final means of pressure.

Along with the feeling that government can be influenced by the people, there should also be some knowledge of and differentiation among the different levels of government. For the native Canadian it is often confusing to sort out the powers of the municipal, provincial, and federal governments and it is hardly surprising if immigrants find it even more so. For the most part, the immigrants who were interviewed were able to differentiate between municipal and federal levels of government, and the responsibilities which are allotted to each. Except for respondents from Germany, experience with federal systems of government is limited, and many commented

_____

24. Campbell et al., The Voter Decides, pp.187-94. See also Angus Campbell et al., The American Voter, pp.103-5.

that they found provincial politics uninteresting, and could not really see their purpose.

4.   The recognition of reliable sources of information encourages participation.   By reliable I do not necessarily mean unbiased or objective, but rather that those making use of the sources see them as trust-worthy.   For the non-English speaking immigrant this may mean reliance on the foreign-langugage press for most of his news. In recent years at least, the political parties in Canada have attempted to encourage and foster the growth of the ethnic press.   Prior to the 1962 election, the Conservatives and Liberals both were active in entertaining ethnic newspaper publishers and providing them with releases for their papers. (25)   It is nevertheless difficult to evaluate the effectiveness of ethnic newspapers as sources of information for their readers.   Among those interviewed who read ethnic newspapers, the feeling was that they were good for homeland news, social events, and special sports coverage, but generally that news coverage was rather limited and dated.   One informant, however, mentioned that a good summary of the week's news was given in the ethnic newspaper that he read.   For the others, if ethnic newspapers were primarily looked at for special items rather than for news coverage or for guidance on political matters, then possibly political parties were paying undue attention to ethnic newspapers rather than to the members of ethnic groups themselves.   In order for a source of information to be influential in drawing groups into the political community, it must both provide information and guide groups in a particular political direction.   If ethnic newspapers are seen either as providing insufficient information, or if they provide it in such a way as to give an undesirably biased picture of political events, then their effectiveness appears to be limited.

Information about political matters need not of course come from the mass media.   It might be provided by friends, relatives, work associates, organizations to which a person belongs, and organizations or groups which are looked to for guidance.   The first requirement is obviously that the immigrant should have people with whom he can discuss politics.   Some immigrants who were interviewed said that politics had been a favourite topic of conversation in Europe, but here they did not notice Canadians speaking about political matters with the same degree of interest or frequency. As hypothesized earlier, a politicized environment encourages participation in that it prepares people to think about events in terms of the distribution of power among different interest groups.   Belonging to politicizing groups also provides information and guidance to those interested in politics.   Identification with an ethnic group may lead to this kind of guidance as well.   As one respondent said

---

25. See Globe and Mail, April 30, 1962, for an article on the Conservatives headed "Spread Gospel According to John, Walker Implores Ethnic Editors," and the same newspaper, May 6, 1962, for one on the Liberals, headed "Political? Perish the Idea."

when asked about the influences of her ethnic group on voting, "If they said that someone was good to vote for and he would do good things for us, then I would vote for him."

II. PARTICIPATION IS ENCOURAGED WHERE THERE IS AN IMMEDIATE CONNECTION BETWEEN POLITICS AND INDIVIDUAL OR GROUP INTERESTS

1.   Immigrants will be drawn into the political community where current political issues are of concern to the individual, his family, or his ethnic group.   Studies done in the United States indicate the role of ethnic groups in attempting to influence policies on matters concerned with their homelands. (26)   Domestic policies also can have their main impact in terms of ethnic identification. (27)   During the 1952 federal election campaign, there were four issues which stood out as of major concern to the foreign-born.   These were governmental policies pertaining to communism, immigration, unemployment, and social welfare.   The first two affect the foreign-born in terms of the strength of his ethnic identification and the others in respect to his present social and economic position.

Those born in countries which are now under communist control have been anxious that the Canadian government take a strong anti-communist stand and they have critically evaluated party pronouncements on this issue.   The level of consistency which some demand of Canadian parties was exemplified by one respondent. While she agreed that Conservatives appeared to be most firm in their stand against communism, she could not reconcile this with their encouragement of trade with communist countries.   In this instance, her solution was not to vote unless the candidate who was running in her riding was ideologically more consistent than his party.

When a respondent who mentioned the offer of some party members to assist ethnic voters was asked about the kind of help that might be provided, she answered, "Immigrants always want to bring someone over."   Canada, throughout her history, has been a country of immigration and, at the same time, has allowed legislation to define the groups and individuals she considers "desirable." (28) Once landed in Canada, the immigrant who wishes to have his friends and relatives join him is faced with differentiating among the parties in terms of the liberality of their proposed immigration schemes.

In 1962, unemployment was the major campaign issue, at least to opposition parties, as it had been the main problem for the economy in the year and a half prior to the calling of the election.

---

26. Gabriel A. Almond, <u>The American People and Foreign Policy</u> (New York, 1960), pp.183-9.

27. Lane, <u>Political Life</u>, pp.237-8.

28. See David C. Corbett, <u>Canada's Immigration Policy</u> (Toronto, 1957), and Vallee <u>et al</u>., "Ethnic Assimilation and Differentiation in Canada," pp.544-5.

Both native- and foreign-born were affected by this problem, but the foreign-born, by virtue of their inferior economic position and limited job skills, often suffered more. While the view of some is that economic hardship is due to such individual failings as laziness and immorality, many foreign-born believed that the government had a responsibility to provide employment and relieve extreme want. According to a disappointed immigrant, "If you invite someone into your home, you can't just leave him alone."

Immigrants accustomed to more comprehensive government social welfare plans in their home country were concerned about the absence of these in Canada. This was especially the case where immigrants could ill-afford medical bills or to support themselves and their families when unemployment insurance ran out. To one immigrant, it was in Canada that he discovered the meaning of freedom - "Here a man is free to be sick or to starve." We normally associate strong anti-communism with right-wing ideologies, but this does not necessarily extend to a distrust of social welfare legislation or economic planning, as several of the respondents in this pilot study indicated.

2.   Participation will be encouraged where individuals and groups have established ties with the community. Political activity to the extent of becoming a citizen and of voting can be seen as an indicator of the degree to which individuals identify with their new home. Strong ties with an ethnic community may also be a means of encouraging participation when this is seen as a way of enhancing the group's status or protecting its interests. A feeling of identification with an ethnic group has implications for partisanship when parties and their candidates seek to capitalize on it by presenting themselves as special protectors of the group. For example, the Conservative candidate in Spadina riding urged Italians to "Elect John Bassett as the member for Spadina in Parliament and be certain that you have elected a friend of the Italians ..."(29) Carried to its conclusion, this view can mean that each ethnic group should have its own representative. In Toronto's Trinity riding, an independent Italian candidate stated, "I feel I have a moral obligation to run. Thirty-five per cent of Trinity is made up of Italian newcomers and Canadians of Italian origin."(30) But those who take such positions infer that each ethnic group is a unified entity and this is rarely the case. Interviews conducted in Toronto produced massive evidence of differences based on the regions from which immigrants came, length of settlement in Canada, immigration experiences, past and present social class, and so on. These internal differences are also relevant to the political activites of the group and the kind of leadership it offers. For example, the Italians are not particularly well organized and there are no strong leaders to direct voting in a particular direction. This likely contributed to the failure of the independent candidate in Trinity to gain

29. Corriere Illustrato, June 16, 1962.
30. Toronto Daily Star, June 4, 1962.

any significant number of votes or of a Conservative candidate of Italian origin in Hamilton East to win.   Another kind of example is presented by the Ukrainians.   Here the newcomers interviewed felt that their group would vote Conservative to a man, but they could not be so sure of pre-1939 immigrants.   The more recent arrivals expressed suspicion of the latter in terms of their political reliability and there was even some "communist" labelling.   Identification, then, need not be with an entire group or community.   In this connection, one German respondent noted how pre-war German immigrants had been overly concerned with their own economic advancement and "missed the chance to act together, to do something about the government's immigration policy ...   The Germans just aren't a united group, like the Ukrainians or the Jews.   The Ukrainians have seen to it that they have representatives in politics."   In contrast to the earlier immigrants, he felt that later ones were much more politically oriented and conceivably would take a more active role in politics.

3.   A further impetus to participation comes where politics is viewed as a channel of mobility, either for the individual himself or for his group.   Oscar Handlin describes this process as more likely affecting the second generation." ... many youngsters growing up in the confused decades after 1850 came to understand that the State might also be a means of their own personal advancement."(31) The possibility of politics being viewed as an avenue of advancement is greatly enhanced when political parties nominate members of different ethnic groups for potential office.   In this way the members of that group have a visible sign that one of their own can achieve. (32)   For some groups achievement is readily apparent and may be identified with one particular party.   In this way, for example, it is said that the Progressive Conservatives have tied up the Ukrainian vote because of the political recognition they have given to Ukrainians, extending to cabinet positions. (33)   The possibility of a member holding political office in Canada may, however, seem remote to some groups.   Some of those interviewed expressed ambivalent feelings about having one of their group run for office, fearing for one thing that such a person would not be acceptable to other Canadians, and that, by extension, other ethnic groups would have the same privilege.   Thus some Hungarians felt that no Hungarian would vote for a German or an Italian, and for this reason a "Canadian" would be preferable.   Within-group jealousies can also be brought to the fore in this way, with distrust for a group member overriding pride in his accomplishments.   This view was expressed by several Italian respondents who did not think Italians would be especially prone to vote for other Italians, since they thought these would "be out for themselves."   But where such sentiments are kept under control, it would appear that the achievements of ethnic group members

---

31. The Uprooted, p.209.
32. Campbell et al., The American Voter, p. 313.
33. Globe and Mail, Jan. 29, 1962.

should serve as a stimulus to participation.

4.   A prior ideological commitment will enhance the likelihood of
participating.   Voters who come on the political scene with an already existing ideological position have ready-made frameworks in
which to fit present party platforms.   Ideologies are viewed here as
relatively consistent attitudes toward, for example, the role of government in social and economic affairs, issues of domestic and foreign
communism, or the importance of social class as a determinant of interests.   These are fairly comprehensive frames of reference which
can be activated by specific party pronouncements.   Those with an
orientation which begins with the premise that governments have
certain welfare responsibilities to their citizens would use this in
judging party platforms and selecting the party which best adheres
to these requirements.   This appeared to be the attitude of some of
the Italian respondents.   In the case of one respondent, at least, an
ideological commitment which was strongly anti-communist led away
from participation since no party was seen as adequate in this respect.   The more usual occurence would be, however, that when a
voter comes with an ideological approach to political questions, he
is more likely to participate than otherwise.

III. WHEN PARTIES AND THEIR CANDIDATES ACTIVELY SEEK TO RECRUIT SUPPORTERS AND TO DIFFERENTIATE AMONG THEMSELVES, THERE WILL BE AN ENCOURAGEMENT OF PARTICIPATION

1.   When parties take issues affecting voters as an important basis
for differentiating their policies, participation will be encouraged.   I
have already indicated the four crucial issues in the past election.
For all of these, the parties made special efforts to appeal to ethnic
voters.   In respect to communism, the Conservatives undoubtedly
preempted the privilege of being more anti-communist than anyone
else.   This distinction was consolidated as the result of a speech by
Mr. Diefenbaker delivered before the United Nations on September 26,
1960, when he urged the dismantling of the Soviet colonial empire. (34)
The Liberal party's image as an anti-communist force suffered from
a remark Mr. Pearson allegedly made in a television interview on
the CBC programme "Closeup," on May 19, 1960.   Several minutes
before the conclusion of the broadcast, Mr. Pearson was asked
what he would do if forced to choose between atomic immolation or
life under communism.   In the brief time left to him, Mr. Pearson
answered that he would "live under Khruschev rather than die, and
do what I could to throw Mr. Khruschev and his ilk out of power."
(35)   From this time, Mr. Pearson had never been considered
quite "safe" and several days before the 1962 election the then Minister of Finance told his constituents, "The man the Russians want
is the man who said - as much as he may regret it - I would rather

---

34. Ibid., Sept. 27, 1960.
35. Toronto Daily Star, June 16, 1962.

be red than dead." (36)   But despite the suspicion with which Mr.
Pearson was regarded by some Eastern Europeans, this view did
not necessarily extend to all members of the Liberal party.   Paul
Martin, for example, has been singled out by some Eastern European groups for the outspokeness of his denunciation of communism.
(37)   Before one ethnic audience he said, "We from the Liberal
party think that merely to condemn the enslavement of Eastern
European countries by Communist colonialism is not enough.   We
feel that some positive steps have to be taken towards the liberation
of these people." (38)   In these terms the Liberal party, and also
Mr. Pearson in particular, attempted to redeem themselves in the
eyes of the anti-communists. (39)   The NDP too attempted to modi-
fy their conciliatory orientation to international affairs in order to gain
the relevant ethnic votes.   For example, the NDP pledge to get out
of NORAD and, under some circumstances, NATO, was so soft-
pedalled by most NDP candidates in the Toronto ridings as to be
almost non-existent.

     Clearly then the political parties felt it important in attracting
votes from those of Eastern European origin to emphasize the one
issue they were certain was of uppermost concern.   In doing so,
they undoubtedly led Canada into a harder cold war stand than was
formerly the case, a position which might not have been pleasing to
other Canadians if they were intensely interested or aware of it. (40)
For the ethnic voter concerned with party attitudes towards communism, however, this movement toward clearer policy positions can
only have aided him in making a choice.

     Parties also attempted to acquire votes through the interest of
many ethnic groups in immigration policies.   In February of 1962
the Conservative government changed immigration regulations by an

---

     36. Ibid.
     37. Oleg Pidhaini, ed., New Review, II, no.3, May, 1962,
p.l.
     38. Translated from Kanadsky Slovak, Jan. 10, 1962.
     39. For example, Mr. Pearson's speech at a Toronto "Free-
dom Festival," Jan., 1962.
     40. "The more substantial indictment of the present government
is that it has accelerated the decline of Canada's influence, part of
which may have been inevitable, by playing to the gallery - by sub-
verting foreign and defence policy to considerations of domestic popularity." Peyton Lyon, Toronto Daily Star, May 16, 1962.
     Some indications of attitudes toward defence generally can
be derived from two Gallup poll surveys.   In one, 31 per cent of the
respondents had no opinion about Canadian defence policies (Canadian
Institute of Public Opinion release, Aug.25, 1962).   In the other, 47
per cent felt the US should stop atomic tests compared to 39 per cent
who wanted them continued.   (Canadian Institute of Public Opinion
release, Sept. 1, 1962).   Both surveys hardly suggest a highly militant climate of opinion.
     For the effects of ethnic groups and "reactionary nationalists"
on American foreign policy, compare Almond, The American People
and Foreign Policy, pp.191, 200-209.

order-in-council to permit a greater number of non-whites to settle in Canada.   The changes were intended to remove some of the ill feelings caused by previous measures, particularly as these affected sponsored Italian immigrants (41) and the inept handling of illegal Chinese immigrants.   The election results appeared to indicate that these moves were still not sufficient.   Roland Michener and Douglas Jung were defeated in ridings with a large proportion of Chinese, and three candidates in Toronto (Morton, Frolick, and Bassett) met a similar fate in constituencies where many Italians reside.   As a symbol of the failure of the Conservative government to appease the ethnic voter on this score, the then Minister of Citizenship and Immigration, Ellen Fairclough, was replaced after the election. (42) Since other parties were not guiltless in terms of desiring restrictive legislation, whether or not restrictions were to be geared to employment opportunities, immigrants concerned about this issue might have found themselves voting against Conservative policies rather than for some preferable alternative.

While the Conservatives tended to play down the significance of unemployment, they were forced to answer at least some of the criticism they received from other parties.   For example, Douglas Morton in Davenport riding stressed the number of new jobs which had been created by the Conservative administration and John Kucherepa in High Park noted such specific accomplishments as the opportunities in construction work which had come from the enlargement of a technical school in his constituency and those which followed from winter works projects. (43)   But it was the Liberal and New Democratic parties which were more successful in appealing to voters with a promise to improve the employment situation.   Here party programmes were often designed not for the ethnic voter as ethnic,

---

41. An April, 1959, order-in-council had limited sponsored immigration, and since most Italian immigrants were admitted under this category, it was at least covertly designed to restrict Italian entry.   Objections were strong and the offending order-in-council was repealed, but not before the development of resentment and suspicion. According to one respondent, "The government seemed to let in all the Germans that wanted to come, but the Italians had to wait many months."

42. "As for the reason why Mrs. Fairclough was shifted from citizenship and immigration to the slot of postmaster-general, a job with no kudos, one has only to remember Diefenbaker's intensive election campaigning for the ethnic vote, and then to recall that it went overwhelmingly against him.   The Chinese- and Italian-Canadian voters, and about every other ethnic group, were apparently dissatisfied with the government's immigration policies.   Those policies were personified, of course, by Mrs. Fairclough," Dillon O'Leary, "They Were Expendable," Star Weekly, Sept. 1, 1962, pp.8-9.   The Toronto Daily Star, June 23, 1962, quotes a Liberal organizer as saying, "Ellen Fairclough was one of our greatest assets."

43. Corriere Canadese, June 13, 1962.

but as a member of a disadvantaged, low-income group. The supposed connection between Conservative governments and hard times did no go unnoticed. An Italian who had arrived in 1954 remarked, "When I came the Liberals were in Ottawa, the country was rich, and it was easy to find a job. Now you have to take whatever you can find." To another Italian, the promises held out by the NDP to solve unemployment crises seemed the most attractive solution. But whatever course the voter took, he saw clear alternatives to the Diefenbaker government.

Parties which held out the promise of increased social welfare assistance appealed to the many immigrants from countries with broader welfare coverage. The Conservatives stressed their achievements in this area in their campaign literature, particularly the reduction in residence requirements for old age pensions. The Liberals were able to refer to past accomplishments in instituting welfare measures as well as future plans. Comprehensive legislation of this nature is widely recognized by both supporters and opponents as one of the major plans in any NDP platform. Despite Conservative actions the general impression was that Liberal and NDP programs were considered more attractive and believable.

2.   Participation will be encouraged where party workers and candidates seek out contacts with voters. Voting studies in Britain and the United States note the importance of personal intervention by the party workers in bringing people to the polls. (44) In the 1962 election the Conservatives, Liberals and NDP all made special efforts, with varying degrees of success, to contact ethnic voters. Since 1953 the Conservative party has had a Metropolitan Toronto organizer whose prime responsibility is ethnic liaison work, although according to the former incumbent of this office, good contacts with ethnic groups were not effected until 1950. (45) The Liberal liaison officer is styled "personal representative to the leader of the Liberal party," but unlike his Conservative counterpart, he must combine his duties with those as a member of the Ontario provincial legislature. The NDP does not have a full-time ethnic contact in Toronto at present, and like the CCF before it, has made no concerted attempt to deal with ethnic groups at the organizational level. It is the Conservative party which appears to have made the most thorough-going efforts to maintain close relations with ethnic voters. These include such things as providing speakers for organizations, supplying press releases for the ethnic press, and serving as a clearing house for reports and recommendations from ethnic representatives. To keep in tune with developments, the ethnic press was carefully scanned, some research was undertaken, and ethnic leaders and party supporters were eagerly sought after for opinions and advice. While the Liberals did not have such elaborate arrangements, they were greatly aided by the personal qualities of their ethnic contact.

44. Lazarsfeld et al., The People's Choice, pp.150-8; R.S. Milne and H.C. MacKenzie, Straight Fight (London, 1954), p.72.
    45. Source: interview by Aubrey Morantz.

Personable and approachable, he established a wide reputation for sympathy with the problems of his ethnic constituents. (46)   The Conservatives, by contrast, were more remote and concerned with contacts at the organizational and leadership levels.   The NDP's activities have been comparatively fewer than either of the two older parties.   Perhaps its most successful contact has been the Brandon Hall Union Group, representing several thousand Italian construction workers.   The leadership of the union has looked to the NDP as a source of political strength in calling attention to the exploitation of immigrant labour.   But the party seems to have few illusions about its chances of winning over ethnic leaders.   "New Democratic Party officials, for their part, say that they have never been able to match the old parties' investment in the ethnic vote, particularly their purchases of advertising in the ethnic press and their hiring of personnel from the ethnic community in their organiation." (47)   While the parties varied in their efforts to contact members of ethnic groups at higher levels of the organizational hierarchy, there were greater similarities at the riding level, at least for those ridings we examined.   At nomination meetings, spokesmen for different ethnic groups participated in the ceremonies, adding a short speech supporting the candidate nominated, while pretty girls dressed in national dress were part of the decor.   Campaign literature translated into languages other than English was generally available for distribution.   Voters' lists were examined and voters separated by supposed origin.   Canvassers of the same background were then assigned to contact them.

It may well be that contact at the face-to-face level is where votes are gained or lost.   But parties which are most adept at making these contacts can suffer boomerang effects.   For the rank-and-file voter, being courted by a party specifically as a member of an ethnic group can lead to feelings of suspicion as to how he is viewed as a Canadian and he may resent the implication that he is under the political control of his ethnic community leaders.   For these leaders, on the other hand, there is a great stake in being differentiated on ethnic lines, for it is in this way that they acquire prestige and influence.   According to one commentator, "The politicians overrate the ethnic group and underrate the individual 'ethnic'. He is fed up with being thought of as a constantly folk-dancing, 'native'-dressed curiosity.   Our newest citizens want to be treated just like other Canadians, and that goes for election campaigns too." (48)   While the Conservative party made the most concerted attempt to attract the ethnic vote, the Liberals calculate that they obtained about 70 per cent of it in Metropolitan Toronto.   According to Robert Campbell, Toronto and Yorks organizer, "The Tories made their mistake in playing with the 'voices' - the ethnic leaders and ethnic newspaper publishers." (49)

45. See the articles by Pierre Berton in the Toronto Daily Star, June 26, 27, 28, 1961.

47. Globe and Mail, March 5, 1962.

48. Bogden Kipling, Toronto Daily Star, May 30, 1962.

49. Ibid., June 23, 1962. Also personal communication with the author.

3.   Where party leaders have a distinct "image," participation is encouraged.   One means of pointing up differences among parties and at
the same time personalizing the political context is through the creation
of distinctive images for party leaders.   Issues may appear complex
and government remote, but the personality of the leader can evoke
immediate response from the voters.   The leader who represents
personally attractive qualities and special skills in dealing with the
problems that the country faces has obvious advantages in gaining
voters' support.   For example, President Eisenhower's vote-getting
ability is generally attributed to the hero worship that he was able to
inspire.   But, at the time he was running for office when foreign policy was a dominant concern, his military background was also seen
as uniquely appropriate to his new role. (50)   The importance of a
political leader in Canadian politics is possibly not as great as in
American politics although some suggest that it is even greater. (51)
In Canada voters do not ordinarily vote for the leader but for candidates who represent the same party.   Then, if a candidate is attractive or if a party's policies are appealing, the leader's personal
attributes or skills may not be too relevant.   Several respondents
indicated that their behaviour would be influenced more by the former
alternatives than by the leader.   But to others the personality of the
leader was a strong drawing force.   The leader can be an important focus for overcoming the handicaps of traditional party associations, as indicated by the success of the Conservative campaigns in
the 1957 and 1958 general elections.   Then the party was often ad-
vertised as Mr. Diefenbaker's party rather than the Progressive
Conservative party.   Some of the immigrants interviewed also
labelled the political parties in this manner.   There was even some
confusion among those voting for the first time who did not realize
that the leader's name would not appear on the ballot.   This was
more likely to occur among politically unsophisticated respondents who
had little interest in their local candidate.   But even the more know-
ledgeable were impressed by the endorsation that an unknown or
otherwise weak candidate received from his leader.

4.   Participation is both encouraged and directed into partisan
lines where parties are perceived as taking different stands on
issues and supporting different interest groups.   The issues considered to have greatest salience in the 1952 election have already
been discussed in some detail, both from the viewpoint of their impact on the ethnic voter and of party activities and policies.   But we
have also had some indication that parties were not uniformly
successful in convincing voters that they had something special to
offer in respect to these issues.   Several respondents, and they
were among the best educated and most articulate ones, said they

---

50. Campbell et al., The Voter Decides, pp.175-7.
51. Alford, Social Class and Voting in Four Anglo-American
American Democracies, p.300.   The federal elections of 1957 and
1958 have been seen as examples of those where issues and party
allegiance were subordinated to the appeal of the party leader. See
Peter Regenstreif, "The Canadian General Election of 1958,"
Western Political Quarterly, XIII, 1950, 1960, p.352.

could discern no differences between the Liberals and Conservatives. Although the NDP was recognized to have clear-cut policy alternatives, these were not taken seriously where informants did not believe that the party would form the next government. For these people at least, a voting decision was difficult to make, and they indicated that, if they did vote, it would be because of the individuals running rather than the parties they represented. Yet even if a party is not completely successful in its presentation of policy alternatives, it too, like a leader, can acquire and promote an "image" which serves to structure political life. Several respondents who could not distinguish too well among platforms still were able to attain a general conception of the different parties which guided them in their voting decision. Thus, those who said that the Liberals were "for the little man", or that Conservatives were mainly rich, English and Jews indicated that they wished to identify with a party that represented interests or groups similar to their own.

CONCLUSION

I began with the acknowledgement that empirical studies of voting behaviour have revealed a connection between ethnic origin and participation and partisanship. But, because the political behaviour of an unknown proportion of the electorate tends to be tradition-ridden in the sense that voters always prefer the same party, or even the party of their parents or grandparents, it is not easy to find the original connection between party preference and origin. For this reason, a study of the foreign-born is advisable. Leading from my observations on the behaviour of the foreign-born, I have attempted to indicate that in order to treat ethnic origin as an explanatory rather than as merely a classificatory device, it is necessary to look at the social meaning which is attached to it. It is this which I have termed life situation. The foregoing hypotheses should be considered as the main components of the ethnic life situation as this pertains to political participation. Life situation has been described in terms of the politicizing influences of the environment, the nature of ethnic identity, and the reciprocal influences of political parties' activities. (52) I have concentrated here on the social structural implications of ethnicity. (53) In so far as these

---

52. A comparable view is expressed by S.N. Eisenstadt, The Absorption of Immigrants (London, 1954), where he emphasizes the importance of looking both at the conditions of the immigrant groups and the absorbing society.

53. A series of hypotheses on non-participation from the point of view of motivation is contained in Morris Rosenberg, "The Meaning of Politics in Mass Society," Public Opinion Quarterly, XV, spring, 1951, pp.5-15, and the same author's "Some Determinants of Political Apathy," Public Opinion Quarterly, XVIII, winter, 1954, pp.349-66. More wide-ranging propositions than our own are presented by S.J. Eldersveld, A. Heard, S.P. Huntington, M. Janowitz, A. Leiserson, D.D. McKean, D.B. Truman, "Research in Political Behavior," in H. Eulau, S.J. Eldersveld, M. Janowitz, Political Behavior (Glencoe, 1956), pp.64-82.

are general propositions which can be applied to native-born or to any other politically relevant groupings, they should have wider application as explanatory devices for isolating and organizing empirical variables. The first requirement is that they be subject to empirical testing.

CONCLUSION: AN ANALYSIS OF THE NATIONAL (?) RESULTS*

J. Meisel

PARTY STRENGTH

It is useful to distinguish between the static and dynamic aspects of election results. The first concerns the votes obtained by the parties in any given contest; the other concentrates on changes over time. We shall take a static view first and then turn to consider the shifts.

The Conservatives held on to 116 seats in the 1962 election, the Liberals won 100 and the NDP and Social Credit parties captured 19 and 30 seats respectively. (1) While party strength in the House of Commons is of critical importance to the functioning of government and of the party system, an election analysis demands that emphasis be placed on the popular vote. Here, of course, the picture was quite different, the main parties having obtained practically an identical number of votes.

Newspaper accounts have uniformly shown the Liberals slightly ahead of the Conservatives (by 1/20 of 1 per cent). If the votes polled by the Independent Liberals and Independent Conservatives are excluded from those obtained by the old parties, however, the Conservatives are seen (Table I) to have outvoted the Liberals by 1/10 of 1 per cent.

With only a little more than one third of the popular vote, neither of the old parties could claim to have obtained anything like national support. The most outstanding feature of the election, as has often been noted, was the widely differering ways in which various provinces and regions of Canada reacted to the issues and personalities before them. Taking the provincial averages as our points of departure, we note, in Table I, that the Conservative proportion of votes in BC (27.3 per cent) was 24.0 percentage points below their maximum of 51.3 in PEI. The Liberal low point was 19.4 per cent in Alberta, and was 39.6 percentage points below their maximum of 59.0 in Newfoundland. The Conservatives won

---

*A part of this paper was presented at the 1963 meeting of the Canadian Political Science Association. I should like to acknowledge the able research assistance of W.P. Irvine, D.H. Burney, and C.W. Gordon.

1. At dissolution the party standings were as follows: Conservative 203, Liberal 51, NDP/CCF 8, Social Credit 0.

Table I
Percentage of Votes and Seats Obtained by Parties*

Area	Conservative Vote %	Conservative Seat %	Liberal Vote %	Liberal Seat %	NDP Vote %	NDP Seat %	Socred Vote %	Socred Seat %
Nfld.	36.0	14.3	59.0	85.7	4.9	–	0.1	–
PEI	51.3	100.0	43.3	–	5.2	–	0.2	–
NS	47.3	75.0	42.4	16.7	9.4	8.3	0.9	–
NB	46.5	40.0	44.4	60.0	5.3	–	3.6	–
Atlantic	45.4	54.5	45.9	42.4	7.2	3.0	1.5	–
Que.	29.6	18.7	39.2	46.6	4.4	–	26.0	34.7
Ont.	39.3	41.2	41.7	51.7	17.0	7.1	1.9	–
Man.	41.6	78.6	31.1	7.1	19.6	14.3	6.8	–
Sask.	50.4	94.1	22.8	5.9	22.1	–	4.6	–
Alta.	42.8	88.2	19.4	–	8.4	–	29.2	11.8
Prairies	44.8	87.5	23.9	4.2	16.1	4.2	14.7	4.2
BC	27.3	27.3	27.3	18.2	30.9	45.4	14.2	9.1
Yukon & NWT	47.6	50.0	45.7	50.0	–	–	6.7	–
BC Region	27.7	29.2	27.7	20.8	30.3	41.7	14.0	8.3
Canada	37.3	43.8	37.2	37.7	13.5	7.2	11.7	11.3

*"Other" candidates excluded. Source: Report of the Chief Electoral Officer. Henceforth cited as RCEO.

more than half the votes only in PEI and Saskatchewan; the Liberals only in Newfoundland. A glance at the table shows how the parties did elsewhere.

A few general observations can be made at the outset about the performance of the parties in the various provinces and regions: in Newfoundland, it was the Conservatives who registered their greatest strength in urban areas and in constituencies containing a high percentage of Roman Catholics. In New Brunswick, on the other hand, the usual stereotypes were re-enforced: the Conservatives did better than their provincial average in English-speaking and Protestant counties.

Social Credit's victories in French Canada, as startling as if some army of Jacks in the Box had sprung out of the Quebec hinterland, can easily be pinpointed to areas of economic under-development. When the vote is broken down into the major economic regions of the province (2) it becomes apparent that Social Credit had its greatest impact in the three remote or economically

2. The areas used are those established in DBS, Statistics of the Economic Regions of Ontario and Quebec (Ottawa, 1956). The constituencies included in each area are listed in the notes to Appendix D in J. Meisel, The Canadian General Election of 1957 (Toronto, 1962). Henceforth cited as Meisel, 1957 Election.

depressed areas: it won about half the votes in the Saguenay-Lac St. Jean, Northern Quebec, and Quebec City regions. The party's next best performance was in the Eastern Townships. It was in all these areas, of course, that the Liberals and Conservatives fared badly, the latter failing to win as much as 20 per cent of the vote. The Liberals polled more votes than the Conservatives here, but these were also their least successful economic regions. It is well known that they did best in Montreal but it may come as a surprise that this was also the area of the greatest Conservative strength in Quebec. Less than 4 percentage points in fact separated the votes of the two old parties in Montreal. In the surrounding metropolitan area, however, the Liberals did considerably better than the Conservatives. The only other constituencies in which the Liberals polled more than their provincial average were either isolated ones, like Iles-de-la Madeleine and Bonaventure, or Gatineau and Hull, where the presence of large numbers of civil servants may have stemmed the Social Credit tide. (3)

In the light of the frequency with which the generalization is made that Conservative strength in Ontario centres on rural areas, it is revealing that the party's weakest vote-getting performance in Ontario was in the economic region of the Lakehead and North. It is also worthy of note that the Conservatives polled a larger proportion of votes than their provincial average in five Toronto constituencies: they were York Scarborough, Broadview, Eglinton, Rosedale, and St. Paul's, each contested by an unusually prominent Conservative candidate. The government's strength in Ontario was, nevertheless, generally greatest in rural areas. The four economic regions where they polled about half the votes were Georgian Bay, Lake Ontario, Lake Erie, and the Upper Grand River. Toronto is now beginning to be thought of as a Liberal stronghold, but the party vote fell below the provincial average in nine of this region's twenty-one constituencies. Of the ten economic regions of Ontario the Metropolitan Toronto region, in fact, ranked only seventh in terms of the proportion of Liberal votes polled there. For the NDP it ranked second, after the Lakehead and North region.

Conservative strength continued to be impressive throughout the prairies. It fell to around 30 per cent in three Manitoba constituencies: in Winnipeg North and Winnipeg North Centre (see paper by Peterson and Avakumovic), won by the NDP and in St. Boniface, captured by the Liberals, who also came second in all but two of the other Manitoba ridings. Outside Winnipeg the highest proportion of votes polled by the NDP was 25.6 per cent. In Saskatchewan (see paper by Ward), the Conservatives carried ten constituencies with clear majorities, but the Liberals replaced the NDP as the second party, winning one seat, admittedly with the aid of what some thought was a second-hand CCF candidate. They also obtained a larger portion of the popular vote than the NDP which, however, came second in nine constituencies, to the Liberals'

---

3. For a detailed analysis of the Quebec vote, see the paper above by W.P. Irvine.

seven. Only the Conservatives and Social Crediters were serious contenders in Alberta, the former winning all but two seats. These were taken by the Social Credit party which also placed second in twelve ridings.

It continues to be an interesting aspect of prairie politics that the NDP fails to make any kind of impression in Alberta and that Social Credit is equally impotent in Saskatchewan. The NDP's highest proportion of votes in Alberta was 14.5 per cent, Social Credit's highest constituency poll in Saskatchewan was 8.3 per cent.

The outstanding features of the vote in BC were the great urban strength of the NDP, the continuing weakness of Social Credit, the major parties being evenly matched in the popular vote and finally, the Liberals placing second in twelve constitiencies (see paper by Young).

It is one of the unwritten laws of political journalism in this country to insist, during the early stages of an election, that the current campaign is one of the dullest within the memory of the newspaper fraternity. The 1962 contest was no exception, the most plausible explanation offered being that many voters were dis- illusioned about the Conservatives but could not become enthusiastic over the Liberals. When the results were finally tabulated, it be- came apparent that the turnout had been higher than ever before. Table II contains the relevant figures. Of the eligible voters, 80.1 per cent cast their ballots. Prince Edward Island successfully defended a long standing record by reaching a 90.0 per cent turn- out. This figure is really quite staggering when it is remembered that mistakes inevitably creep into voters' lists, that deaths occur after enumeration and that other unavoidable reasons prevent even

Table II
Turnout

Area	% Voting	Change '58 - '62
Newfoundland	72.0	-6.6
PEI	90.0	+1.8
Nova Scotia	83.6	-0.6
New Brunswick	83.4	-1.5
Atlantic	81.3	-2.1
Quebec	77.6	-1.8
Ontario	80.0	+0.5
Manitoba	77.2	-2.9
Saskatchewan	84.9	+3.1
Alberta	74.3	-0.1
Prairies	78.3	-0.1
British Columbia	77.6	+1.8
Canada	80.1	+0.1

Source: RCEO

the most ardent of partisans from casting their ballots.   The lowest
provincial turnout was registered in Newfoundland where 72.0 per
cent voted.   The highest constituency turnout was 92.6 per cent in
Kings; the lowest, recorded in Hochelaga, was 59.3 per cent.

SHIFTS IN THE VOTE

So far we have looked at the results from the point of view of
the proportion of votes obtained by the various parties in the 1962
election.   It is, of course, equally important, and perhaps more
interesting, to compare the outcome of an election with the results of
the preceding one.   And since we have just been talking about turnout, we might continue this theme by examining whether changes in
party fortunes, from 1958 to 1962, were affected by changing rates
of turnout.   In the 1957 election which, in toppling a well-entrenched
government resembled that of 1962, a very high correlation pre-
vailed between turnout and Liberal losses and Conservative gains.
At that time the Conservatives did unmistakably better in ridings
where the percentage voting had increased; the Liberals did correspondingly worse.   The relationship is revealed dramatically in
the accompanying Table III.   No such relationship between the rise
and fall of party fortunes and turnout was observed in the 1962
election.   Table IV shows the median change in turnout for various
intervals of Conservative losses.   The median change in turnout is
quite high in the eight constituencies in which the Conservatives
gained, then drops for increasing losses, but starts to rise again
for constituencies where Mr. Diefenbaker's party lost from 15.0 to
19.9 percentage points and continues to rise until it falls again in
areas where the losses exceeded 30.0 percentage points.   We have
a U curve here which in the end becomes tired and simply drops.
It tells us that increases in turnout were recorded in constituencies

Table III
1957 Turnout and 1957 Liberal Losses

Liberal Loss	None	0-4.9	5-9.9	10-14.9	15-19.9	20+
Median percentage change in turnout	1.4	4.2	6.1	7.9	9.1	13.6

Source: RCEO.   Cf. Meisel, 1957 Election, p. 250.

Table IV
Turnout and Change in Conservative Vote (1962)

Conservative loss	None	0 to 4.9	5 to 9.9	10 to 14.9	15 to 19.9	20 to 24.9	25 to 29.9	30+
Median percentage change in turnout	+4.8	+1.0	-0.2	-1.7	-0.4	+0.7	+1.7	-0.6
Number of constituencies (263)	8	23	44	61	45	45	24	13

Source: RCEO

where the Conservatives gained or lost very little, and in those where they suffered large but not overwhelming losses. Where the losses were really enormous, there was a slight drop in turnout. Comparable figures for changes in the Liberal vote are equally inconclusive.

In 1957 two trends moved in parallel fashion to give a clear-cut national relationship between changes in turnout and the gains and losses of the old parties: distaste for the Liberals and the Diefenbaker appeal led to an impressive increase of 6.2 percentage points in turnout, practically all of which seems to have favoured the Conservatives. Furthermore, the shift was reasonably uniform throughout the country. In the 1962 election, on the other hand, turnout rose by only 0.1 percentage points over the previous election, and the flight from the Conservatives moved in all directions. There were regional differences in the change in turnout and, of course, astonishing regional variations in who benefited from Conservative losses. The highest increase in turnout occurred in Saskatchewan, for example, where the Conservatives suffered their smallest losses. The second largest increase in percentage voting was recorded in BC, the province in which the Diefenbaker forces endured their worst defeat. In view of the foregoing it therefore appears clear that if turnout can be related to changing party fortunes at all, in the 1962 election, it is not possible to do so at the national level. Regional variations are too great.

Table V
Party Gains and Losses, 1958-1962*
(in percentage points)

Area	PC	Lib.	NDP	Socred	NDP & Socred gain
Nfld.	-9.2	+4.6	+4.6	+0.1	4.7
PEI	-10.9	+5.8	+4.9	+0.2	5.1
NS	-9.7	+4.0	+4.9	+0.9	5.8
NB	-7.6	+1.0	+3.5	+2.9	6.4
Atlantic	-8.8	+3.6	+4.5	+1.5	6.0
Que.	-20.0	-6.5	+2.1	+25.4	27.5
Ont.	-17.1	+9.1	+6.5	+1.6	8.1
Man.	-15.1	+9.5	0.0	+5.0	5.0
Sask.	-1.0	+3.2	-6.3	+4.2	4.2
Alta.	-17.1	+5.7	+4.0	+7.6	11.6
Prairies	-11.0	+6.0	-0.6	+6.2	6.2
BC	-22.1	+11.2	+6.4	+4.6	11.0
Canada	-16.3	+3.6	+4.0	+9.1	13.1

*"Other" candidates excluded.   Source: RCEO

Of the 16.3 percentage points loss of the Conservatives, the Liberals gained only 3.6 percentage points, well below the Social Credit gain of 9.1 and even under the NDP's modest increase of 4.0 percentage points. The figures given in Table V show, in

fact, that in six provinces, the NDP and Social Credit parties together gained more from Conservative losses than did the Liberals.
The country as a whole rejected the Conservatives, but it did not
embrace the Liberals.

That Social Credit should have gained more than the Liberals
in the prairies was perhaps not surprising, but the better performance
of the NDP in the Atlantic provinces was quite unexpected. One
should not be carried away by these figures because, of course,
they simply represent shifts. It was easier for James J. Walsh, the
NDP candidate in St. John's East, to gain 1.5 percentage points by
winning 435 votes in a constituency where there was previously no
NDP candidate, than for the Liberal in Bonavista-Twillingate to
prevent his loss of 1.0 percentage point. Mr. Pickersgill still polled
75.0 per cent of the 15,458 votes cast.

Nevertheless, the inconclusive results of the 1962 election were
caused by the almost equal showing of the Liberals and Conservatives
and by the impressive strength of the NDP and the Social Credit
parties, pinpointed in a few regions where they wrested seats from
their old rivals. Previous threats to two-party domination had always
come from the concentrated discontent of one region. The innovation
of 1962 was that the hegemony of the Liberals and Conservatives
was threatened in several centres simultaneously.

The most significant fact of the 1962 election, as has often been
noted, may in the long run prove to be the way it has affected the
traditional bases of party support (see paper by Regenstreif). The
Conservatives were able to minimize their losses in Saskatchewan,
the Maritimes, and also in some of the rural areas of Ontario. They
suffered most grievously in British Columbia, Quebec, Ontario and
Alberta, the most rapidly expanding and industrialized provinces.
This pattern has been widely recognized and interpreted as indicating
that the Conservative party has been transformed and that it now
appeals to an economically less favoured portion of the electorate
than before Mr. Diefenbaker became leader. This interpretation
will be examined later.

An even more startling change in support seems to have be-
fallen the Liberals and the NDP. One would have expected them to
benefit throughout the country from the disfavour into which the Conservatives had clearly fallen by the opening of the 1962 campaign.
They not only did not profit from Conservative misfortunes in anything like uniform fashion but they suffered most seriously in areas
which were formerly their strongholds. The Liberals lost support
in one province - Quebec. The only decline of the NDP was in
Saskatchewan; the province where it obtained the same proportion
of votes as in the disastrous 1958 election was Manitoba, which the
CCF once viewed with considerable optimism. At any rate, the
Liberals and the NDP both seemed to do rather badly in agricultural and rural areas, and to thrive in urban, fast-growing communities like the most densely populated sections of Ontario and BC.

No one can question the _rough_ accuracy of the description just
given of the shifts in party support in Canada. And yet there are
significant exceptions to these generalizations which make it desirable

to examine more closely the nature of party support in recent elections.

The Conservatives did noticeably better than the Liberals in some of the urban centres in the Atlantic provinces. In Quebec (see papers by Dion, Irvine, and Lemieux), Conservative losses were heaviest in an area stretching roughly northeast from a point about half way between Montreal and Quebec. The party lost less than its provincial average in Montreal itself, and lost most in the eastern rural areas, like the Gaspésie, except for such isolated constituencies as Bonaventure, Gaspé, and Iles-de-la-Madeleine. This pattern is obviously affected by the forces which have fanned the Social Credit flame, but there may be other factors as well. The influence of isolation on the rate of political change, for instance, may be of some relevance to the shifting fortunes of our parties. (4) Or, to put the same point more broadly, the key may be the effectiveness with which an area can communicate with the centres of power. This may be affected by a subtle and complex set of factors related to ethnicity, rurality, sheer distance, or the type of persons able to seek political careers.

A close look at what happened in Toronto underlines our argument. It has often been remarked that it was something in the metropolitan conditions of Toronto that was somehow responsible for the Liberals and the NDP making such an excellent showing in the 1962 election. But there is something else of interest about Toronto. Despite the relative staying power of the Conservatives in rural Ontario, the party lost less than its provincial average in two Toronto ridings, Spadina and Trinity. In three others, Davenport, High Park, and Parkdale, its loss was only slightly greater. Now obviously some factor other than whatever political attitudes thrive in an urban or metropolitan centre must be at work to explain this minor but interesting deviation. In this instance, it may be a difference in economic conditions or - much more likely - in the ethnic composition of the population of these constituencies. The percentage of people of non-British origin is extremely high in these five constituencies: Spadina and Trinity have 67.7 per cent each, Davenport, High Park, and Parkdale 60.1, 53.8, and 45.5 per cent respectively. If it is the ethnic factor, then we are confronted by another problem: what of the widely held view that the Conservative government failed in its bid to press the new Canadian voters into a new Conservative coalition? The Liberals and the NDP are said to have benefited most from the votes of the new Canadians. What are we to make, then, of the curious pocket of Conservative "strength" in these strongly non-British ridings of Toronto?

Enough has been said to suggest that many of the generalizations often made about party patterns in recent elections are perhaps too crude to lead to a satisfactory reading of events. As a

---

4. See J. Meisel, "Analysing the Vote", Queen's Quarterly, LXIV, no. 4, winter, 1958, pp. 494-5. Cf. Regenstreif and Lemieux papers in this volume.

modest preliminary step towards a more refined understanding, some of the prevailing views have been tested, using the 1962 election results either exclusively, or in conjunction with 1961 census data. A few of the relevant findings of the Canadian Institute of Public Opinion have also been applied to our problem.

PROPORTION OF URBAN POPULATION
IN CONSTITUENCY

Let us return to the question of the extent to which Conservative support can be classed as rural, and Liberal strength as urban. I shall again distinguish between the static and dynamic approaches. A chi square test, performed on the relation between the proportion of the vote obtained by the Conservative party in each of the 263 constituencies and the proportion of urban voters, as defined by the Chief Electoral Officer, gave a significant result at the 1 per cent level. It showed, in other words, that the size of the Conservative vote was related to the proportion of urban dwellers in the various constituencies. The table used in this test is presented as Table VI in a somewhat simplified form, for quick reading. It tells us that in the 105 constituencies in which the Conservatives received less than 35 per cent of the vote, more than half had populations which were from 60 per cent to 100 per cent urban. In the 158 ridings, on the other hand, where the Conservatives polled over 35 per cent, seventy-seven constituencies were only 30 per cent or less urban. There is therefore no question that for Canada as a whole the Conservatives did better in rural areas and worse in urban ones.

Table VI
Percentage Urban and Conservative Vote

| PC vote | % Urban | | | |
	0-29.9	30-59.9	60+	Total
0-34.9	23	22	60	105
35+	77	33	48	158
Total	100	55	108	263

Source: RCEO

A similar test applied to the Liberal vote failed to produce any results. There seemed no relation, nationally, between the proportion of urban dwellers in each constituency and the vote of the Liberal party.

The performance of the NDP on the other hand, can be related to the proportion of urban voters. Table VII shows the median percentage of votes polled by the NDP for constituencies grouped in 10 per cent intervals according to their proportion of urban dwellers. The lowest median performance, 5.9 per cent, was obtained in electoral districts containing less than 10 per cent of urbanites. The median vote fluctuates between 7.0 and 10.7 for

Table VII
Percentage Urban and NDP Vote

	0 to 9.9	10 to 19.9	20 to 29.9	30 to 39.9	40 to 49.9	50 to 59.9	60 to 69.9	70 to 79.9	80+
% Urban									
Median NDP vote	5.9	10.7	9.5	7.0	10.2	8.3	22.7	17.9	17.0
No. of constituencies	29	25	17	15	19	10	6	17	78
N=216									

Source: RCEO

constituencies which are from 10 per cent to 59.9 per cent urban. But where the urban population composes over 60 per cent of the ridings, the NDP median strength was near 20 per cent.

The Gallup poll figures showing party support for communities of various size (Table I in paper by Regenstreif, Cf. Table VIII in paper by Alford) leave little doubt about the relation between the degree of urbanization and party performance. Combined with other material he has assembled, they led Regenstreif to formulate some imaginative and revealing interpretations about Canadian electoral behaviour. But these national figures are also misleading because they gloss over some extremely important regional differences.

Alford's breakdown of the final Gallup poll survey into regions Table XIX, p.227) indicates, perhaps not surprisingly in the light of the results, that the Conservatives did better than the Liberals in communities of over 30,000 in Manitoba, Saskatchewan, and Alberta. The Liberals on the other hand, were shown to exceed the Conservatives in rural centres in BC and also, of course, in Quebec. The subtle and sometimes strongly localized influences of rural and urban settings on the voters' choices are illuminated in several papers in this volume, notably those by Lemieux, Peterson and Avakumovic, Smith, Irvine, Ward, and Young.

ETHNIC ORIGIN

The importance to the election outcome of ethnic groups, other than the British and French, was measured by finding the median percentage of members of these groups for constituencies grouped according to the size of the Conservative or Liberal vote in them.(5) Thus in Table VIII we see that 1.8 was the median percentage of non-Anglo-Saxon and non-French citizens in the eighteen constituencies in which the Conservatives won less than 20.0 per cent of the vote. Virtually all of these constituencies were, incidentally, in Quebec. The table does not reveal any noticeably consistent re-

---

5. The framework required for an infinitely more refined and fruitful manner of analysing the so-called "ethnic" vote is outlined in the paper by Schwartz.

Table VIII
Ethnic Groups Other than British and French and Conservative Vote

	0 to 19.9	20 to 24.9	25 to 29.9	30 to 34.9	35 to 39.9	40 to 44.9	45 to 49.9	50 to 54.9	55+
PC vote									
Median %									
"Other"	1.8	18.4	27.1	15.2	20.8	30.2	18.5	20.8	27.2
N(263)	18	9	34	35	30	45	37	32	13

Source: RCEO, 1961 Census.

lation between Conservative performance and the presence in the constituencies of voters whose background is neither British nor French. The median is highest in constituencies where the Conservatives polled from 40.0 to 44.9 per cent of the vote, second highest where the Diefenbaker forces won 55 per cent or more, and third in ridings in which their share of the total was only from 25.0 to 29.9 per cent.

A much clearer picture emerges from a comparable examination of the Liberal vote. Table IX convincingly reveals that the areas of Liberal strength were ones in which there was a low proportion of non-British and non-French voters, and that their weakest terrain contained a high proportion of what we have come to call "others." The chief reason for this seems to be the absence of enthusiasm for the Liberals in the prairies, an area rich in Slavs, Scandinavians, and other minorities. The evidence contained in Table IX is particularly interesting because politicians and others assume that in Canada as a whole the Liberals have done better among the ambiguously named "ethnic" voters than the Conservatives. The table seems to put this in question. At any rate, as we have seen, the voting habits of various ethnic groups vary with a number of other factors, of which rural or urban residence may well be one.

Table IX
"Other" Ethnic Groups and Liberal Vote

	0 to 19.9	20 to 29.9	30 to 34.9	35 to 39.9	40 to 44.9	45 to 49.9	50+
Lib. vote							
Median %							
"Other"	48.1	32.3	22.2	17.6	19.7	13.5	14.4
N(262)	21	54	36	38	40	35	38

Source: RCEO, 1961 Census.

One of the reasons for the general impression that non-French and non-British voters prefer the Liberals to the Conservatives may be the result of a careless interpretation of the Gallup polls. The question of defining ethnic origin is, of course, an exceedingly difficult one. The usual way out is to ask for a person's mother tongue. This means that many second-, third-, and fourth-generation Canadians whose forefathers came from Continental Europe or other remote places, and who are thoroughly "Canadianized" do not show up

as being of non-British or non-French stock. Many of the descendants of prairie settlers may well belong to this group. In any
event, the Gallup poll shows a marked preference for the Liberals,
over the Conservatives, among the people whose mother tongue is
"other."

Tables (not reproduced) drawn up to examine the shift in the
vote from 1958 to 1962, in relation to ethnic origin, fail to reveal
much of interest. The poll findings are to some extent confirmed,
in that there is absolutely no indication that the Liberals gained less
in constituencies where there were large numbers of non-French
and non-British citizens. Furthermore, the Conservative table indicates that a fairly large number of constituencies where the Diefenbaker losses were high did contain a large proportion of
"others." But these are only modest indications requiring further
examination.

It is difficult to estimate how much of the so-called "new
Canadian" vote is composed of non-British and non-French persons.
The French component is, of course, small, but in the immediate
post-war years the British element was enormous. It has con-
tinually declined in favour of an ever larger portion of people whose
origin was on the Continent. The non-British proportion of new
Canadians is smaller among those possessing the franchise than
among all new Canadians because the most recent arrivals are not
yet eligible to vote. The new Canadian vote can, nevertheless, be
considered as containing a high proportion of non-Anglo-Saxons.
As part of our inquiry into the relation between voting and ethnic
origin the percentage of new Canadians in each constituency was
therefore compared with the proportion of votes obtained by the
Conservatives, Liberals, and NDP. New Canadians are defined
as those immigrants identified in the 1961 census as having arrived
in Canada since 1946.

Table X
"New Canadians" and Conservative Vote

	0 to 19.9	20 to 29.9	30 to 34.9	35 to 39.9	40 to 44.9	45 to 49.9	50 to 54.9	55+
PC vote								
Median % New Canadians	0.9	9.0	7.3	8.1	9.7	3.7	2.8	3.8
N(263)	18	54	33	30	46	37	32	13

Source: RCEO, 1961 Census

Table X relates the median percentage of new Canadians to
constituencies grouped according to the Conservative vote polled in
them. The first column, for instance, tells us that for the eighteen
constituencies in which the Conservatives polled up to 19.9 per cent
of the vote, the median percentage new Canadians was 0.9. The
table indicates that except for these eighteen ridings the proportion of
new Canadians was rather steady in all constituencies in which the
Conservatives polled up to 44.9 per cent of the vote, dropping to
7.3 per cent in one category and rising to 9.7 in another. But in
all the constituencies in which the Conservative poll was highest,

that is in those where the proportion of the vote exceeded 44.9 per cent, there was a markedly smaller new Canadian component. The eighty-two constituencies in which, as grouped here, the median percentages of new Canadians were 3.7, 2.8, and 3.8 were distributed geographically as follows: 19 were in the Atlantic provinces, 7 in Quebec, 29 in Ontario, 25 in the prairies, and 2 in BC. The small proportion of new Canadians in the Maritimes and rural Ontario Conservative strongholds was largely responsible for these three medians being so low.

Liberal strength seems to have been influenced less by the percentage of new Canadians present in the various constituencies.

Table XI
"New Canadians" and NDP Vote

	0 to 3.9	4 to 6.9	7 to 10.9	11 to 14.9	15 to 19.9	20 to 29.9	30+
NDP vote							
Median % new Canadian	1.4	3.7	6.3	11.1	10.0	8.0	12.0
N(216)	27	40	39	16	32	40	22

Sources: RCEO, 1961 Census.

Table XI shows how strongly NDP support was associated with the presence of new Canadians. The highest vote was generally polled in the urban centres of Ontario and BC, or in the mining centres of Northern Ontario, all of which have attracted large numbers of recent immigrants. Further analysis is required before one can say to what extent the presence of new Canadians was a reasonably independent and potent variable favouring the NDP. Those wishing to muse over this question further will find some useful information in Table XII which lists the NDP's ten best Toronto constituencies in order of the proportion of the vote polled by the party and which also gives for each riding the percentage new Canadians and the percentage of those belonging to ethnic groups other than British or French.

Table XII
NDP Vote, New Canadians and Ethnic Origin

Constituency	% NDP Vote	% New Canadian	% "Other" Origin
York South	40.4	30.3	54.2
Greenwood	37.7	21.6	32.3
Danforth	35.0	16.9	22.6
York Centre	34.2	21.0	46.3
York Humber	27.3	21.8	31.9
Broadview	24.3	41.3	60.1
Davenport	24.3	22.3	33.1
York East	24.1	17.8	25.0
Parkdale	22.4	29.7	45.5
York Scarborough	21.7	14.4	21.7

Sources: RCEO, 1961 Census.

The need to distinguish between the static and dynamic approa-

ches becomes evident as we turn to an examination of the proportion
of new Canadians in relation to shifts in votes, rather than to the
percentages obtained in one election.   This analysis indicates that
the Conservatives suffered their greatest losses in constituencies
where the proportion of new Canadians was high, and that a more
modest decline in their vote occurred in ridings where there were
relatively fewer new Canadians.   But the most impressive result of
this investigation concerned the Liberals.   They did least well in
ridings where there were few new Canadians and made their
greatest advances in constituencies with a high component of new
Canadians.   In part this was so because of the great losses suffered
by the Liberals in Quebec outside the Montreal region, but even if
this is made allowance for, the degree to which the two factors
seem to be associated is really striking.   Table XIII, which is the
table used in computing the highly significant relevant chi square
test, makes the point abundantly clear.   In addition to the important
exploration of the ethnic vote by Schwartz, highly informative descriptions and assessments of it are to be found in papers by
Alford, Irvine, Peterson and Avakumovic, Regenstreif, Scarrow,
Young, and Ward.

Table XIII
"New Canadians" and Changes in Liberal Vote

% new Canadian	Liberal change		
	Loss	00-4.9	5.0+
0-2.5	53	22	15
2.6-5.0	17	15	10
5.1-7.5	8	6	18
7.6+	5	12	81
N(262)	83	55	124

Sources: RCEO, 1961 Census.

The relation between ethnic origin and voting cannot be discussed without some reference to the electoral preferences of French
Canada.   The flight from the old parties in Quebec, examined in the
papers by Dion, Lemieux, and Irvine, robs the normal type of test,
applied to national results, of any meaning.   The Gallup poll shows,
not unnaturally, that for Canada as a whole those whose mother
tongue was French displayed a strong preference for the Liberals,
then came Social Credit and the Conservatives were third.   But in
Quebec, as Irvine shows, the Liberals did best in constituencies
peopled by a high proportion of non-French voters.

CLASS

Voting studies in Britain and the United States have shown
that electoral behaviour in both these countries is intimately related
to class or to SES - socio-economic status.   Robert Alford's comparative studies of class and voting indicate that class is far less
important in Canada, but most of his evidence was collected before

the 1962 contest. (6)   Some observers have recently detected increasing class influences in this country and have argued that the
traditional class support of the major parties is changing.   The Liberals are, according to this view, becoming the party drawing
greater support than heretofore from the more privileged groups.

Public opinion polls show that both the executive and professional groups and those in white collar and sales occupations preferred the Conservatives to the Liberals in 1962, but that labour
gave decisive support to Mr. Pearson's party.   Nevertheless,
Alford's analysis of the polls in this volume shows that these relationships are, by no means, evident in all the provinces and that
regional and religious variations are far more important.   The influence of class factors in particular regions or constituencies is
demonstrated in a number of the present papers.   Young's analysis··
of the British Columbia voting is particularly illuminating in this context.   Several of the papers in fact challenge the still widely held
myth which asserts that Canadians form a classless society.   Class
was not infrequently an important determinant of voting choice but its
influence was not uniform.

RELIGION

Even the significant and consistent relationship between religion
and party preference is not uniform in Canada.   In Saskatchewan
the Catholics seemed to divide evenly between Liberal and Conservative, according to the polls, and in Alberta they gave a decided
edge to the Conservatives.   This is not surprising, of course, in
view of Conservative strength in the prairies and the Liberals'
corresponding weakness.   Many normally pro-Liberal Catholics in
the prairies were almost certainly under considerable cross-
pressure in recent elections.   The evidence of regional variations
in the relationship between religion and voting presented by Alford,
Regenstreif, and notably by Perlin adds weight to the argument
that Canada's political life is distinguished by the degree to which
every national trend in the voting behaviour of its citizens is contradicted by some important regional or provincial exception.

CONCLUSION

It is not surprising that when even the influence of religion was
blunted by regional pressures, other characteristics of the population
also defied enshrinement into neat generalizations about their effects
on the national outcome of the 1962 election.   We have seen that
almost any statement made about Canadian voting behaviour as a
whole can be shown to be strongly contradicted in some region or
among some section of the population.

Under these circumstances, would it be wise to stop genera-
lizing altogether about politics in Canada?   Is Professor Frumhartz

---

6. R.R. Alford, Party and Society (Chicago, 1963).

right in urging that "a general picture and a broad overview are not among the more useful contributions of contemporary social science"? (7)   The answer must be an emphatic "No!"   For the lives of Canadians are affected vitally by federal (i.e., national) politics, emerging from a Canadian Parliament and a Canadian cabinet, however much these are sensitive to regional pressures and whatever the difficulties they pose for social science.   Many uniformities do in fact emerge and, as the present papers show, some national patterns do exist.   Furthermore, the nature and significance of a unique or atypical occurrence can often be identified and understood only if it is considered from the perspective gained by first obtaining "a general picture and a broad overview."   What is required, is larger numbers of behavioural studies undertaken at both the national level and on a smaller scale.   Political behaviour, like any other human act, takes place against an institutional background and within the matrix of a given community.   In Canada the variation in institutional and regional backgrounds is so great that a sound development of political studies demands that national behavioural studies be supplemented by inquiries probing into the same questions at the local and regional levels.   This volume shows that a beginning has been made in this area, by a few scholars.   In relation to the information required, however, it is at best a modest beginning.

But it is not only the field of study which requires some redefinition.   The theoretical frame of reference within which the studies are undertaken merits examination.   Life in Canada and many of its leading institutions has tended to assume its identity in relation to British or United States reference points.   Various phenomena have been described as Canadian primarily not because of any inherent qualities, but because of the differences they display when compared with British or American prototypes.   This has been particularly true of our political institutions and practices, and for obvious and compelling reasons.   It is possible that this tendency has been reinforced by the fact that most Canadian scholars have received their graduate training in other countries.   This may have led to a neglect of some distinctly Canadian realities and also of distinctly Canadian problems.

There is a pronounced tendency in Canada to discuss the political scene in terms of such concepts as the Left and the Right, the nationalization of politics, the Americanization of our parties, or in terms of the comparison of our two major parties or of the personalities of our politicians.   These are important questions, but are they at the heart of the problem of Canadian politics?

In Canada we have a highly developed system of parties; we have numerous national political institutions but in what sense can it honestly be said that there exists a Canadian nation?   The most distinctive feature of the party system is not that it has four or five

---

7. In a review of my book on the 1957 election, <u>Canadian Journal of Political and Economic Science</u>, XXIX, no. 3, Aug., 1963, p. 396.

members but that among its chief tasks is that of promoting a sense of national community. This is the key to an understanding of Canadian parties and elections. More evidence than is now available is required on the degree to which there exists in the various parts of the country a national secular culture and on the degree to which elections foster it. It would also help if it were possible to devise at least a rough measure of the relative strength in the various regions and provinces and of the centrifugal and centripetal national economic and political forces, or if we could determine, for the different regions and provinces, the degree to which party support is prompted by local or national sentiment. These, and equally important gaps in knowledge will be filled when behavioural, ecological, and institutional studies of politics are combined and when they are undertaken not only nationally, but also at the regional, provincial and local levels. The papers in this volume offer some evidence of the usefulness of such inquiries and they point to at least some of the questions which might fruitfully be tackled in the future.

www.ingramcontent.com/pod-product-compliance
Lightning Source LLC
Chambersburg PA
CBHW080556030426
42336CB00019B/3206